TRANSFORMATION

MAGIC

INTENTION

ELIEF

*objects*

VISIBILITY

VOICE

LITY

LANGUAGE

AESTHETICS

OF CONCERNS

# Glenn Kaino

## This Book Is A **Promise** Memory

DelMonico Books • D.A.P. New York | Massachusetts Museum of Contemporary Art

This Book
Is A
**Promise**

# FOREWORD

## Joseph C. Thompson

In her monographic survey of artist Glenn Kaino's work contained in this beautiful catalogue, MASS MoCA senior curator Denise Markonish describes the richness of his practice and the remarkable array of form, technique, scale, and ideas that infuse it. Glenn is a superb sculptor, a cunning visual punster, a dramaturge, an elegant poet of shape and shadow, a magician, a graphic designer, a videographer, a social media interlocutor supreme, a skilled artistic director, and a collaborator comfortable in arenas both intimate and vast.

Denise's fine essay captures all that, alongside Glenn's belief that art can provoke change, fulfill promises, and give concrete form to hazy dreams. Having watched Glenn develop his idea for this current exhibition in our signature gallery—the football-field-sized Building 5—what I learned is that each and every one of his works of art is like a Russian doll, containing within it another work, and another, each iteration emerging out of itself. Or perhaps a flip-book is the better metaphor here, his ideas animating one another, shape-shifting over time. It may be that his evolving online platform, _Ships, will capture a little of that iterative energy as well; but for now, let me point out that this exhibition—which starts with fire and proceeds with shadow play, music, a ghostly boat, and the casting of stones—began as a massive waterfall, some twenty years ago.

*In the Light of a Shadow* is not the first proposal Glenn made to MASS MoCA. That ur-waterfall—a crashing cascade of water flowing endlessly over the western mezzanine of our largest gallery, disappearing miraculously into its floor—morphed into at least six other free-standing ideas. Each of these was as beautiful, startling—and complicated!—as bringing an actual waterfall into a nineteenth-century mill building. Every one of his ideas, in a way, hovered around his same grand subject matter—the complex interactions between ambition and achievement, between individual freedom and public responsibility, between promises delivered and promises denied. A flip-book of that progression of ideas would be a beautiful thing indeed.

MASS MoCA first met Glenn in his home, before he had a studio, when a small group of Museum trustees, staff, and supporters were making the rounds in LA in 2003. This was just after the most ebullient moment of the dot-com frenzy, when every Silicon Valley start-up had Sergey Brin and Steve Case on the brain. Herman Miller's Aeron chair had become a coveted fashion statement for digital entrepreneurs, a sure signal that some sort of end was nigh. Glenn felt the quivering of the dot-com bubble early. With his typical economy of means, and his devilish sleight of hand, he had mounted the iconic Aeron chair on a fast-spinning turntable (*The Siege Perilous*, 2003; see Memory page 56). With the flip of a switch, the chair spun as if on a potter's wheel, its curving mesh back and organic armrest blurring, seemingly becoming a solid body, transfiguring before our eyes into a perfect trophy urn or Holy Grail.

Other works by Glenn we saw that day were small, detailed constructions made from model car and airplane kits, which came to be known as his "kitbash" or "pin" drawings. In these works, he takes various commercial model kit parts and transforms them into three-dimensional maps, both real and metaphorical. But these were the California low-riders of kitbashing, beautifully crafted conversions that transformed objects of pop and commercial culture into breathtaking things of beauty and wonder.

Glenn's work between that 2003 visit and today is well-illustrated in this publication, as are examples of his innate entrepreneurial spirit. If *The Siege Perilous* was a finger in the ribs of Silicon Valley, Glenn also drank of that well in the sense that he understands better than most artists the power of disintermediation, social media, and the affecting connection between pop culture, politics, and power. He is an artist, to be sure, but he is also a producer, a software designer, and a storyteller par excellence. He's as comfortable talking about Hollywood and show business as he is talking about art. His studio practice feels, to me, utterly sophisticated, and of this time.

Over the years of knowing Glenn, I have experienced his almost frenetic energy up close: his ideas come fast, and in shorthand form, eliding from one cultural reference to the next, equally attuned to both high art and pop culture, while frequently skipping whole sentences, generously assuming we are filling in the gaps ourselves. He can often barely stay seated. And yet, at his core, Glenn is an exceedingly patient man who works at the speed of art, which is sometimes measured in months, years, or, in our case, even decades. The interplay between Glenn's rapid-fire brainstorms—which come in torrents that remind me of his first waterfall idea—and their meticulous development, testing, and execution over time (always with the help of many hands and many collaborators, within his studio operation and across the museum staff, to whom he always gives credit) has been a joy to watch unfurl.

For me, *In the Light of a Shadow* will be the last exhibition realized as I conclude my three-decade tenure at MASS MoCA, and I could not imagine a better capstone. It's also telling that after Glenn and I tried to bring several of his earlier ideas to life—but could not quite find the magic elixir of space, time, form, and budget—it was left to Glenn and Denise (and an amazing team of art fabricators, studio collaborators, and exhibition planners) to actually pull it off. If that's not a signal that it's the right time to exit stage left, I don't know what is.

After first thanking our wonderful colleague and curatorial impresario, Denise Markonish, for her superb work in bringing this great exhibition to fruition, allow me now to join with her in thanking the many who helped: from MASS MoCA (Richard Criddle, Megan Tamas, Tavish Costello, Peter Mahoney, Kathryn Carter, Brad Dilger, Amy Chen, Chris Nelson, Azariah Aker, Richelle Soper, Jenny Wright, Mike Kurpiel, and many more); from Glenn's studio (Gideon Webster, Riley Ogden, Brooke Baker, Joe Fellows, Alison Klein, and Deon Jones); the catalogue essayists: Stacey Abrams, Amir Ahmadi Arian, Kimberly Juanita Brown, Mike Caveney, Brian Dooley, Laura Fried, David Gruber, Deon Jones, Janna Levin, and Chus Martínez; the team at Cultural Counsel; and the generous funders: Nicole Deller and Matthew Bliwise, the National Endowment for the Arts, the Barr Foundation, Horace W. Goldsmith Foundation, and Mass Cultural Council, with additional support from Parsons Audio LLC and Genelec Inc., and Crystalle Lacoutoure and Scott Stedman.

Finally, I join our staff and Board of Trustees in thanking Glenn for the current torrent of ideas (which proved a modicum easier to realize than Niagara Falls), his patience, his remarkable generosity, and ultimately his inspiring sense of optimism. The COVID era has been an especially interesting time to make a complex work of art, and an equally interesting time about which to make it. I'm deeply honored to have spent some of that time with Glenn and our respective creative teams, both as an antidote and as a beacon of truth and light, right when we needed it most.

***Sunspot (Syria + Ferguson)***

*2019, Found asphalt, meteorite, copper, paint, high-density urethane, 40 x 40 x 4.5 inches*

*Photo: John Davis*

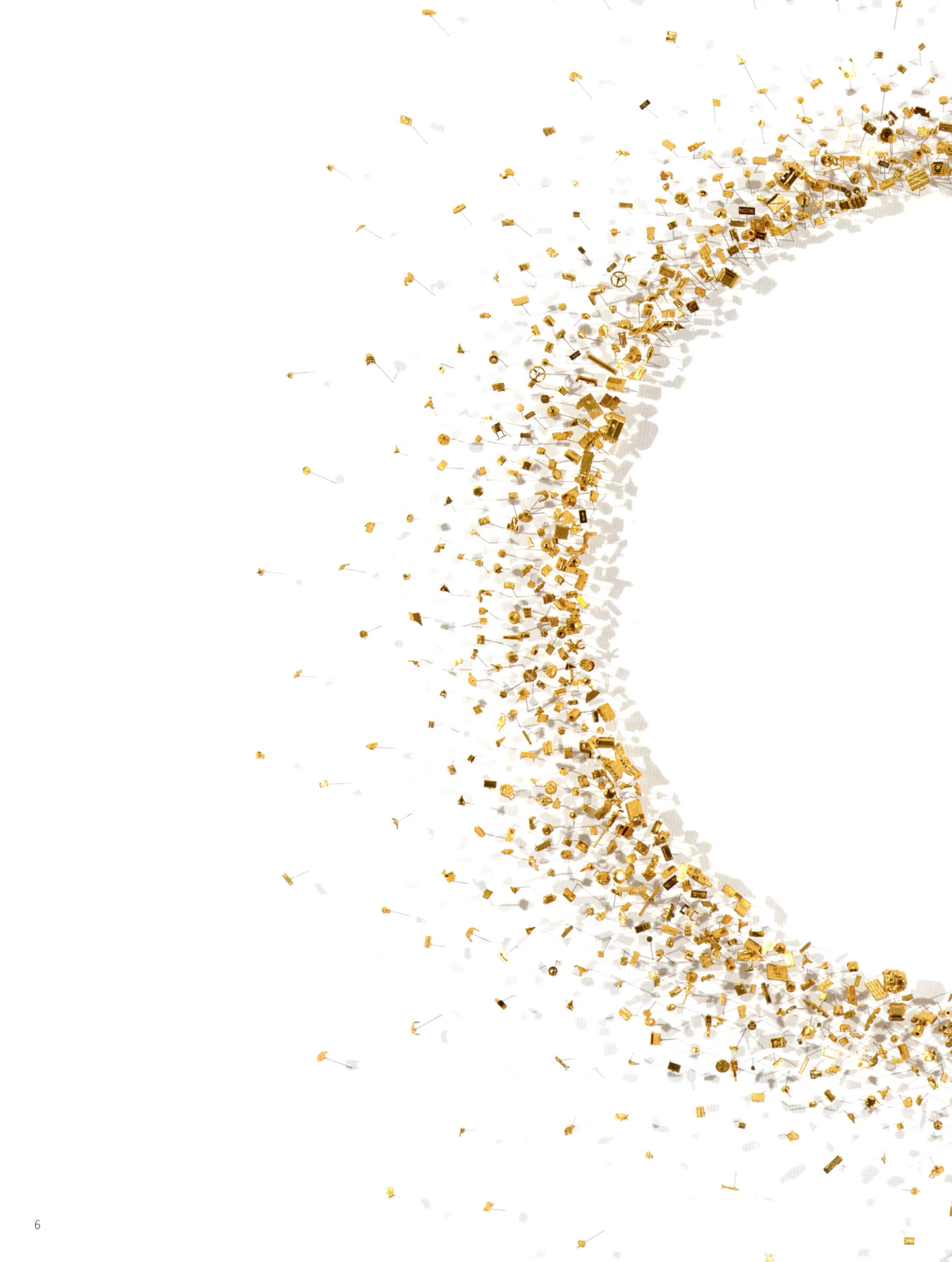

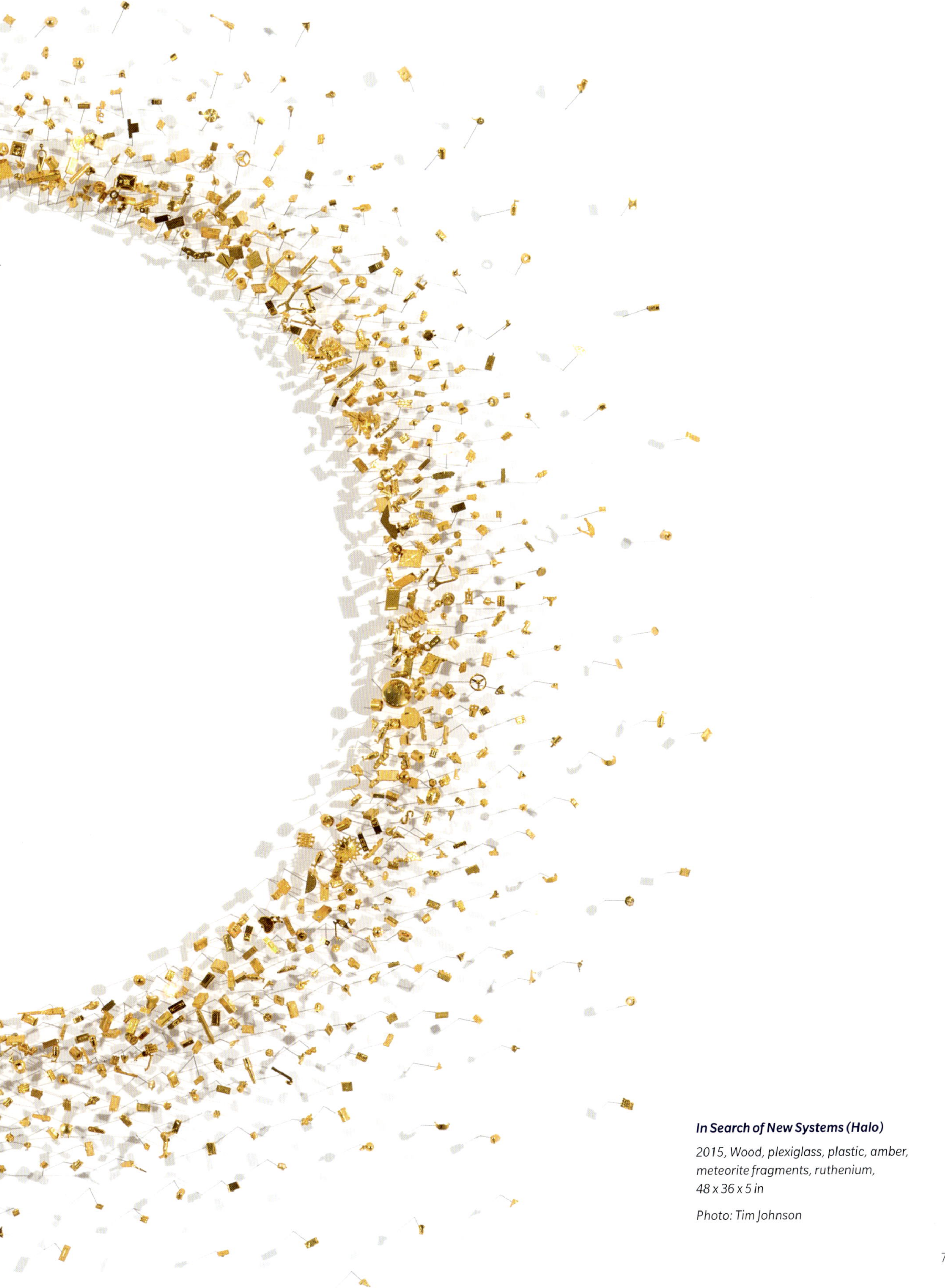

***In Search of New Systems (Halo)***

*2015, Wood, plexiglass, plastic, amber, meteorite fragments, ruthenium, 48 x 36 x 5 in*

*Photo: Tim Johnson*

# Chapter 1

# Promise

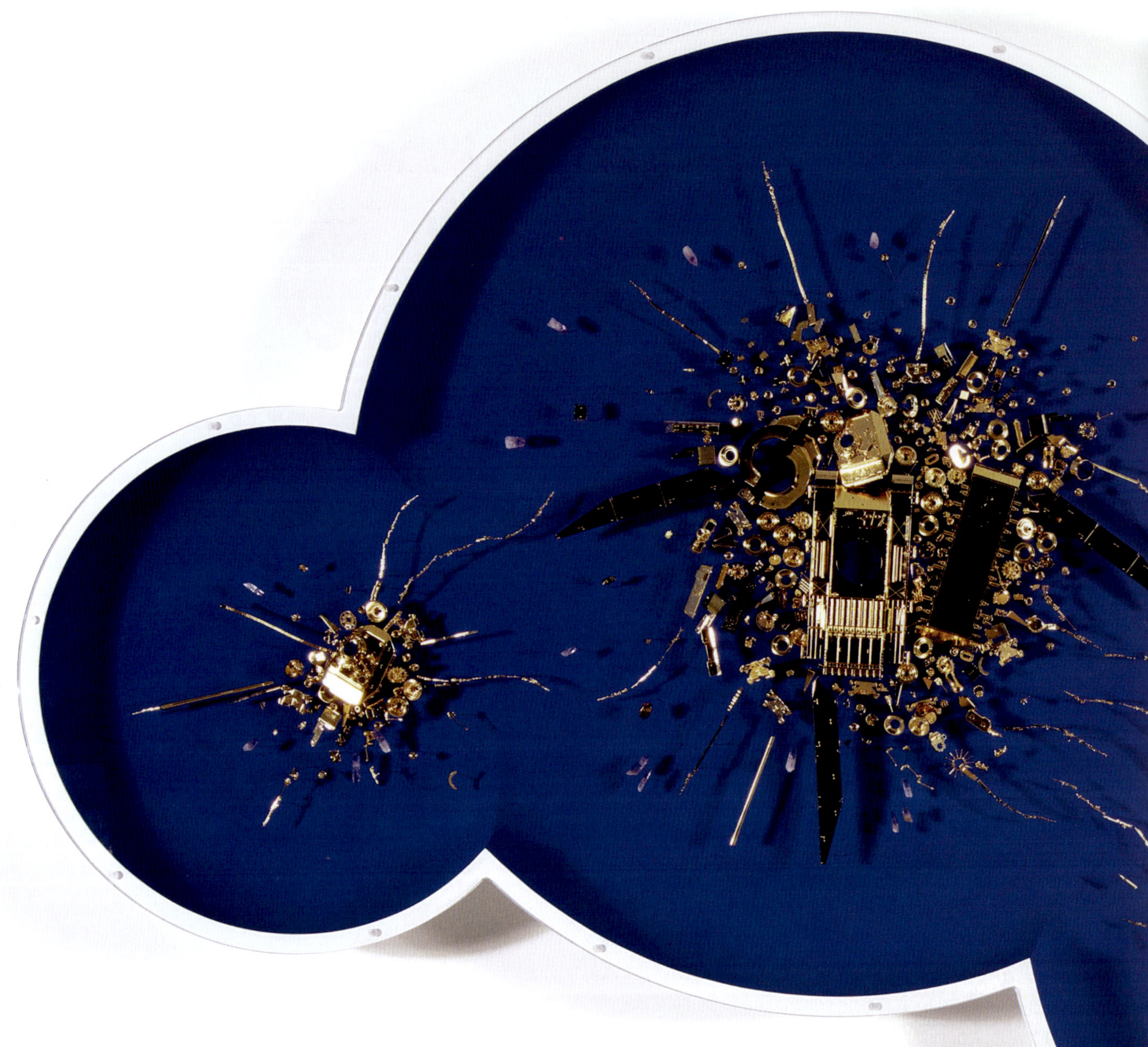

## Kitbash Drawings

Thousands of parts from toy model kits of tanks, planes, and other machinery are cast in gold and used as sculptural gestures for pin drawings of various geographies, both real and imaginary. Mobilizing a sculptural language of disassembling and reassembling that anchors the artist's studio practice, this ongoing series of works takes particular cities such as Los Angeles, Cairo, New York, and others as points of departure to re-inscribe layered histories and re-chart distinct places. Selecting particularly charged sections of these terrains, which often have contradictory historical narratives, Kaino layers the various accounts and relationships that make up those places in order to put forth new possible readings of a site. Los Angeles depicts a cancer cell-like structure that also stands in for Dodger Stadium and the displaced communities of Chavez Ravine that once occupied the site, while Cairo is represented as a series of inscriptions tracing the movement of people through Tahrir Square during the eighteen-day Lotus Revolution.

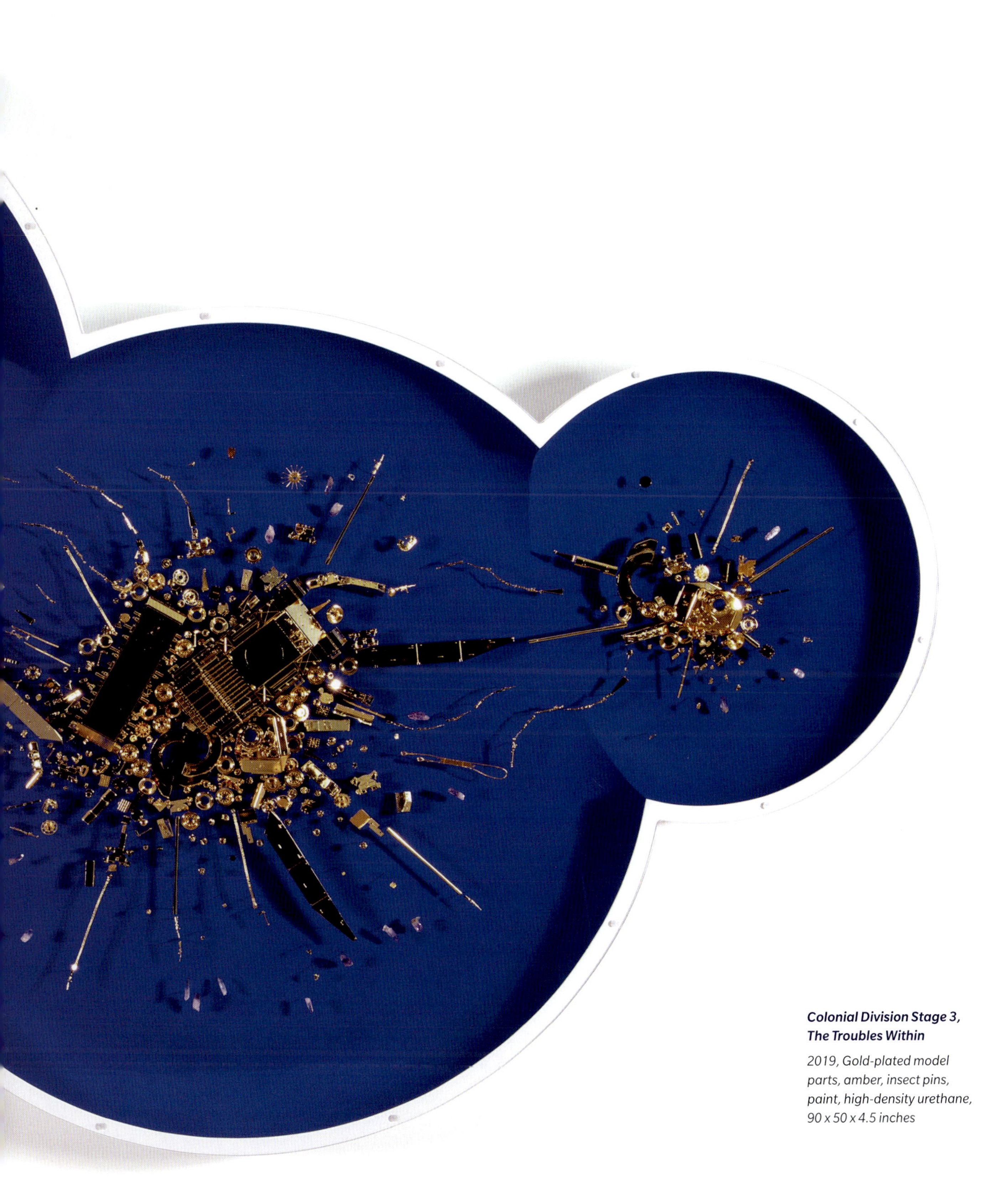

**Colonial Division Stage 3, The Troubles Within**

*2019, Gold-plated model parts, amber, insect pins, paint, high-density urethane, 90 x 50 x 4.5 inches*

**_In Search of A New Model (Mexico City)_**

*2011, Gold, silver, steel pins, plastic, foam, wood, Plexiglas, white paint, 72 x 48 inches*

*Photos: Joshua White*

**_In Search of New Systems (Logarithmic)_**

*2015, Gold, nickel, and ruthenium-plated model parts, meteorite, cotton, insect pins, paint, high-density urethane, 72 x 72 x 6 inches*

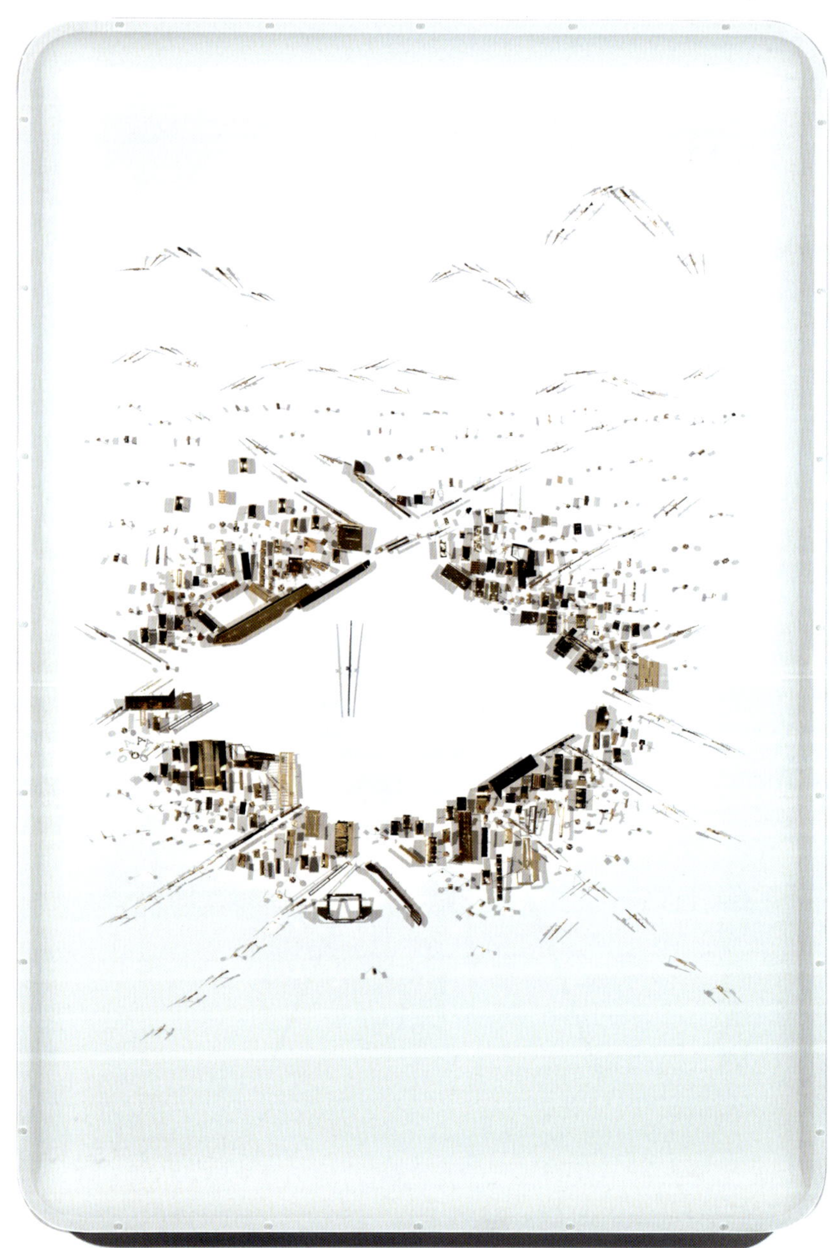

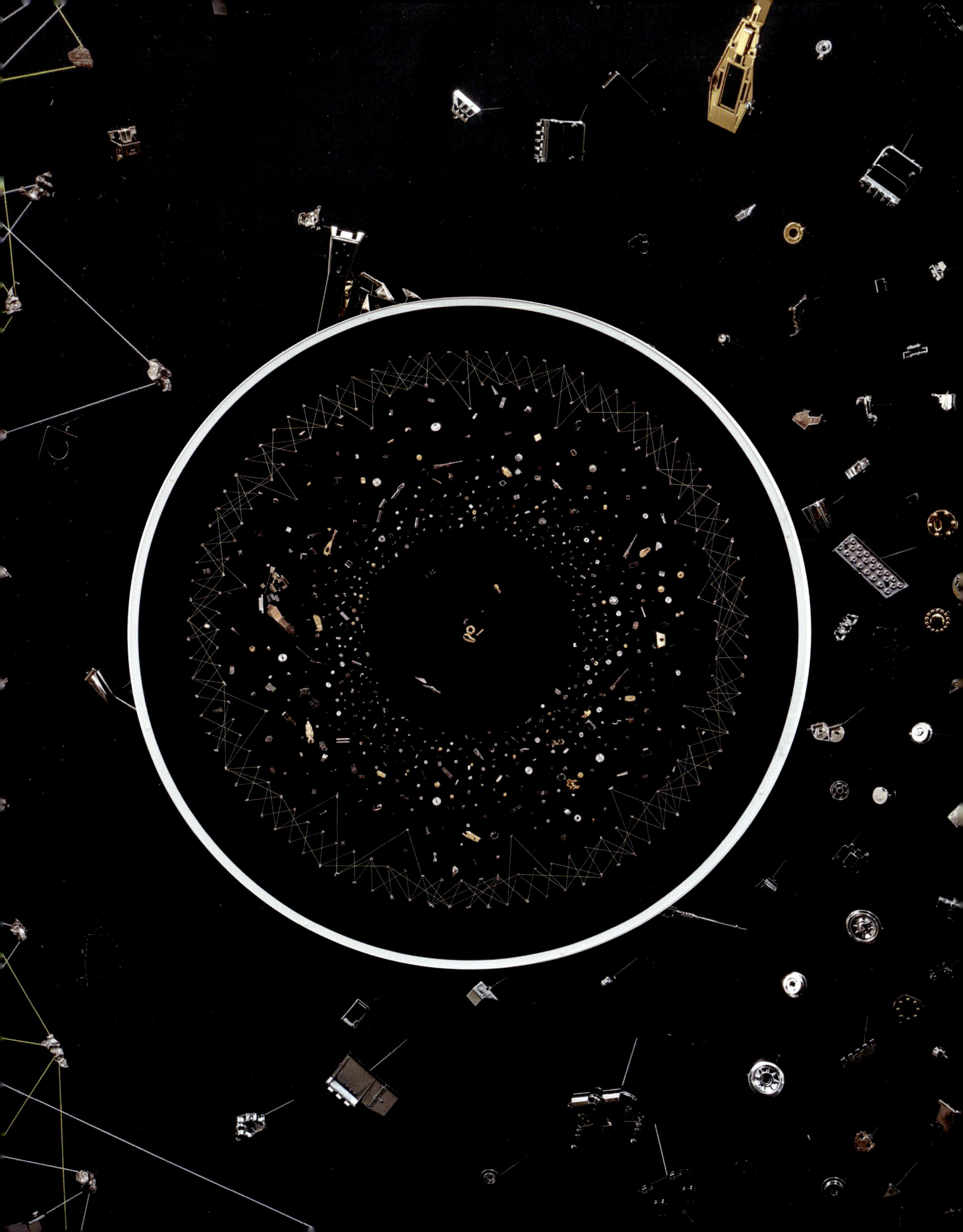

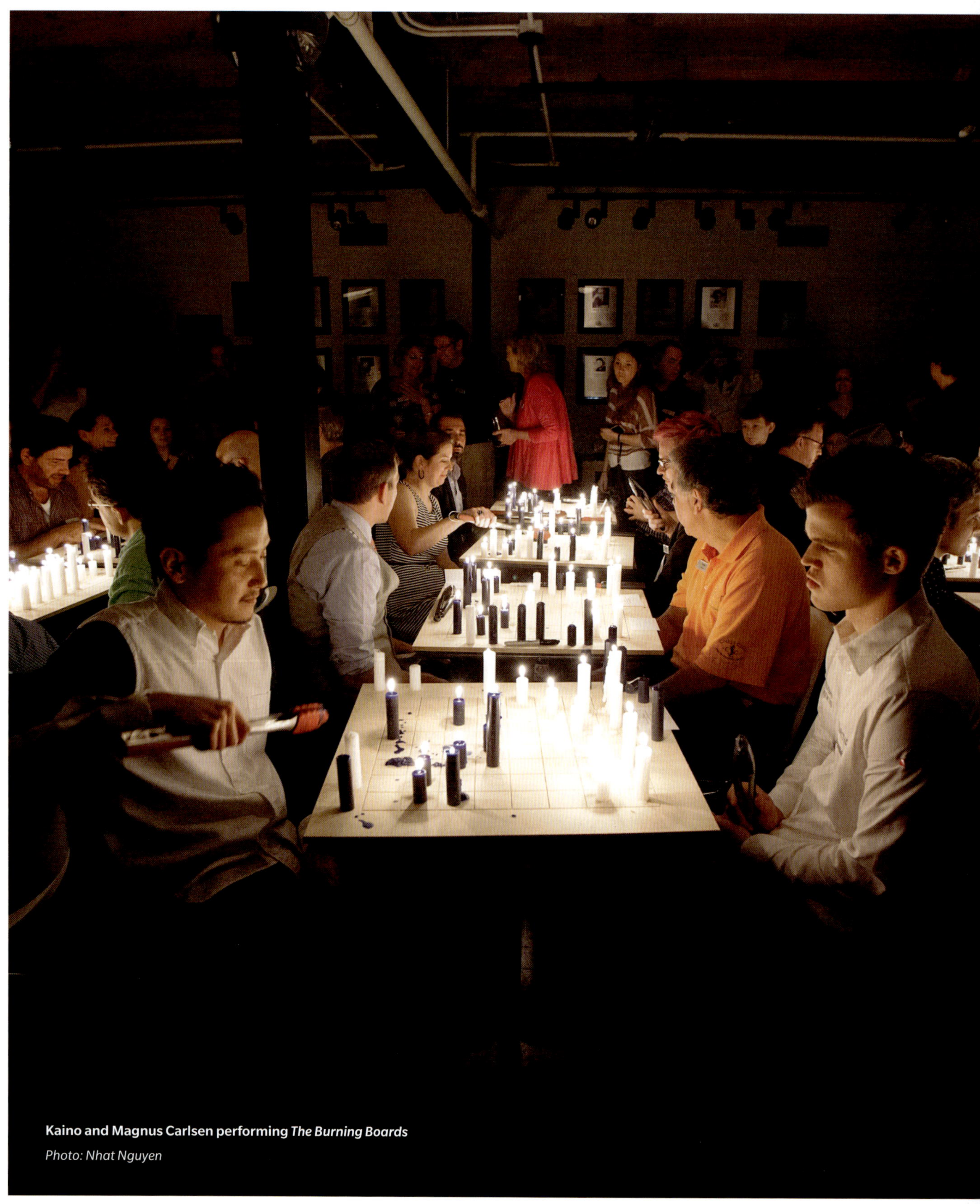

Kaino and Magnus Carlsen performing *The Burning Boards*

*Photo: Nhat Nguyen*

# Dreamweaver: The Promises of Glenn Kaino

Denise Markonish

*"Is it possible to create a Secret Theater in which both artist & audience have completely disappeared—only to re-appear on another plane, where life & art have become the same thing, the pure giving of gifts?"* – Hakim Bey, "Secret Theater," 1985[1]

Belief, hope, magic, and kept promises seem hard to come by these days. So, would you believe me if I told you that the secret theater Hakim Bey describes does exist, that it is in Los Angeles in an artist's studio, and that the artist who harbors this secret theater is a magician, both in the actual and the metaphoric sense? Would you still believe me if I told you that he was in gangs in LA growing up and that art helped him escape; that he was a junior-high DJ who went on to play a pivotal role in the growth of Napster and the creation of streaming music; and that he got Jimmy Iovine into technology? This same artist started journaling at the age of sixteen and later ran businesses for Oprah Winfrey; he was also a competitive surfer who eventually helped to rebuild the World Surf League; and even before he himself was represented by a commercial gallery, he started some of the most important alternative spaces in LA, such as Deep River and LAXART. As if the list isn't long enough already, this very same artist got former Olympic athlete Tommie Smith on a Wheaties box and once challenged grandmaster Magnus Carlsen to a game of chess. Just for starters. I promise you, this is all true.

Please believe me when I also tell you that this artist uses the power he finds in art—the power of creation to instigate change—to help make other people's dreams come true. In a time of so much sadness and unrest, we need an artist who can provide magic to a world that is sorely in need of something dear to hold on to, something to believe in and to hope for. Everything on these pages is true—even though it sounds like the start of a "one that got away" big fish tale—and it is true because the artist I am talking about, Glenn Kaino, keeps his promises, and it is he who holds the secret theater in his pocket.

As this brief introduction evidences, Kaino's practice is impossible to wrap one's mind around, because it doesn't follow a single thread or pathway. It is better understood as a galaxy—a constellation of concerns—rather than a linear trajectory. The spiral arms of this universe can be broken down into their own nebulae: BELIEF, SPACEMAKING, VISIBILITY, EQUITY, FUTURE PROMISES, REGENERATION.

Kaino utilizes these overlapping ideas when he creates what he refers to as "hopeful objects." You will notice that this is a decidedly un-art-world brand of thinking, and, thankfully, Kaino's galaxy creates its own art world rather than following the norms of a questionable system that already exists and has cracks in its foundation. The traditional art world just doesn't know what to do with an artist who quits making art to learn magic, who sees developing popular apps and being in the Whitney Biennial as equally important artistic endeavors. The art world is more apt to reward convention and repetition than to give in to an unknowable new galaxy of ideas. It is no wonder, then, that Kaino prefers the term "kitbashing" when referencing his varied approaches to assembling these diverse tangents. The term "kitbash" comes from the model-making community and refers to taking disparate parts of commercially available model kits and mixing them together to create hybrid forms—like a mash-up or remix. So, it is this contrarian nature—the desire to make a new whole from a broken bag of parts, alongside the embrace of the unknown—that makes Kaino's practice as wondrous as exploring the galaxy itself.

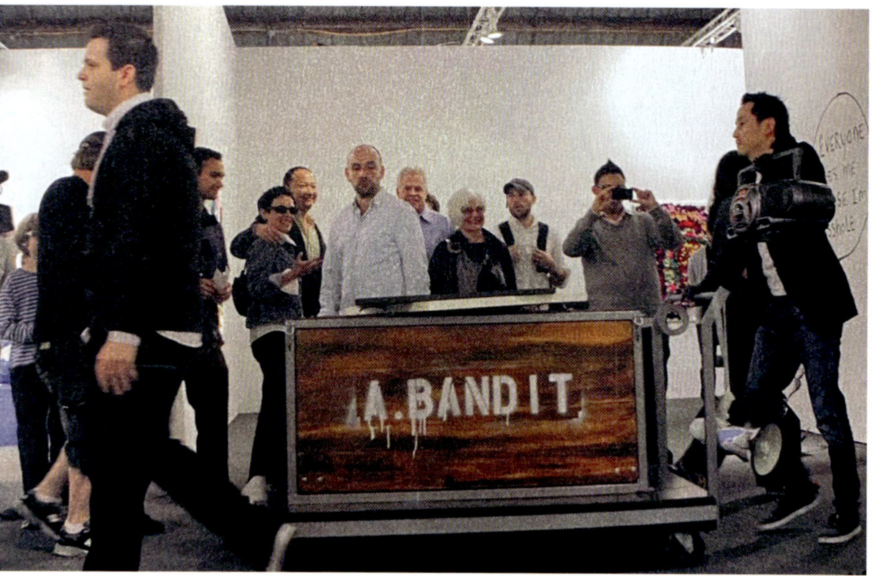


**A.Bandit, *My House Will Be Called A House of Art*, 2011**

*Photo: Kim Dziura*

So, before I get into the depths of Kaino's work, I end this introduction with notes to both Glenn and my readers.

To Glenn: You are a dreamweaver, a maker (and fulfiller) of promises, a keeper of secrets, a creator of rad things, a conjurer of hope, and this text is my promise to you that I will grant the world access to your enduring magic.

To my readers: Join me on this cosmic adventure through Kaino's unique star system, where I promise you we will enter the secret theater to find a place where "life and art have become the same thing, the pure giving of gifts."

## BELIEF

The embrace of belief is not widely prevalent in an art world more apt to discuss money and cynicism than emotion. This is something Kaino picked up on after attending his first art fair in 2008, Art Basel Miami. The experience left Kaino feeling dismayed. He says, "On the plane ride home with my former gallerist, I said I needed something new and that I was going to press pause. He asked what I wanted, and I blurted out: 'I'm going to hang out with a bunch of magicians!' He asked why, and I responded that I thought they might know something about believing in what they do, and that the notion of trading secrets and learning about secrecy was important."[2] Kaino began asking around, searching for magicians who would make him believe again. Soon after, he commenced training with champion magician Shoot Ogawa, who helped him earn admittance to the prestigious Magic Castle in Los Angeles. Then he was introduced to Derek DelGaudio, a young prodigy, well respected in the world of magic, who was having a similar crisis of belief in his own field. The two became fast friends, and a partnership formed that would forever change the world of magic (and art). The two identified that the art world "had become hyper-professionalized," while the world of magic was "a handful of professionals in a sea of hobbyists."[3] They sought to address these issues from each other's vantage point. DelGaudio, who is now esteemed as a transcendent performer and artist, recalls that in one of their early meetings Kaino said to him, "You're not a magician. You're an artist trapped in a magician's history,"[4] recognizing that his conceptual approach was more akin to an art practice. Their meeting was fortuitous, and both realized they could learn to

believe again by revealing the art of magic and the magic of art.

Soon after, Kaino and DelGaudio formed A.Bandit. The name is short for "Alexander's Band," which references the area that light cannot reach between the arcs of a double rainbow. Of their work, magician Max Maven wrote that "asking if magic is art is like asking if the sky is blue. Most of the time it is, but only if you look at it. Of course, most people don't bother to look, and they are steered away from looking by magic's own practitioners, most of whom haven't thought to look either."[5] Kaino and DelGaudio don't ask, or even tell; rather, they show us what we didn't know we could see, and help us to believe that their magic is real.

As they began their performative explorations, Kaino and DelGaudio quickly dismantled conventional notions of value, replacing commonly held art world concepts with their own logic of belief. Two projects in particular address the problematic idea of "service entertainment," or "performing on cue," that is prevalent for both artists and magicians. *My House Will Be Called A House of Art* (2011), the first-ever public performance by A.Bandit, fittingly took place at an art fair (the first Los Angeles Contemporary Art Fair). Kaino and DelGaudio walked up and down the aisles of the fair pushing a wooden crate and carrying a boombox playing "C.R.E.A.M." by Wu-Tang Clan. They stopped at different booths, and distributed ransom notes asking the galleries to hand over artworks. Some actually obeyed and gave them works, which were stacked inside the crate. Kaino then shouted over a megaphone, "My house will be called a house of art, but you are turning it into a den of thieves," as the crate was hoisted into the air. At this point DelGaudio took the ransom note and stabbed it to the wall, just as the raised crate burst wide open, revealing that all the contents had vanished.

*The Trials of Slydini* (2012) began with a similarly ubiquitous art world event: a fundraising dinner. At a studio visit, patrons asked A.Bandit to produce a magic show for a dinner party at their home in support of the Los Angeles County Museum of Art (LACMA). The two immediately declined, stating that they do not do birthday parties or perform on cue; but they did agree

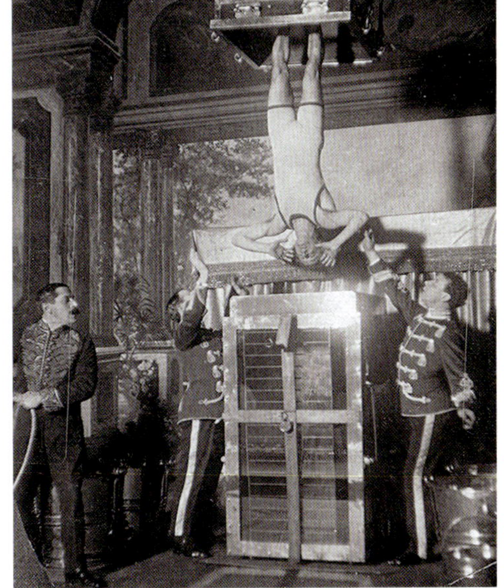

to participate in their own way, with an original commissioned artwork. When the day of the event arrived, they began with a short history of A.Bandit before asking the guests to follow them to the pool. There, they proceeded to tell a story about Harry Houdini's water-torture cell, one of the magician's most iconic performances, in which he was shackled and hung upside down in a tank of water. Houdini would ask his audience members to raise their hands and hold their breath when he was submerged, only lowering their hands when they gasped for air. When the final hand was lowered, Houdini would emerge. As Kaino and DelGaudio told the story, they asked the guests to raise their hands and hold their breath, and just as they neared revealing Houdini's secret, the last patron dropped their hand. Kaino and DelGaudio ended the story abruptly, not revealing Houdini's trick, leaving the audience unsatisfied. The two then proceeded to take the patrons, in their formal gala dress, on a tour through the property, telling them similarly frustrating stories with all of the actual magic withheld. The final stop was the stables at the back of the property, where they told the tale of Slydini, a world-famous magician who was known for putting guests at parties through trials before agreeing to perform. Slydini would hold his own agency, telling the audience when he was ready to present his act, not the other way around. At the conclusion of the story, Kaino and DelGaudio let the audience know that, despite their patience, because of the disparity between the patron and artist, and the context around the instrumentalization of art for casual spectacle, there was no way that they would earn

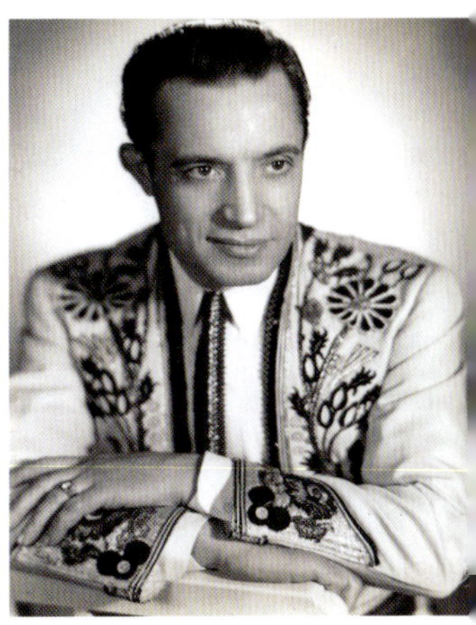

**Tony Slydini (1960s) was a magician's magician who elevated the principles of misdirection to a fine art**

*Photo: Mike Caveney's Egyptian Hall Museum*

**(above left) Harry Houdini hanging above his famous Chinese Water Torture Cell, c. 1913**

*Image: public domain*

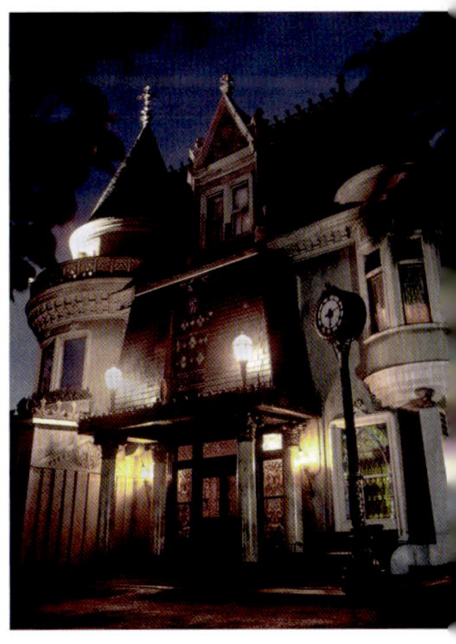

**A nighttime view of the entrance to the world-famed Magic Castle, a private nightclub for magicians and magic enthusiasts in Hollywood**

*Photo: Michele and Tom Grimm / Alamy Stock Photo*

a performance that evening. They then left the dinner guests to make their own way back to the house, walking hundreds of yards for their meal.

Four years later, these guests received an invitation informing them that it was finally time for the performance. The reward was well worth the wait, as they were invited to view the latest theatrical production from A.Bandit, *In & Of Itself* (2016), at the Geffen Playhouse in Los Angeles (the show later traveled to the Daryl Roth Theatre in New York City).[6] As in most things A.Bandit, *In & Of Itself* is impossible to describe.

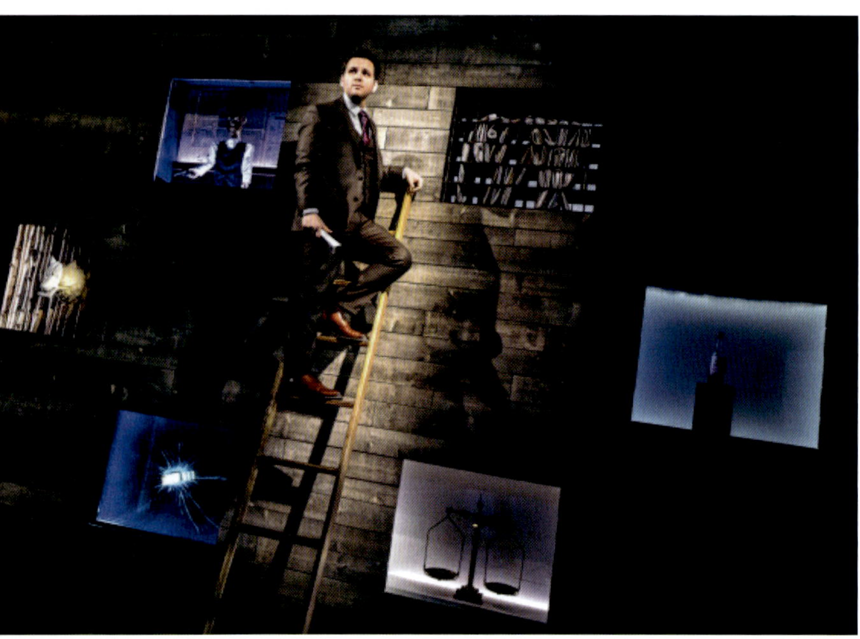

**A.Bandit, *In & Of Itself*, 2016**

*Photo: Matt Murphy*

Produced in Kaino's studio, it is equal parts magic show and conceptual performance about identity and belief—revealing truths to others and understanding truths about ourselves. It is also DelGaudio's first one-man show, directed by Frank Oz with music by Mark Mothersbaugh; all the sets, illusions, and production for the show are artworks created with Kaino, many of which mined his studio's extensive catalogue of works. Perhaps the easiest element of the show to describe is centered around a brick. DelGaudio begins by telling the story of a brick thrown through a window of his childhood home after his mother came out as gay. There is an actual brick incorporated into the set, painted gold, which DelGaudio eventually vanishes during a poetic monologue. While this seemingly simple vanish is fun to watch, the real moment of magic is hearing DelGaudio tell the audience that the brick is not gone, but is now out in the city (at the corner of two streets named by different audience members). If you took him seriously, if you truly believed him, then you would go to the intersection after the show, where you were rewarded. Impossibly the very brick you saw vanish would be lying on the street, exactly where predicted. In this one act, suddenly the hugeness of Los Angeles or New York City became intimate and connected, as a brick sitting on the ground—overlooked by most—became a truth known by only a few. One wonders what the dinner guests who were "Slydinied" learned about themselves from this experience.

For Kaino, it's not magic tricks, but magic as a vehicle for belief that propels him. This is evidenced in solo projects such as *The Burning Boards* (2007–ongoing) and *Safe* (2010). *The Burning Boards* is a performance about trust and equity, and an embrace of ephemerality in the form of a chess tournament. However, this is no ordinary tournament, for Kaino designed the simple wooden boards to be played with pieces made out of lit candles, all of the same shape but differing in lengths as they relate to each standard piece. As the candles melt at different rates due to proximity and warmth, the identity of each piece is obscured and the game becomes one of trusting your opponent while you try to best them. "The possible ranks higher than the actual" is a quote from German philosopher Martin Heidegger's book *Being and Time* (1927) that Kaino uses when describing the multitude of imaginaries played out in the minds of chess players, who only reveal to the world their one decision at the moment of play. Additionally, this work also brings to mind Marcel Duchamp (1887–1968), who famously gave up art-making to play chess (in a move not unlike Kaino's shift into magic). Duchamp once stated that "not all artists are chess players, but all chess players are artists," further confounding just what it means to call oneself an artist and recalling Kaino's own observation about his partner, DelGaudio.

*Safe* is also a work about trust, this time involving both a group of collaborators and, separately, an audience. It embodies the value of secrets that Kaino learned from magic. *Safe* is both a sculpture and a performance, which took place

over the course of a year. During this time, Kaino gathered more than 220 secrets from artists, entertainers, businesspeople, fashion designers, politicians, etc. Participants recorded their secrets on audiocassettes that were then stored inside a safe, never to be opened again. No one but the participant has ever heard them, including Kaino himself, instituting a lifelong pact to keep the knowledge unknown. Each secret was labeled with the participant's name, along with a title alluding to, but not revealing, the secret, and the titles were illustrated in a notebook that accompanied the strongbox. The resulting sculpture was a paradox: what good is a safe that can never be opened? The work denies us knowledge revealed—asking how much is knowledge, or a secret, worth. By keeping the secrets secure, Kaino reminds us that he has proven he can always keep a secret: from never revealing the hidden surf spots of his youth, to the technological innovations of his studio, and now the unheard histories of his peers.

So, you may ask, what does this ongoing commitment and exploration of the world of magic teach Kaino about belief? He states: "In learning magic, I gained the ability to simultaneously believe and disbelieve in what I do. I gained access to a form of creation that is simultaneously high technical and incredibly mysterious. Historically, magic has been used as a means of reconciling seemingly irreconcilable gaps—for example, between science and religion. I think magic is the key link between art and everyday life. In magic, secrets are not simply withheld information; they are truths that exist only within the imagination. Easily manipulated, they have generative powers, especially in the realm of performance."[7]

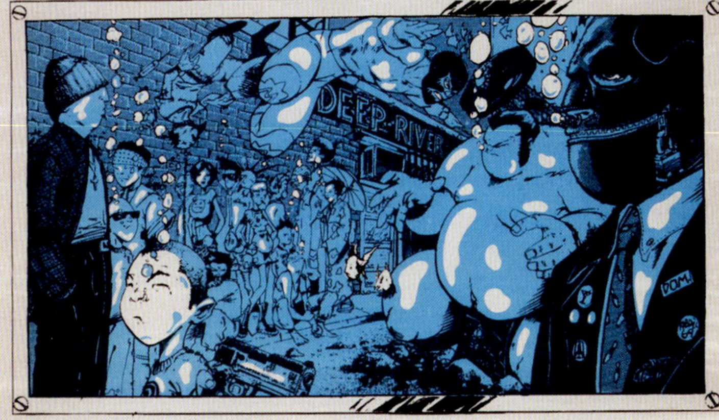


## SPACEMAKING

This belief and trust confirmed for Kaino the importance of ethics within his career. His reliance on ethical collaboration—giving credit where credit is due, understanding with whom he is working, and being accessible—engenders trust in the communities with whom he engages (whether individuals or collectives). To do this—and this is the real magic of Kaino's work—he makes promises you want him to keep, not ones that serve his artistic ego. In many ways, his early life in gangs and his later work with magicians continuously drew upon and developed his respect for relationship and community building, and what he often refers to as "building family" and "honor among thieves."

This generosity of spirit is nowhere more evident than in Kaino's continued work around spacemaking across Los Angeles. In 1997, at just twenty-five years old, Kaino, along with artists Rolo Castillo, Daniel Joseph Martinez, and Tracey Shiffman, started Deep River.[8] An artist-run space that was neither for-profit nor nonprofit, Deep River functioned as an experimental laboratory for "social sculpture"—a phrase borrowed from German artist Joseph Beuys (1921–1986) to describe art that has the potential to transform society. The main goal of the endeavor was to create community, making accessible alternate pathways for the creation and presentation of art outside the constraints

of the established art world. The history of Deep River speaks for itself (as outlined in Laura Fried's essay in this volume) and includes giving some of today's most successful artists, such as Kori Newkirk and Mark Bradford, their first solo exhibitions, alongside over forty others during the course of its brief five-year history.

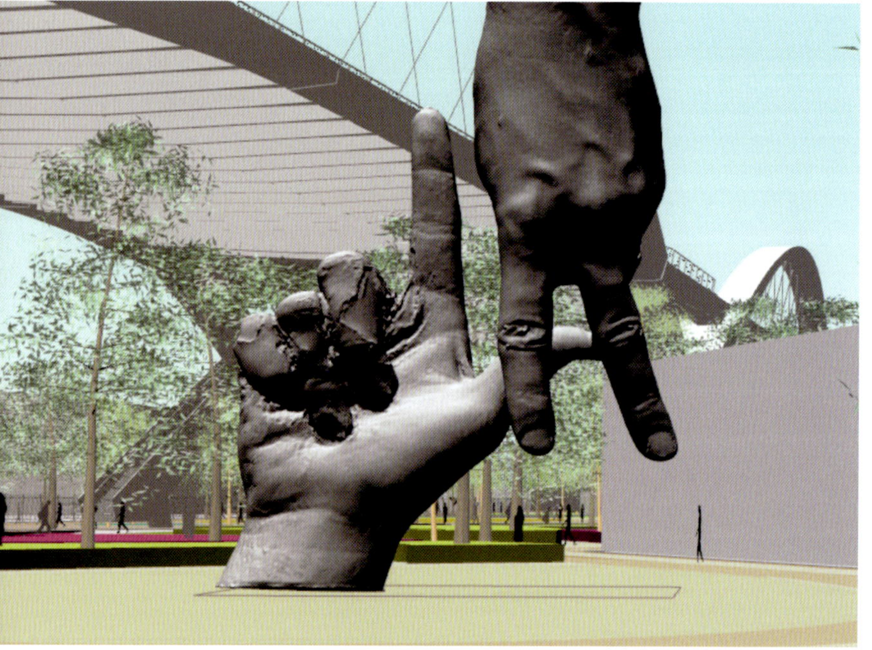

***LA Hands*, Public artwork in progress, 2022**

For many, one collective art gallery would be enough, but Kaino's commitment to people and ideas often lasts lifetimes; and his promise to the city of Los Angeles, and its artists, endures. In 2014, Kaino and curator Cesar Garcia formed The Mistake Room, after collaborating on Kaino's exhibition for the 13th Cairo Biennale. Identifying the need in LA for a platform that would increase the representation of international artists in the city, while also creating a global discourse for local artists, The Mistake Room calls itself "a platform for art, ideas, and practices fueled by radical imagination."[9] The name of the space derives from a 2011 performance by A.Bandit in which Kaino and DelGaudio created an environment where failures—mistakes—are embraced. The artist magicians sat in a small room with a one-way mirror that allowed visitors to witness them performing tricks repeatedly, even as human error set in. This performance peeled back the curtain, revealing that art, magic, and performance—indeed, all aspects of life—are not without mistakes, becoming a fitting moniker for the ensuing nonprofit's experimental and risk-taking nature. The first iteration of *The Mistake Room* performance took place at LAXART—another Los Angeles-based nonprofit Kaino had helped to found in 2005, as a board member for curator Lauri Firstenberg.

More recently, in 2019 Kaino co-founded Active Cultures with curator Laura Fried. Active Cultures is an institution created to explore the convergence of food and art. Inspired by Kaino's ongoing collaboration with two-starred Michelin chef Niki Nakayama, it includes programs like *The MSG Club*—a dinner series wherein the collaborators invite guests to share their food dislikes and then cook a meal with those very ingredients in order to help them expand their taste. This work is a performance about tolerance in the form of a group-therapy supper club. Active Cultures functions as a bridge between the shared concerns of the art and food worlds, including how to connect creative thinkers across disciplines; the exploration of globalism in how we produce and consume both art and food; and, not dissimilar to Kaino and DelGaudio's work in magic, the utilization of the best of both fields in the service of addressing their shortcomings. Most notably, Active Cultures seeks to create a more just and hospitable art world, by utilizing culture to further legitimize the culinary arts. This is evidenced in their recent release of a series of pandemic meal kits, designed by Kaino and Nakayama, to encourage the cooking of restaurant-quality food at home.

Alongside his work with Active Cultures, Kaino is also in the process of designing two public art installations for Los Angeles, both of which aim to bring its citizens together. *LA Hands* (2022) is a monumental public sculpture that draws upon the community's collective pride for their city as a unifying element in these divisive times. The work is created from two hands—one making a gun with thumb and index fingers and the other making a peace sign over the thumb with the middle and index fingers. When assembled, these two opposing gestures take another form, that of an "L" and an "A." This ubiquitous symbol is used across the city as a source of pride and is immediately recognizable to its denizens. As Kaino consistently allows for the right person to hold the spotlight at the right moment, and

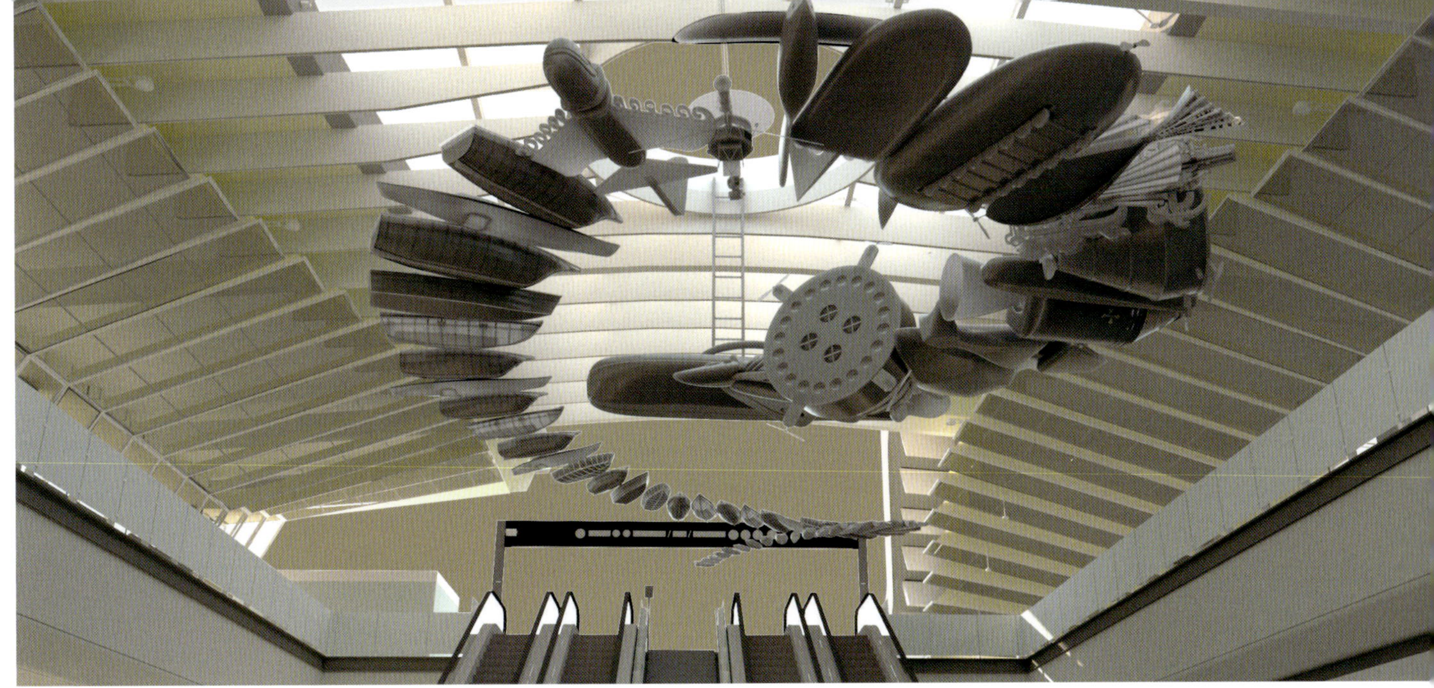

*The Distance of the Sun (Spot)*, **Public artwork in progress, 2023**

does not believe in half measures, he cast the hands of hundreds of Angelinos from both sides of the LA River—oppositional communities fighting for and against gentrification—bringing them together to create a symbol of unity. Kaino invited time and participation from the mostly Latinx neighborhood into which he was born, and, because communities of color rarely directly participate in the creation of their own monuments, the life casts of their hands were returned to the models, so they can share with future generations the proof of their contribution. The final sculpture, which will be placed in a new park adjacent to the rebuilt Sixth Street Viaduct, is composed from the hands of two different residents who, though ideologically opposed, collaborated to create the iconic gesture. This gesture will live on in a more personal way via the small casts in people's homes and the stories that go along with them—proving again that opponents can be simultaneous collaborators across the city.

Kaino's second public work, *The Distance of the Sun (Spot)* (2023), is being created for the Los Angeles Airport Metro Connector. This work begins with two inspirations: Italo Calvino's short story "The Distance of the Moon" (1965) and the total solar eclipse in the summer of 2017.[10] Calvino's story describes a time when the earth and moon were so close you could row a boat and with a ladder climb onto the lunar surface. Calvino's narrator, Qfwfq, states: "The whole business of the Moon's phases worked in a different way then: because the distances from the Sun were different, and the orbits, and the angle of something or other, I forget what; as for eclipses, with Earth and Moon stuck together the way they were, why, we had eclipses every minute: naturally, those two big monsters managed to put each other in the shade constantly, first one, then the other."[11] In the story, the moon and earth drift apart, leaving people stranded on one side or the other. Kaino was reminded of Calvino's narrative when the moon completely eclipsed the sun in 2017, a phenomenon that had not been visible across the entire United States since 1918. Watching that moment at the Griffith Observatory in Los Angeles, Kaino was struck by the collective activity of people staring into the sky. He began to think about people across the US imagining the unknown, dreaming together while looking up.[12] He recalled asking his two daughters what they thought of seeing the sun (through their coated glasses). One told him that the sun looked smaller than she thought, and the other that it looked bigger. "It was a realization of a moment when an idea became an object," Kaino remembers.[13] This shared experience staring at the sun created an interconnectedness across the world, one that Kaino asks us to remember in the face of so much division. For the installation, Kaino will create an oculus in the ceiling of the building from which hangs a ladder; swirling around the ladder is a levitating spiral pathway

constructed from different vessels based on stories of indigenous spacecraft from around the world. The oculus to view our shared sun becomes a path to understanding our history of dreaming about the sky—all in a location representing travel and hope—creating a collective dream of our galaxy.

## VISIBILITY

Kaino's spacemaking in Los Angeles dovetails into the next twin arms of his spiral galaxy: visibility and equity. Throughout his work, Kaino strives to make visible the unseen or the forgotten in an interrogation of the politics of presence and knowing. This is evident in both the studio artworks and his forays into the larger sphere of culture. The latter platform led to his collaborative development of a series of apps in the last five years, such as Ebroji, BLeBRiTY, and Ya Tu Sabes. These apps, co-developed with actor and activist Jesse Williams, are housed under their company Visibility, founded in 2015. For Kaino, the work of Visibility is about creating "interventions into a larger media landscape that prove diversity can be both popular and profitable, in order to make significant positive change in our world."[14] For Ebroji, Kaino and Williams aimed to "bring language to life" by utilizing and making available a new set of emoticons, GIFs, and memes particularly geared toward African American culture. BLeBRiTY and Ya Tu Sabes are charades-like games of Black and Latinx culture respectively, that have been played over five million times. All of these projects are also aimed at filling a void in the field of technology for content created authentically for consumers of color.

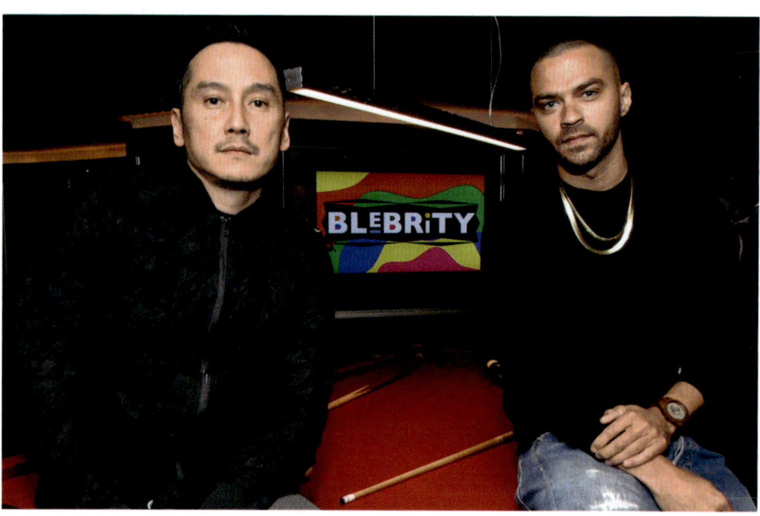


**Kaino and Jesse Williams, founders of BLeBRiTY**

Alongside these wide-reaching public endeavors, Kaino explores this concept of visibility through the materialization of form from a seemingly disparate and damaged set of source materials with his series of kitbash or "pin" drawings (2004–ongoing). For these works, Kaino takes discarded parts from toy models of tanks, planes, and other militarized vehicles, gold-plates them, and subsequently attaches them to delicate pins, transforming these small fragments from symbols of power and infrastructure into a kind of raw jewelry. Kaino then reassembles the pieces to create maps of both real and imagined spaces, often providing his audience insight into the hidden histories of place revealed through cartography. For example, in one kitbash drawing, Kaino depicts a cell-like structure—a cancerous growth—whose shape echoes the form of Dodger Stadium. This map further represents the conflict between the majority Latinx community that was displaced near the Chavez Ravine in Los Angeles to facilitate construction of the ballpark in 1962. In another work, the small model parts become stand-ins for people gathering in Egypt's Tahrir Square during the Lotus Revolution, inspired by Kaino's visit to Cairo on behalf of the US Department of State on the occasion of representing the States at the 13th Cairo Biennale. These micro views of macro moments allow us to intimately consider the changes in the world around us, whether through displacement or political action.

Kaino also uses sculpture to reveal some of the invisible systems of art-making; in particular, the ways in which projects get supported and artists get paid. By exposing these channels of financing, Kaino produces a metaphoric critique of art as a globalized system of political capital. But even in so doing, Kaino's wit and love of popular culture creates wider access points to the narratives of the work. Of *Untitled (Reverse Inverse Ninja Law)* (2006), Kaino states: "'The Inverse Ninja Law' is a pop-cultural theorem of collectivity. It dictates that, in the movies, a ninja is only as effective in combat as one divided by the number of ninjas in the room.

This logic makes for exciting storytelling, as a lone protagonist often beats impossible odds to win our hearts and make it to act three. ... The Inverse Ninja Law is a flawless model for imperialist propaganda and an effective hegemonic gesture."[15] Kaino inverted this "flawless" model into one of collectivity when he was commissioned to create a new sculpture for the Museum of Contemporary Art San Diego. Rather than having the museum manage the budget and purchase materials, Kaino requested that all funds come directly to him, whereupon he re-allocated them to supporters of the Zapatista Army of National Liberation (EZLN) in Chiapas, Mexico. Founded in 1994, EZLN is a Mexican Indigenous movement fighting against the state. The Zapatistas, as they are known, "Produced and leveraged a new form of revolutionary communication through the Internet. The distribution of information, actions, images, and video spread throughout the world in real time, bringing awareness while building solidarity for what the *New York Times* called 'the first postmodern revolution.' Positioning itself as a struggle against neoliberalism and waged against five hundred years of oppression, Zapatismo has employed new technologies of information distribution in order to articulate its wants and beliefs to a global audience."[16] The Zapatistas are also known for making woven dolls (clad in balaclavas and holding rifles), which they sell to tourists to support their cause. Kaino gave his commission budget to the Zapatistas by purchasing as many dolls as his money could buy, then bound the dolls together in the form of a hammer. This gesture completed the alignment between Kaino's subversion of the art world and the Zapatistas' reliance on nontraditional revolutionary tactics. Of the resulting work, Kaino states that he was also interested in implicating "the institution—raising questions about the ability of cultural production to generate multiple economies of value" and that the form the sculpture takes is "a symbol associated with the resistance against capitalism, but made tangible here through hoardable commodities."[17]

One of Kaino's most poignant exercises in visibility and seeing is *Spontaneous Combustion* (2017). Like all of his works, *Spontaneous Combustion* begins with an object we see regularly that is never as innocuous as it appears: the American flag. Kaino had a dozen hand-sewn, white-on-white flags created, which he wrapped and tie-dyed using a historic Civil War-era recipe for tarring. Just like a painter's rag covered in turpentine, if left alone the tarred flags will smolder and then spontaneously combust. For Kaino, his artistic gesture exists in extinguishing the flags, which he then unties to reveal a spiral black pattern made of tar and areas singed by heat. Upon first look, the stars and stripes are all but gone, replaced by a circular target pattern, but, as the viewer changes vantage points, they magically reappear as shadows upon the wall on which they hang, reminding us that hope can be found, and that democracy can shine through the charred remnants of our past. Kaino doesn't deny the pain of this symbol of America, but does suggest that by revealing its checkered past, by making it visible, we can understand it and carve better paths toward the future.

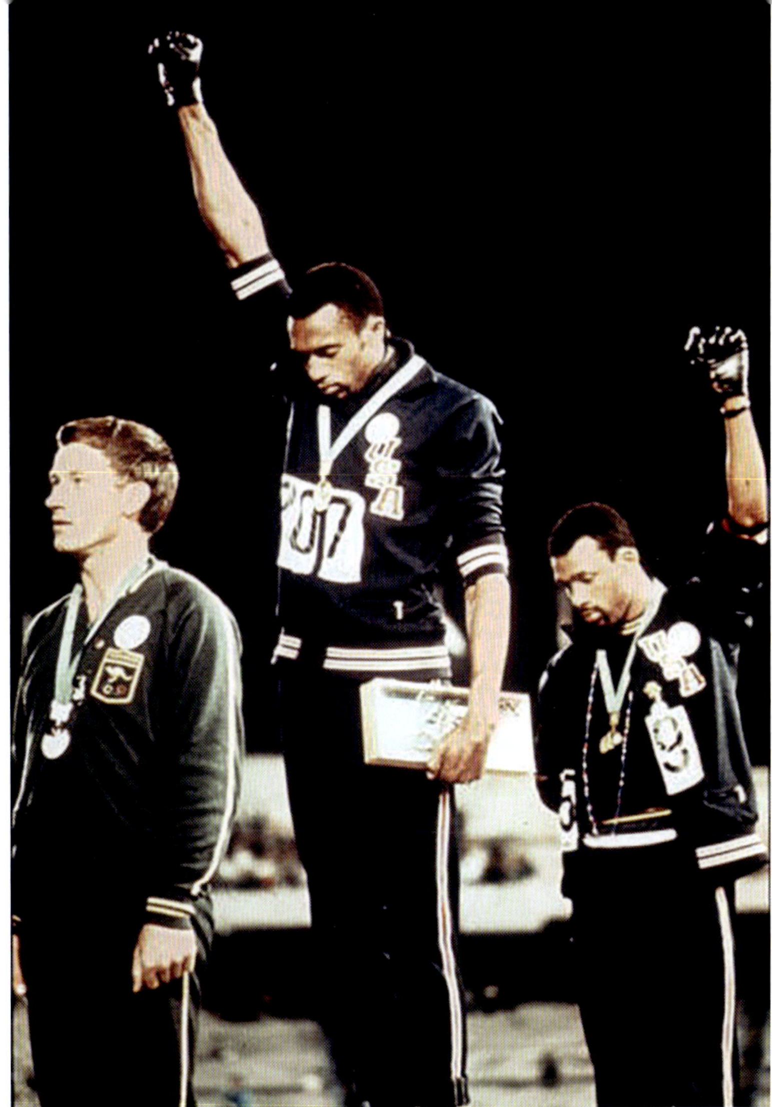


**1968 Olympic Games, Mexico City, 200-meter race gold medalist Tommie Smith (center) and bronze medalist John Carlos of the USA give Black Power salutes in a civil rights protest as they share the podium with Australian silver medalist Peter Norman**

*Photo: Rolls Press/ Popperfoto via Getty Images/Getty Images*

## EQUITY

By making the invisible known, Kaino's work furthers a commitment to equity. This is nowhere more evident than in *With Drawn Arms* (2013–2020) and *Revolutions* (2020). In 2013, Kaino's friend noticed a picture taped to his computer of Olympic champion Tommie Smith. At the 1968 Mexico City Summer Olympics, Smith won the 200-meter race in 19.83 seconds, becoming the first person to break the 20-second barrier. His fellow teammate John Carlos won the bronze, and in an act of visibility and solidarity with US civil rights activists (and a nod to student protests happening in Mexico during the Games), Smith and Carlos took to the medal stand, shoes off, heads bowed, and each raised one black-gloved fist into the air as the National Anthem played. Prior to working with Kaino, Smith had not been vocal about the true intention of the salute, but through their collaboration revealed that this gesture was not merely about Black Power, but also equity for all. This silent moment would change Smith's life forever, as he and Carlos were subsequently banned from the Games and denied the accolades of their fellow Olympians, effectively ending their careers. The photograph that Kaino had in his studio was of the medal ceremony, and Kaino's life too would change when his friend simply reacted, "Coach Smith! Want to meet him?" The familiar phrase "Coach Smith" intrigued Kaino, in that it humanized the person apart from the gesture, and that moment eventually led to an introduction between the two. Kaino didn't predetermine where this meeting would take him, but recognized the major omission of Smith's full story from mainstream cultural history, especially relevant at a time when athletes such as Colin Kaepernick and Megan Rapinoe were similarly protesting civil rights in the realm of sports. By investing in the telling of Smith's story, Kaino made a promise that the sacrifices Smith made—and those of others following in his (huge) metaphoric footsteps—would no longer be ignored by the history books.

When Kaino visited Smith for the first time in Georgia, he told the Olympian he wanted to figuratively take the arm off his body, to remove it from that singular moment and give it agency in contemporary society. Kaino did just that by casting Smith's arm, making two hundred copies and turning them into the horizontal rungs of a sculpture called *Bridge* (2013). This metaphoric gesture of a bridge communicates how Smith's salute inspired a lineage of athletes to stand up to the injustices of the world. With this first monumental transformation, Smith soon realized that art had the power to reinvest his story with meaning. In a 2020 interview, Smith stated,"I didn't throw a rock, and hide my hand. I just held a hand up for everybody to help . . . consciously to view the possibility of an ongoing positive. You see, that's why it needed to be told from an artistic intellectual view and not just me running and holding my fist up and saying, I want to raise my fist and let's do better. It goes much further than that, and you will see as time goes by how far it has gone and what it's going to lead to. We're already seeing what it's leading to."[18]

But Kaino didn't stop with *Bridge*; instead he took it upon himself to fulfill Smith's dreams, which included meeting Oprah Winfrey and then President Barack Obama, and facilitating the donation of some of his memorabilia to the Smithsonian Museum of American History. The first effort was a miss of incompatible scheduling, but Kaino fulfilled the latter two bucket-list items by bringing Smith to Washington, DC, to meet the president and donate to the Smithsonian. While in the Oval Office, Kaino and Smith presented President Obama with a drawing they made based on one of Smith's relay races. The image depicted the first time a US team won the 4 x 100 meter men's relay in world-record time. On the back, Smith inscribed to the president, "I can only imagine the length of passage, but most importantly, the baton was not dropped. Congratulations on a magnificent '8.'" Just weeks later, President Obama invoked very similar language at a speech at the Democratic National Convention, and in subsequent speeches and writings, such as in *The Economist*, when he said of his time in office that it is "a relay race, requiring each of us to do our part to bring the country closer to its highest aspirations."[19]

Never one to rest on his laurels, Kaino had further promises to grant Smith, including bringing his story to mainstream light. With that, he and co-director Afshin Shahidi worked

tirelessly over more than six years to create their feature documentary *With Drawn Arms* (2020), which was produced by Visibility. The film illustrates how that single gesture shaped not just Smith's and Kaino's lives, but also shaped our nation, including the work of countless athletes and activists. Some of the documentary's key moments take the form of artworks. The first is the 2018 exhibition *With Drawn Arms* at Atlanta's High Museum of Art, which included *Bridge*, drawings, and sculptures, as well as workshops with local youth. When Kaino and Smith take the elevator to the museum's second-floor gallery and at last the doors open, Smith sees *Bridge* roll out before his eyes, and grabs his head in disbelief, connecting the audience and Smith in a moment of shared astonishment. In a later scene, also at the museum, Kaino and Shahidi capture a parade of youth raising their fists in Smith's iconic gesture in front of a mirrored silhouette monument of the athlete, called *Invisible Man* (2016). We are reminded that his gesture, his sacrifice, was—despite the controversy surrounding it—for all of us. And finally, in perhaps the most moving passage of the film, and one that was a tremendous surprise to Smith himself, Kaino had secretly been working behind the scenes with General Mills to finally—more than fifty years after his Olympic victory—get Smith on the cover of a Wheaties box. The title of the work is simply *Champion* (2020). Seeing the tears in Smith's eyes as the box, complete with the iconic image of his raised fist, is presented to him, is emotional to say the least. In this one gesture, Kaino fulfilled a promise that hadn't even been requested.

When Kaino first proposed the idea for what would eventually become his 2021 exhibition, *In the Light of a Shadow*, for MASS MoCA's football field-sized Building 5 galleries, he was deep in production for *With Drawn Arms*, and therefore thinking of equity and fairness in relation to the current politics of the United States. About eighteen months before the 2020 presidential election, Kaino knew that part of his project (which was initially slated to open in October 2020, but was postponed to April 2021 due to the COVID-19 pandemic) had to address both the historic and present issues around voter rights in our country. This history, stretching back well before the 1960s, came to a head on March 7, 1965, when civil rights activists John Lewis and Hosea Williams organized a "Walk for Freedom" from Selma to Montgomery, Alabama, with six hundred participants. The goal was to peacefully exercise their constitutional right to vote in an era of segregation. When the group reached the Edmund Pettus Bridge, they were met by state troopers and deputized members of the Ku Klux Klan (gathered by then Dallas County Sheriff Jim Clark) who brutally attacked the unarmed marchers in an event thereafter known as Bloody Sunday. A week later, President Lyndon B. Johnson sent the Voter Rights Act (VRA) to Congress after condemning

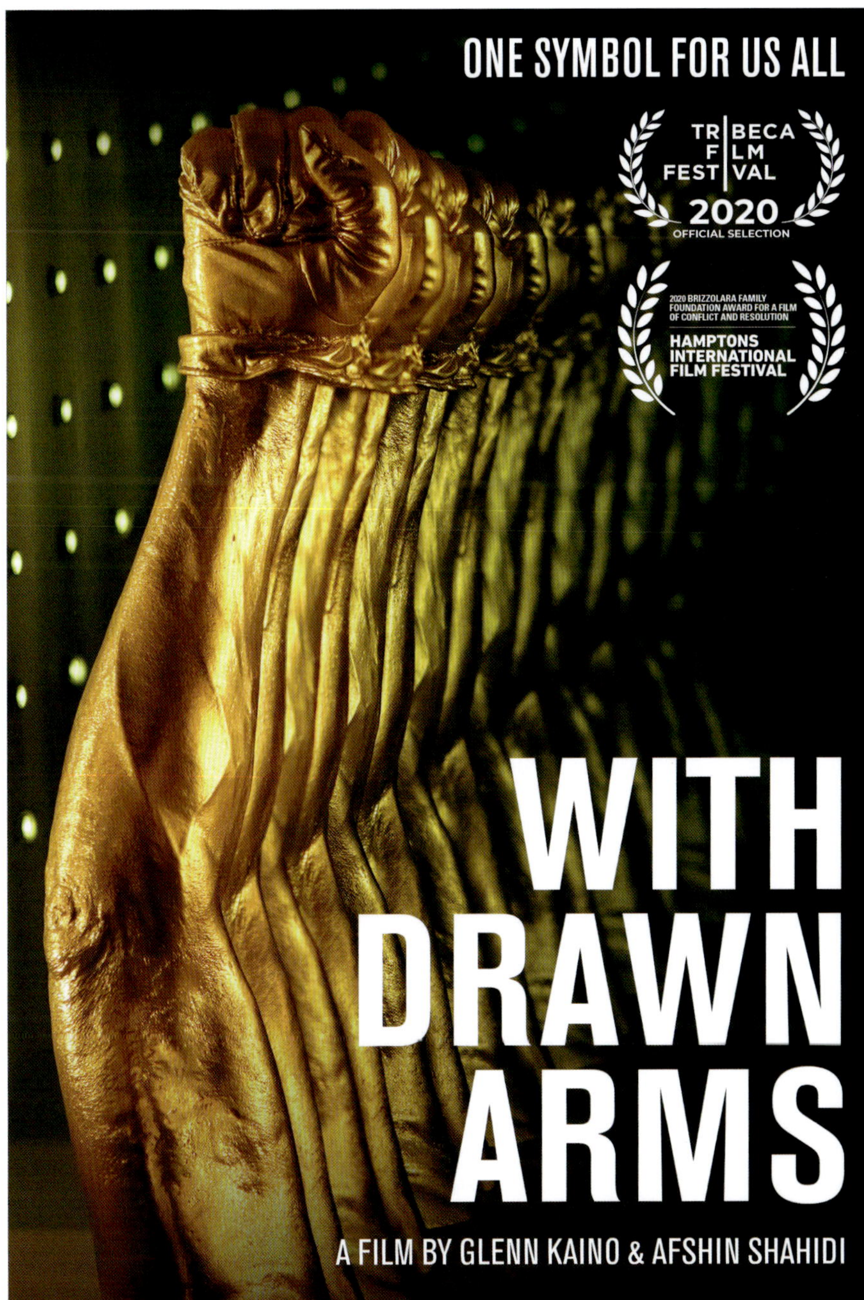

the violence. Aimed at outlawing "devices like literacy tests, transferring voter registration authority to the federal government when necessary, and applying federal standards to state elections, the VRA would succeed where previous laws had failed."[20]

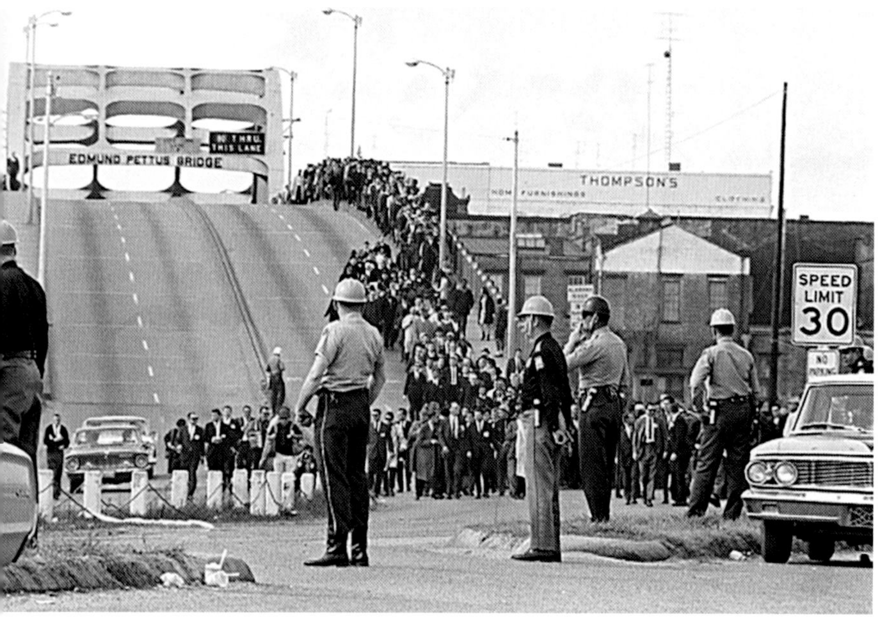


**State troopers watch as marchers cross the Edmund Pettus Bridge over the Alabama River in Selma, Alabama, as part of a civil rights march on March 9, 1965**

*Photo: Bettmann / Contributor, Getty Images*

John Lewis, who suffered a skull fracture that day, and would be elected to Congress from 1987 to his death in 2020, fought his entire life for civil rights. In his book, *Across That Bridge*, Lewis speaks of hope instead of pain, resilience instead of conceit, writing, "People ask me, 'How could you be arrested forty times in the movement and never press charges, never fight or strike back?' When people ask these questions, they perceive that I was being abused, when in reality, I was being freed. By the time I stood on the Edmund Pettus Bridge, in Selma, I had no fear of physical harm or death. So when people ask me how I managed my fear in that moment, I can truthfully say I was not afraid. I knew by that time that no one has the power to injure me. I had taken that power away by experiencing the worst they could do and discovering it did not diminish me; it did not harm me; it set me free and moved my soul beyond the fear of death."[21] Lewis became a guiding light in the fight for equality throughout his tenure in Congress, and it is difficult to see his hard-fought battle continuously challenged by the sustained voter disenfranchisement and police brutality that is all too prevalent against the African American community today, most recently culminating in the Black Lives Matter protests across the country in 2020.[22]

Voter issues were far from solved with the passing of the VRA. As we know from elections in the past two decades, faulty voter cards, broken voting machines, increased gerrymandering of districts to ensure a lack of minority power in the polls, and outright voter fraud have been all too common. To combat this, Kaino's studio mobilized volunteers, such as actors Will Ferrell and Rosario Dawson, to engage crowds as they stood in hours-long lines to vote in the Georgia gubernatorial race in 2019 (only to find that not enough machines had been supplied; associates of Kaino got inside some of the district voting stations and demanded more). Kaino then realized that art needed to do more than just say "get out the vote." A critic of art that merely looks the part rather than truly creating change, Kaino conceived of an art action that would actually drive people to the polls. The idea was called *Deep Waters*, and would center on a "souls to the polls" effort in the state of Florida. After a series of strategic assessments, Florida had been chosen for numerous reasons: it was on the verge of being a swing state demographically; Kaino and his team had numerous relationships with political organizers and activists there; Kaino had done several projects in South Florida over recent years; and the state had been the focus of many scandals around voting, most notably the 2000 presidential election between George W. Bush and Al Gore, which necessitated a recount. In 2000, *Meet the Press* moderator Tim Russert, reporting on the importance of Florida in the election, wrote on a small whiteboard the infamous "Florida Florida Florida."[23] Kaino and his studio's political director, Deon Jones (who previously worked for then Vice President Joe Biden during the Obama administration), realized that no one had ever lost Florida in the last four elections by more than 18,000 votes. So, the two began conceiving of ways they could narrow this slim margin. Kaino's idea was to use the power of art to draw people to vote by opening pop-up galleries across the state in as close proximity as possible to early voting sites. The galleries were designed by the Los Angeles-based architect Michael Maltzan, with the intent that the temporary spaces, utilizing shipping containers, could be repurposed as

public housing after the election. Drawing upon Kaino's extensive history of creating community exhibition spaces, each gallery would show the work of local artists, who would, in turn, encourage their networks of supporters to come to the art opening when casting their votes. Set to take place in the three weeks leading up to the November 2020 election, this project was sadly cancelled due to the complications surrounding gatherings of people amidst the pandemic. One can only imagine what the outcome could have been in one of the United States' most surreal elections in history.

Although *Deep Waters* remains unfulfilled as of yet, Kaino didn't give up on supporting the voter process in this contentious time, and was inspired by Stacey Abrams and her work in helping with the voter effort in her battleground state of Georgia,[24] along with her organization, Fair Fight Initiative, which seeks to change the US justice system—in particular, mass incarceration, violence, and corruption.[25] Kaino, Jones (whom Abrams has known since childhood), Will and Viveca Ferrell, and their mutual friends, Phil Mercado and Todd Quinn, held fundraising events in Los Angeles for Abrams and Fair Fight after her stolen run in Georgia. Kaino and his studio's most recent support of Fair Fight unfortunately arose from a situation of violence and corruption with regard to the LA protests after the murder of George Floyd in the spring of 2020. On May 30, Jones was peacefully protesting as part of the Black Lives Matter demonstrations at Pan Pacific Park when police blocked him in and fired rubber bullets directly at his face, an action that is against the rules of engagement. Rubber bullets are meant to be shot only on the ground so as to ricochet into crowds, not to be aimed directly at any civilian. Jones's doctors told him, "One inch higher, and you would have lost your vision. One inch lower, and you would be dead."

Taking this traumatic event as inspiration, and channeling injustice into healing creativity, Kaino and Jones mobilized by recording a new version of the iconic U2 song, "Sunday Bloody Sunday" (1983),[26] along with an accompanying video. The original song memorialized the events of January 30, 1972, when 15,000 protestors marched from Bishop's Field in Derry, Northern Ireland, in protest of violations of civil rights by the British government. On that day, the British military opened fire, killing fourteen unarmed protestors and injuring dozens more. In Ireland, this date is referred to as Bloody Sunday, just as in the United States it is used in reference to the march across the Edmund Pettus Bridge in Selma in 1965.

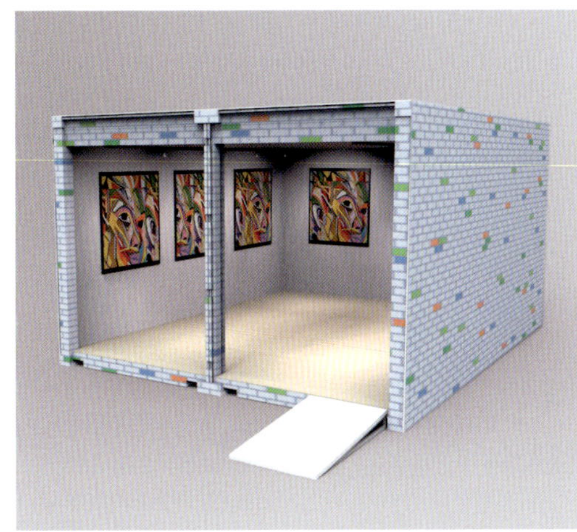

**Container gallery rendering for *Deep Rivers* Florida voter initiative, designed by Michael Maltzan**

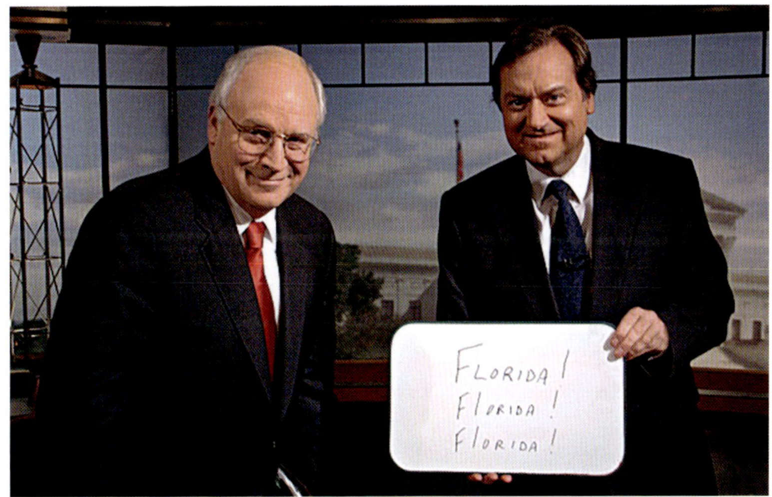


**WASHINGTON, JANUARY 28, 2001: Moderator Tim Russert (right) poses with Vice President Dick Cheney as he holds up a whiteboard with the words "Florida! Florida! Florida!" after a taping of *Meet the Press***

*Photo: Alex Wong/Getty Images for Meet the Press*

Kaino was inspired by the parallels between these events, and the cyclical history embodied by the song's refrain: "How long must we sing this song?" To that end, the centerpiece of the song's remake, and a critical part of the exhibition *In the Light of a Shadow*, is *Revolutions*, a circular sculpture Kaino created from a series of suspended metal bars, conjuring the intimidating structures often used in political suppression and border division. Each length of steel is crafted to play a specific musical note when hit with a baton. Struck in sequence, the bars play the melody of "Sunday Bloody

Sunday." Immediately following Jones's attack and recovery, Kaino rallied an all-star cast of collaborators—including producer Butch Vig, cinematographer Larry Fong, and musicians Jon Batiste and Glenn Kotche—to re-imagine and re-contextualize the U2 song around Jones's experience. The song begins with the sculpture as an instrument, played by Kotche, expands with Batiste on the piano, and then is fully realized with Jones's singing. The accompanying video, shot within the sculpture, honors history and illustrates the complicated story of its inspiration. As he sings, Jones becomes part of an unfortunate lineage, as images of both Bloody Sundays play behind him, including a historic clip of Lewis asking, "How long must we be patient?" an eerie precursor to the U2 lyrics. We become immersed in this history immediately as Jones sings, "I can't believe the news today. I can't close my eyes and make it go away." He sings again and again, "How long must we sing this song?" A refrain seemingly meant for this moment, but tragically nearly forty years old.

All proceeds from this recording have been donated to Fair Fight, reinforcing Kaino's belief and model that art has a purpose toward helping those for whom equity is a dire need. You can feel the weight of history on Jones's shoulders as he sings with passion and despair, channeling his responsibility as a public voice in a chorus speaking out against police violence.

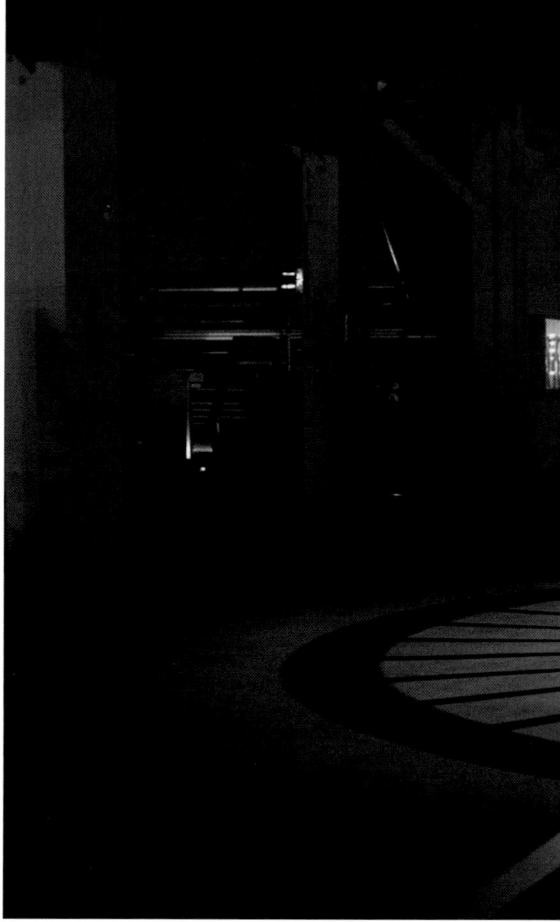

## FUTURE PROMISE

*Revolutions*—a promise by Kaino to help ensure the future of voting rights and ensure that civil rights are still taken seriously—sits within the larger exhibition *In the Light of a Shadow*. This exhibition encompasses Kaino's entire constellation of concerns in one place, making it both a reflection on his commitment in the past, and his promise to us for the future. *In the Light of a Shadow* was inspired by the connection between global protests, specifically those in response to tragic events known as "Bloody Sunday" all around the world, in addition to those in Selma and Derry. By making evident the parallels between these events, Kaino reminds us that "the struggle for equality is universal, as we have seen from numerous uprisings from people of every nation and generation, fighting to have their voices heard. *In the Light of a Shadow* is a meditation on the perpetual motion of change. It is a metaphor for the spirit of insurrection in the face of oppression, and it is an access point to the promise of the future, built on the memories of our collective past."[27] The installation in the main gallery of the vast Building 5 is viewed via an elevated 200-foot-long pathway spanning nearly the entire length of the exhibition space. This pathway bisects a levitating galaxy of rocks floating in the darkness—at once an asteroid field and a meteor shower; it also recalls rocks thrown in protest.

The politicization of rocks is not new to Kaino. For example, in the sculpture *Suspended Animation* (2014) he illuminated the precarity of political action. The piece consists of a 14-foot-long conveyor belt (similar to those used in construction to remove detritus) that is delicately balanced on just two wheels, seemingly about to obey the laws of gravity and topple. Instead, on top of the belt, which protrudes into the gallery like a jetty, are rocks that perfectly balance the piece. The rocks

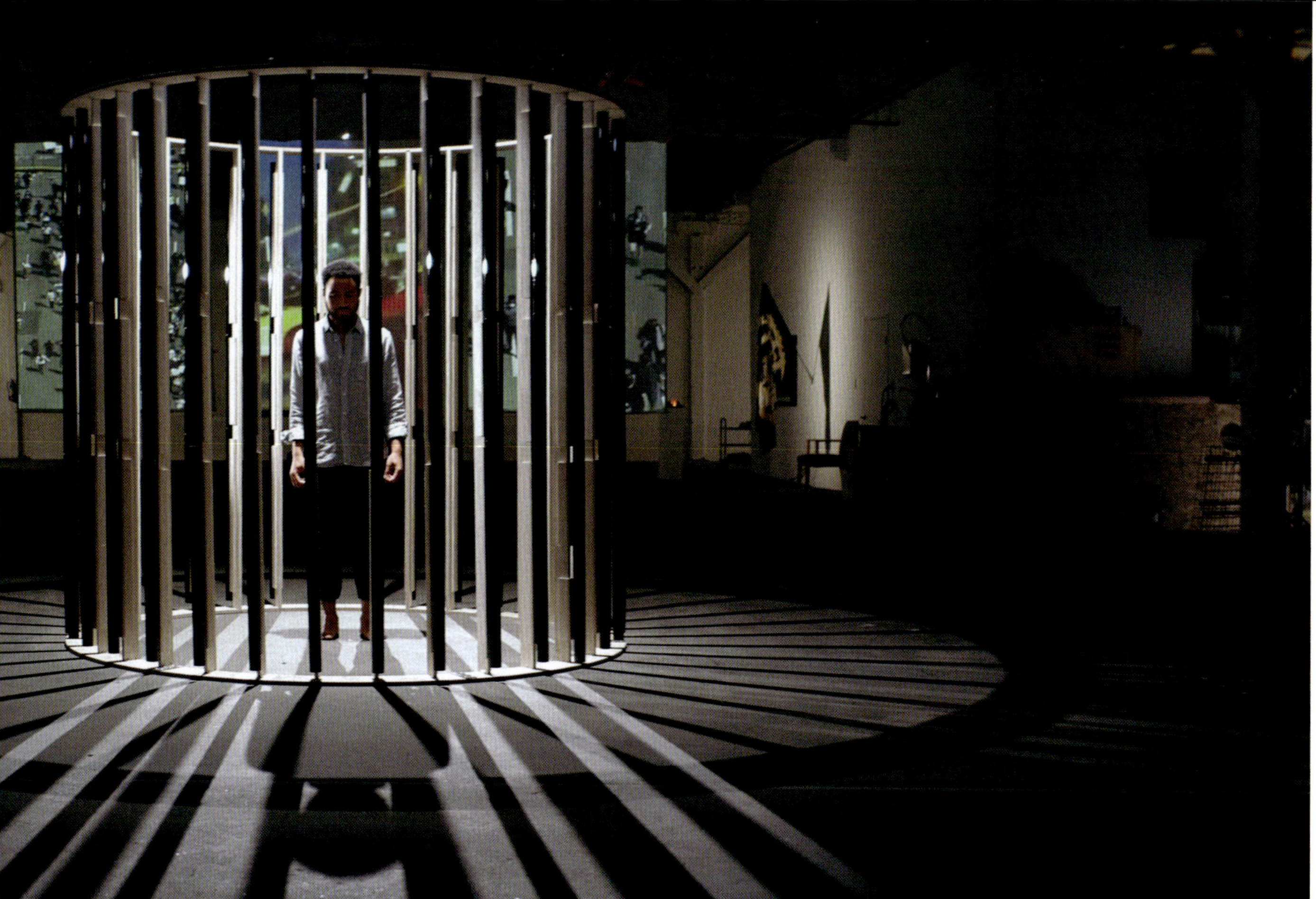

**_Sunday Bloody Sunday/ Revolutions_**

*2020, Paint, wood, metal, dimensions variable*

were collected by a network of people Kaino contacted across the globe, who hail from sites of protest and government oppression, including Tahrir Square in Cairo, Egypt; Benghazi, Libya; and Ferguson, Missouri. The action of the rocks, in balancing the very machinery that intends to displace them, reminds us that the most powerful mechanism is the human ability to rise up in the face of oppression. In an earlier work, *In Revolution* (2003), Kaino takes his title from a quote by Napoleon which states: "In revolution, there are two types of people: those who create it and those who profit from it."[28] For the sculpture, Kaino created another balancing act in the form of an A-frame fitted with a propeller arm—on one end is a massive rock, while the counterbalance contains an image of a suburban house, complete with a swimming pool filled with actual water. The centripetal force of the piece keeps the water in place, creating a status quo referencing the stasis of our political systems.

Unlike the heaviness of rocks in these previous works, the rocks for *In the Light of a Shadow* appear weightless, as if Kaino conjured his knowledge of magic to make them levitate. In transforming the rocks, Kaino turns these static objects into carriers of pure potential. In his book *Stone*, Jeffrey Jerome Cohen writes that "you expect stone to be heavy, but it is light. You presume that stone possesses fact; it holds stories. If stone had a voice it would be less ponderous than your own. If your hurried heartbeat did not bind you to your swift smallness, you would know the affinity that binds you with stone."[29] Kaino reminds us that rocks tell stories and can be lifted from their own weight. These rocks are both real and 3D printed, and they swirl above our heads in a spiral galaxy. The real rocks take the form of a fleet of ships, a nod to the Paradox of Theseus, which poses the question: if you take a boat and rebuild it over time, plank by plank, is it still the same boat in the end? Each of these small ships incorporates broken pieces of larger geological wholes, and their sails contain postcards collected by Kaino. For him, these postcards exist in a moment between a promise and a memory—traveling and sending a postcard is a promise to ourselves and our loved ones of the

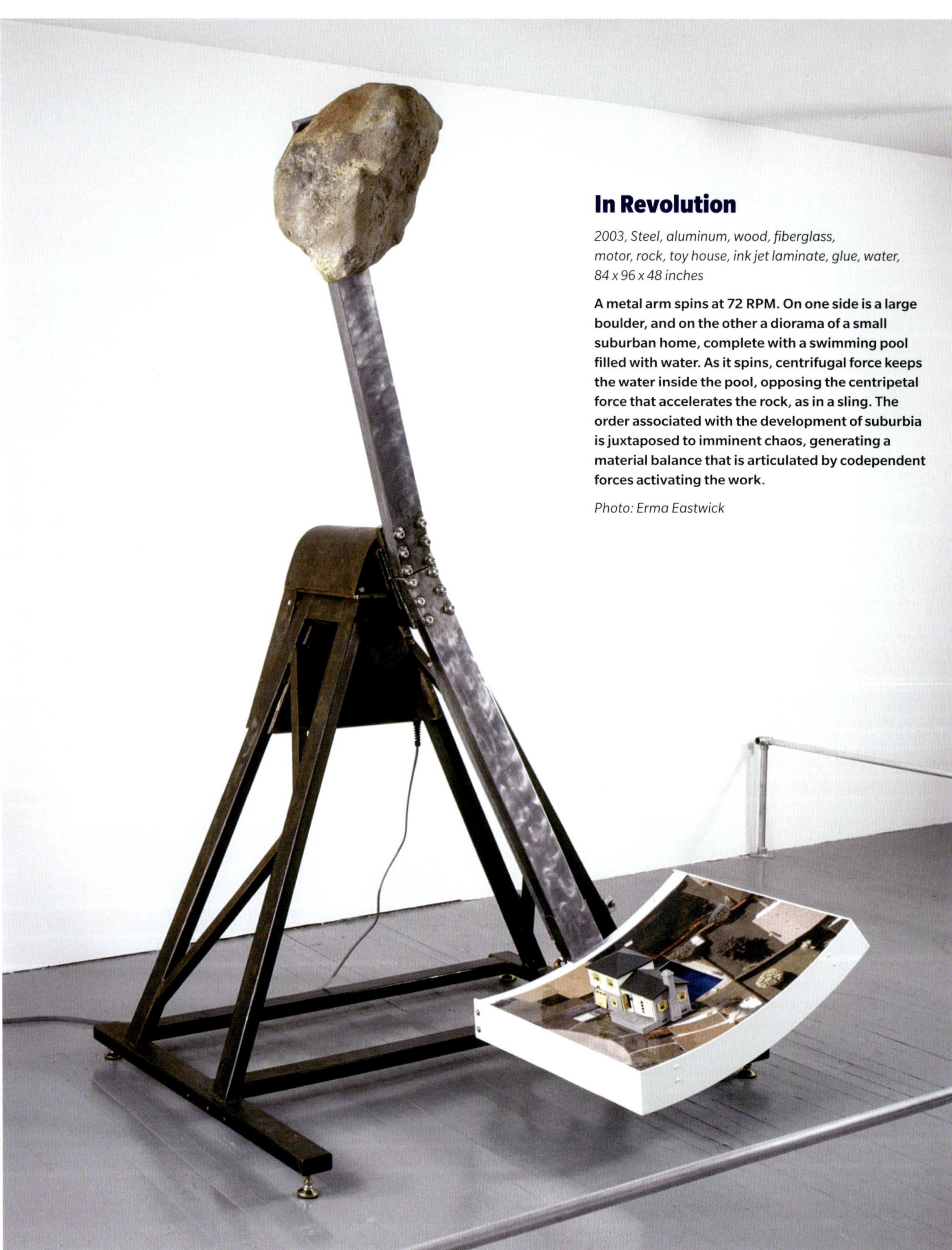

## In Revolution

*2003, Steel, aluminum, wood, fiberglass, motor, rock, toy house, ink jet laminate, glue, water, 84 x 96 x 48 inches*

**A metal arm spins at 72 RPM. On one side is a large boulder, and on the other a diorama of a small suburban home, complete with a swimming pool filled with water. As it spins, centrifugal force keeps the water inside the pool, opposing the centripetal force that accelerates the rock, as in a sling. The order associated with the development of suburbia is juxtaposed to imminent chaos, generating a material balance that is articulated by codependent forces activating the work.**

*Photo: Erma Eastwick*

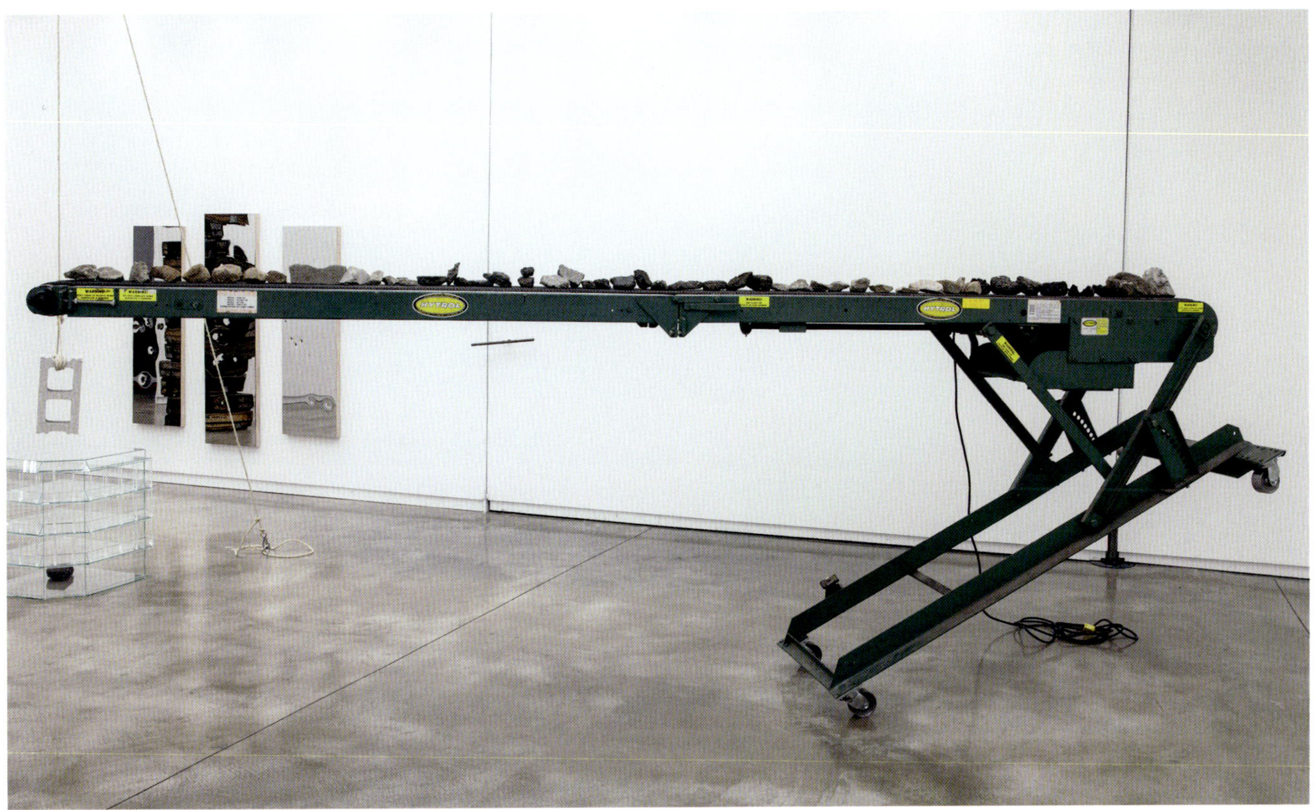

## Suspended Animation

*2014, Found rock conveyor, rocks, 63 x 173 x 41 inches*

*Suspended Animation* is a precariously balanced, 14-foot-long, found rock conveyor belt—the kind of machinery typically used to move heavy building and quarry materials. The frame of the conveyor is suspended off the ground, impossibly balanced on two small wheels, threatening all nearby with intense potential energy. The structure is counterbalanced by a pile of rocks collected from global sites of protest. These rocks were secured by a network of international agents from Tahrir Square, Yemen, Ferguson, Benghazi, and other locations that have seen massive protests against governmental oppression, and which have become a symbol threaded throughout Kaino's work about political agency—they function as not only sculpture and medium, but as a call to action. The rocks are imbued with energy—inert objects that have been lifted through mechanized force to increase their power, a collective threat that has toppled the very machinery itself into a precarious balance. The sculpture, in its suggestion of interrelated forces of movement, power, and precarity, calls into question the tensions between activist acts and the potential for change. It captures a moment of uneasy stasis in the midst of intense action—a balance that cannot hold.

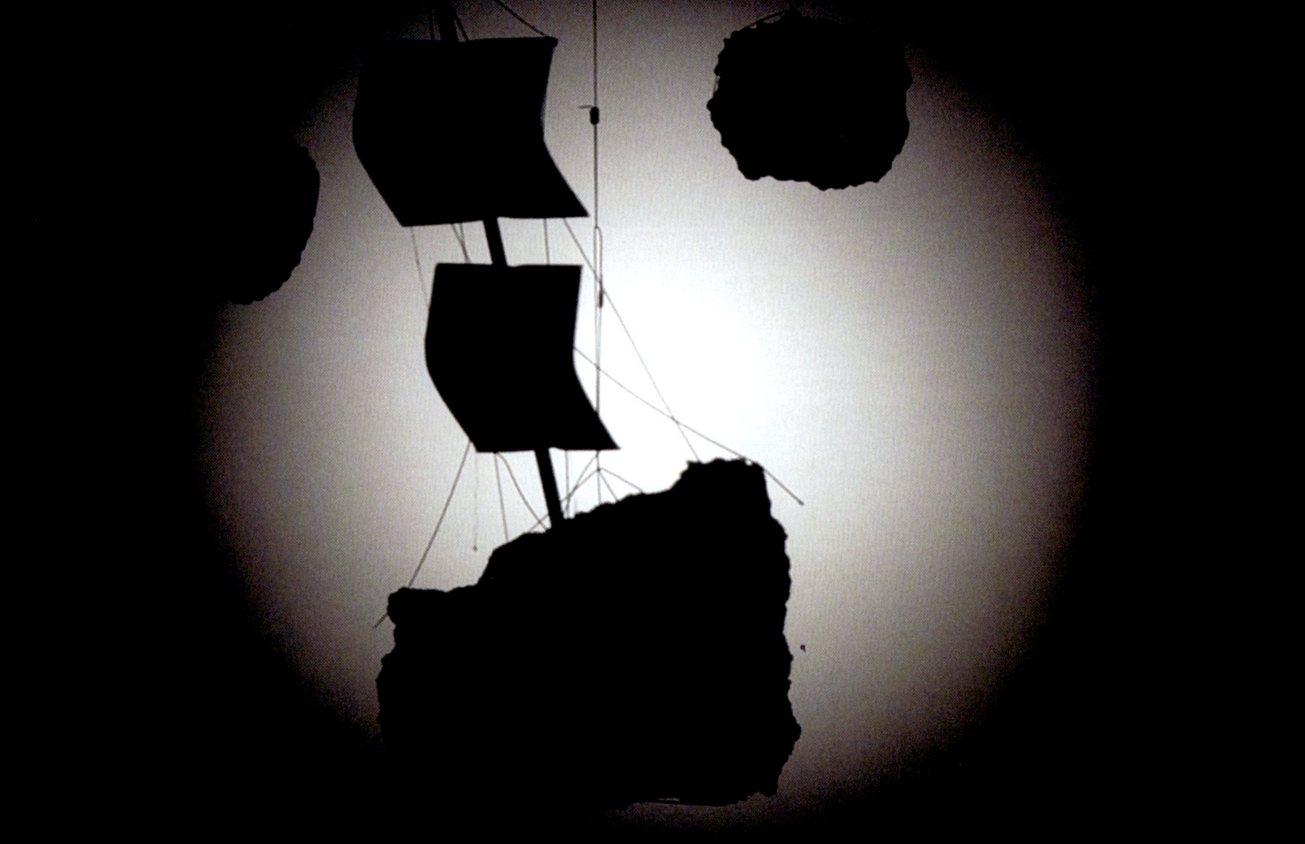

*In the Light of a Shadow*
**Fabrication detail**

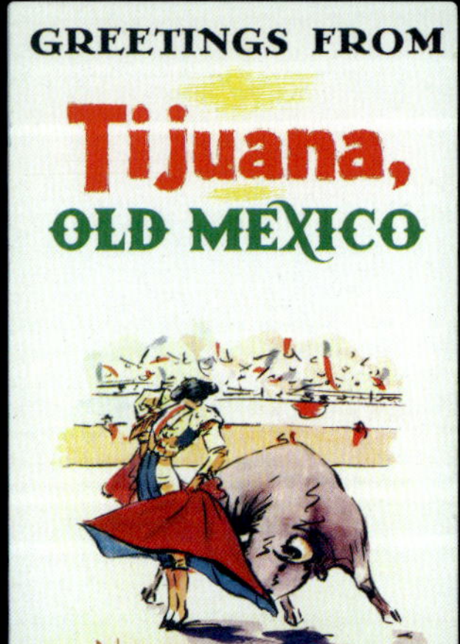


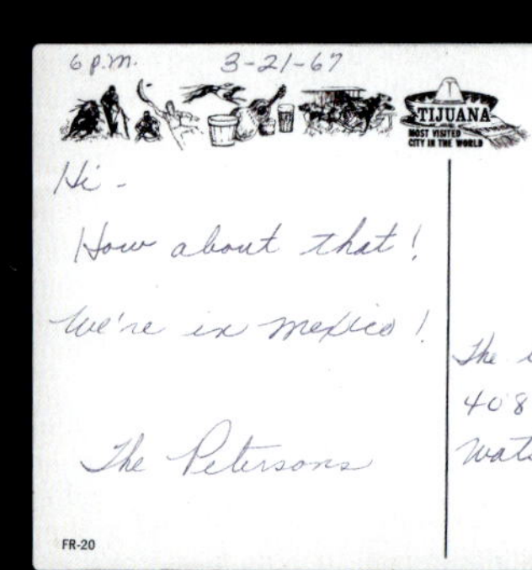

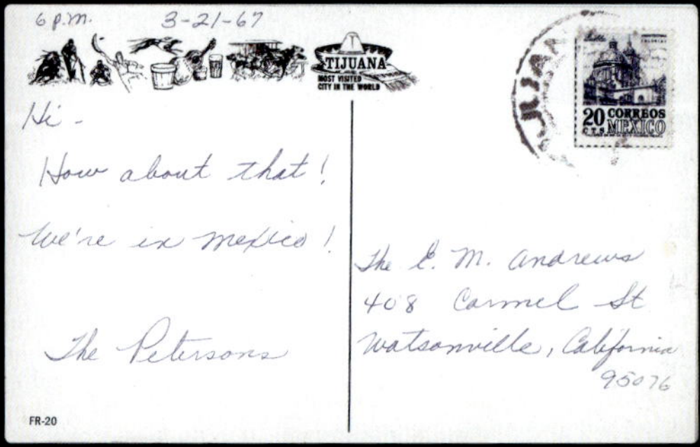

experience we are having, while in retrospect these moments become fleeting memories boiled down to phrases like, "How about that, we're in Mexico." These short dispatches are paradoxical; equally colonial, curious, and hopeful. Similarly, Kaino believes that the value of protest rocks exists only when they are in the air. Rocks (including material such as concrete and asphalt) on the ground are detritus, rocks in hand are not guaranteed to have agency, but when a rock is flying it is the symbol of hope for change against the odds. These rocks thrown in the face of protest begin as promises for change, for revolution, which in the end stand in the history books as memories. The rocks of Kaino's fleet come alive in the air of the exhibition space, and we see them magically transform into the revolutions they inspire.

Kaino's galaxy is not made up of rocks alone, at its center is a re-creation of the *Shadow V*, the fishing boat on which Louis Mountbatten, 1st Earl Mountbatten of Burma (and Queen Elizabeth II's second cousin) was assassinated by the Irish Republican Army (IRA) on August 27, 1979, in Mullaghmore Harbor on Ireland's northwest coast. Mountbatten, who had a home in Ireland close to the border with Northern Ireland, was seen as a target representing the unwelcome militarization of the North by the British forces, and the subsequent repression of the minority Irish Catholic population. The Provisional IRA, a paramilitary group protesting British (and Protestant) rule, planted a bomb on Mountbatten's fishing boat, killing him, his grandson Nicholas Knatchbull, Paul Maxwell (a young Irish boat hand), and Lady Doreen Brabourne. Additionally, Mountbatten's daughter Patricia, her husband John, and their son Timothy (twin of Nicholas) were injured. Following the bombing, the IRA issued the following statement: "In claiming responsibility for the execution of Lord Mountbatten the IRA state that the bombing was a discriminate act to bring to the attention of the English people the continuing occupation of our country. The British Army acknowledge that after 10 years of war it cannot defeat us, but yet it continues with the oppression of our people and torture of our comrades in H Block. Well, for this we will tear out their sentimental imperialist hearts. The death of Lord Mountbatten and tributes paid to him will be seen in contrast to the apathy of the British Government and English people to the deaths of over 300 British soldiers and the deaths of Irish men, women and children at the hands of their forces."[30]

This was one of the most visible moments of "the Troubles," the decades of conflict in Northern Ireland over civil rights. The political strife in Northern Ireland started well before the 1960s, when it became widely publicized outside the country due to the prevalence of televised media. While the conflict can be traced back to the 1916 Easter Rising, the matter was further confounded in 1921, when "Great Britain partitioned Ireland into two separate entities, six counties in the north-eastern historical region of Ulster remained under British rule (Northern Ireland), while the Irish Free State was established to the south. The new province of Northern Ireland was created so that the Protestants loyal to the British Crown, about two-thirds of the local population, could retain their political and cultural union with the United Kingdom. The remaining one-third of the population, the Irish Catholics, instead identified politically and culturally with what would later become the Republic of Ireland in the south."[31] This was followed in 1922 by the passage of the Civil Authorities (Special Powers) Act. "Originally intended to last for a year, it was renewed until 1933 and then made to last indefinitely. It permitted the authorities various powers, including the right to search and arrest without warrant, imprison without trial, and allow punishment by flogging. While citizens of Northern Ireland could lawfully be whipped with a cat-o'-nine-tails, those in the rest of the United Kingdom could not, as the Act only applied to the six counties ruled by the Stormont parliament."[32] These two moments, among others, set the stage for a sectarian battle between the Protestants and the Catholics in Northern Ireland, with the latter group being the ethnic minority. The peak of the Northern Ireland civil rights movement was not unlike its counterpart in the United States, and included pleas for voter rights and equitable housing, which were affected by the gerrymandering of the democratic process.

For Kaino, re-creating the *Shadow V* was not intended to be a straightforward gesture, for the events and interpretation of all radical politics are far from straightforward. Therefore, he chose to rebuild the boat to represent this

complication, and shaped it as an ouroboros—a snake eating its own tail—reminding us of the cyclical nature of conflict. When the IRA killed Lord Mountbatten—the highest-ranking British official to show empathy toward the group—they succeeded in their most visible victory, while at the same time turning the public against them. Kaino sees the rebuilding of the boat itself as an act of restitution, one that began by the artist and me traveling to Northern Ireland in 2017 to speak to constituents on both sides of the conflict about what it would mean to resurrect the boat. Everyone agreed that a rebuilding and re-imagining of the boat—representing the violent past eating itself alive—would be a welcome symbol of the future. Additionally, Kaino's version of the *Shadow V* is partially transparent, though there are burnt planks attached at the point where the two sides crash together, emblazoned with text from protest posters. Kaino then placed lights inside the vessel, choreographed to pulsing sound, bringing the heartbeat of the boat to life in the gallery.

For *In the Light of a Shadow* Kaino takes two of the most visible moments of the Troubles,[33] Bloody Sunday, and the bombing of the *Shadow V*, and aligns them with the US civil rights movement. The IRA openly borrowed tactics from people like Martin Luther King Jr. and John Lewis (until the Troubles turned away from civil disobedience toward violence). Alongside the parallel Bloody Sunday events, Brian Dooley outlines other ways in which the African American and Northern Irish communities found alignment. He begins his book, *Black and Green: The Fight for Civil Rights in Northern Ireland and Black America*, by writing: "The Irish Times is a famous Irish bar in Washington, DC, opposite Union Station and just a few hundred yards away from the US Congress. It displays all the usual Irish-American memorabilia found in Irish-American bars all over the country—pictures of John F. Kennedy, of Michael Collins, of James Joyce. Next to a mirror promising Jameson's Irish whiskey, there is a portrait of black American Frederick Douglass, and at first glance the picture seems incongruous—a nineteenth-century black face looking down from a row of Irish heroes. But for many years former slave Douglass agitated in Washington for Irish independence, visited Ireland twice and spoke at a political meeting with Daniel O'Connell in Dublin. Douglass is one of the largely forgotten links between black American and Irish politics, part of a tradition which goes back several centuries and which inspired the civil rights movement in Northern Ireland in the 1960s." He goes on to note that "civil rights activists in Northern Ireland borrowed slogans from black American protestors, called themselves 'white negroes' and identified in a positive way with the struggle across the Atlantic led by Martin Luther King."[34] In addition, during the march from Belfast to Derry in Northern Ireland in 1969, marchers sang the US civil rights protest song, "We Shall Overcome," and referred to the march as "Selma to Montgomery."

**Young Catholic rioters hurl projectiles at British soldiers in Londonderry on March 2, 1972, during a rally protesting the January 30 "Bloody Sunday" killing of thirteen Catholic civil rights marchers by British paratroopers in the city**

*Photo: BONI DE TOROUT/ AFP via Getty Images*

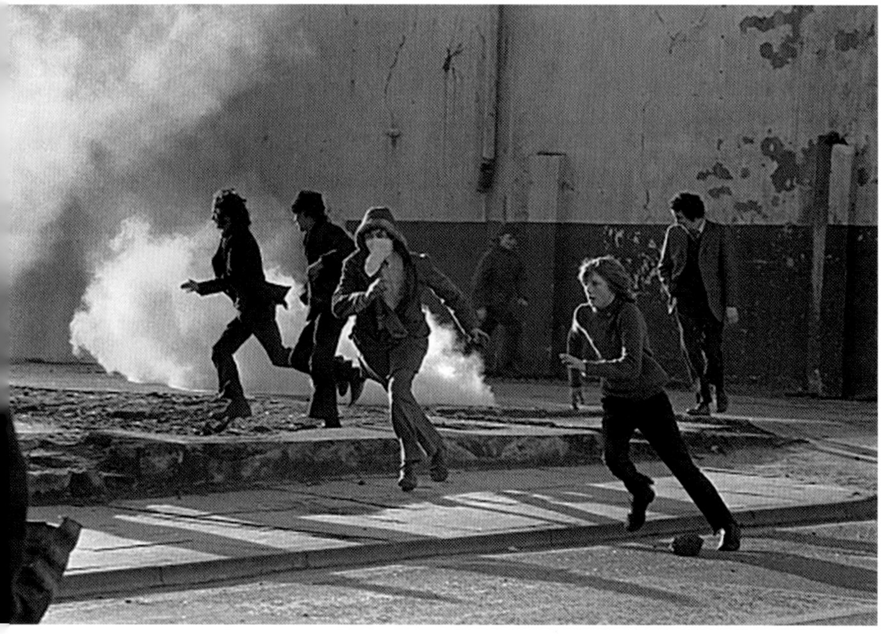

These twin histories are even more personal for Kaino. In 1994, he was invited to a dinner in Los Angeles with Gerry Adams, a former member of the IRA and at that time president of the Sinn Féin political party in Northern Ireland. Years later, while making his documentary with Tommie Smith, Kaino was able to speak with Congressman John Lewis.[35] Hearing firsthand accounts of both events allowed Kaino to reflect on the similarities of struggle and the cyclical nature of protest and revolution. Of the ineffability of revolution, one of the founders of the Occupy Wall Street Movement, Micah White, writes that "revolution is a grand overturning, a magical moment when the status quo is heaved

long enough for a new way of being to emerge. Many revolutions last only a minute and take place in the mind as an epiphany that shatters an old way of thinking. Others hold for weeks, and the epiphany spreads from mind to mind, taking the form of a social movement. And only a very few revolutions cement into a permanently new social order. Revolutions are a dynamic and complex human phenomenon. Although unpredictable—revolutions tend to appear spontaneous and are therefore notoriously difficult to forecast—they follow discernible patterns and obey physical and biological limits."[36] Kaino tests these limits in his exhibition by using shadows to illustrate the ephemerality of revolutionary moments. His shadows are not static, for he takes the rocks that form his galaxy and transforms them into the tellers of stories and carriers of both promise and memory by formally experimenting with the physical relationships between object and light.

Shadows are the stuff of dreams, nightmares, and magic, but they are also the stuff of daily life, art, and science. The allure of shadows goes as far back as Plato (though, no doubt, even further) and his "Allegory of the Cave." The story comes from *Republic* (514–520 CE) and in it Plato states: "Picture men dwelling in a sort of subterranean cavern with a long entrance open to the light on its entire width. Conceive them as having their legs and necks fettered from childhood, so that they remain in the same spot, able to look forward only, and prevented by the fetters from turning their heads. Picture further the light from a fire burning higher up and at a distance behind them, and between the fire and the prisoners and above them a road along which a low wall has been built, as the exhibitors of puppet shows have partitions before the men themselves, above which they show the puppets."[37] For Plato, this narrative uses the men who see the shadows and believe them to be true, rather than projections of the actual objects, as an allegory for false knowledge. Later, Pliny tells a story of shadows in his *Natural History* (77–79 CE) about Dibutades or the Maid of Corinth. "We know very little about the birth of painting, said Pliny the Elder. . . . One thing, however, is certain: it was born the first time the human shadow was circumscribed by lines."[38] As Pliny's story progresses, we learn that Dibutades faithfully traced her lover's shadow on the wall as he left for war—cited as one of the first shadows in art. Further, Dibutades's father then pressed clay over the tracing to create a relief of the outline, considered the first sculpture. The history of and fascination with shadows was further explored by artists such as Leonardo da Vinci and scientists such as Galileo as a way to understand the world around them.

Shadows in art provide one history, but Kaino's work also explores shadows in magic. Of this history, Marina Warner writes: "In Paris soon after the Revolution, the showman and inventor Étienne-Gaspard Robertson staged a son-et-lumière Gothic moving picture show, under the name of 'Fantasmagorie'; coined from the Greek, phantasmagoria means an 'assembly of phantasms.' Robertson used a projector, a Fantascope, dispensed with the conventional theater's raised stage, the puppet shadow box, and the proscenium arch, and concentrated his lighting sources and effects in the projector itself by placing it behind a large flat screen, like a theatrical scrim. He also mounted his newfangled magic lantern on rollers, so that when, concealed behind the screen, he pulled

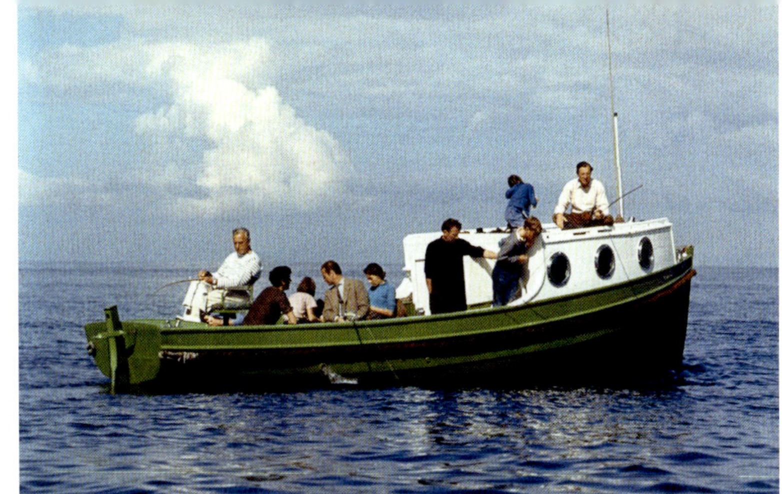

**Lord Mountbatten fishing with family and guests off the Irish coast from *Shadow V*, which was blown up in his assassination**

*Photo: Malcolm Aird, 1970, Co. Sligo, Ireland. Robert Estall photo agency/ Alamy Stock Photo*

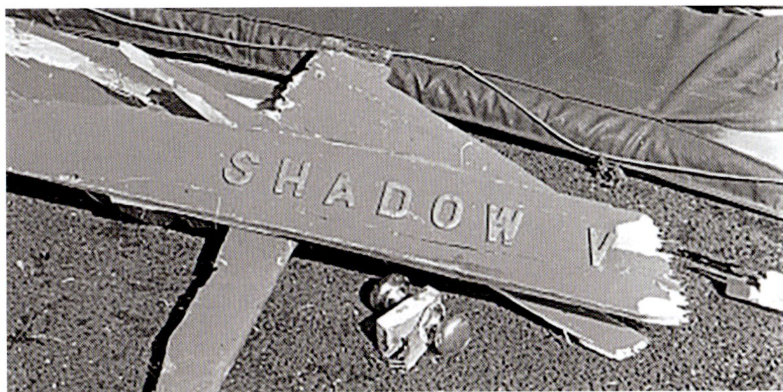


**Part of the wreckage of the *Shadow V*, in which Lord Mountbatten was assassinated by the IRA at Mullaghmore Harbor, Co. Sligo, in August 1979**

*Part of the Independent Newspapers Ireland/ NLI Collection. Photo: Independent News and Media/Getty Images*

back from the audience, the image swelled and appeared to plunge forward into their ranks. With a true impresario's flair for catching the mood of the public, Robertson deliberately excited screams and squeals."[39] For *In the Light of a Shadow*, Kaino explores the liveliness of shadows and further confounds what a shadow can do by bringing to life these dark spots, these stand-ins for the real, in order to march across the walls of the gallery. In his book *Seeing Dark Things*, Roy Sorensen states that "no part of the shadow acts. Shadows are creatures of omission. Shadows are where the inaction is." He continues with, "Philosophers are especially suspicious of rotating shadows. We can explore why with the help of the flowing question: A sphere casts a shadow. If the sphere spins, does its shadow also spin? This riddle bears on the classic controversy about how objects change."[40] Kaino turns to the realm of magic to prove that shadows are far from inert and that they are, in fact, exactly where the action lies. Drawing on his magic knowledge, Kaino understands that shadows can do more than illustrate an object. His favorite shadow-related performance artwork is an illusion from the magician Teller called "Shadows." For this piece, Teller inverts the causality of how we understand shadows as reflective of a moment by making evident the possible agency of the shadow over the object, rather than the other way around. In the performance, Teller stands before a rose in a vase as its shadow is cast on a piece of paper placed behind it. Teller then takes a knife to the shadow and mimes cutting off the shadow rose's leaves. To the audience's disbelief, the actual rose sheds its leaves without the magician ever touching it.

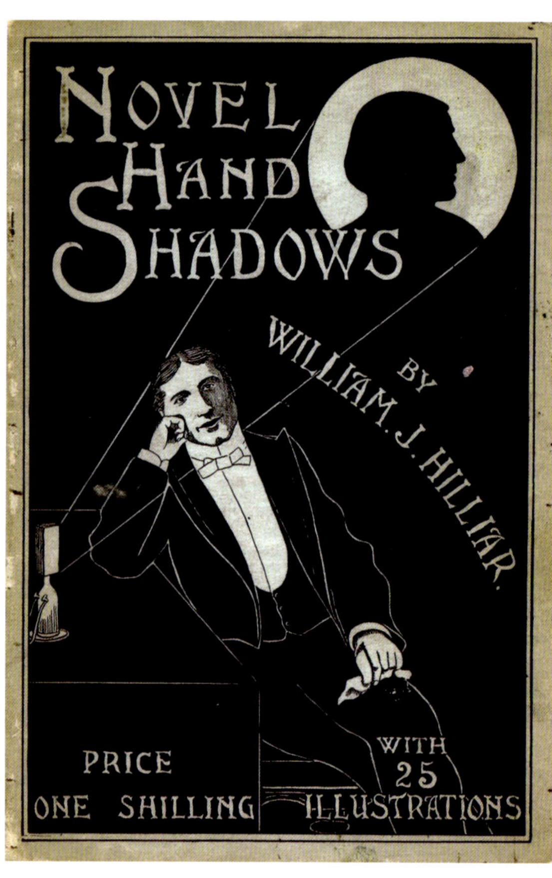


***Novel Hand Shadows* by William J. Hilliar, 1900. Hilliar was a multi-talented magician, who spent part of his career managing the sideshow for the Barnum & Bailey Circus**

*Photo: Mike Caveney's Egyptian Hall Museum*

To imbue agency and life into his own shadow compositions, Kaino sought the help of magician and historian Mike Caveney, who described to him a performance by magician Sonny Fontana, in which Fontana made a hand puppet shadow of a rabbit jump around the theater. Kaino was inspired by this conversation to push the medium forward. For *In the Light of a Shadow*, Kaino takes both rock and shadow—two seemingly static objects—and brings them both alive. Alongside representing the rock thrown in protest, the promise and memory of the history of revolution, Kaino's rocks tell the stories that are held within their lithic nature. So as the visitors move through the exhibition they are met by a sequence of choreographed shadows—accompanied by a soundtrack by the musician Dave Sitek—that emerge from these seemingly inanimate objects, forming the images of protest marchers such as those in Selma and Derry alongside images of Tommie Smith's raised fist, Colin Kaepernick's bended knee, the protester facing a tank in Tiananmen Square, etc. Further, we experience the shadows of ships sailing through the gallery as if they are stars flying by us in the galaxy, while our own shadows join the throngs, placing us in the midst of our own revolution. At one point, the shadows merge to become maps, while others take the form of texts serving as bridges to highlight the intentionality of the project. Phrases such as "you are not alone," "Black lives matter," "transparency now," "march for our lives," "yes we can," and "we shall overcome" emanate from the installation itself, as the shadow maps and texts suggest pathways for the future. This is a new kind of psychogeography, inspired by ideas found in Hakim Bey's *Temporary Autonomous Zone* (1991) and Guy Debord's *Naked City* (1957), both of which posit new ways of looking at the experience of place and its associated politics. Within these maps, Kaino reminds us that we can find light in the darkest of times, in the shadows, through unity and empathy. This was made plainly clear at President Joe Biden's inauguration on January 20, 2021, when the first-ever National Youth Poet Laureate, Amanda Gorman, spoke the phrase, "Where can we find light in this never-ending shade,"

and then ended with, "There is always light, if only we're brave enough to see it. If only we're brave enough to be it."[41] All of this aligns with the poetic turn of Kaino's title, for this light, brave enough to be seen, is found in the shadow.

It is no coincidence that all of these elements—rocks, shadows, revolutions—come together at MASS MoCA to form a galaxy, which is also the structural principle of Kaino's practice. When you trace the history of revolution, shadows, and Kaino's studio, all have celestial connections. Literary critic Hannah Arendt, in her text *On Revolution* (1963), states: "The word revolution was originally an astronomical term which gained increasing importance in the natural sciences through Nicolaus Copernicus' *On the Revolutions of Heavenly Spheres*. In this scientific usage, it retained its precise Latin meaning, designating the regular, lawful revolving motion of the stars, which, since it was known to be beyond the influence of man and hence irresistible, was certainly characterized neither by newness nor by violence."[42] Further, Italian Renaissance author Leon Battista Alberti writes of shadows in *De Pictura* (1435) that "some lights are from the stars, as from the sun, from the moon, and that other beautiful star Venus. Other lights are from fires, but among these there are many differences. The light from the stars makes the shadow equal to the body, but fire makes it greater."[43] And finally, suggesting that the study of shadows is linked to the study of astronomy, the epitaph on seventeenth-century German astronomer Johannes Kepler's grave reads, "I used to measure the heavens, now I shall measure the shadows of the earth. Although my soul was from heaven, the shadow of my body lies here."[44] In one epic gesture, Kaino brings the galaxy together—like Carl Sagan's reminder that "we are all made of star stuff"—weaving a new celestial sphere out of rocks, revolution, and shadows.

As viewers walk to the end of Building 5, before moving to the smaller mezzanine spaces (where *Revolutions* is placed) rocks make a penultimate apparition, reminding us of the path we have to take in both the gallery and history (a memory, and a promise to hold that memory in infinite time). At the back of the gallery, Kaino attempts something never before considered: he makes the enormous exhibition space even bigger. He does so by installing a monumental replica of the wall in Derry where Bloody Sunday took place, in the form of a steel mirror. The original wall is painted with the phrase, "You are Now Entering Free Derry," whereas Kaino's mirrored counterpart doubles the gallery while also creating a space for the viewer to become part of the universe reflected in its surface. Kaino's mirrors are not conventional glass mirrors; instead, they are built from a special configuration of materials so that they bend

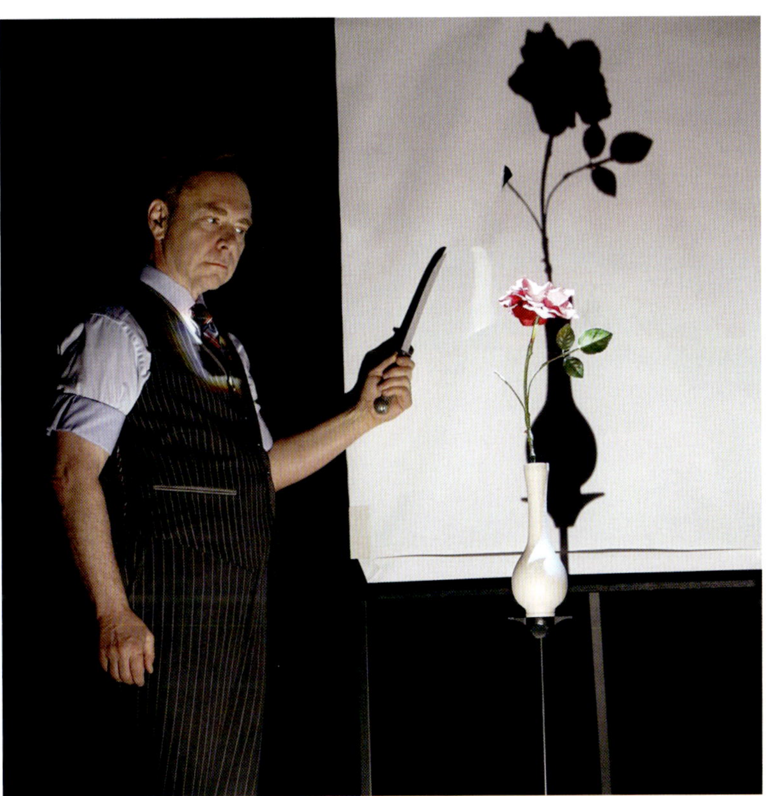

**Penn and Teller, *Shadows***

*Photo: Joan Marcus*

softly, and anything that hits them ripples, rather than shatters, the surface. This ripple technique was invented by Kaino for a body of work that he refers to as "dent paintings," in which a highly polished surface becomes embedded with liquid-looking dents when rocks are thrown at it. Kaino first used this method in *Now Do I Repay a Period Won* (2014), for which he used rectilinear shapes based on the doors and windows of US embassies that have been attacked across the world. We don't ever see the rocks, but rather witness the trace of their existence, and are left to wonder what kind of projectile could ripple, not fracture, matter. For the "Free Derry" wall at

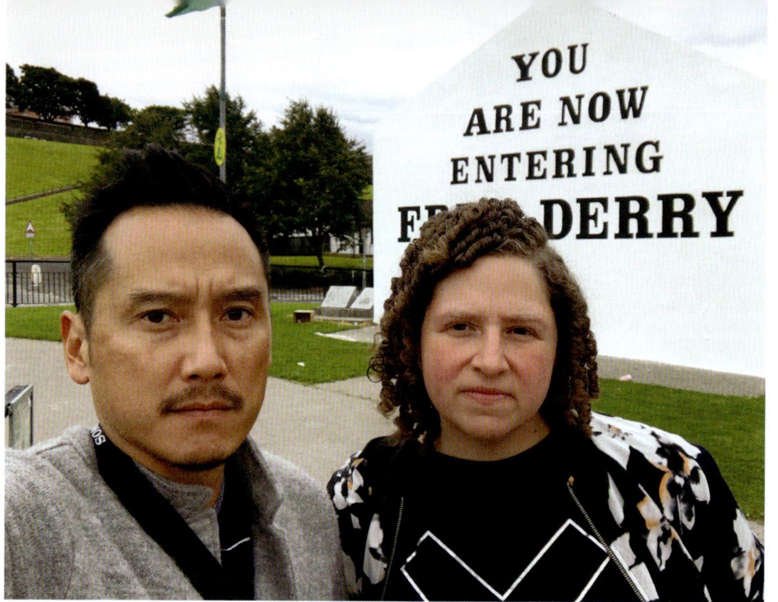


**Kaino and Markonish in Derry, Northern Ireland, 2017**

*Photo: Glenn Kaino*

MASS MoCA, Kaino expands this technique in two ways. First, by doubling the size of the gallery and mirroring the galaxy behind us, he allows us to bear witness to our own experience, as his fleet of rocks perpetually hurl themselves toward the liquid dents. Second, when we stand before the wall toward the end of the shadow show, the fourteen dents—one for each victim of Derry's Bloody Sunday—slowly light up. As each light hits the marred surface, a reflected "X" pattern apears on the floor, and soon the anthem "We Shall Overcome" fills the space. The first verse is sung by the Silverlake Conservatory of Music's youth choir, while the second verse is a historic recording of the song sung by protestors in Derry on the day of Bloody Sunday. The reckoning that takes place in front of the Derry wall—of history and the present, and of the use of this iconic song in both Selma and Derry —recalls art critic Harold Rosenberg's 1960 statement that "the differences between revolution in art and revolution in politics are enormous; revolution in art lies not in the will to destroy but in the revelation of what already is destroyed."[45]

The final act of the shadow show is a series of ships made from rocks and postcards that slowly voyages across the room—their sails facing forward and back—and functions simultaneously as a retrospective elegy and a path forward. In the end, the largest gallery of the exhibition, not just the ship and the shadows, functions as an ouroboros or a palindrome. It can be read forward and back, in cycles and reflection, reminiscent of Chris Marker's film *La Jetée* (1962) and the phrase "twice-lived fragment of time."[46]

For Marker, this notion relates to time travel and re-living the past, while understanding and being haunted by memory; in Kaino's hands, it is the bridge between promise and memory, that space of both future and past made hybrid through the double nature of shadows and reflection, revealing the cyclical nature of history.

## REGENERATION

After revealing what has been destroyed, Kaino turns to regeneration. The final artworks of *In the Light of a Shadow* bookend the main gallery, illustrating how regrowth comes from ashes. Regeneration has been a part of Kaino's work for years, used to explore ecology through the lens of decolonizing nature. Of this theory, T. J. Demos writes: "Political ecology necessitates engagement with these inequalities of our neocolonialist present, just as centuries of colonialism initiated climate change. Accumulation by dispossession occurs when the fossil fuel economy in so-called developed nations creates the atmospheric pollution that, in causing global warming, now threatens the existence of small island nations, such as Kiribati and the Maldives, creates havoc in the Bangladesh's delta, and melts permafrost in Alaska." He goes on to say that "decolonizing nature entails no longer placing ourselves at the center of the universe and viewing nature as a source of endless bounty."[47] That is exactly what Kaino does in *Tank* (2014), which consists of a series of aquarium infinity tanks, inside of which he grows coral. However, the corals grow on fragments cast from decommissioned M-60 Patton military tanks.[48] The M-60s were sunk to construct artificial reefs, rendering machines of destruction into life-affirming ecosystems. Kaino took casts of a tank before it was submerged, and uses the pieces for his own coral-growing venture. What was fascinating to him was that "the vibrant colors that the viewers encounter in these tanks are not, however, entirely peaceful; as the polyps grow, they encroach on each other's boundaries, thereby creating new visual demarcations of color and density while simultaneously exposing a slow-motion war for survival."[49] Corals are in fact colonists that war at their borders with other corals in order to defend their territory. For Kaino, the tank is an apt metaphor for nature finding its way.

For *In the Light of the Shadow*, Kaino further explores ideas of regeneration. Before arriving at the galaxy of rocks, visitors encounter two small artworks at the entrance to Building 5, the sculpture *We Shall Overcome, We March With Selma, Free Derry* (2021), and the painting *Ours to Eat, Brotherhood* (2020). The allusion to fire is one that holds many reference points at present, from the burning forests of California and Australia as a result of climate change, to fires in locations such as Ferguson and Minneapolis in protest of police violence. But one is also reminded of the regenerative qualities of fire, in particular the slash-and-burn techniques used by Indigenous populations to cultivate and control flammable ground cover. For this sculpture, Kaino presents a small bonfire. But as in all of his work, things aren't quite what they seem, and we are confronted with what the artist refers to as a poetic contradiction: we can see the flames but there is no heat. Instead, the illusion of fire is created by the very matter that is used to extinguish it: water. The fuel/firewood also tells a story, for it is created from sticks that have been carved with words taken from cross-generational global protest posters, such as "overcome," "the police," and "continues." The painting similarly utilizes these burned planks to create intersectional poetry in the form of an arrow pointing to the exhibition entrance. The seemingly burning remnants form an eternal flame, as the sticks that once held posters aloft smolder in perpetuity. The work recalls the Latin palindrome *In girum imus nocte et consumimur igni*: "We wander around in the night in circles and get consumed by fire," a fitting epitaph for the history of protest.

Kaino does not leave us in the ashes, for in the upper mezzanine gallery of Building 5 we are confronted with a platform levitating off the gallery floor. On top is a Zen garden with two non-traditional components. The first is a series of cloud chambers—tanks that hold frozen alcohol vapor that creates an environment in which usually invisible particles are made visible, such as alpha particles, muons, electrons, and more. As the mist created by the vapor falls slightly, we see trails of the zipping particles manifest before our eyes, becoming a miniaturized version of the galaxy we just traversed. Accompanying the cloud chambers are more rocks. Echoing the galaxy below (which is visible from the mezzanine's balcony) these rocks, much like the shadow producers on the lower floor, are far from inert. Out of each rock sprouts new growth in the form of plants based on precolonial tropical species; regenerating from a seemingly barren landscape, they remind us that nature—both human and the flora/fauna variety—can persevere. This is an apt reminder that work on this exhibition, though five years in the making, was completed in the middle of a global pandemic. The timing necessitated that Kaino make radical shifts in the project to accommodate the inability of his studio team and MASS MoCA's fabricators to come together in person, instead building sculptures apart and over Zoom. It is also a reminder that in the midst of this pandemic, though we have seen some of the darkest times in our society—from the Black

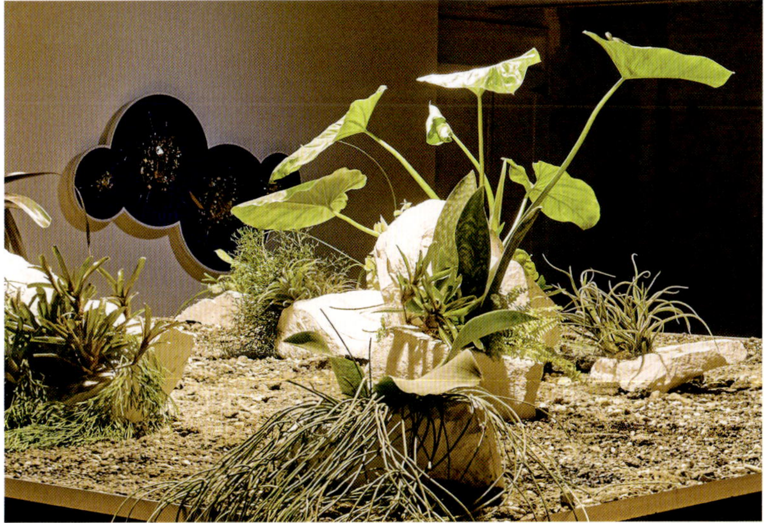

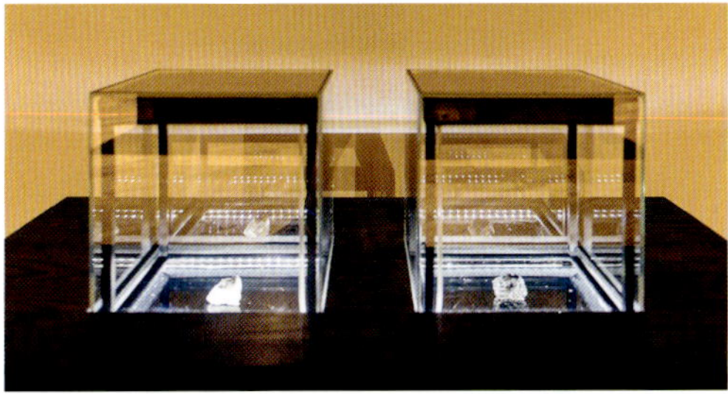

***In the Light of a Shadow*** **Installation views of plants and cloud chambers, 2021**

*Photos: Tony Luong*

Lives Matter protests to the fraudulent claims of election fraud and the shocking insurrection at the US Capitol—we have also experienced bright spots on occasion, such as nature's ability to repair itself as we humans slow our destructive tendencies.

## HOPE

Finally, since Kaino is in the business of making promises, his work, though addressing complicated politics, strives to find hope. Though Kaino does not list hope as one of the studio's core concerns, I would argue that it is, because everything he does, the very center of his galaxy, revolves around the concept—producing it, highlighting it, reminding us that, in the darkest of days, anything is achievable. Rebecca Solnit writes that "hope locates itself in the premises that we don't know what will happen and that in the spaciousness of uncertainty is room to act. When you recognize uncertainty, you recognize that you may be able to influence the outcomes—you alone or you in concert with a few dozen or several million others. Hope is an embrace of the unknown and the unknowable, an alternative to the certainty of both optimists and pessimists."[50] It is hope as a catalyst for action that is particularly important to Kaino, for a lot of art and a lot of artists merely illustrate the politics of our time rather than acting to change them. Kaino's fostering of belief, his support of community through spacemaking, his granting of visibility and equity to those who have been forgotten, and his reminder that through the darkest of times we can regenerate, all allow us to locate hope through art that is action.

In 2014, Kaino made a work titled *Excalibur*. The sculpture is a slingshot embedded into a wall with a waiting stone. Like the sword in the stone, or the slaying of Goliath, the rock waits for the right person to free it. The person to liberate the slingshot—and who in turn would surely promise to show us how to free it as well—is Kaino, and he uses this perceived weapon to engender hope in the world. In emancipating the idea of a rock, Kaino channels Congressman John Lewis, who encouraged people to get into "good trouble." Lewis writes: "This planet can smolder with imagination, burn with creativity, reverberate with love, oneness, and peace. The infinite is possible, but this beauty can only manifest through us."[51] So, with this beauty, this love—and a dash of magic—make a wish; if you are lucky, Kaino might ensure that it comes true, for he will weave your dreams into memories while ushering you through the door into the secret theater. Believe me, it is all true.

[1] *http://ratconference.com/secretth.htm. This quote appears on a deck of cards Kaino created in 2010 with magician Derek DelGaudio for their collaborative,* A.Bandit.

[2] *"Origins of A.Bandit," an interview with Denise Markonish in Glenn Kaino and Derek DelGaudio,* A.Bandit: A Secret Has Two Faces *(Munich, London, New York: DelMonico/Prestel, 2017), p. 19.*

[3] *In a note to the author, January 2021.*

[4] *"Origins of A.Bandit," in* A.Bandit: A Secret Has Two Faces, *p. 20.*

[5] *Max Maven, "Mystery Loves Company," in* A.Bandit: A Secret Has Two Faces, *p. 14.*

[6] *When the show moved from LA to New York City it became one of the longest and most successful off-Broadway productions in the theater's history. The show ran, between the two cities, from May 11, 2016, to August 19, 2019. A film based on the play, directed by Frank Oz, was released on Hulu in 2021.*

[7] *Glenn Kaino, "Secrets Keeping Secrets," in* A.Bandit: A Secret Has Two Faces, *p. 239.*

[8] *Deep River closed in 2001.*

[9] *http://www.tmr.la/about.*

[10] *Kaino was introduced to the Calvino piece during one of our early working sessions, when he inquired about a tattoo on my arm illustrating the story, created by the artist Eva Karabudak.*

[11] *Italo Calvino, "The Distance of the Moon," in* The Complete Cosmicomics *(Boston: Mariner Books, 20020), p. 3.*

[12] *Kaino's interest in art and science will be seen in an exhibition he is curating about the intersections of climate and astronomy for the Hammer Museum, Los Angeles, on the occasion of 2024 Pacific Standard Time (PST), an initiative of The Getty Foundation to unite Southern California cultural institutions around shared themes.*

[13] *From the artist to the author, January 2021.*

[14] *From the artist to the author, December 2020.*

[15] *"Ninjas and Pirates, Revolution and Romanticism: In Conversation with Glenn Kaino," by Lauri Firstenberg, in* Communicating Rooks: The Work of Glenn Kaino *(Berlin: Hatje Kantz, 2008), p. 18.*

[16] *Marc James Leger and David Thomas, eds.,* Zapantera Negra: An Artistic Encounter Between Black Panthers and Zapatistas *(Brooklyn: Common Notions), p. 1.*

[17] *From the artist to the author, December 2020.*

[18] *Mike Fleming Jr., "Defined by 1968 Olympics Silent Podium Protest Whose Message is Now Crystal Clear,"* Deadline.com, *June 9, 2020, https://deadline.com/2020/12/tommie-smith-1968-olympic-sprinter-gold-medal-protest-bounce-trumpet-awards-with-drawn-arms-1234655132/.*

[19] *Barack Obama, "The Way Ahead,"* The Economist, *October 8, 2016, www.economist.com/by-invitation/2016/10/08/the-way-ahead.*

[20] *Ari Berman,* Give Us the Ballot *(New York: Farrar, Straus and Giroux, 2015), p. 34.*

[21] *John Lewis,* Across That Bridge: A Vision for Change and the Future of America *(New York: Simon and Schuster, 2015), p. 34.*

[22] *The most recent protests came after the killings of George Floyd and Breonna Taylor, just two of countless victims of police violence in 2020 alone.*

[23] *www.today.com/news/election-night-2000-tom-brokaw-others-look-back-nbc-news-t192646. Later, "Unwindulax," a 2012 episode of the TV show 30 Rock, would spoof Russert by calling Florida the "armpit of America" in a scene about election results.*

[24] *Most recently seen in the 2021 Senate run-off races and the subsequent victories of Jon Ossoff and Raphael Warnock, the first Democrats elected to the Senate from Georgia since 2000, which also led to Democratic control of the Senate.*

[25] *www.fairfightinitiative.org/.*

[26] *"Sunday Bloody Sunday," written by Bono/Adam Clayton/The Edge/Larry Mullen Jr., was released by Island Records in 1983 on the U2 album* War.

[27] *From the artist to the author, December 2020.*

[28] Communicating Rooks, *p. 77.*

[29] *Jeffrey Jerome Cohen,* Stone: An Ecology of the Inhuman *(Minneapolis: University of Minnesota Press, 2015), p. 30.*

[30] New York Times, *August 31, 1979, www.nytimes.com/1979/08/31/archives/statement-by-ira.html.*

[31] *Lorenzo Bosi and Gianluca De Fazio, "Contextualizing the Troubles Investigating Deeply Divided Societies through Social Movements Research," in* The Troubles in Northern Ireland and Theories of Social Movements, *ed. Bosi and De Fazio (Amsterdam: Amsterdam University Press, 2017), p. 18.*

[32] *Brian Dooley,* Black and Green: The Fight for Civil Rights in Northern Ireland & Black America *(London: Pluto Press, 1998), p. 40. See also Dooley's essay in this volume.*

[33] *The third would be the hunger strikes at the Long Kesh prison just south of Belfast, including the death of Bobby Sands. Sands went on a hunger strike for sixty-six days in 1981, protesting the shifting of his status from political prisoner to part of the general prison population. The official reason he was jailed was that he was found riding in a car with an unloaded weapon.*

[34] *Dooley,* Black and Green, *p. 1.*

[35] *Kaino later heard vocalist Bono's account of the U2 song, "Sunday Bloody Sunday." A report on Adams's visit, which was granted by Bill Clinton, can be found at www.latimes.com/archives/la-xpm-1994-09-24-mn-42433-story.html.*

[36] *Micah White,* The End of Protest: A New Playbook for Revolution *(Toronto: Knopf Canada, 2016), p 59.*

[37] Plato: Collected Dialogues, *ed. Hamilton & Vairns, trans. P. Shorey (New York: Random House, 1963), p. 747.*

[38] *Victor I. Stoichita,* A Short History of the Shadow *(London: Reaktion Book, 1997), p. 7.*

[39] *Marina Warner, "Darkness Visible," in* Cabinet, *Issue 24: Shadows, Winter 2006–7, p. 75.*

[40] *Roy Sorenson,* Seeing Dark Things: The Philosophy of Shadows *(Oxford: Oxford University Press, 2011), pp. 74 and 76.*

[41] *www.npr.org/sections/inauguration-day-live-updates/2021/01/20/958743170/poet-amanda-gorman-reads-the-hill-we-climb.*

[42] *Hannah Arendt,* On Revolution *(London: Penguin Classics, 2006), p. 42.*

[43] *Stoichita,* A Short History of the Shadow, *p. 137.*

[44] *Roberto Casati,* The Shadow Club: The Greatest Mysteries of the Universe—Shadows—and the Thinkers Who Unlocked Their Secrets *(New York: Knopf, 2003), p. 128.*

[45] Lapham's Quarterly, *Volume VII, No. 2, Spring 2014, Revolutions, p. 127.*

[46] *www2.hawaii.edu/~meidor/art_101/la_jetee.html.*

[47] *T.J. Demos,* Decolonizing Nature: Contemporary Art and the Politics of Ecology *(Berlin: Sternberg Press, 2016), pp. 17 and 19.*

[48] *Infinity tanks have no tops, and the water flows right to the surface, creating a glass-like surface tension that allows for a clear bird's eye view.*

[49] Glenn Kaino *(Chicago/Berlin: Kavi Gupta Gallery, 2014), unpaginated.*

[50] *Rebecca Solnit,* Hope in the Dark: Untold Histories, Wild Possibilities *(Chicago: Haymarket Books, Second Edition, 2016), p. XIV.*

[51] *Lewis,* Across that Bridge, *p. 201.*

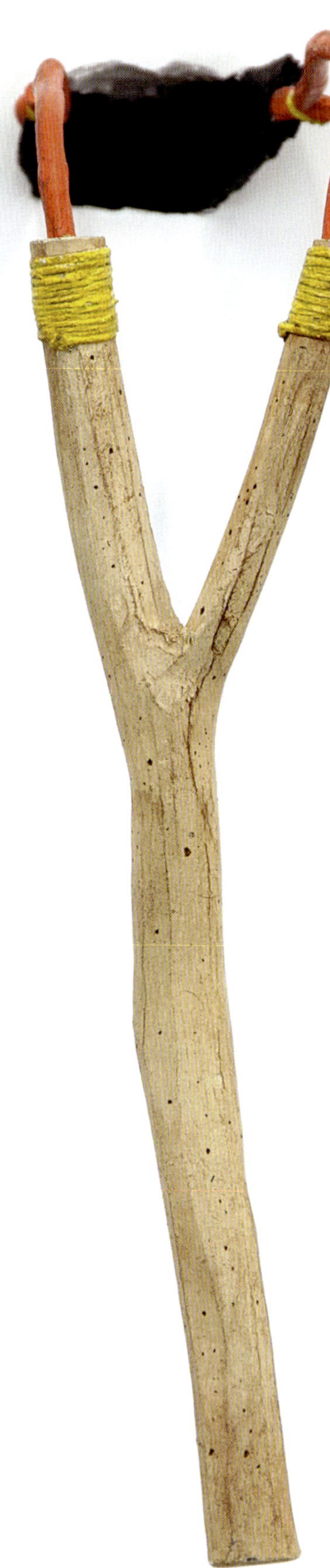

## Excalibur

*2014, Painted bronze, 11 x 7.75 inches*

Instead of a sword stuck in stone, awaiting a true leader to liberate it, *Excalibur* is a slingshot embedded in the wall. Purveyor of rocks, tools of political agency, this sculpted weapon challenges the viewer to consider his/her own complicity in systems of social currency and exclusionary power. Who will pull it out and become a change agent rather than a passive consumer? Like Joseph Beuys's multiples, this edition invites action through the spread of objects, questioning the relevance of art as political provocation. This piece is hopeful, wishing to imbue art with agency and purpose, but resigned to its limitations. It is up to the viewer to make viable the capacity for social change latent in all of us.

*Photo: Joseph Rynkiewicz*

OF A SHADOW

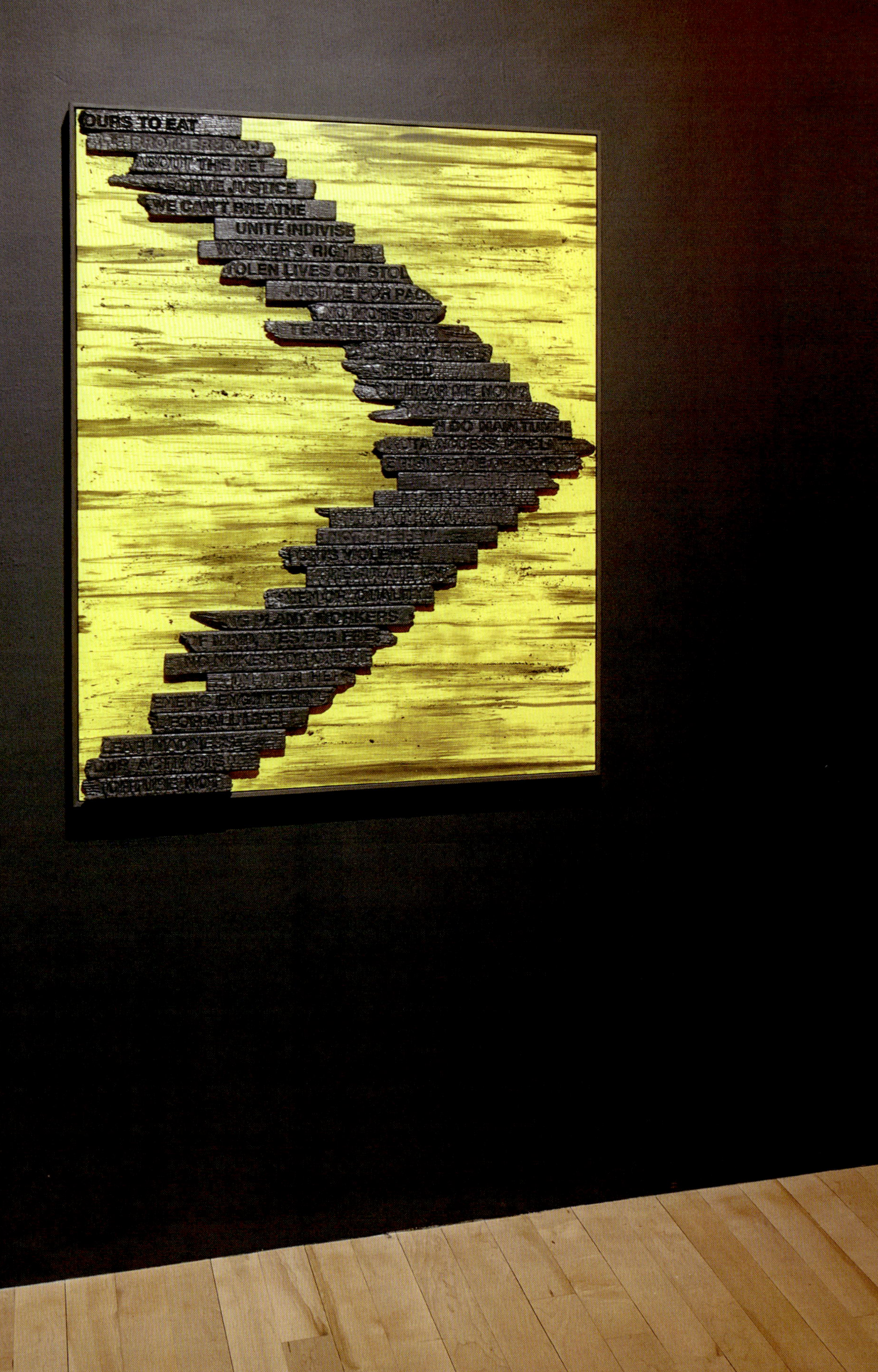
OURS TO EAT
WE CAN'T BREATHE
UNITÉ INDIVISE
WORKER'S RIGHTS

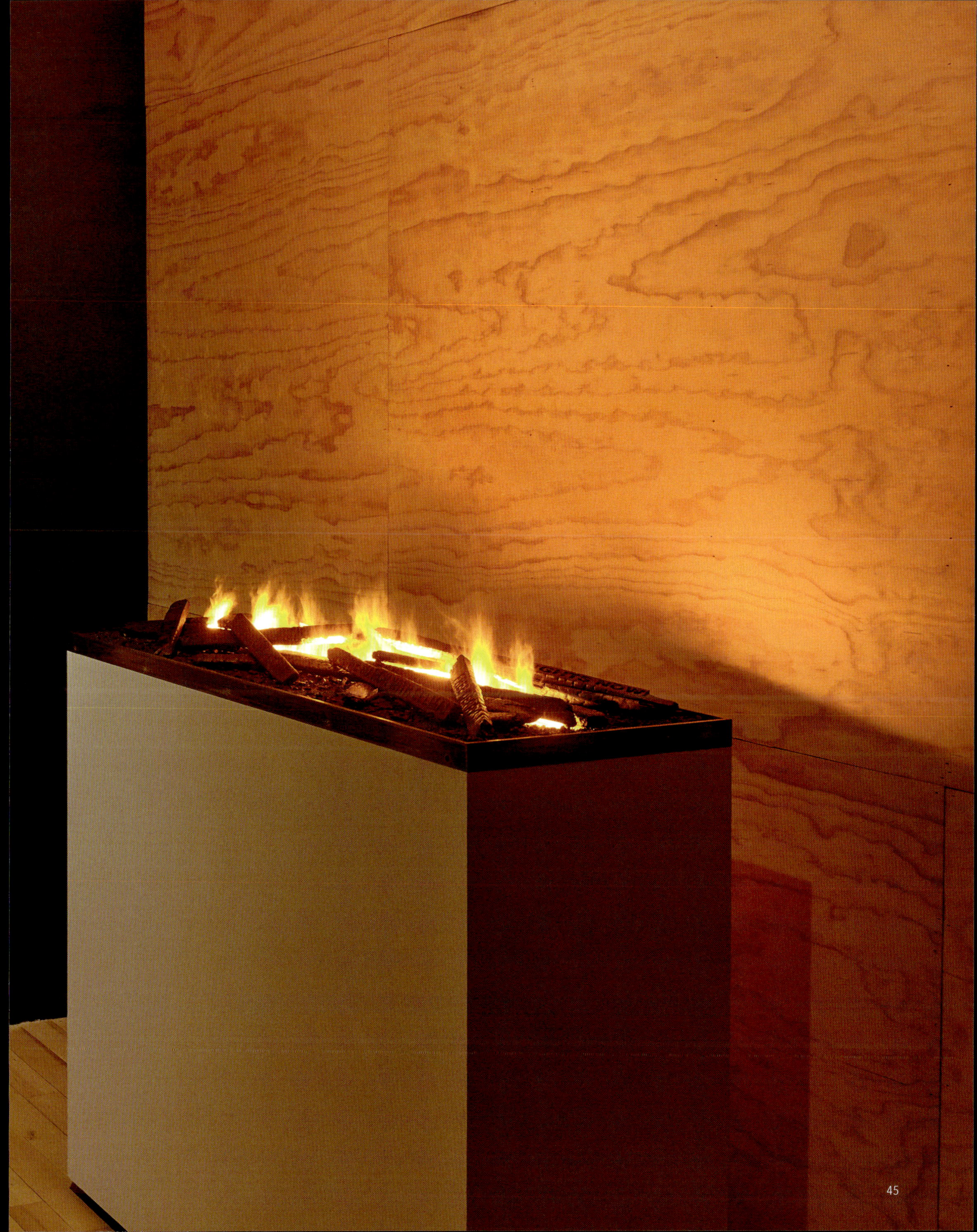

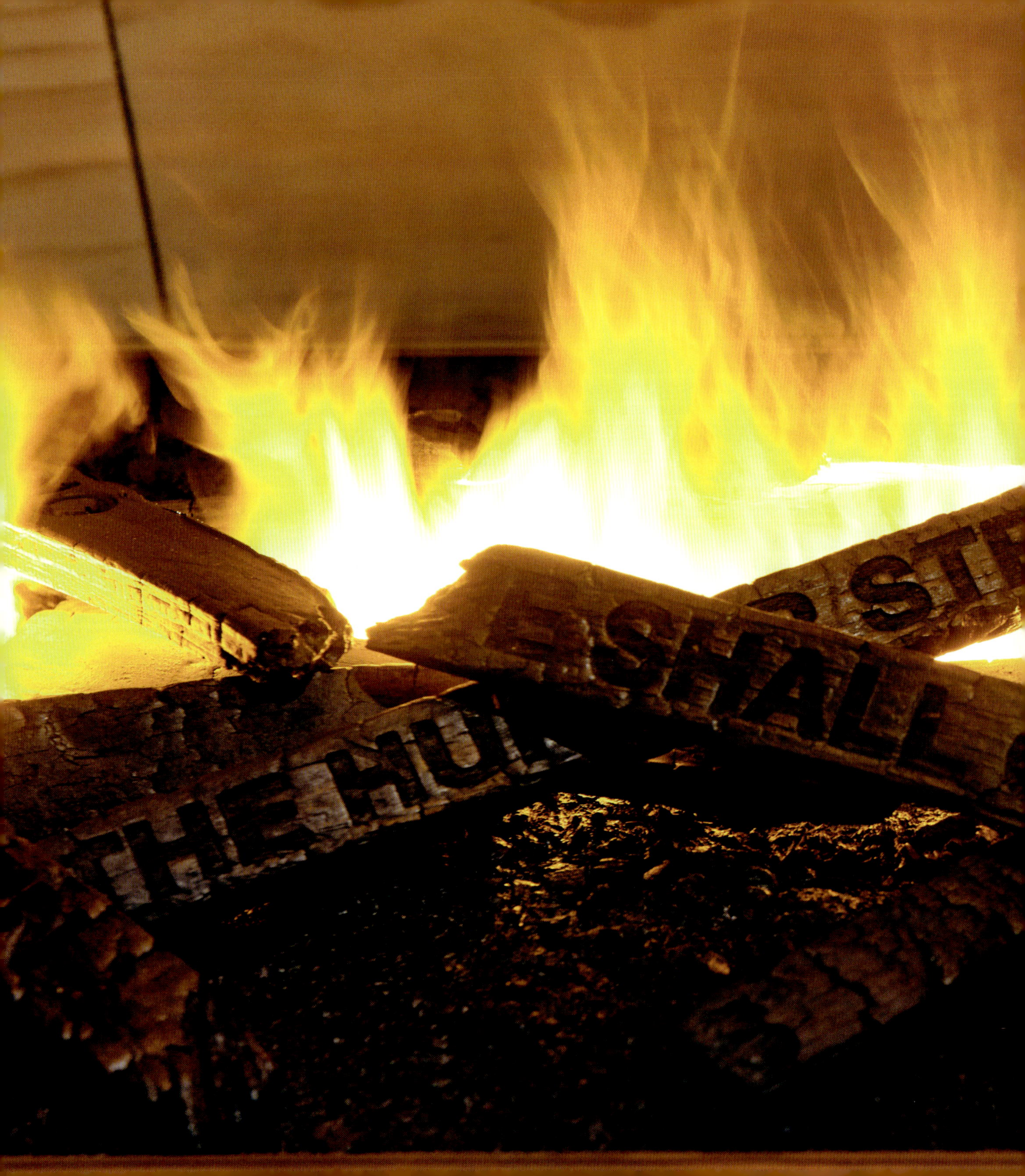
THE
SHALL

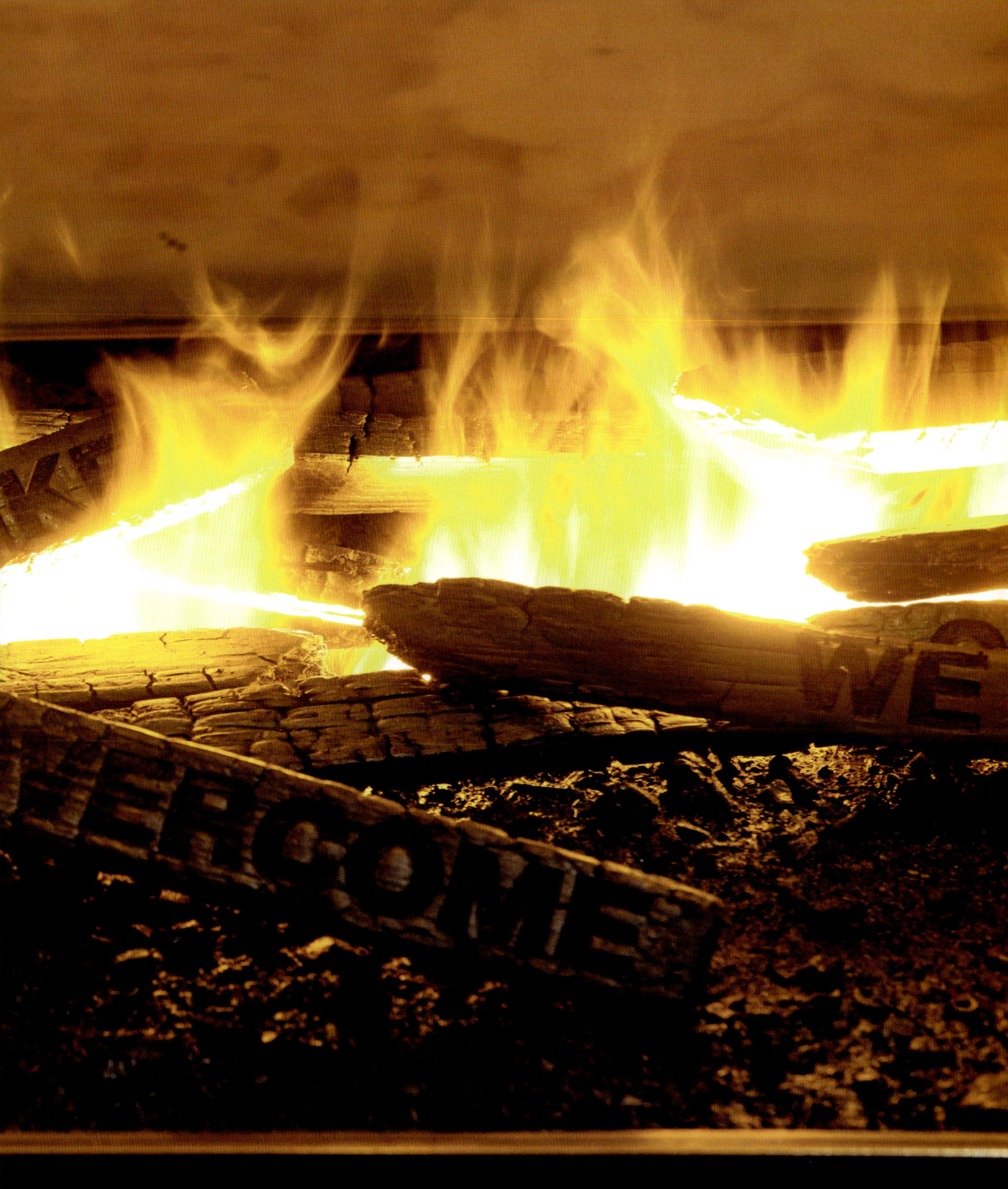
WE
ELCOME

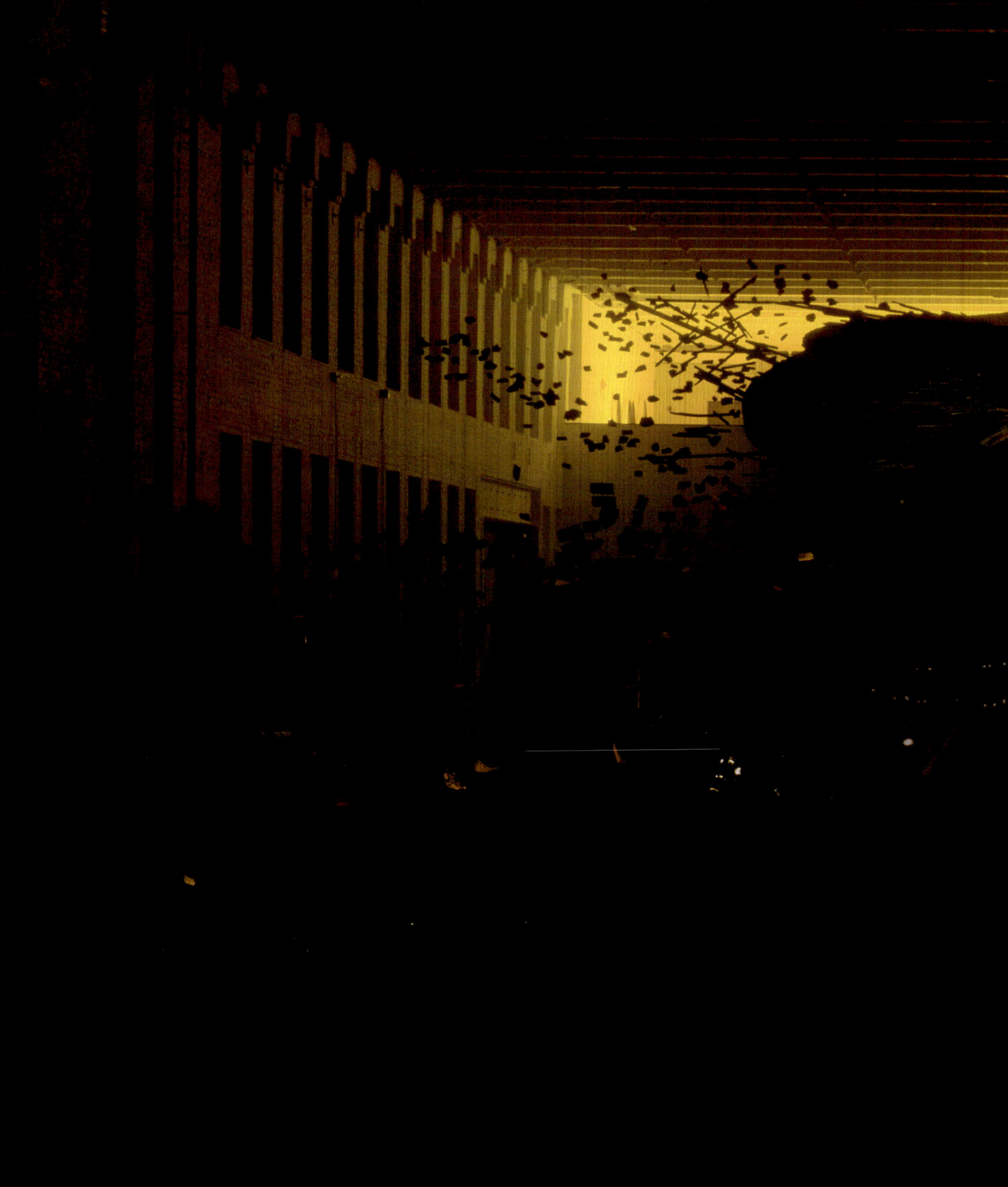

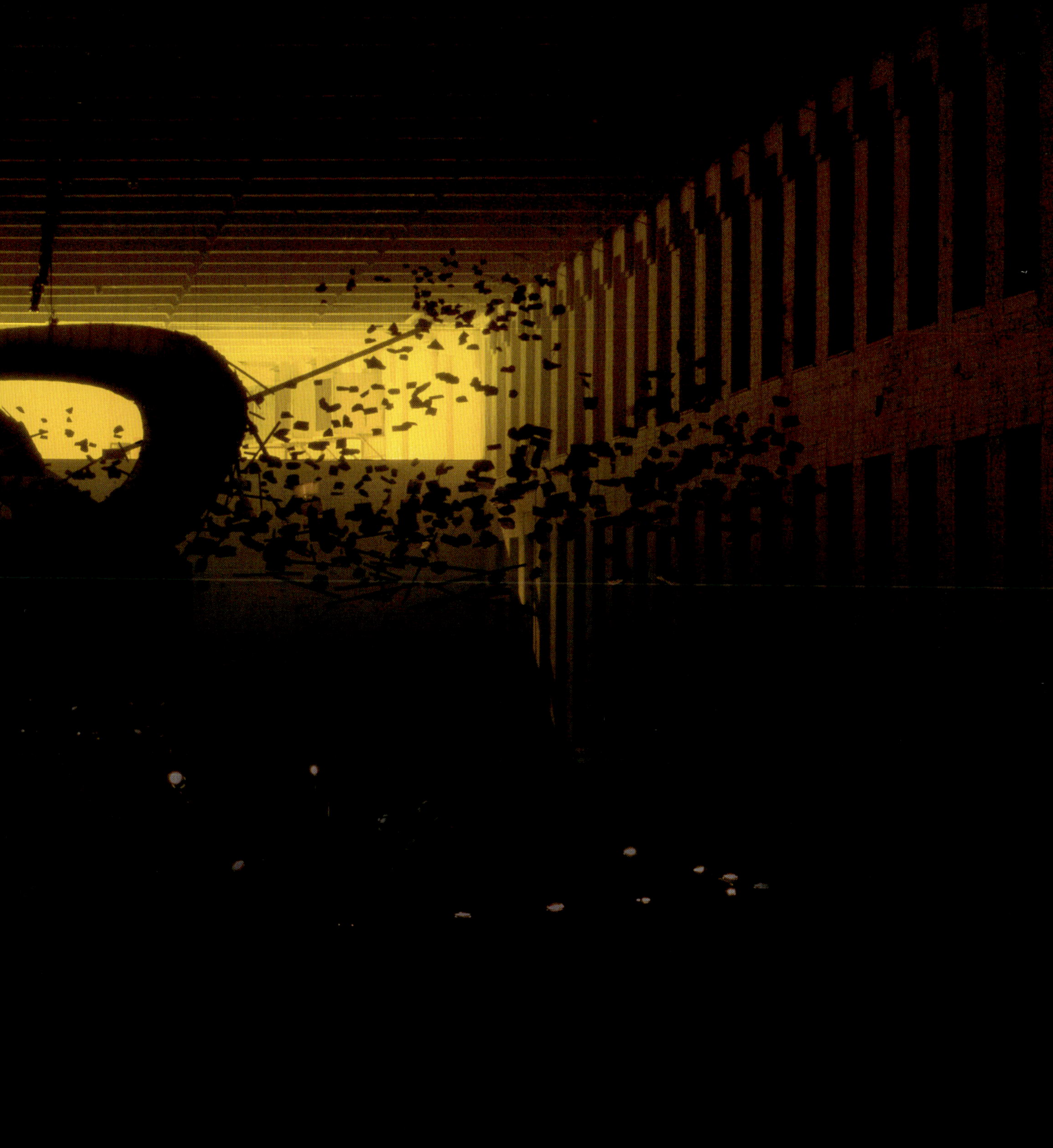

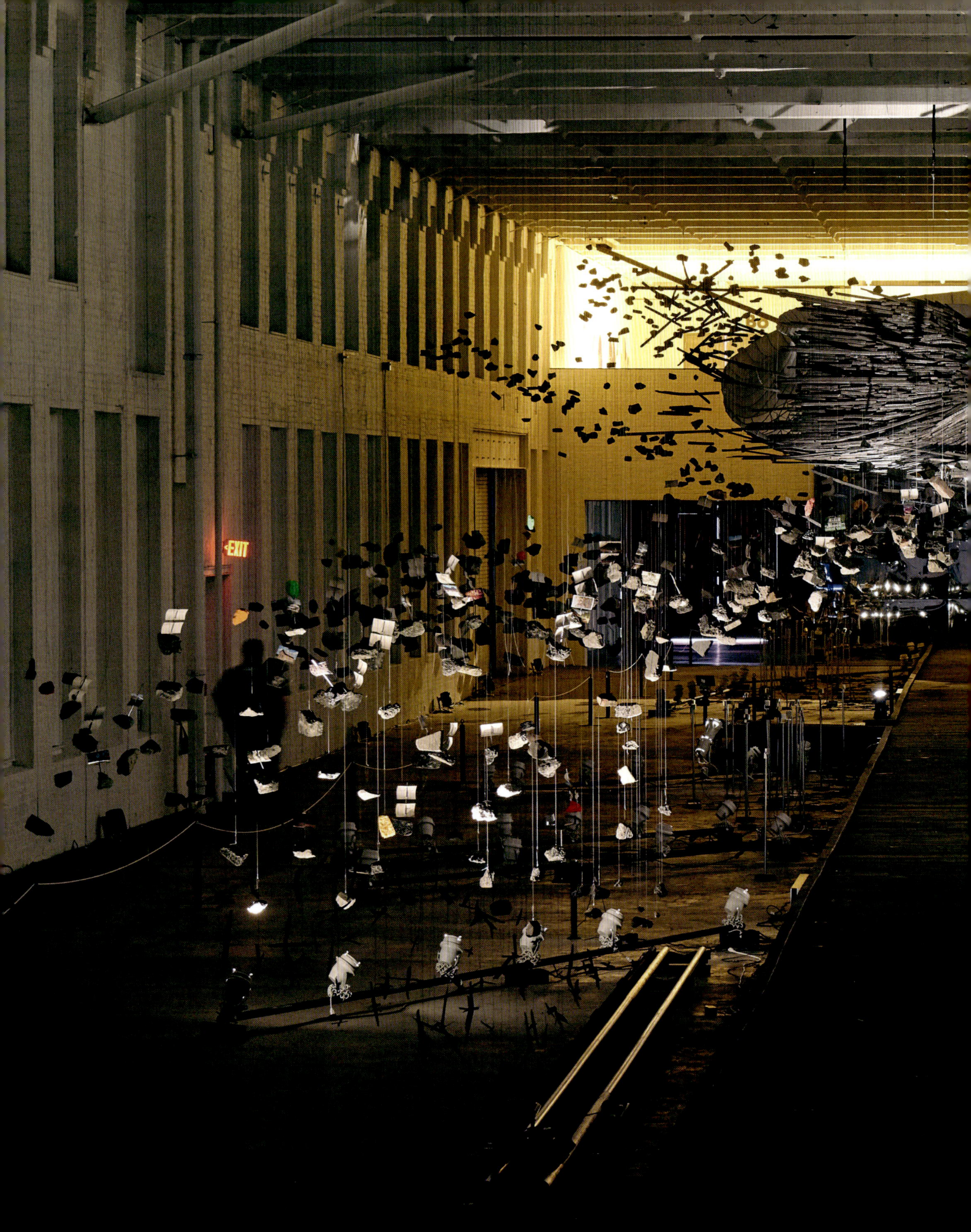
EXIT

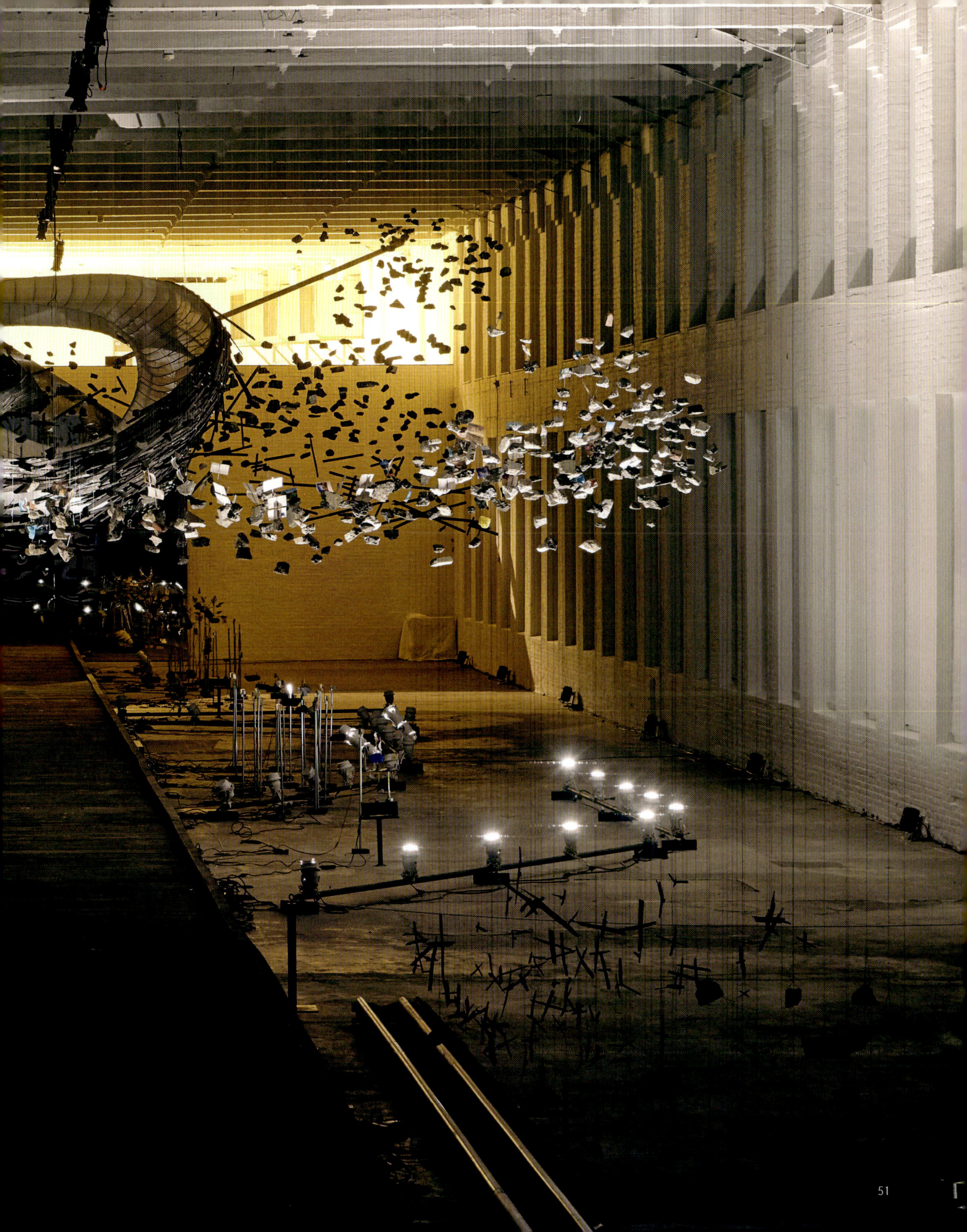

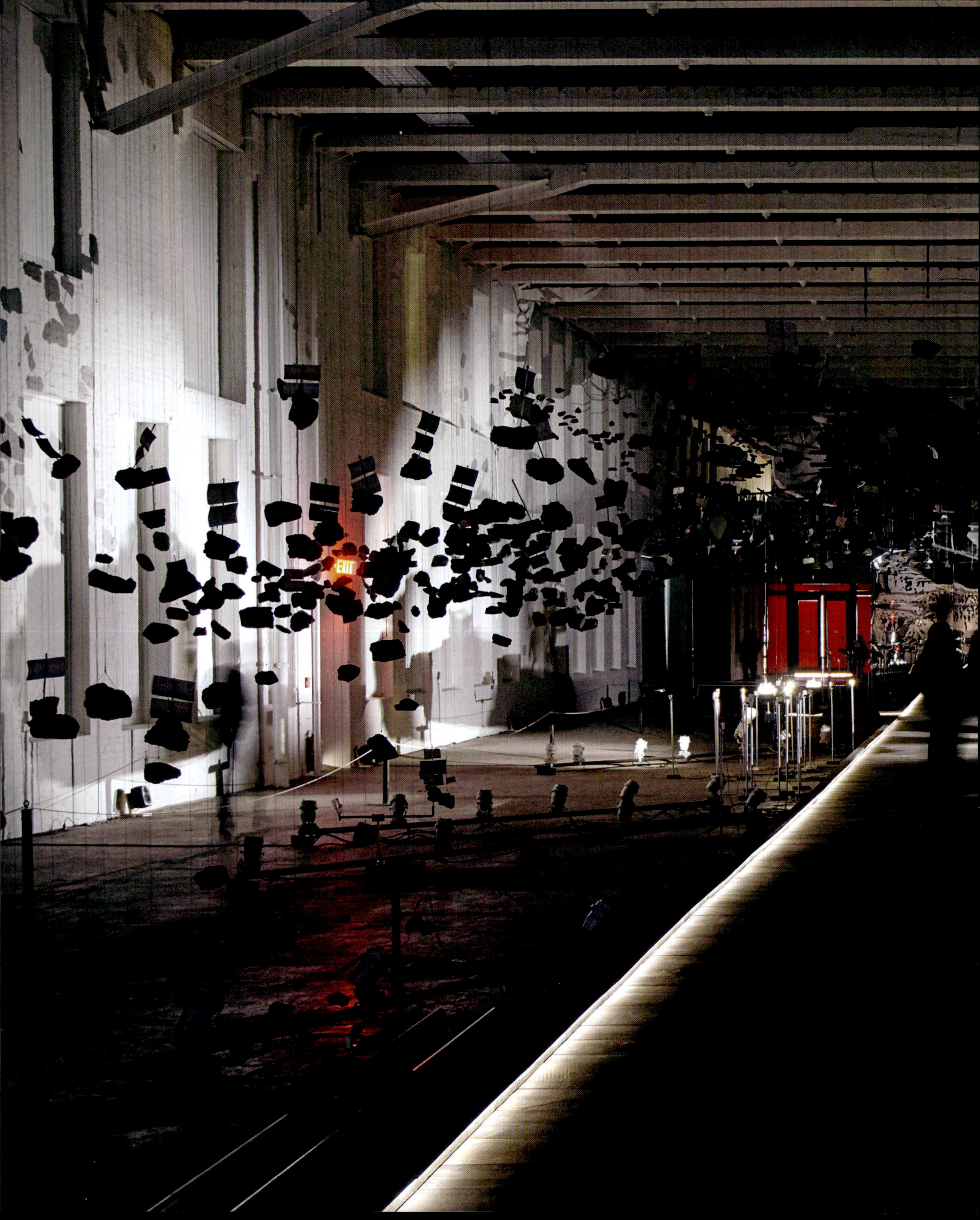
EXIT

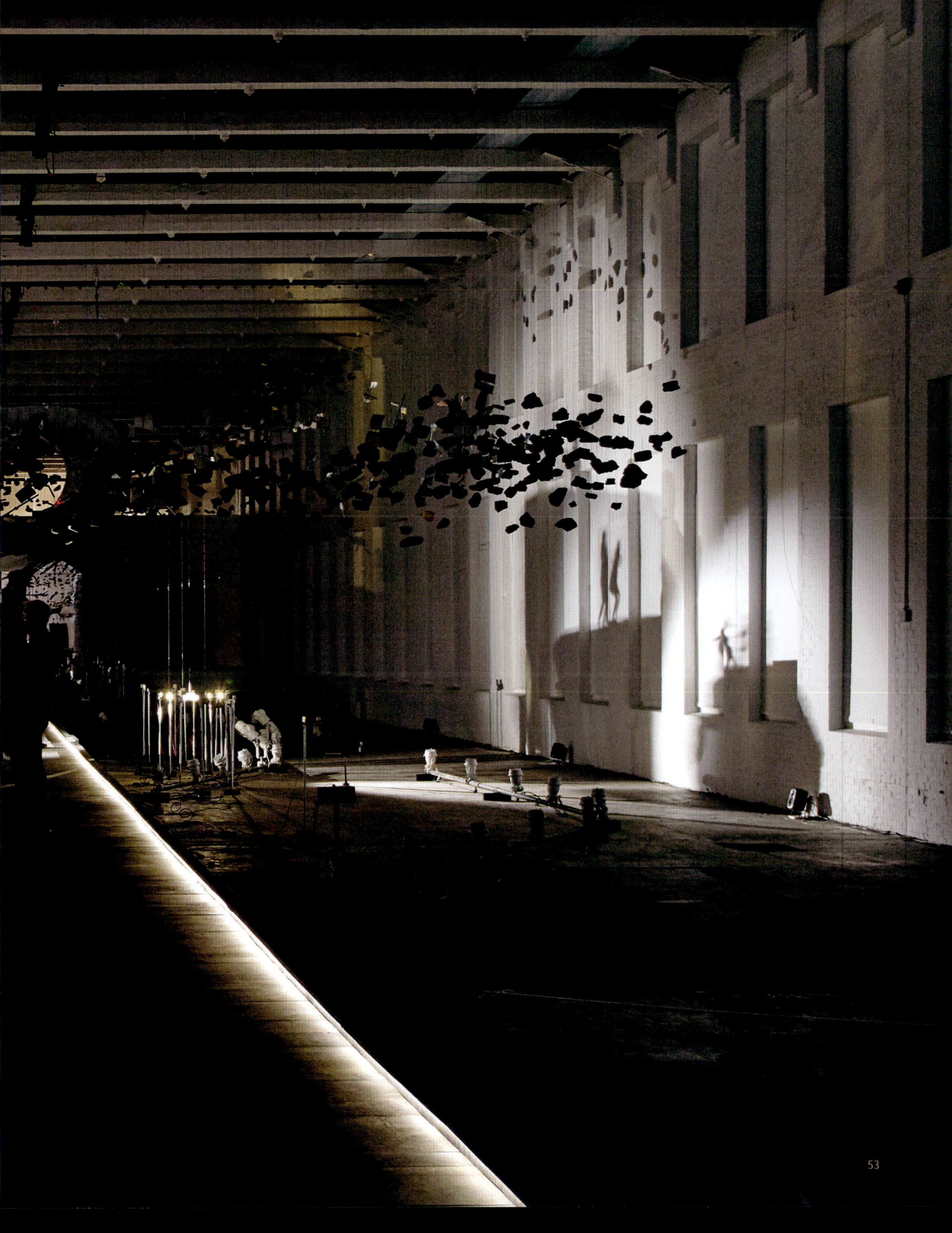

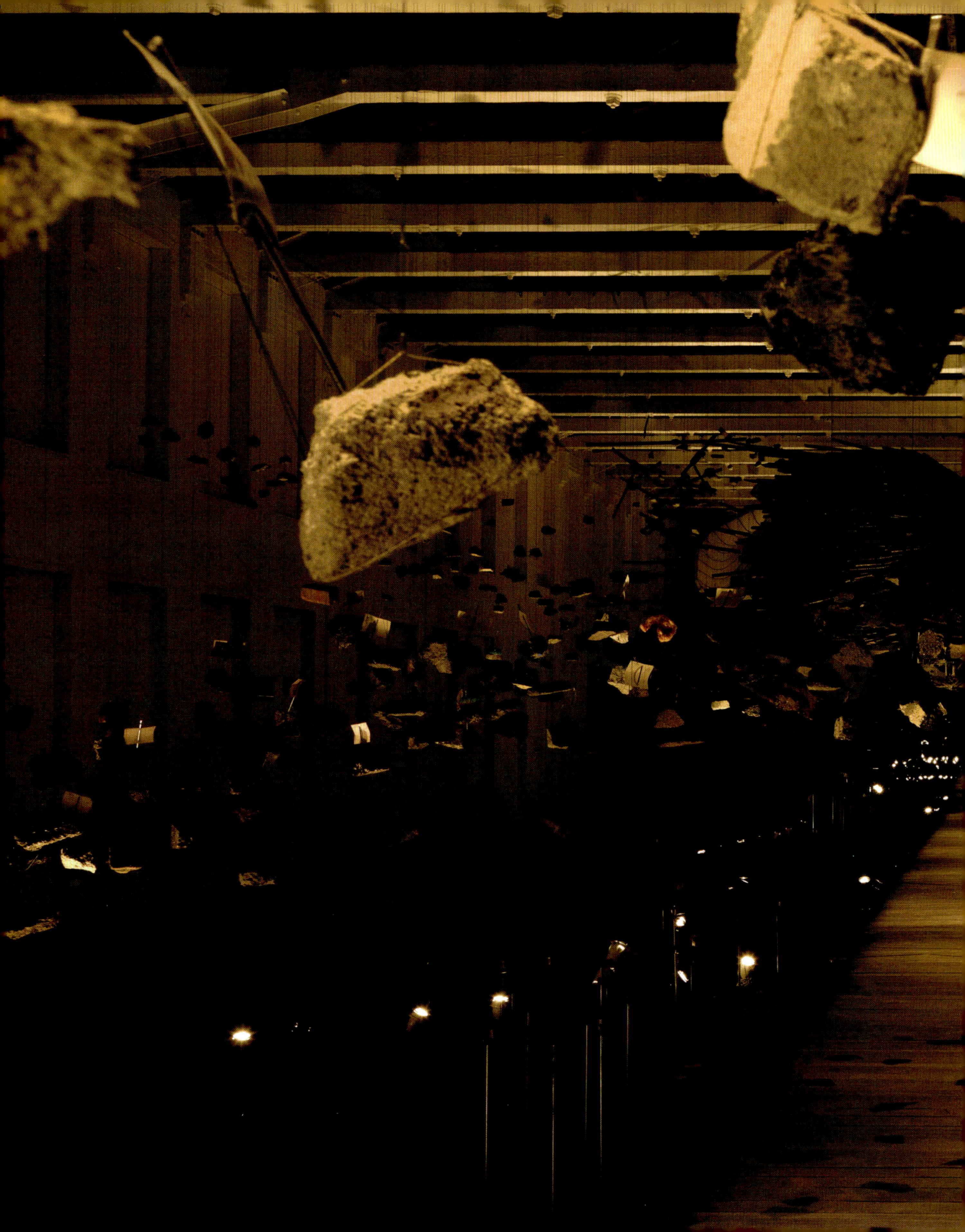

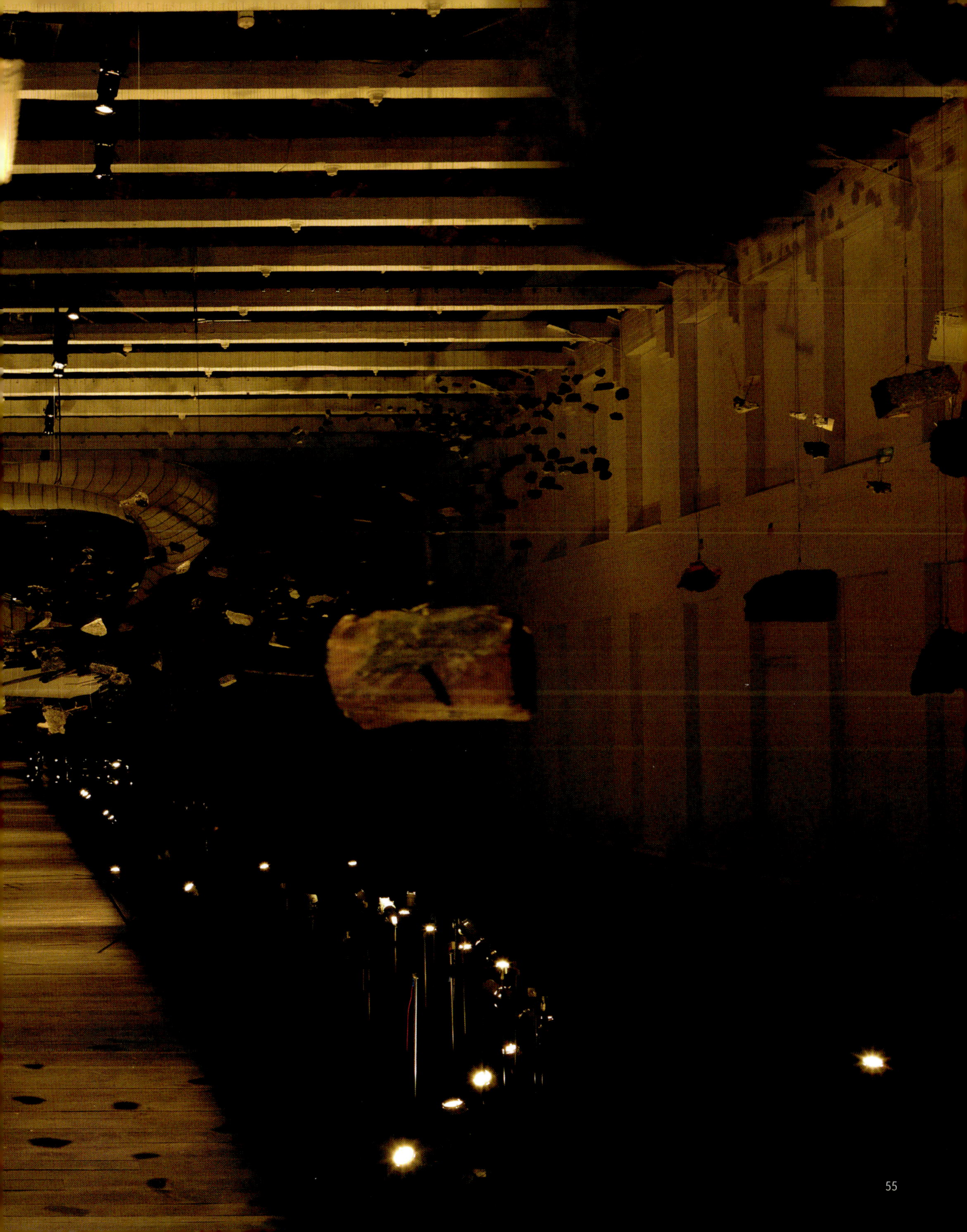

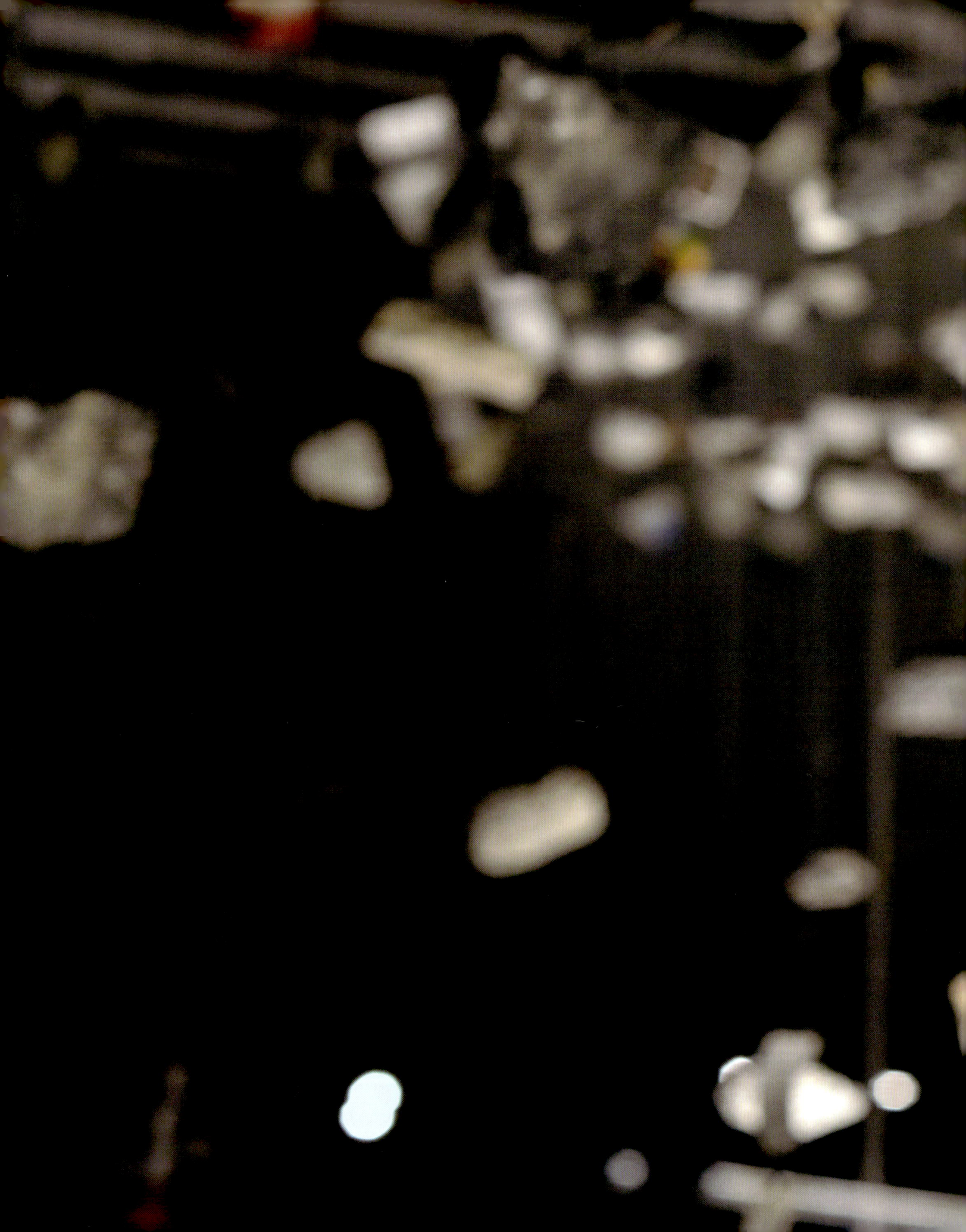

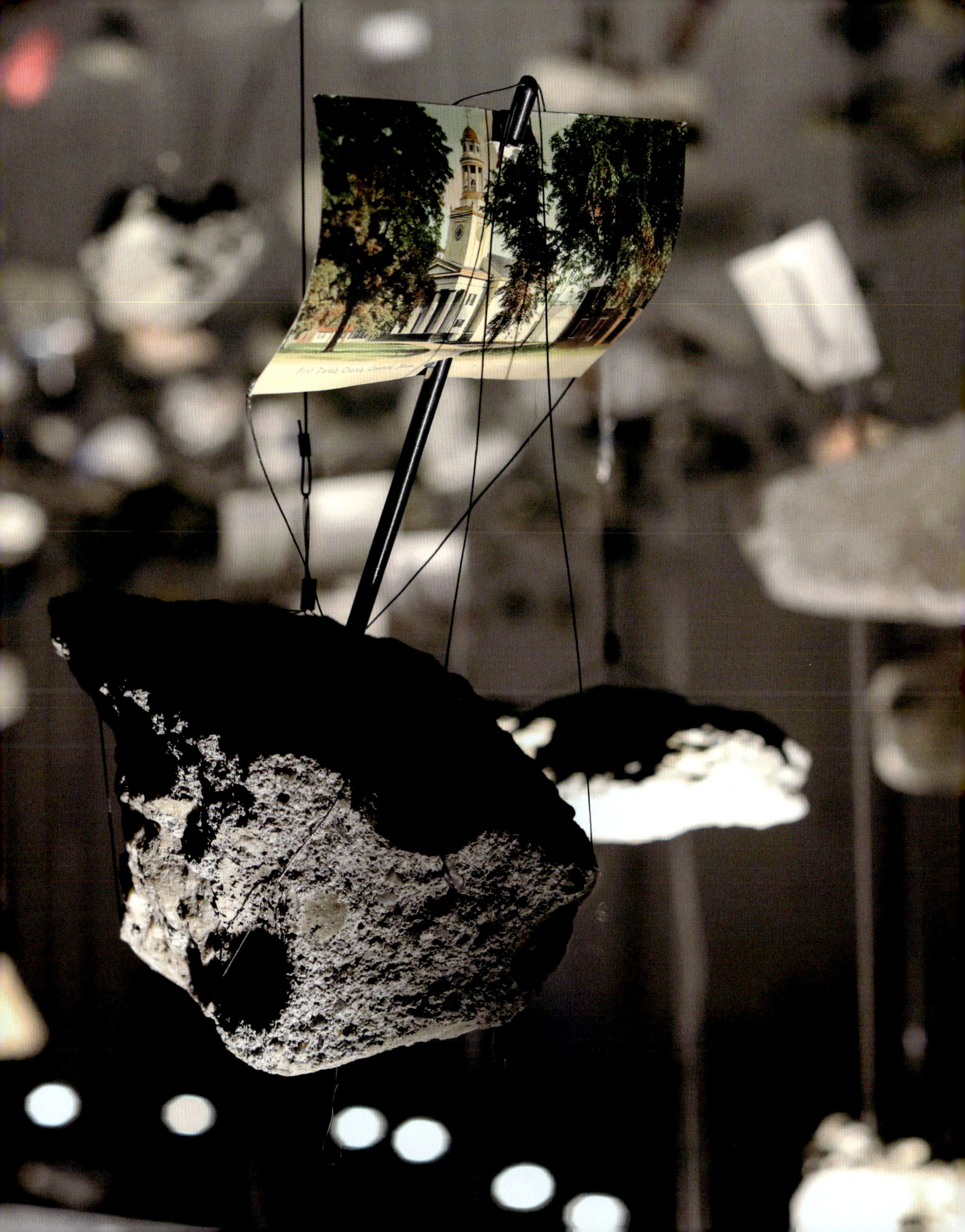
First Parish Church, Concord, Mass.

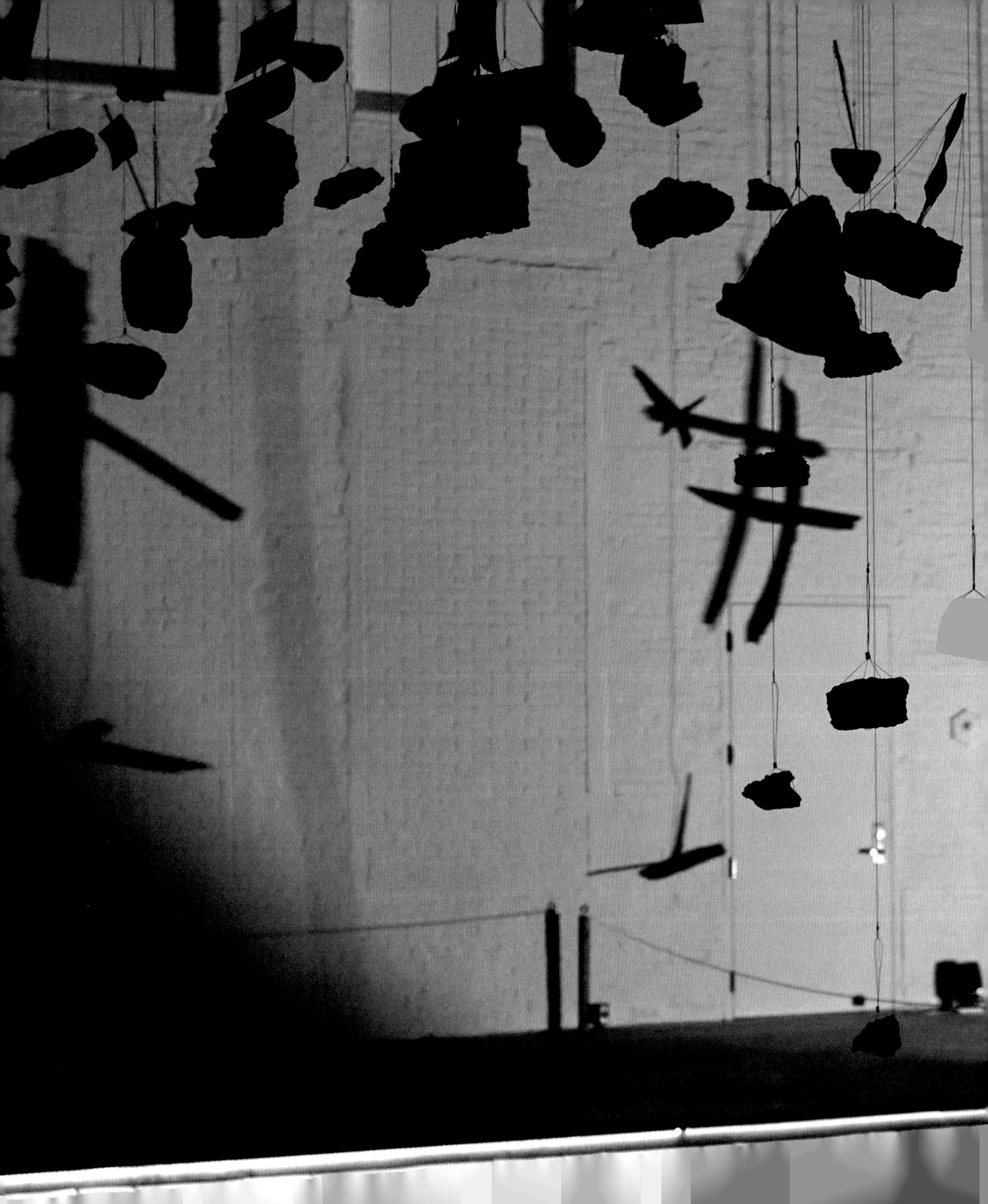

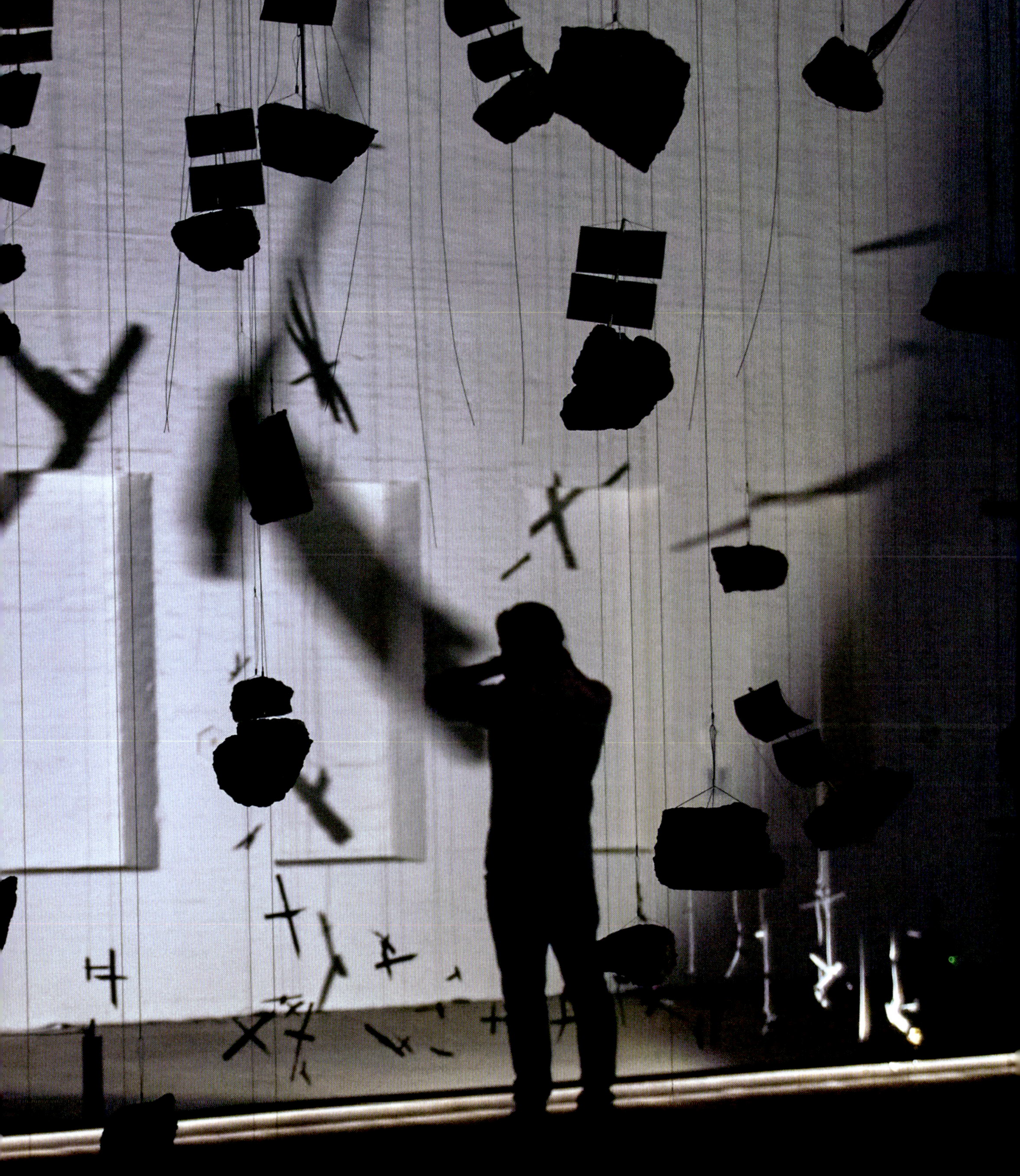

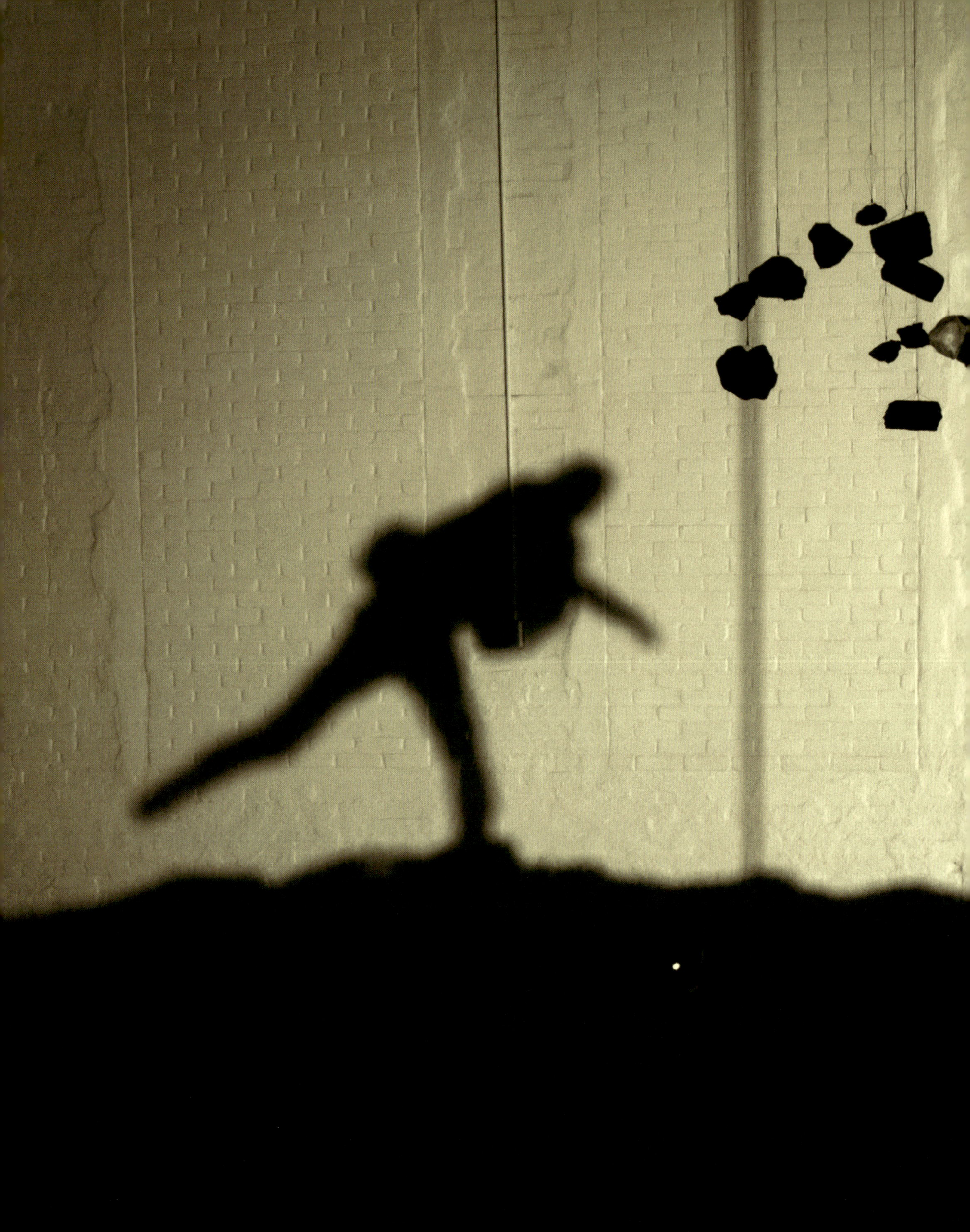

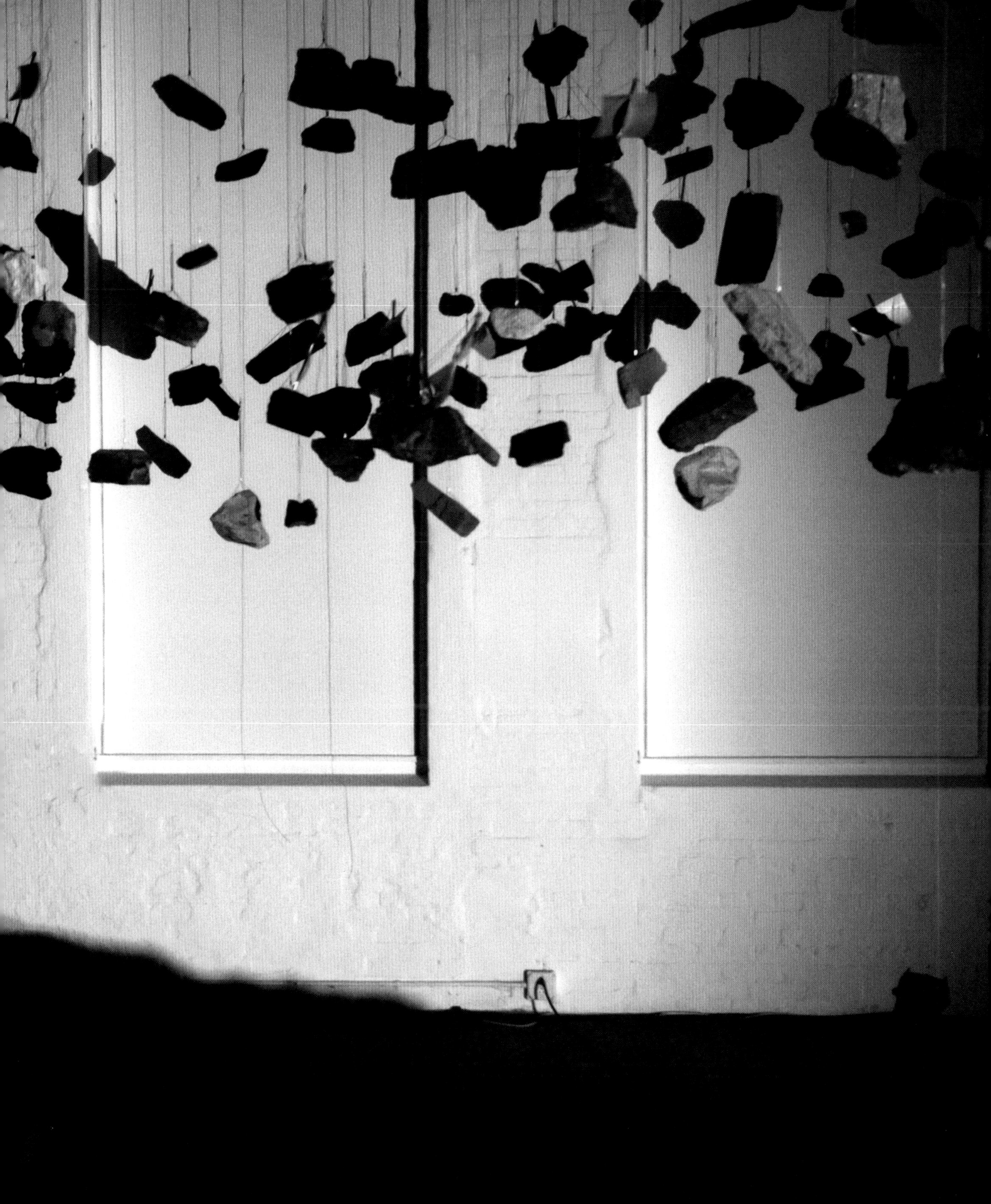

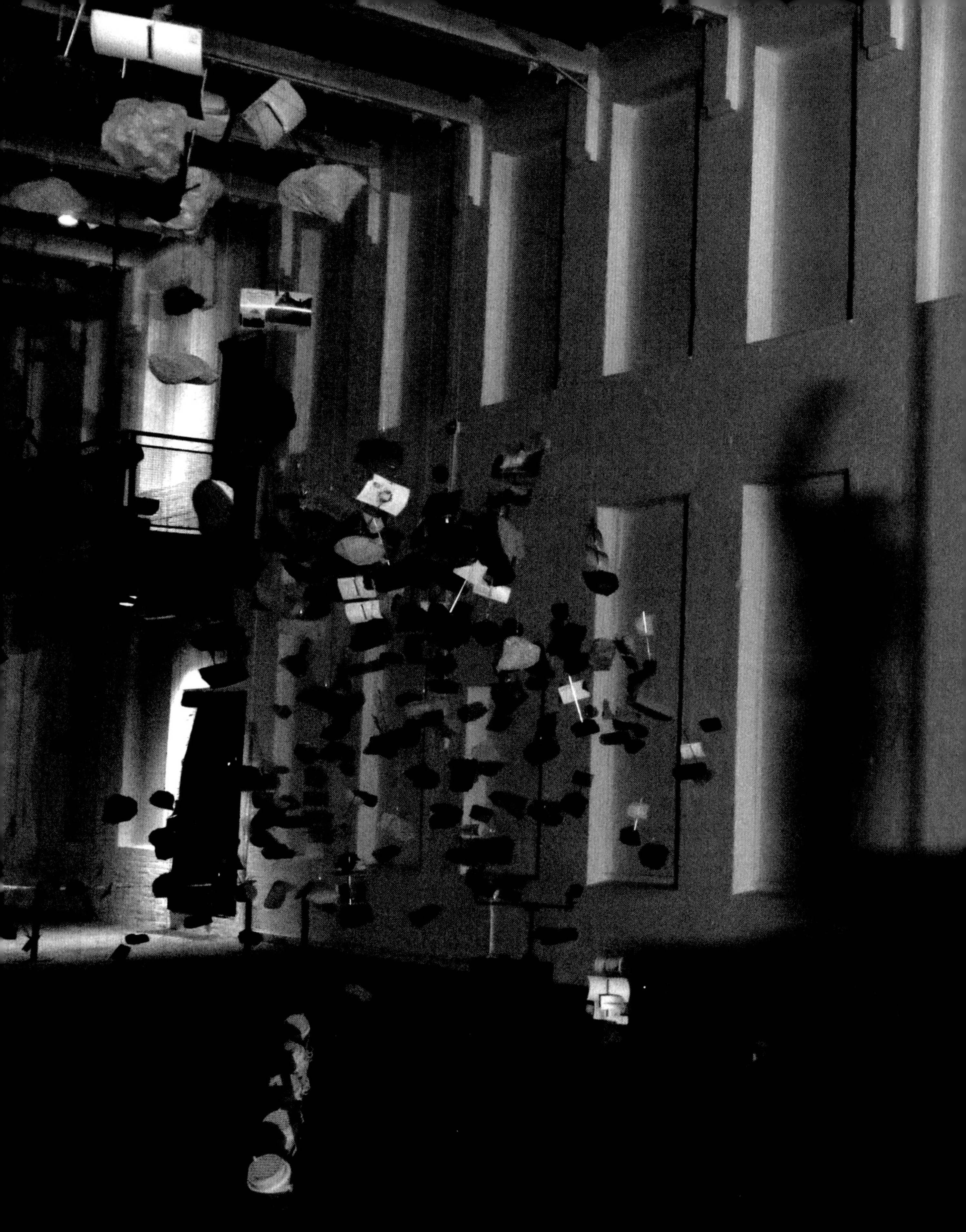

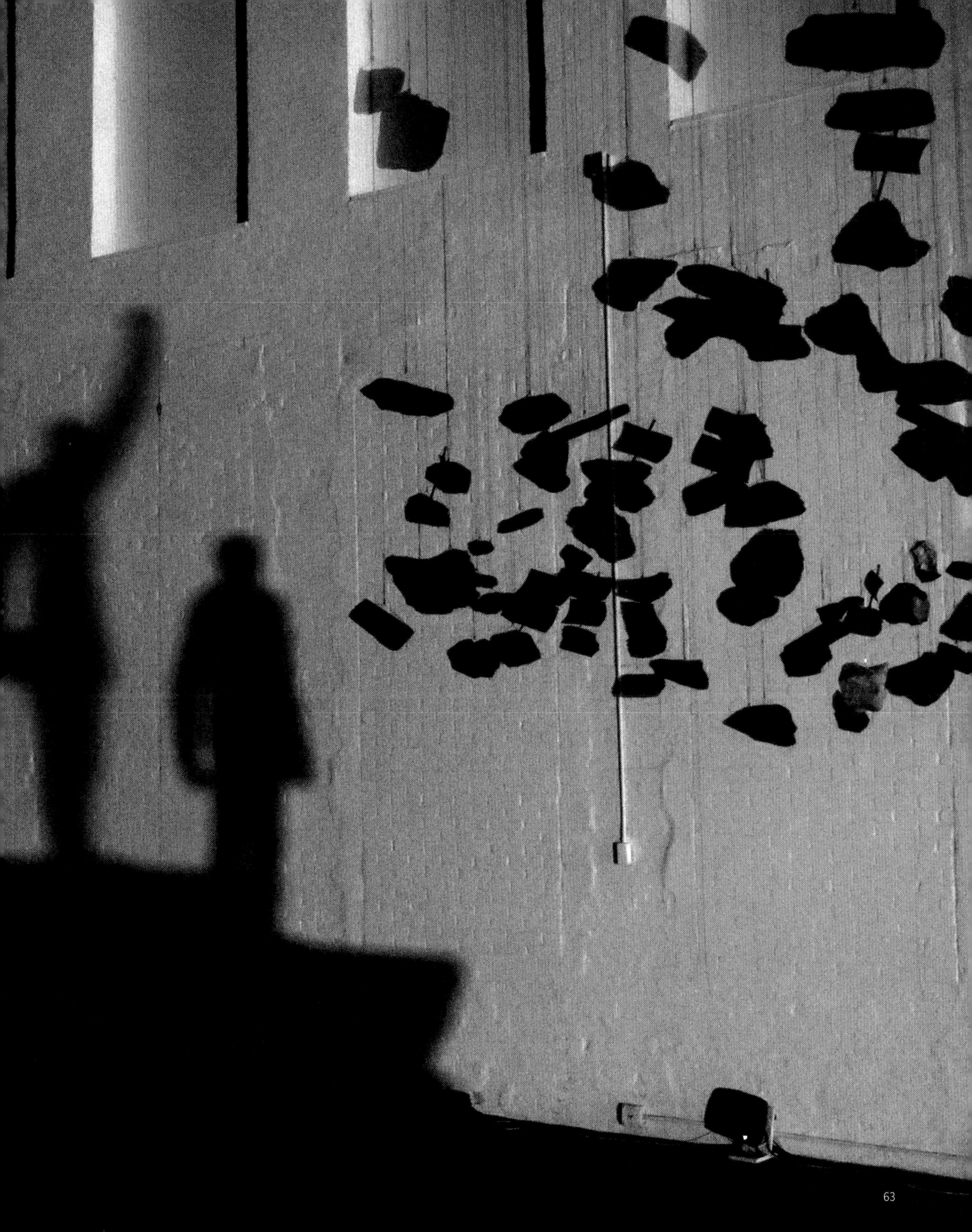

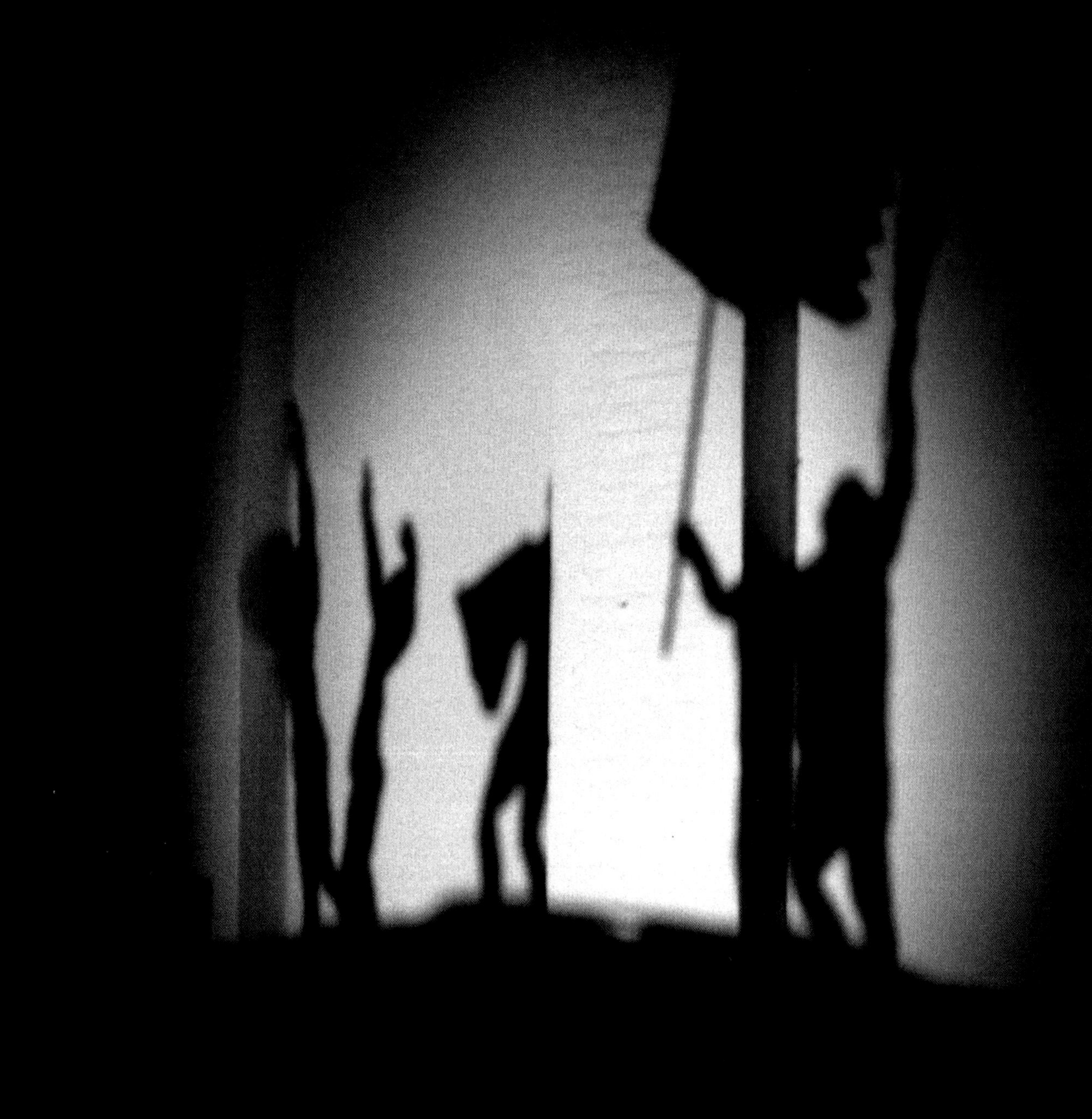

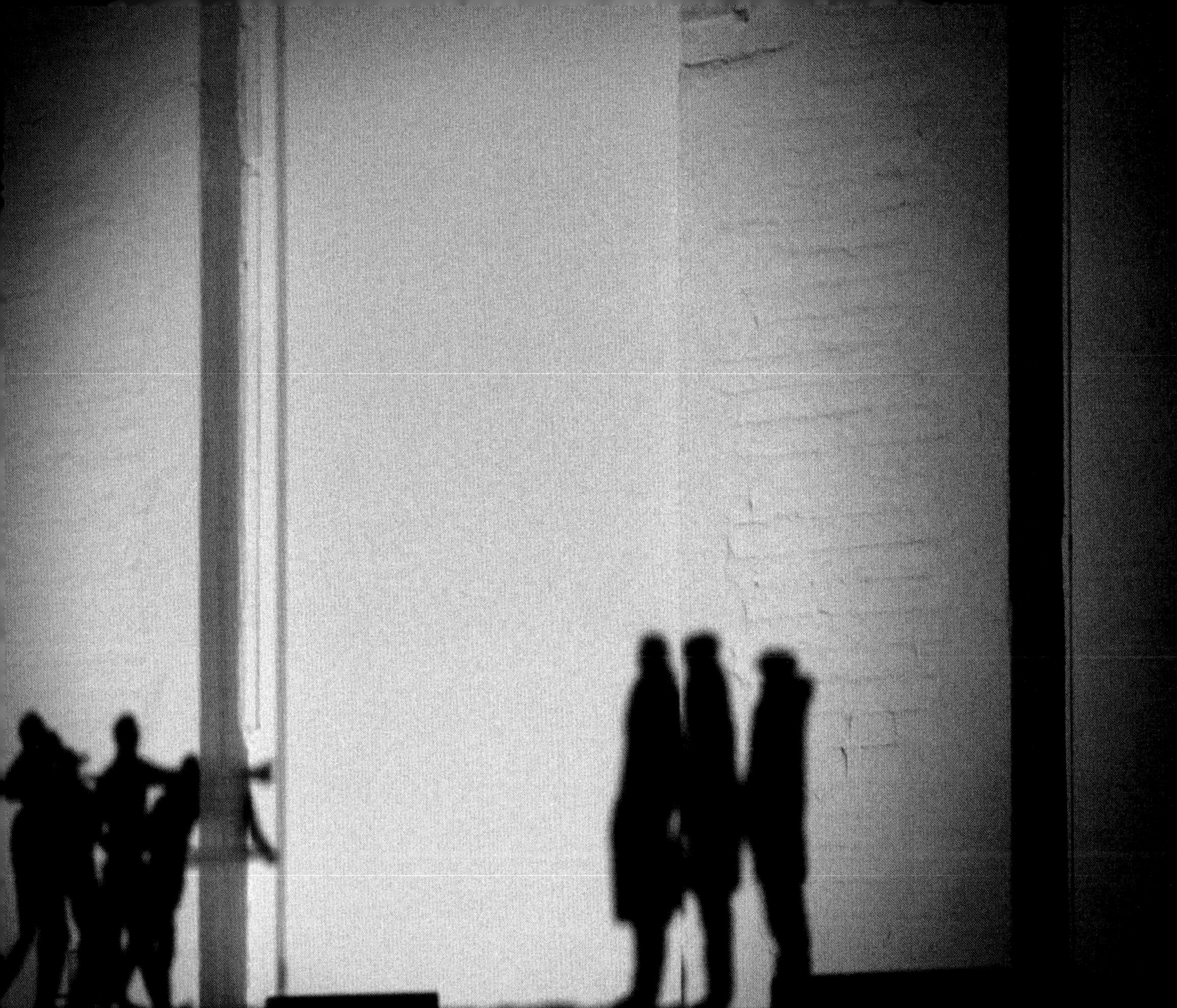

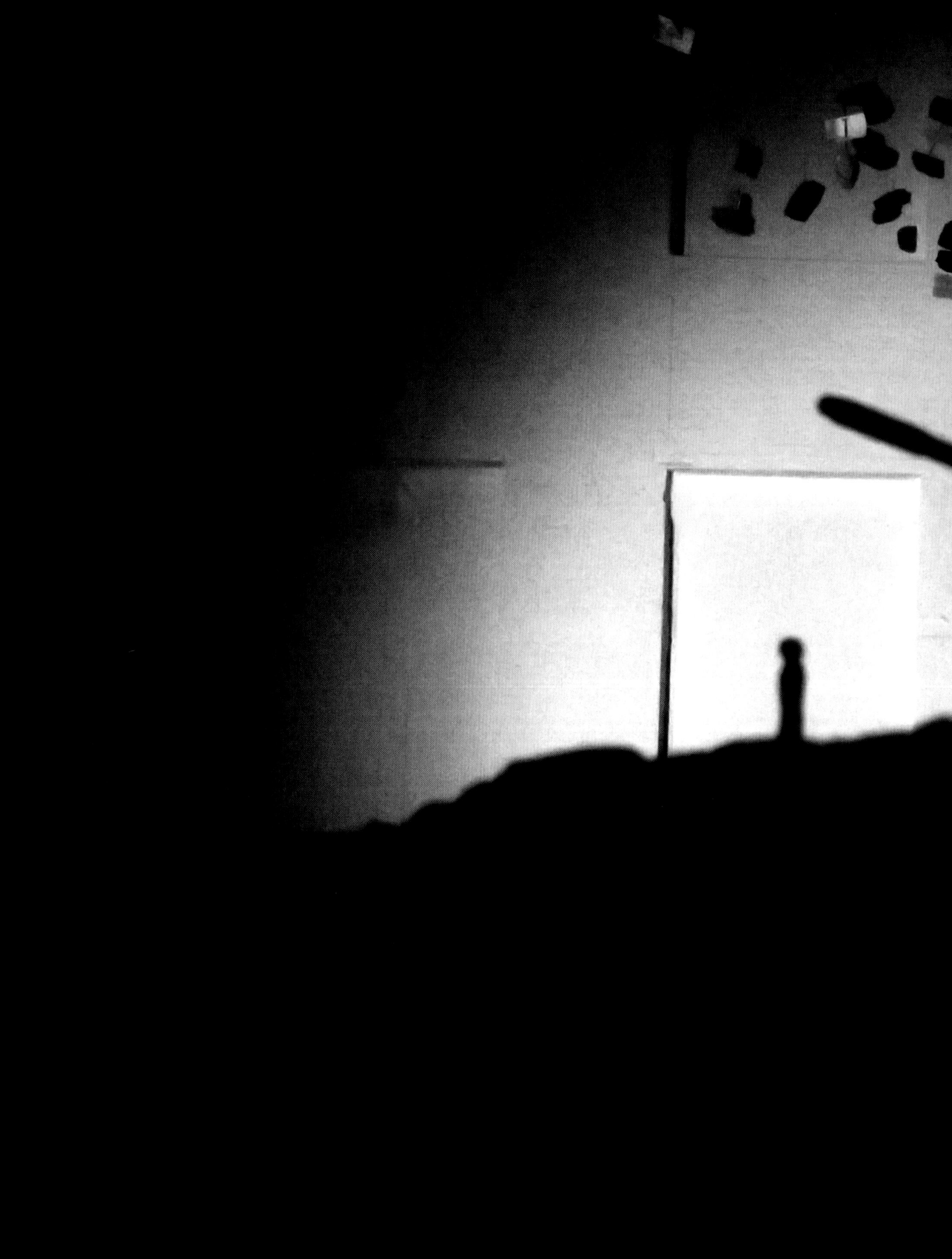

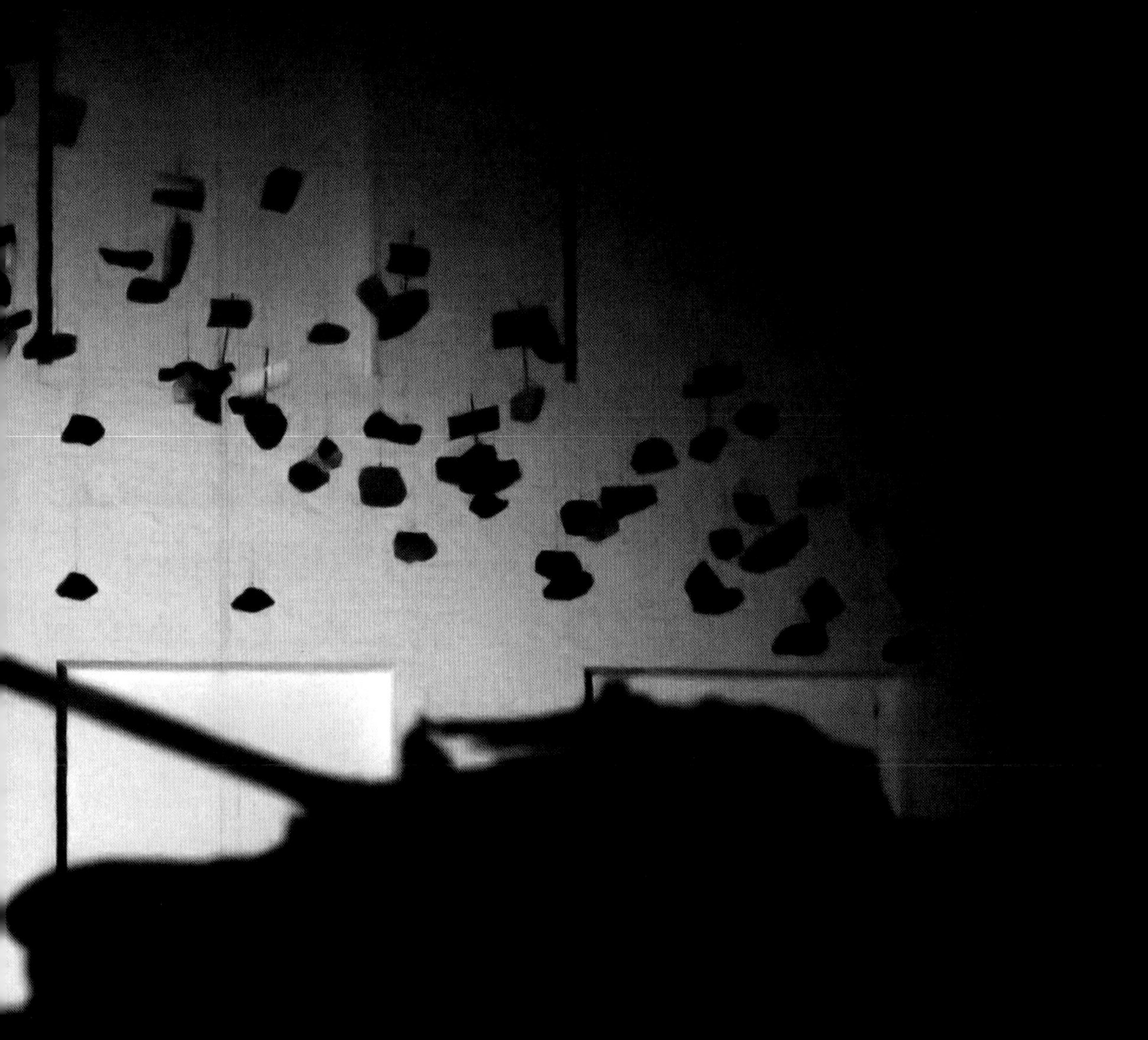

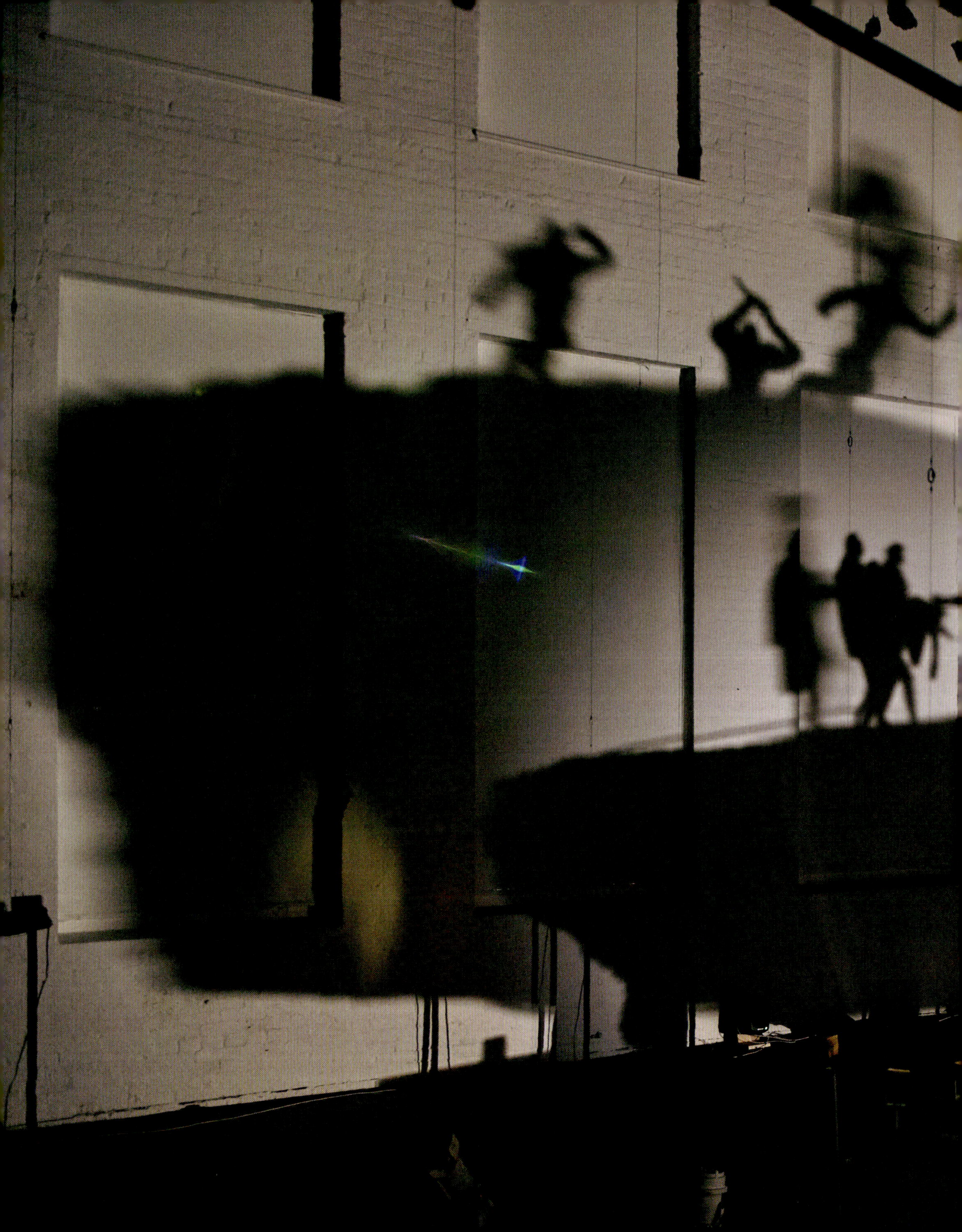

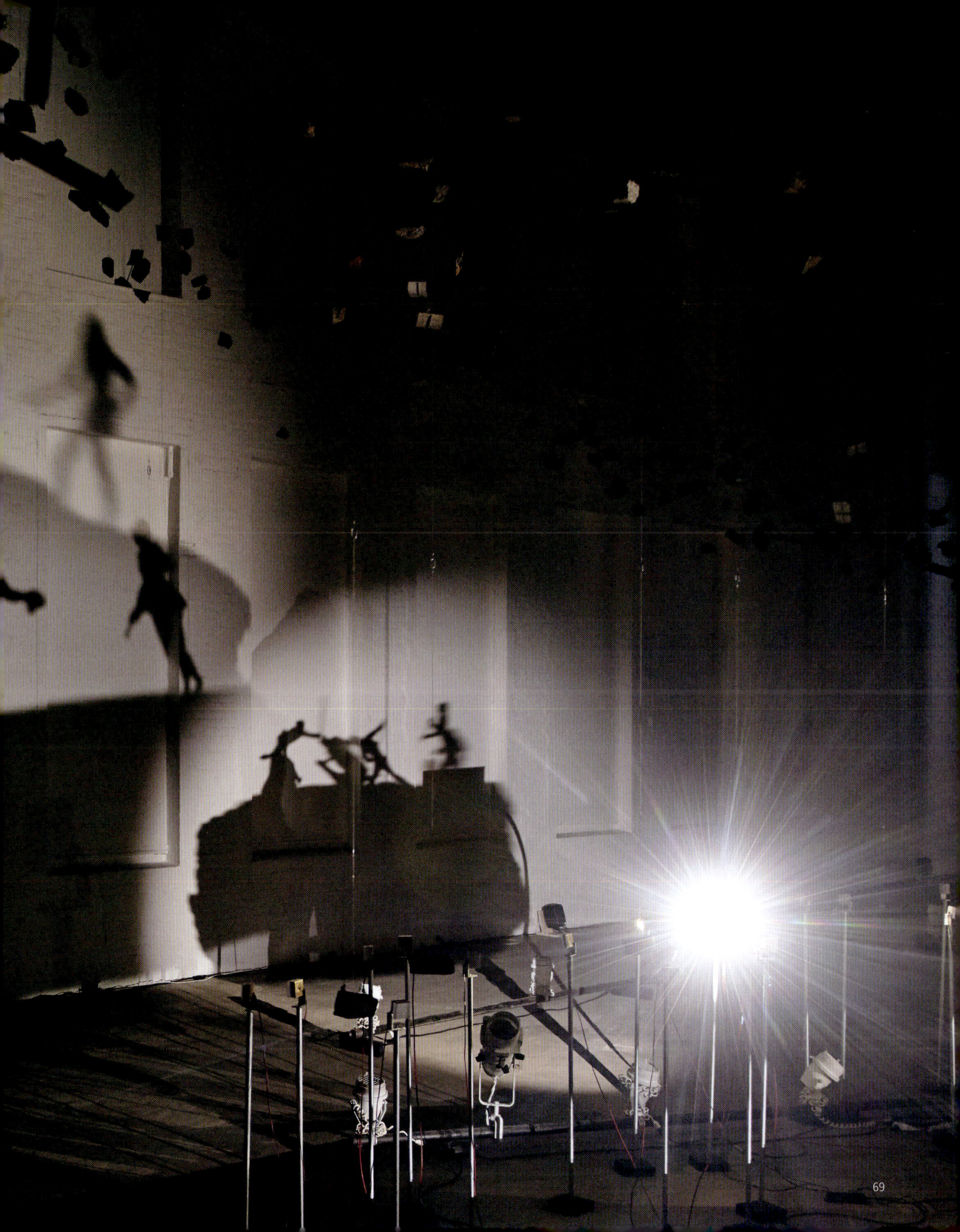

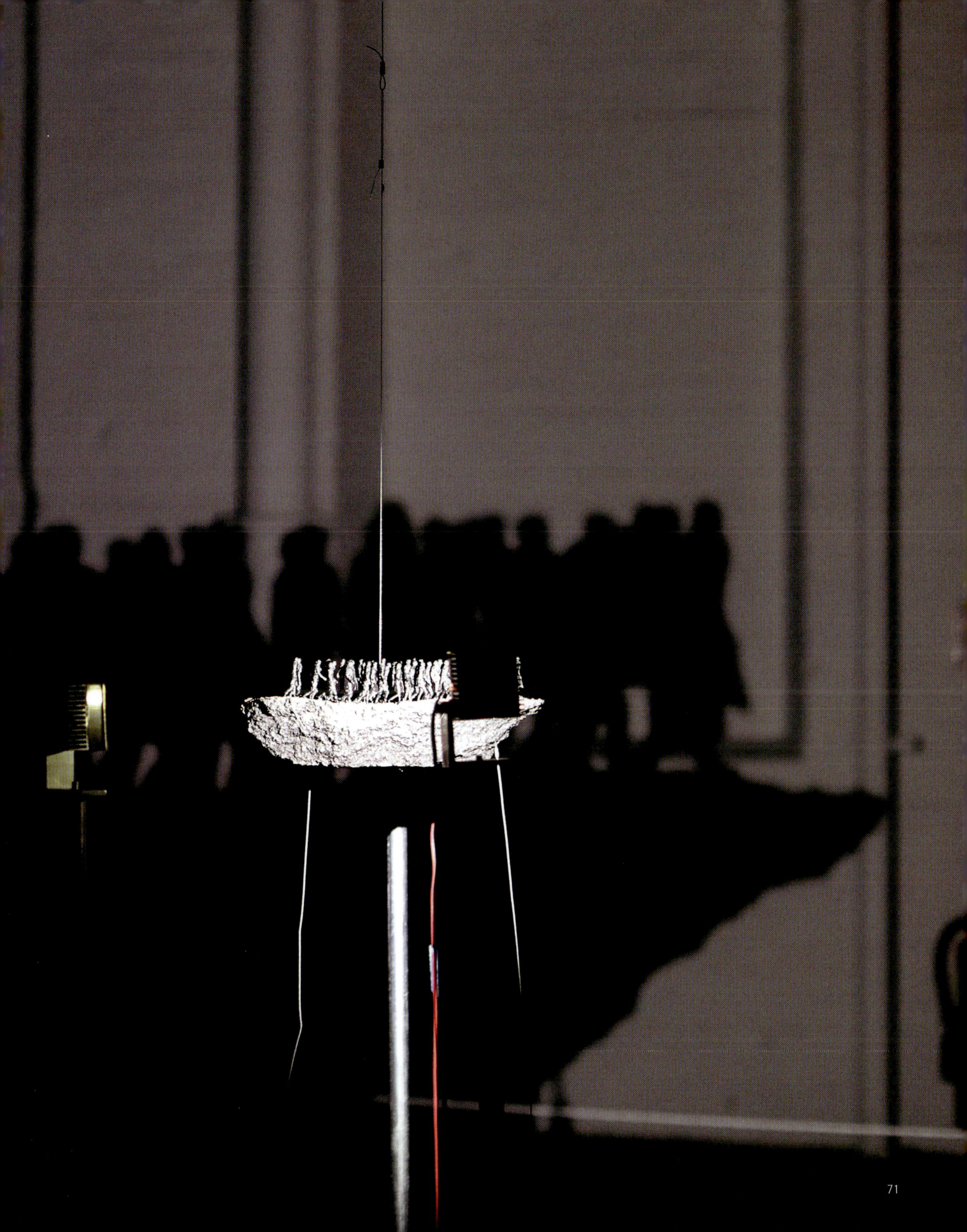

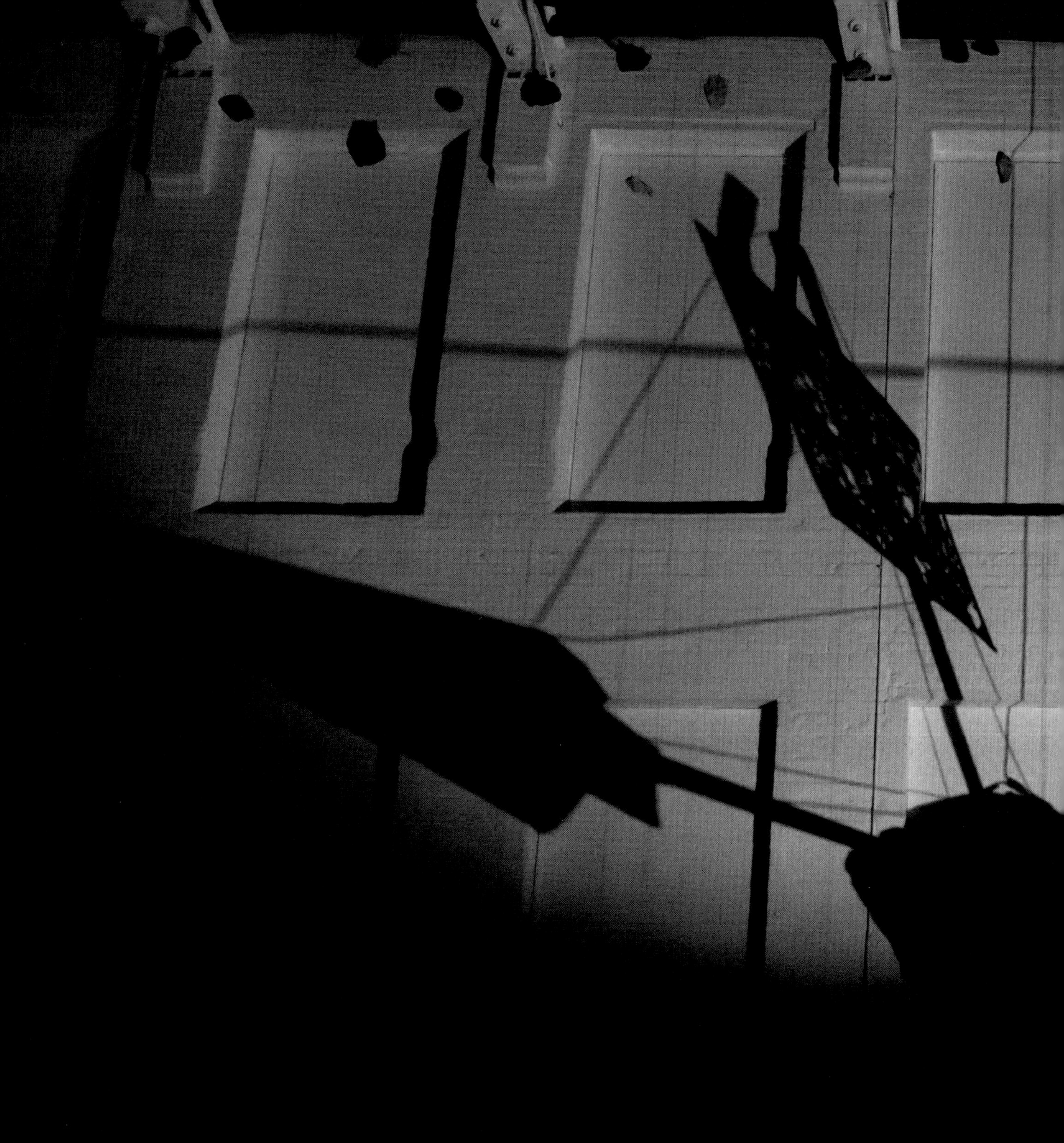

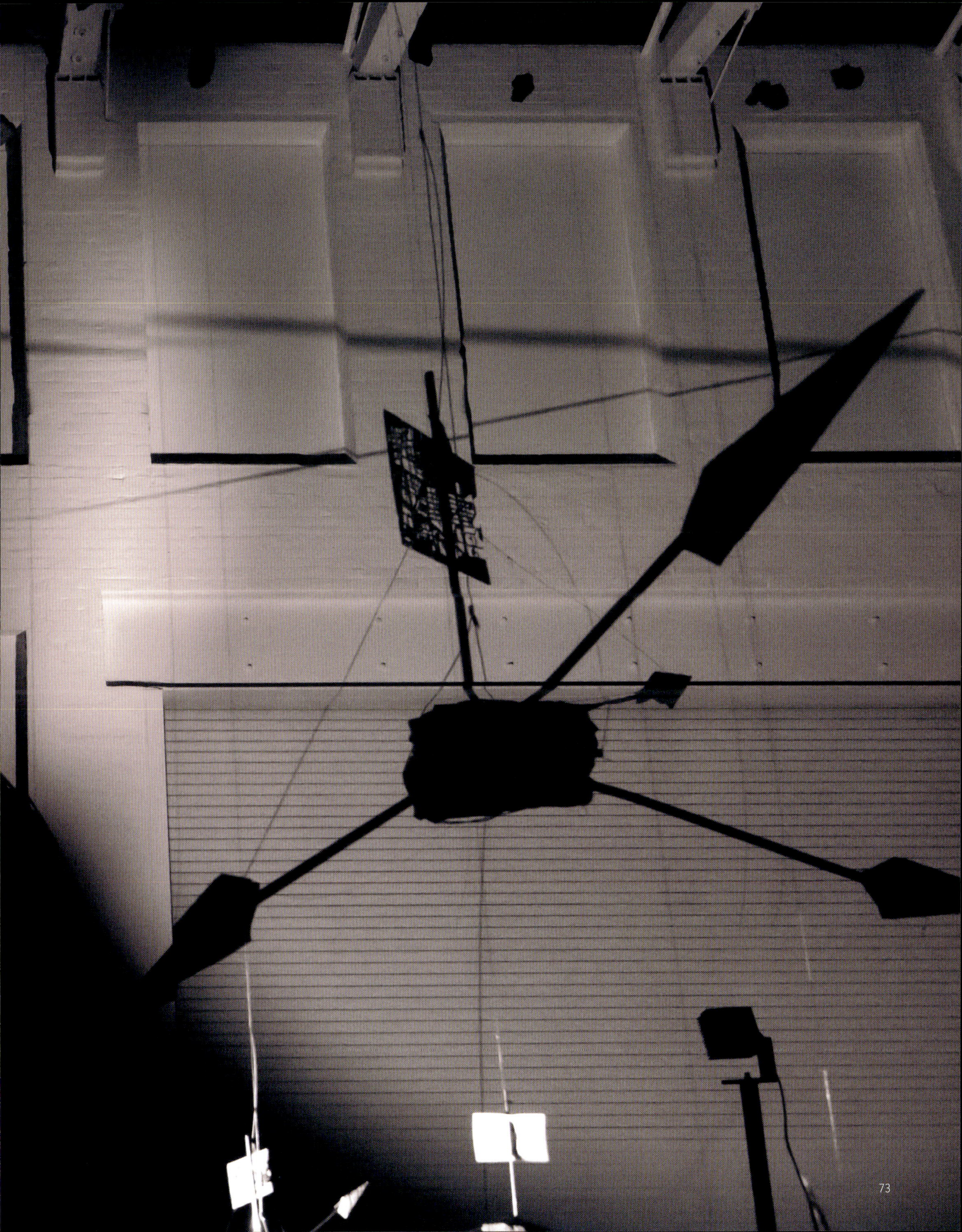

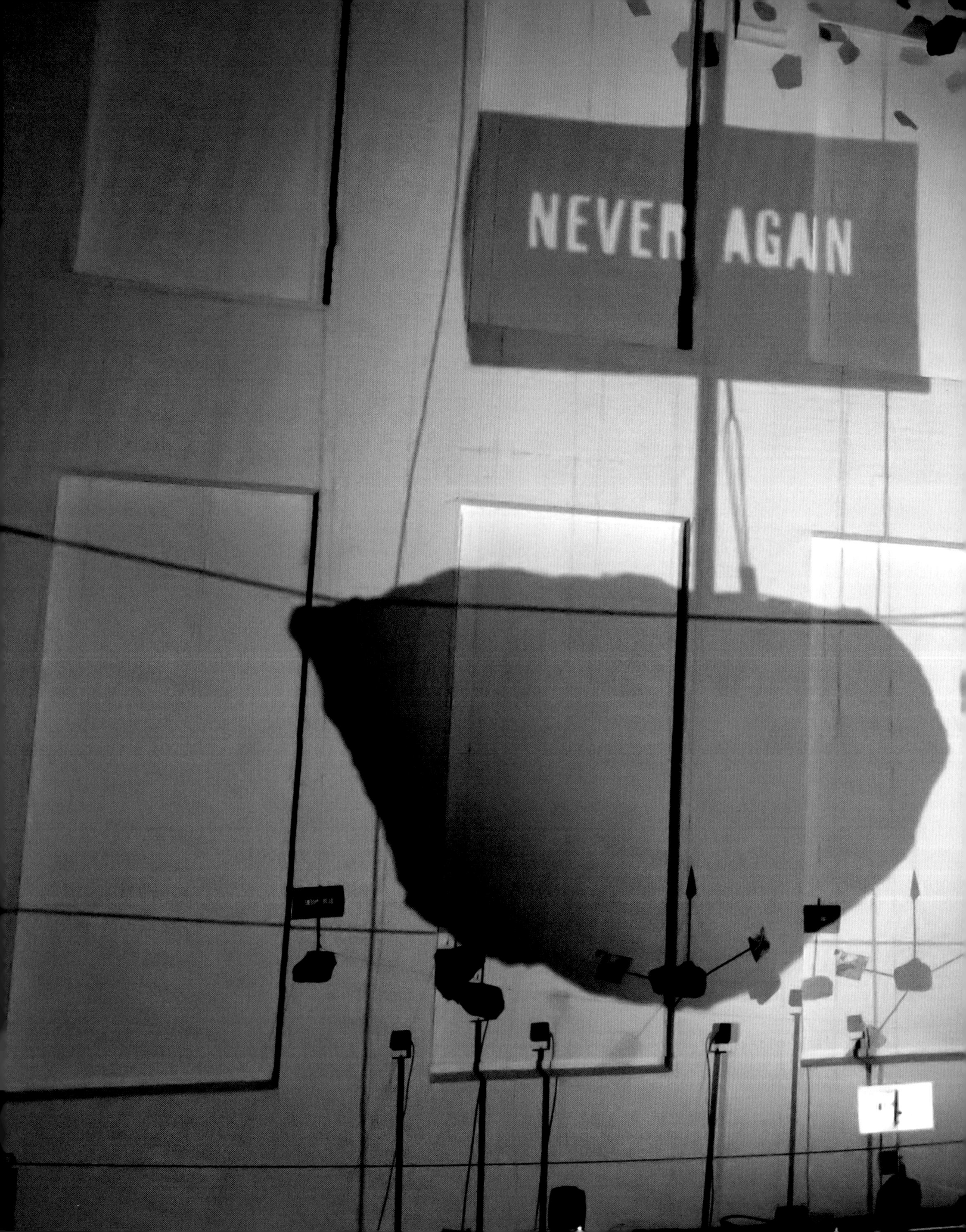
NEVER AGAIN

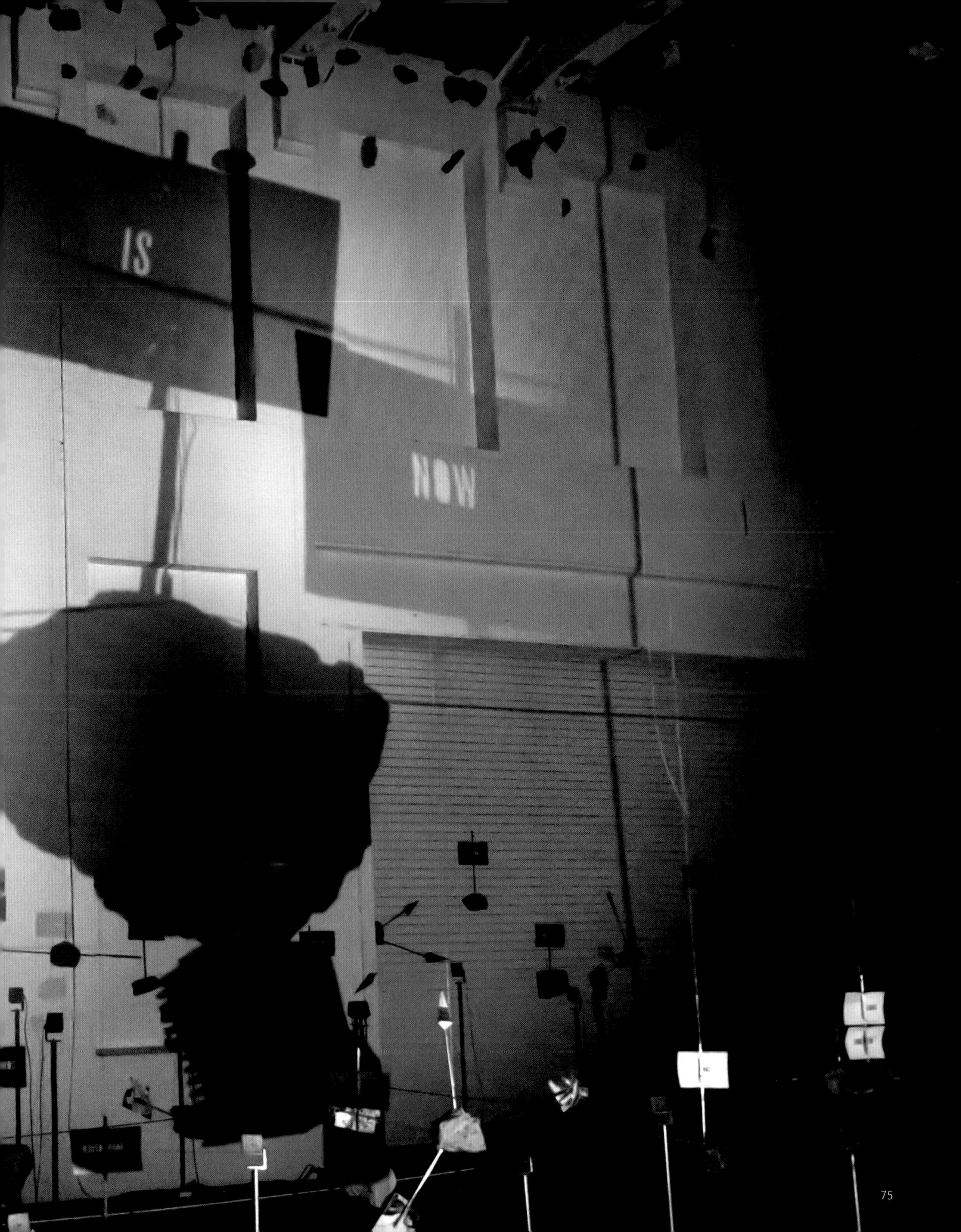
IS
NOW

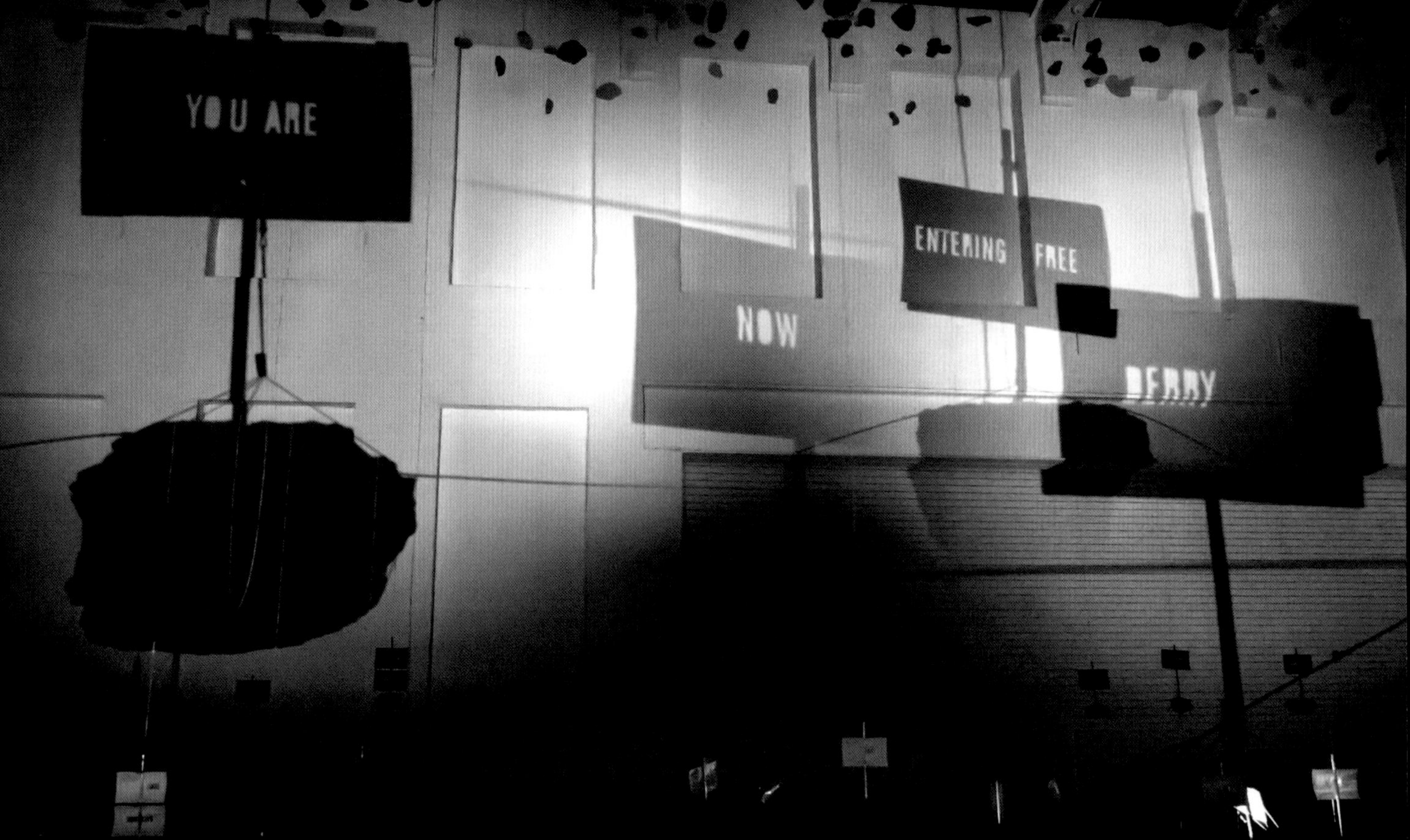

YOU ARE
ENTERING
FREE
NOW
DERRY

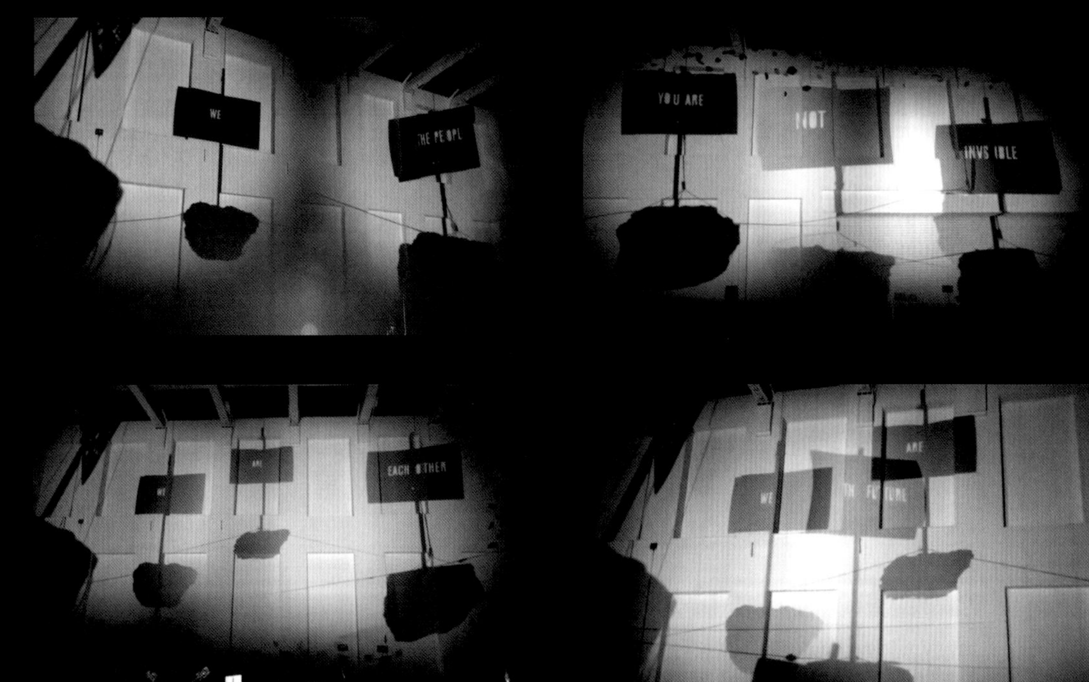
WE
YOU ARE
NOT
ARE
EACH OTHER
ARE

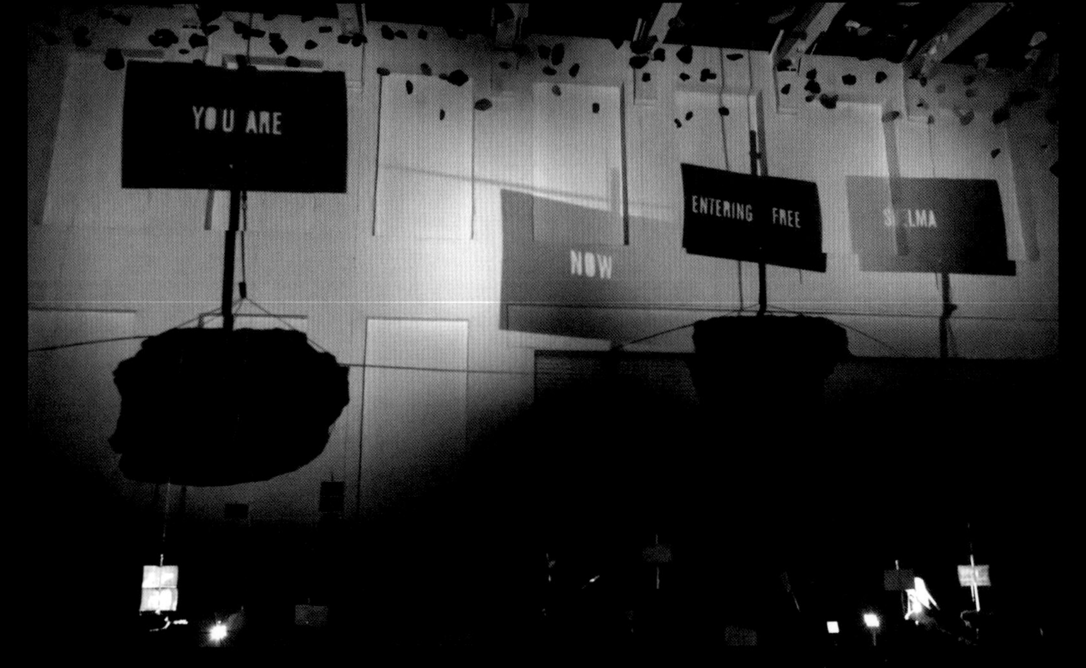
YOU ARE
NOW
ENTERING FREE
SELMA

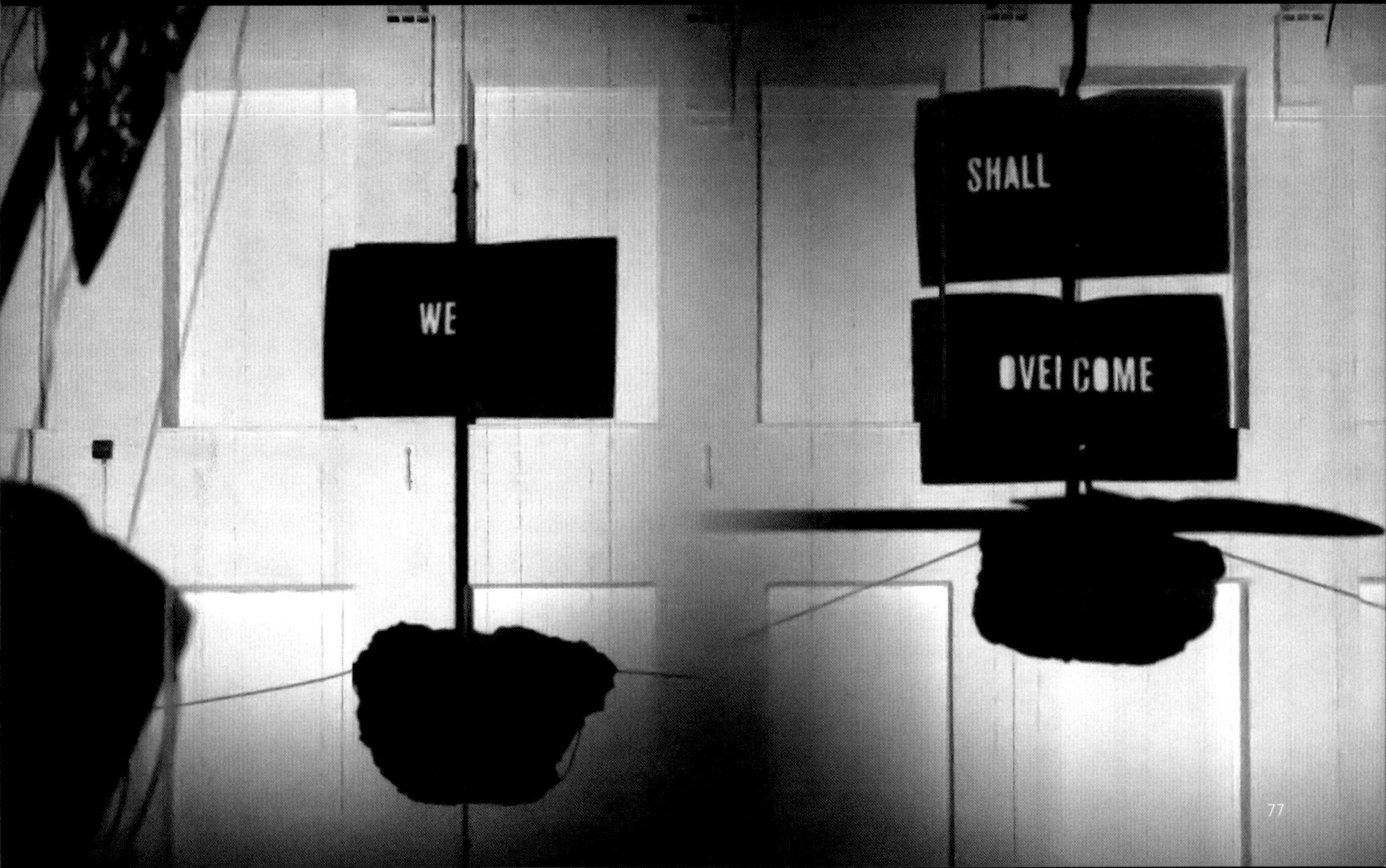

WE
SHALL
OVEI COME

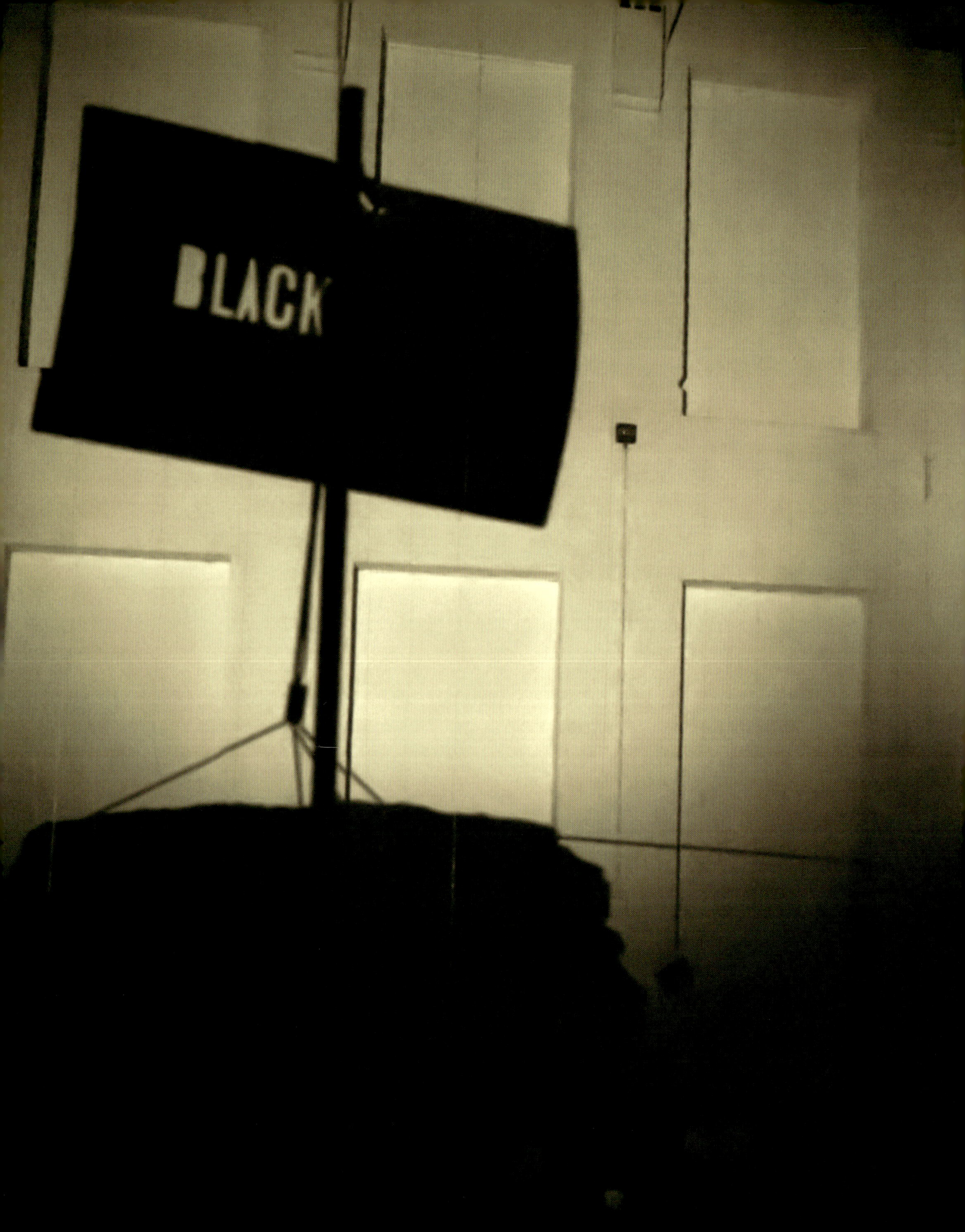
BLACK

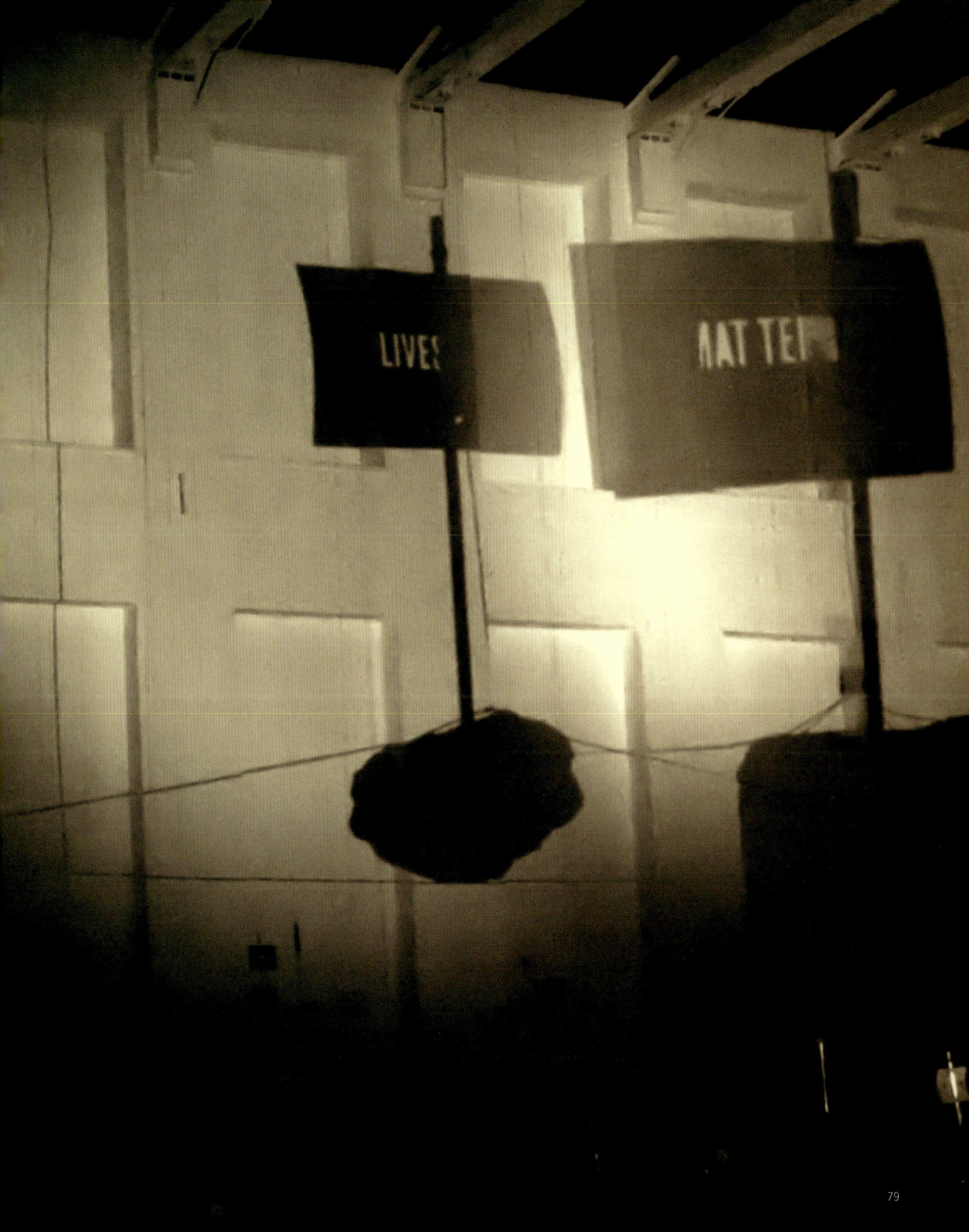
LIVES
MAT TE

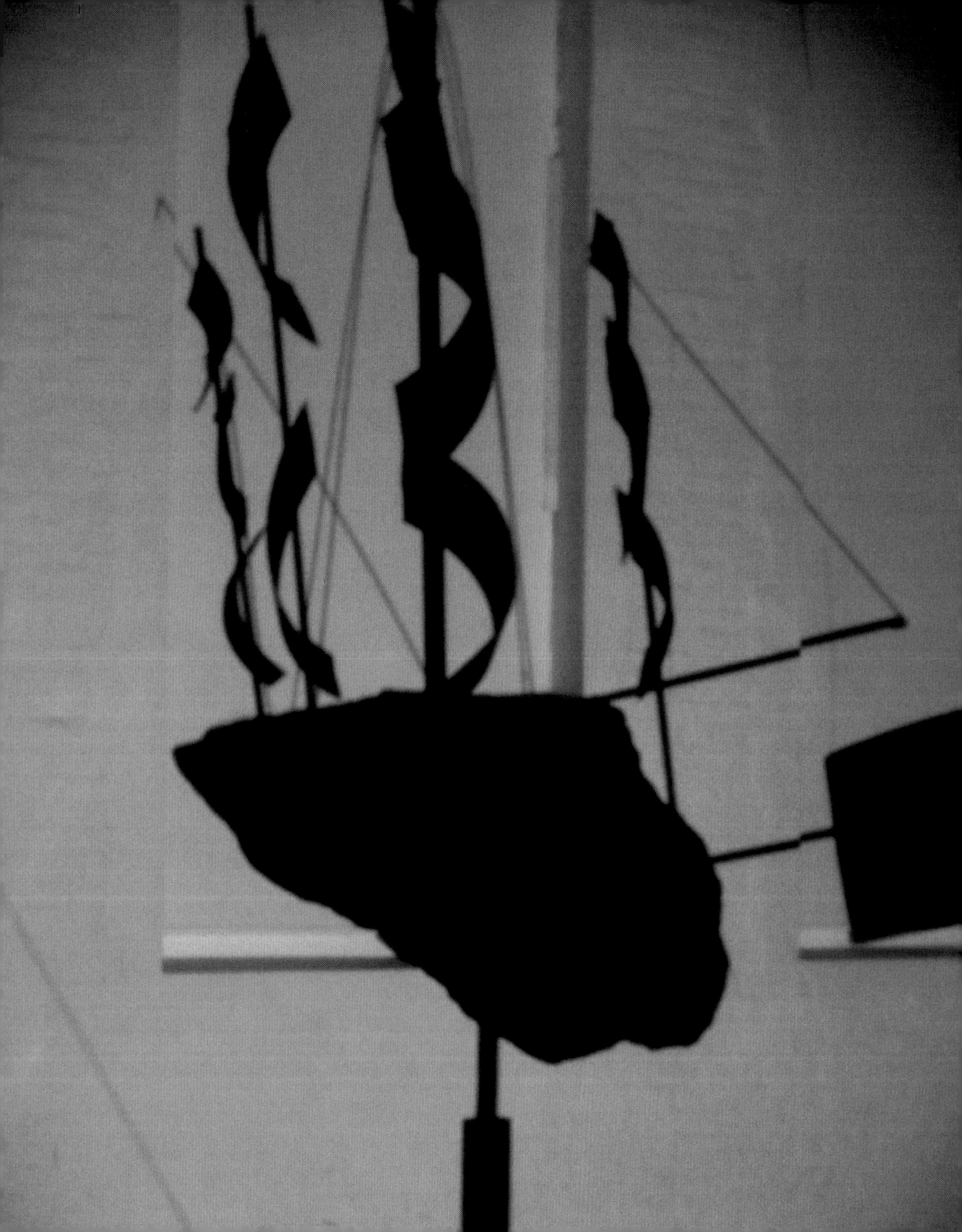

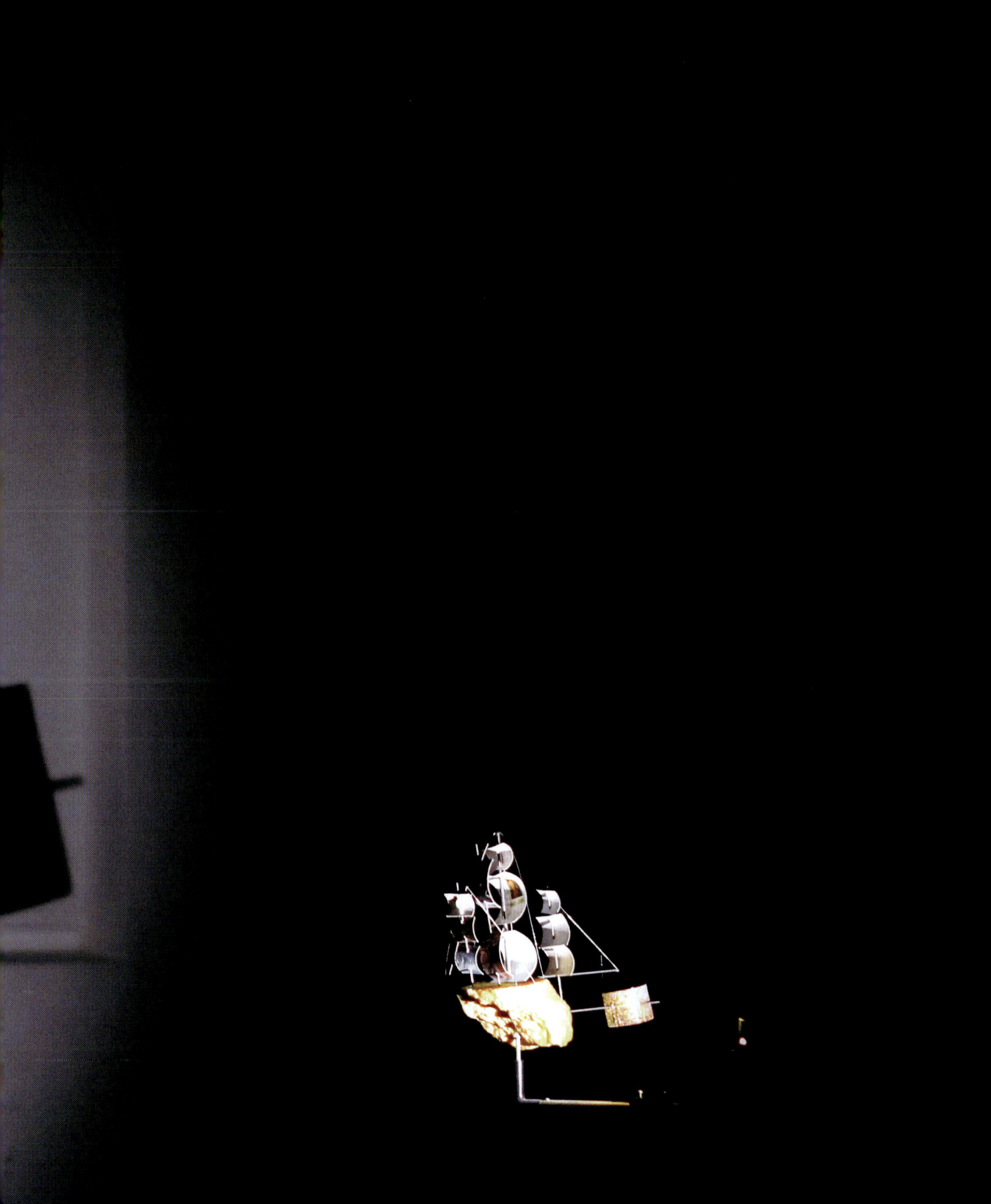

# Black, Green, and the Shared Palette of Struggle

Brian Dooley

At 4:10 pm Irish time on January, 30, 2021, people all over the world placed candles in the windows of their houses. At that moment, on every continent, the shooting of dozens of unarmed civilians by British soldiers in Derry exactly forty-nine years earlier was quietly marked.

Each of the tiny flames, framed against glass, reflected a simple, powerful expression of the art of remembrance.

Bloody Sunday 1972 has scarred Irish and British history for half a century, and resonates hard with many others struggling for rights across the world. The phrase is now part of a shared lexicon of activists everywhere, reverberating across vast geographies, reaching across generations. There have been at least a dozen Bloody Sundays, human rights tragedies dating back more than a century, from Russia to Germany to Turkey. Ireland has endured several.

And then there is Selma in 1965, Alabama's Bloody Sunday, when dozens of civil rights marchers were bludgeoned on the Edmund Pettus Bridge, another commonality binding the two civil rights movements across the Atlantic.

The Irish struggle for rights has swapped and shared its ideas with its Black American cousin for centuries. Frederick Douglass toured Ireland in the 1840s, advocating for support to end slavery in the US. In turn, he became a leading voice for Irish independence from British rule, developing a close personal and political relationship with the Irish emancipator Daniel O'Connell.

The thread between the Irish and Black American struggles has grown and strengthened across every decade since. The father of Black nationalism in the US, Marcus Garvey, modeled much of his movement on the young Sinn Féin organization he'd seen in London in the early 1900s. In 1921, he sent a telegram to Irish Republican prisoner and hunger striker Terence MacSwiney, offering support and the "sympathy of 400,000,000 Negroes."[1]

The connections were often artistic, and the Harlem Renaissance of the 1920s included a strong Irish dimension. One of the key literary vehicles of the renaissance, *The Survey* magazine, devoted an edition in 1921 to Ireland's cultural resurgence, featuring some of Ireland's leading writers and nationalists, and explored whether the Irish experience was predominantly national or racial.[2]

American artiste Harry Belafonte and author James Baldwin cited strong Irish influences on their work, as did Black Panther Party founder Huey P. Newton, who reflected that as a teenager he "identified very strongly" with the central character in James Joyce's *Portrait of the Artist as a Young Man*.

When Rosa Parks refused to budge on the Montgomery bus in 1955, she sparked a mass protest of civil disobedience which used a tactic—the boycott—that had been created, named, and developed seventy-five years earlier in the west of Ireland, when local farmers refused to pay land agent Captain Boycott.

By the 1960s, when there was a surge in agitation for civil rights in the north of Ireland, activists reached across the Atlantic for inspiration, strategy, and solidarity. Protestors campaigning about unfair housing allocations in Tyrone in 1963 carried placards saying "Racial Discrimination in Alabama Hits Dungannon" and in Derry banners were painted with "Derry's Little Rock Calls for Fair Play."

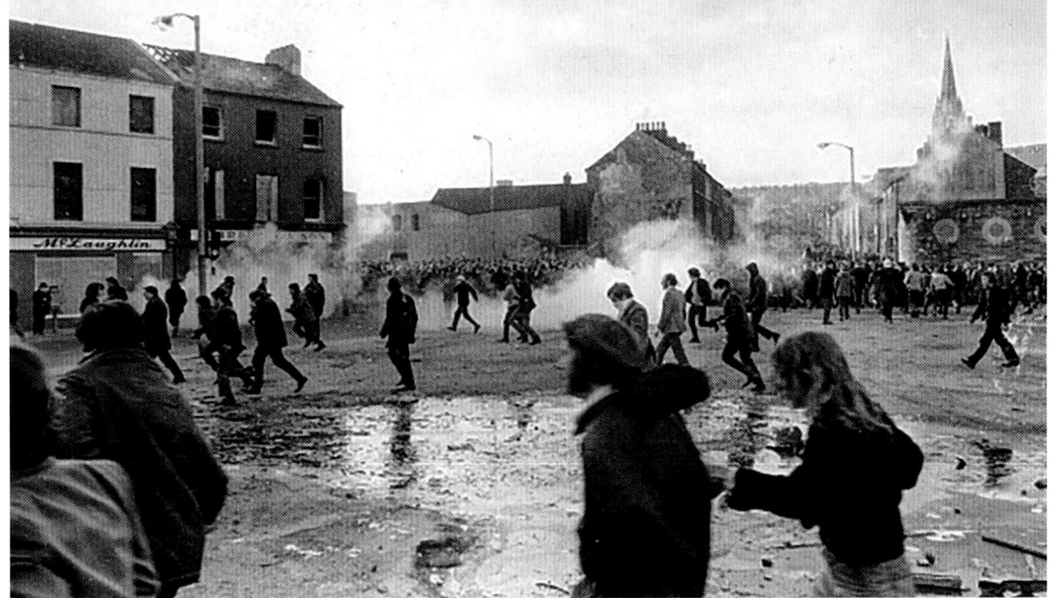

**NORTHERN IRELAND JANUARY 30, 1972 Demonstrators run after tear gas explosions on Bloody Sunday**

*Photo: PL Gould/Images/ Getty Images*

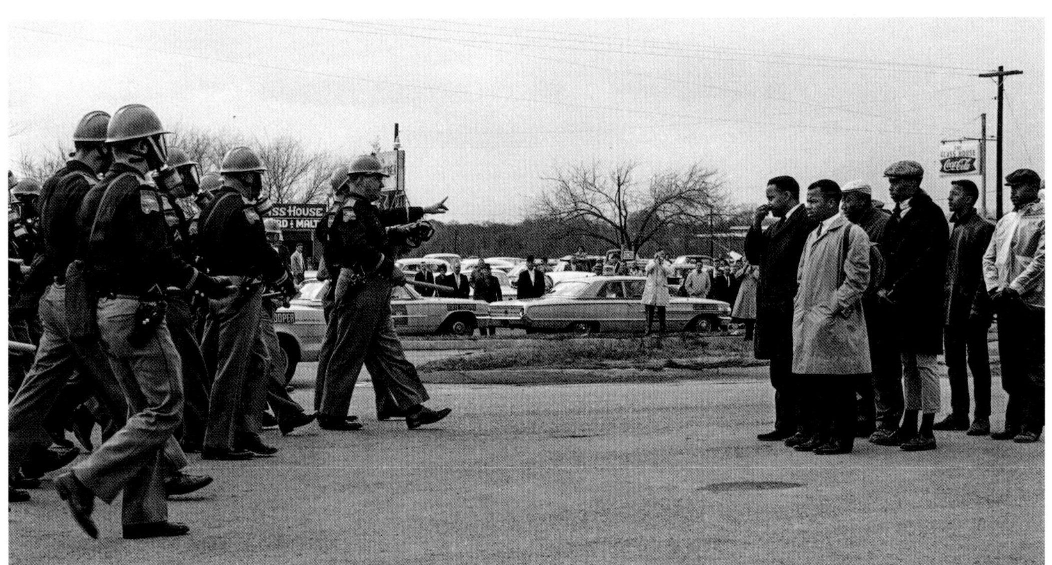

**Two Minute Warning, Police confront John Lewis in Selma, Alabama, on Bloody Sunday**

*© 1965 Spider Martin*

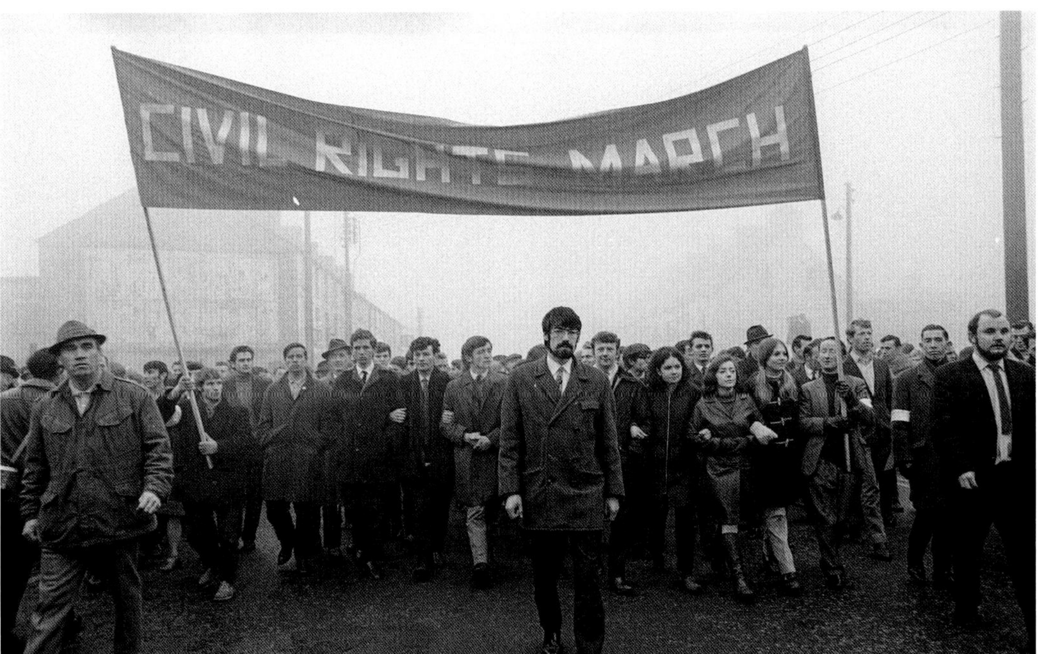


**Tom Keane leading the Civil Rights March, Newry (1969)**

*Ref 2605 055, RTÉ Archives*

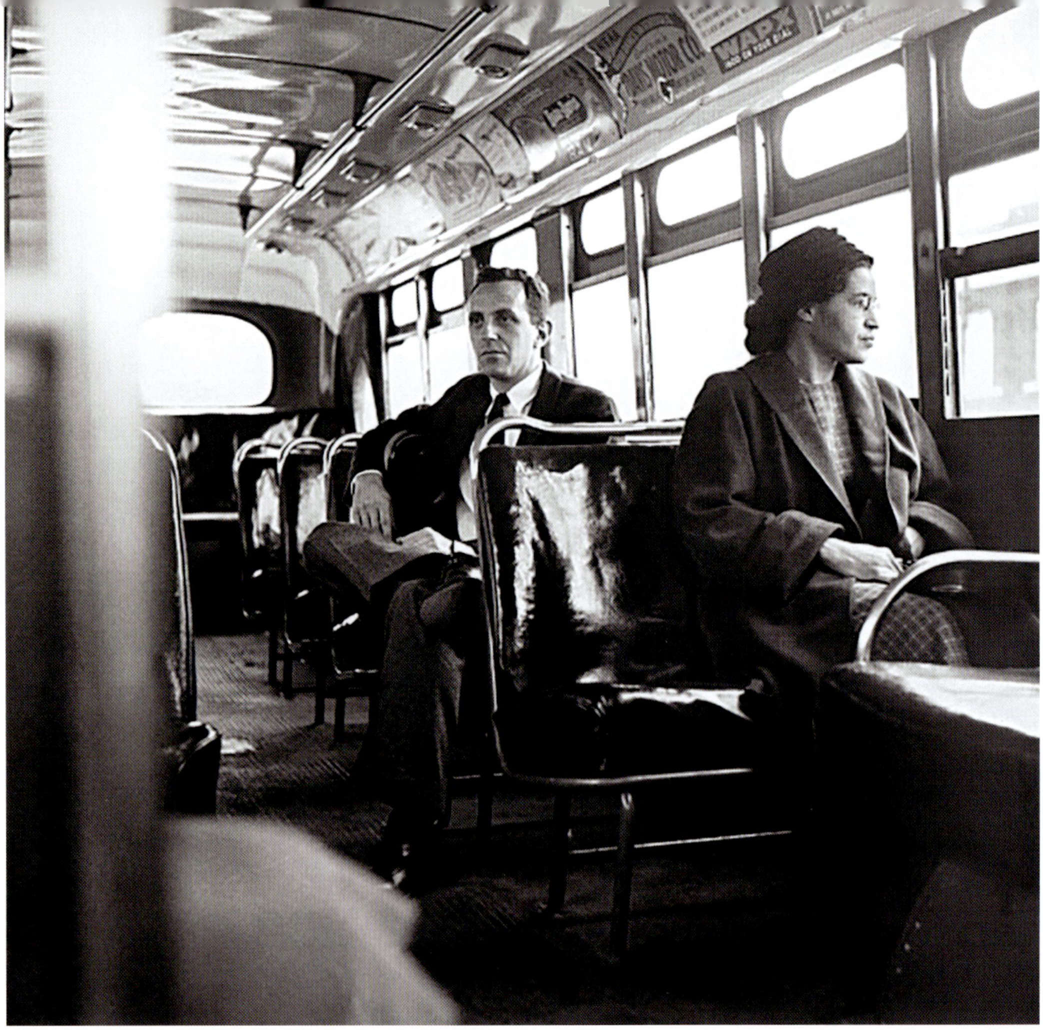

**American civil rights activist Rosa Parks sits in the front of a bus in Montgomery, Alabama, after the Supreme Court ruled segregation illegal on the city bus system on December 21, 1956. Parks was arrested on December 1, 1955, for refusing to move to the back of a Montgomery bus**

*Bettmann/Contributor, Getty Images*

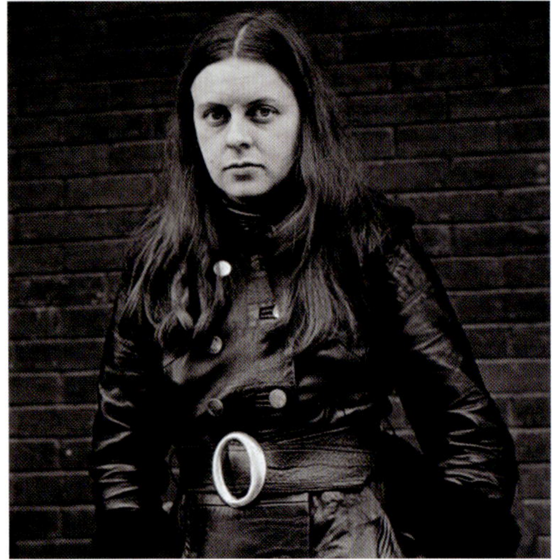

**Irish civil rights activist and politician Bernadette Devlin upon her return from the US, March 12, 1971**

*Photo: Daily Express/ Getty Images*

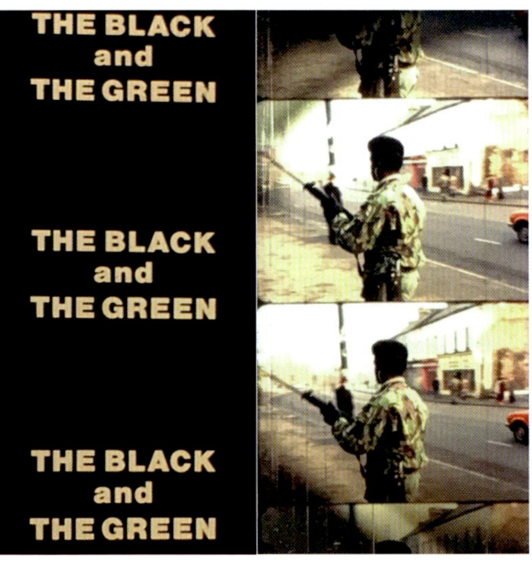


**St. Clair Bourne, *The Black and the Green*, 1983**

*Courtesy: Chamba Mediaworks & Judith Bourne*

John Hume of Derry became a civil rights leader early in the movement, and a prominent political leader. He was a key architect of the Good Friday Agreement, for which he won the 1998 Nobel Peace Prize. At the University of Massachusetts in 1985, he explained that "the American civil rights movement gave birth to ours. The songs of your movement were ours also."

Activists in Ireland adopted the American civil rights anthem "We Shall Overcome," the (now-dated) slogan of "One Man One Vote," and copied the tactics of their American counterparts, including staging sit-ins. The American protestors "sat down, so we sat down," civil rights leader Bernadette Devlin McAliskey explained to me.

Irish activists marching from Belfast to Derry in early 1969 chanted "On to Selma" in imitation of the American civil rights demonstration of 1965. International media described Catholics in the north of Ireland as "Ulster's White Negroes" to explain similar experiences of discrimination.

But these connections were far more than rhetorical. Devlin McAliskey visited Angela Davis in prison in California in 1971, where the Black civil rights icon was charged with murder and kidnapping. "Angela Davis and I are involved in the same struggle . . . for the liberation of our own people," said the Irish activist.

Davis told me how, during the visit, "We talked about the similarities of the situations in Northern Ireland and in the US with respect to African Americans and people of color." Devlin McAliskey's identification with Davis and other Black civil rights figures shocked much of Irish America, whose relationship with the civil rights movement in the US was complicated—part hostile, part supportive.

The Boston busing controversy of the mid-1970s exposed one strand of Irish American racism, confirming the views of many Black American activists about Irish America. Former Black Panther official Kathleen Cleaver told me that during the 1960s and 1970s, "There were too many Irish policemen who conveyed racist attitudes."

On St. Patrick's Day in 1969, the Philadelphia chapter of the Irish American organization Clan na Gael agreed that a civil rights banner could be carried in the local parade as long as it was clear it supported civil rights in Ireland, and not in the US.

Other Irish Americans were more supportive. An Irish priest in San Francisco, Father Eugene Boyle, was the first to open his doors to the Black Panther Party's free breakfast program when it began in 1969. The Black Panther newspaper reported that he allowed his Sacred Heart parish hall to be used for Panther political meetings, and appeared as a character witness for Black radical leader Bobby Seale when he was on trial for murder.

Bobby Kennedy, too, eventually understood and addressed structural white racism in a way few white politicians—or people—grasped then or now.

But despite the complicating influence of Irish America, the connection between the two struggles endured. The 1972 Bloody Sunday killings in Derry resulted in worldwide media coverage. British soldiers killed thirteen children and adults, civilians at a civil rights march, on that day. Another man died later.

International reaction was swift, and both Massachusetts senators responded strongly. Democrat Edward Kennedy compared the event to the massacre by American soldiers of hundreds of Vietnam civilians at My Lai four years earlier. Republican (and African American) Edward Brooke called on the European Commission on Human Rights to intervene.

And the Southern Christian Leadership Conference, founded by Martin Luther King Jr., dispatched senior officials to Ireland to join protest marches. The delegation included Juanita Williams, Bernard Lee, a veteran of sit-ins in Atlanta and a close associate of King, and Juanita Abernathy, who told a civil rights meeting in Belfast that "the struggle for Irish freedom is the same struggle that is going on in the United States."

But for many, the 1972 Bloody Sunday murders spelled the end of peaceful resistance and the civil rights movement in the north of Ireland. The killing of unarmed protestors by the state convinced many that the non-violent struggle was futile. The IRA was inundated with recruits in the weeks after Bloody Sunday, and "Brits Out" slogans replaced those about housing or voting rights.

However, the political and artistic connections between the Black American and Irish activists persevered, even during the bleakest days of the Troubles. In the early 1980s, African American

filmmaker St. Clair Bourne filmed a group of Black American civil rights activists visiting the north of Ireland in the immediate aftermath of the prison hunger strikes there.

He told me how, during the making of the documentary, locals in Belfast told the group that "the British were like White Southerners during the American civil rights era," and that "they hate us for no reason, they're racist." Bourne noted that for those they met in Ireland, the Black American activists "were the standard of oppression, both heroically and as victims."

In 2011, President Barack Obama visited Ireland, and cited the Black American-Irish relationship of the 1840s. In a speech in Dublin, he noted the "unlikely friendship" between Douglass and Irish rights leader O'Connell. "When we strove to blot out the stain of slavery and advance the rights of man, we found common cause with your struggles against oppression," he said. "Frederick Douglass, an escaped slave and our great abolitionist, forged an unlikely friendship right here in Dublin with your great liberator, Daniel O'Connell. His time here, Frederick Douglass said, defined him not as a color but as a man. And it strengthened the non-violent campaign he would return home to wage."[3]

Art has continued to fuel the identification across the Atlantic between the two struggles. In 2019, Helen Cammock received a major art award, the Turner Prize, for her installation *The Long Note* (2018), which traced the involvement of women in Derry in the civil rights movement. It includes the influence of civil rights activists in the US, and of Selma's Bloody Sunday, on Irish activists.[4] Cammock's work also highlights how the history of both struggles has often minimized the central role played by women over decades of activism.

Representatives of the Black Lives Matter movement have been regular speakers in Derry at Bloody Sunday commemoration events for several years. Both struggles remain connected with shared issues of pursuing justice for past police violence and killings. The Bloody Sunday families in Derry continue to campaign for the prosecution of those who killed their loved ones almost fifty years ago.

The Free Derry Museum has become an educational center for the history of the civil rights movement in Ireland, and is engaged on a project with the Hush House Black World Community Museum in Detroit to further explore the connections between the two struggles.

Legendary Massachusetts Congressman Tip O'Neill was half right when he famously said that all politics is local. That's true, but struggles for rights are global too.

While the civil rights movements in the US and Ireland have influenced each other over many decades, and still do, they in turn help inform and shape struggles for rights all over the world. Through shared vocabulary, tactics, and arts, they show how their activism is simultaneously local and international.

Art—and museums—play a central role in affirming and developing this long history of solidarity between Irish and Black American civil rights activists. January 2022 will mark the fiftieth anniversary of Derry's Bloody Sunday, and the small city and what happened there in just ten minutes that afternoon will again become the focus of international attention. Commemorations organized by the Free Derry Museum will educate, inspire, and encourage activism for rights throughout the world.

At MASS MoCA, Glenn Kaino will present *In the Light of a Shadow*, an exhibition that celebrates and strengthens this spirit of resistance shared across the Atlantic. Commencing in 2021, and running through the fifty-year anniversary of Bloody Sunday in Derry, it reminds us how the act of making art can be one of memory and purpose, whether by creating large-scale immersive installations, or by lighting candles in our windows.

[1] *Unless otherwise noted, all quotes in this essay come from research and the published book: Brian Dooley,* Black and Green: The Fight for Civil Rights in Northern Ireland & Black America, *(London: Pluto Press, 1998).*

[2] *Tracy Mishkin,* The Harlem and Irish Renaissances *(University Press of Florida, 1998).*

[3] *https://obamawhitehouse.archives.gov/the-press-office/2011/05/23/remarks-president-irish-celebration-dublin-ireland.*

[4] *www.tate.org.uk/whats-on/turner-contemporary/exhibition/turner-prize-2019/helen-cammock.*

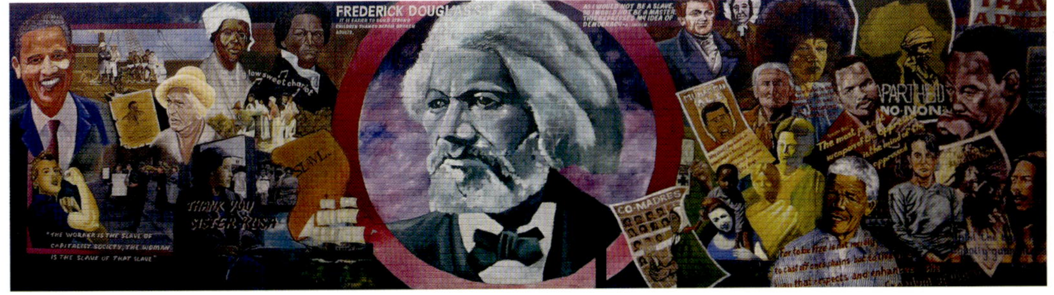

**Mural of Frederick Douglas, Belfast, Northern Ireland, March 17, 2017**

*Photo: Keith Ruffles*

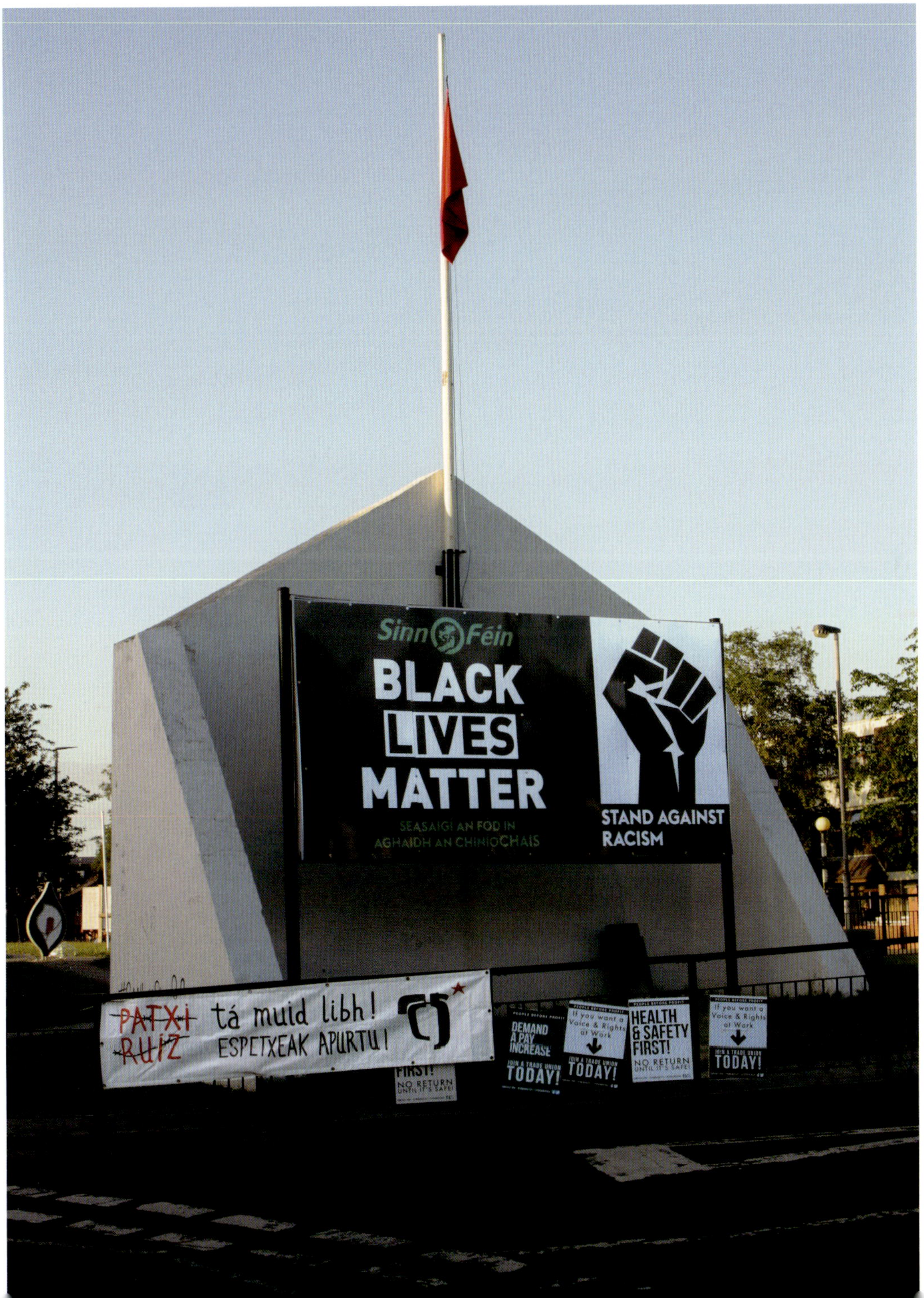

**"Seasaigí an fód in aghaidh an chiníochais—Stand [your ground] against racism." A Sinn Féin billboard in support of the protests sparked by the killing of George Floyd in Minneapolis has been erected at the back of Free Derry Corner, in Northern Ireland**

*Photo: Andy McDonagh, Photojournalist & Photographer, Eclipso Pictures, Belfast/Derry, Northern Ireland*

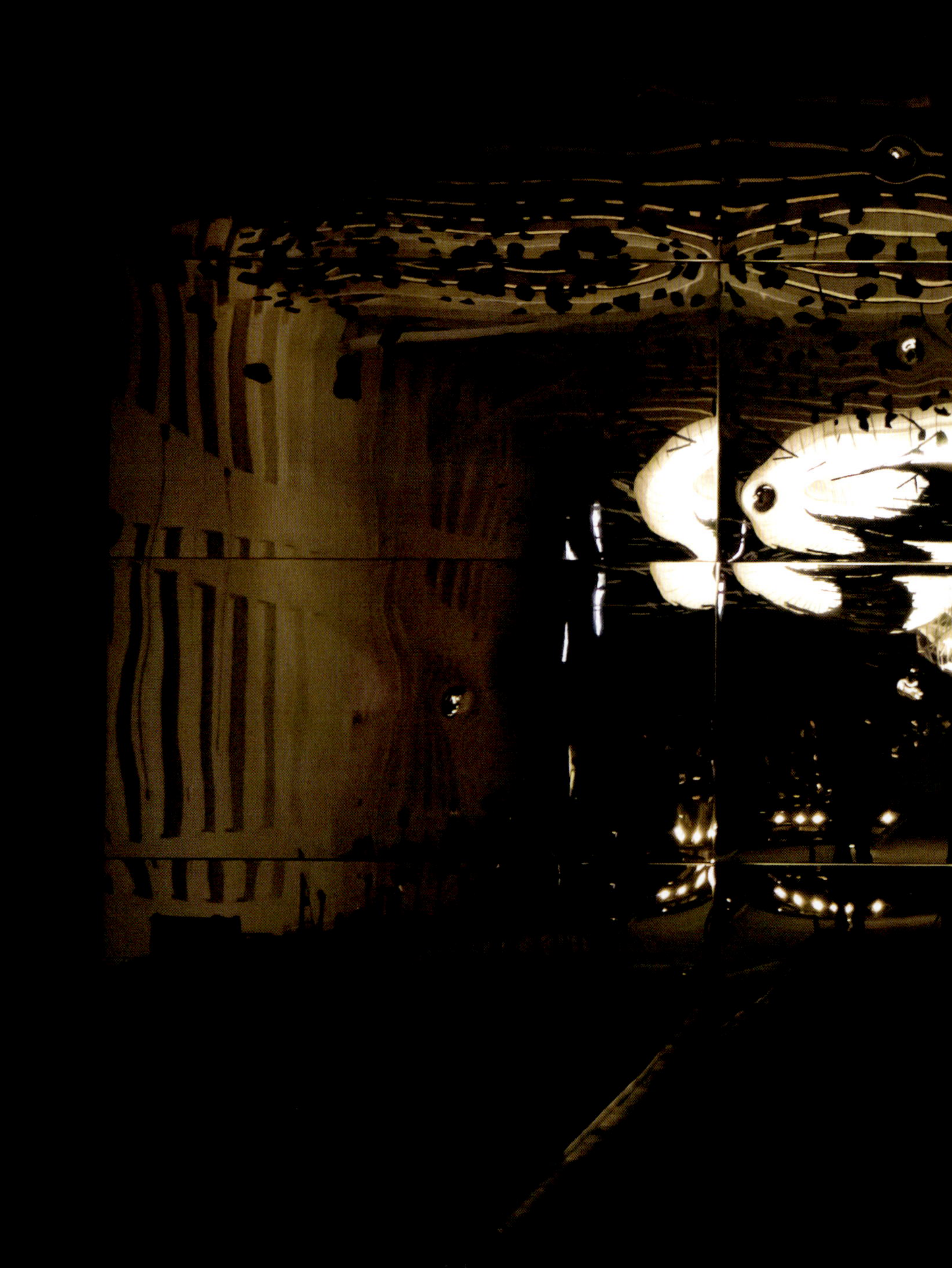

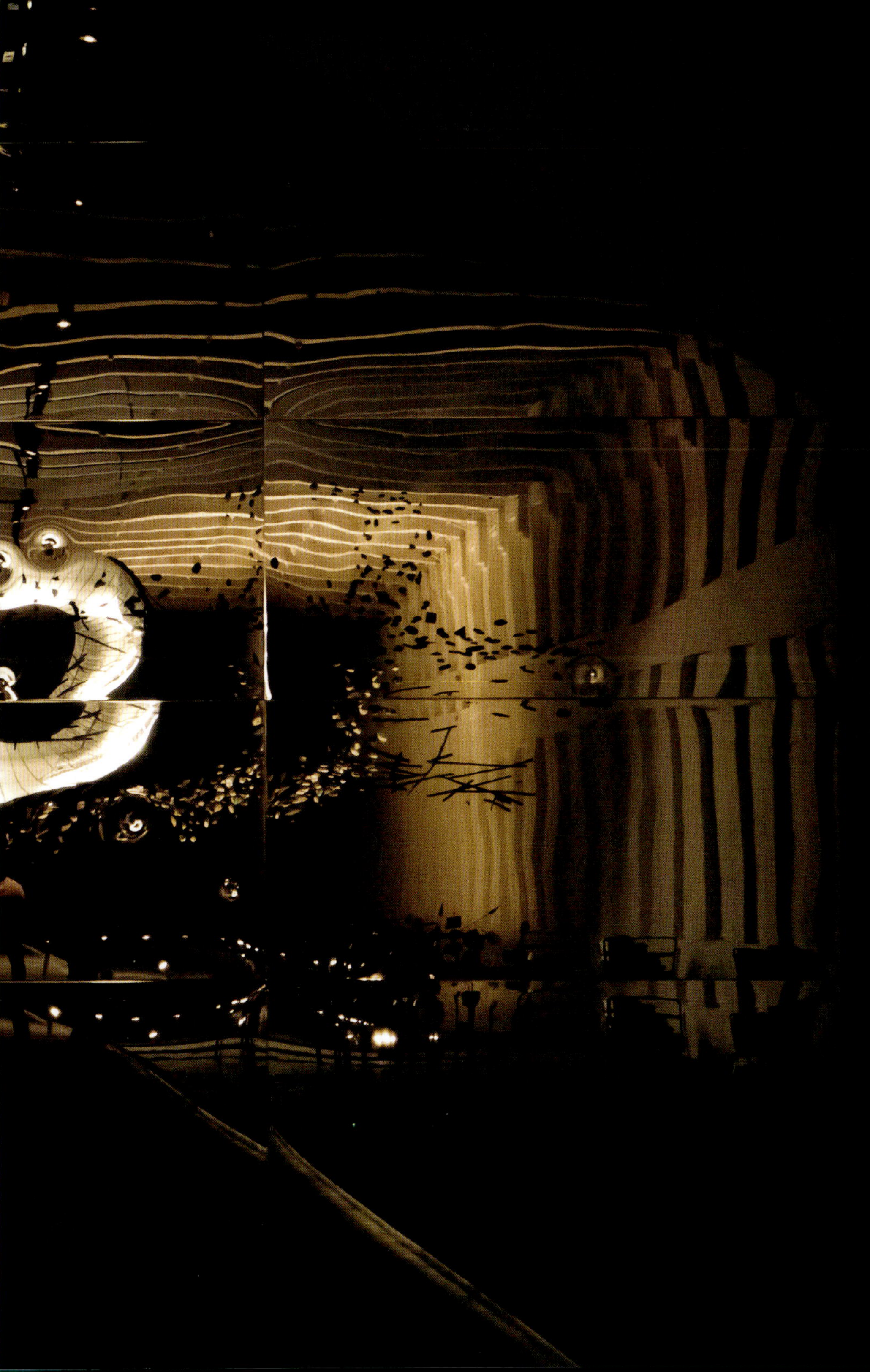

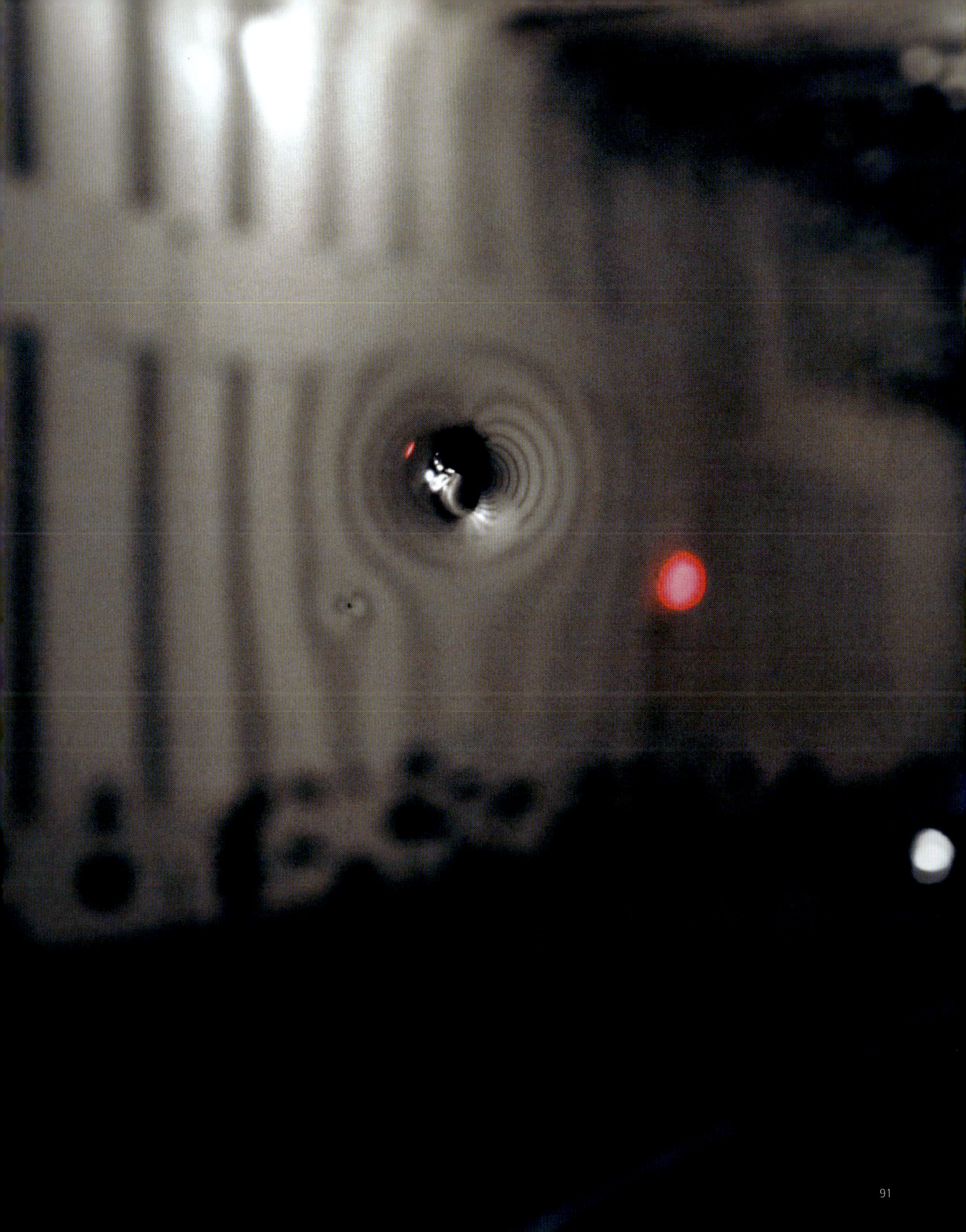

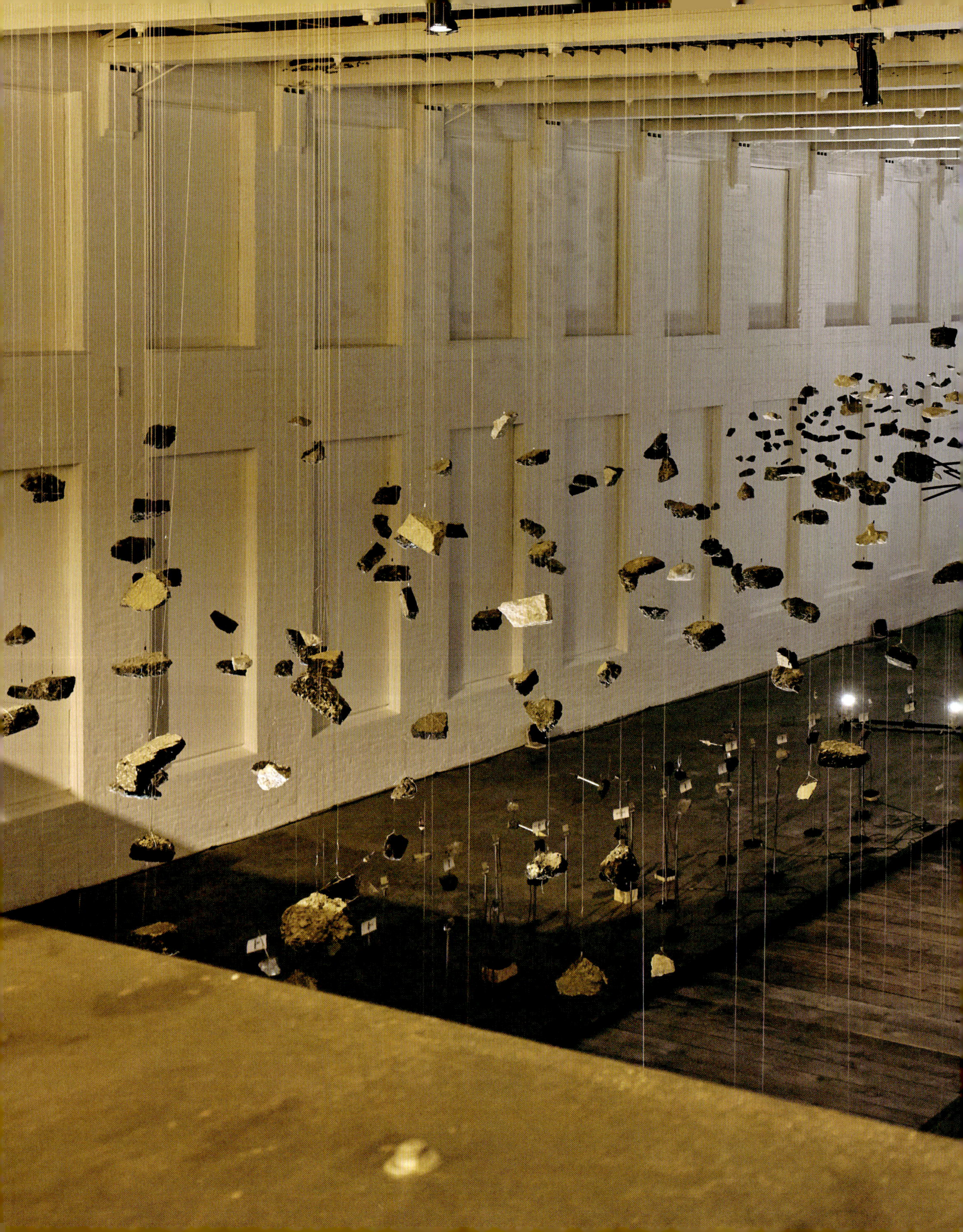

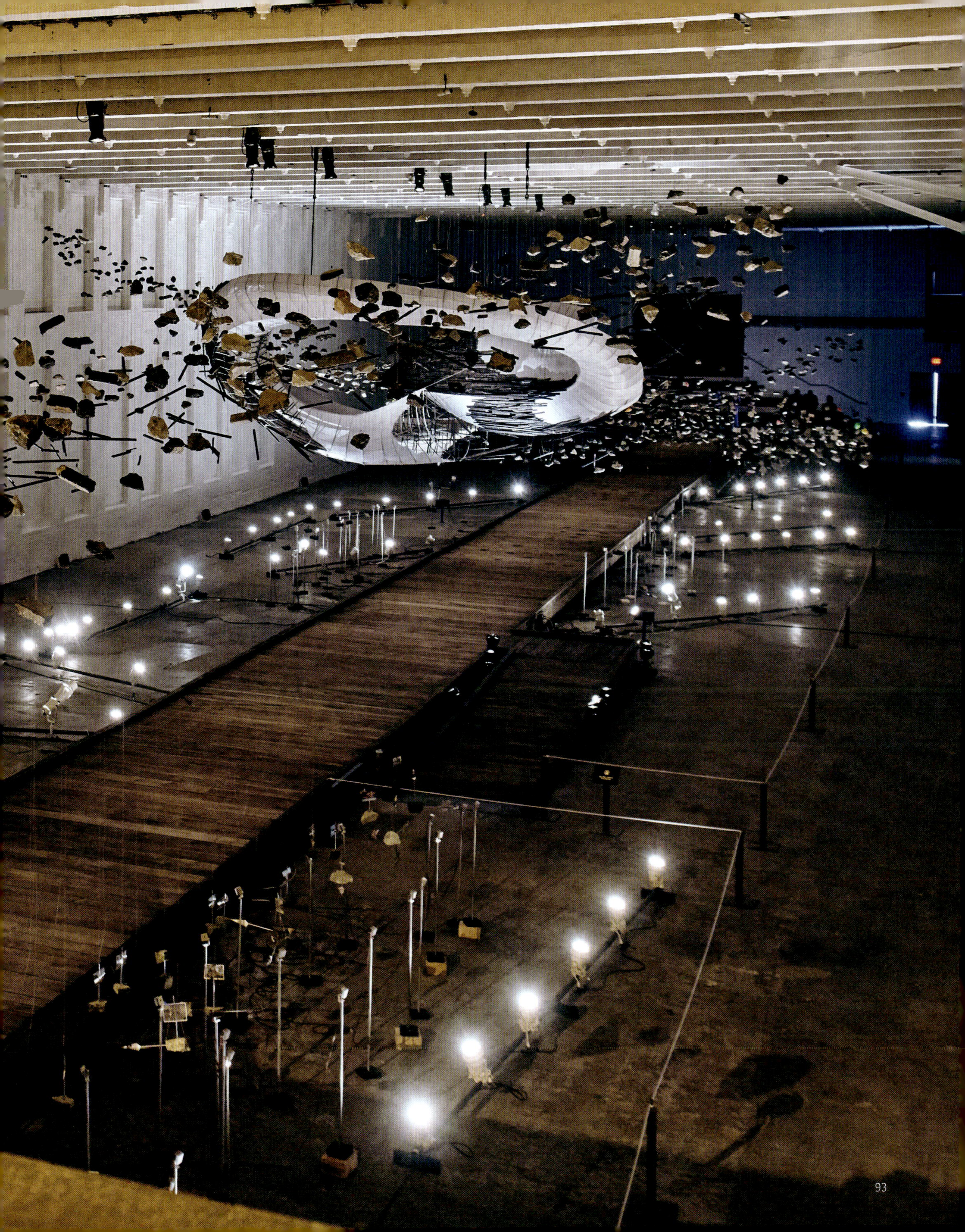

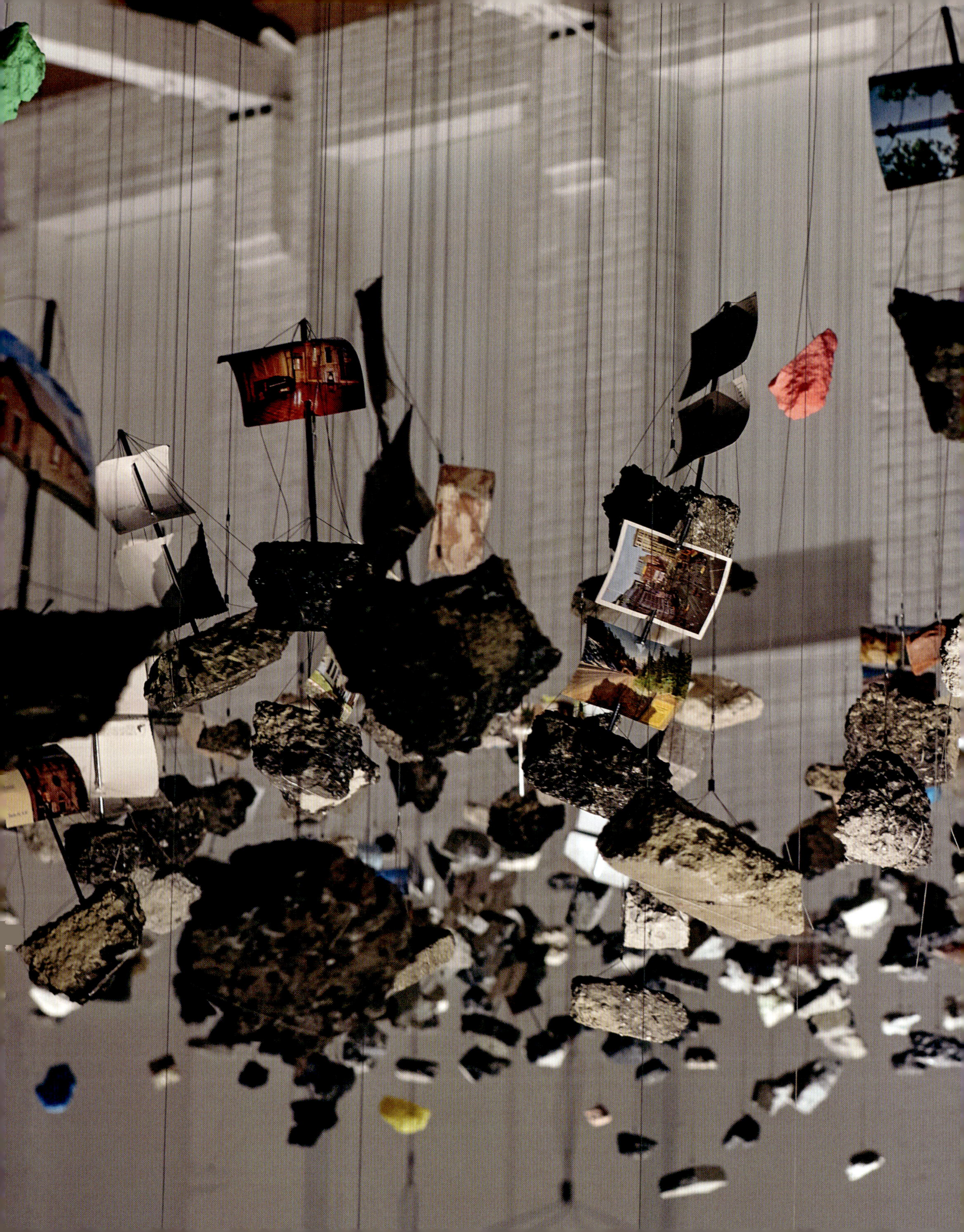

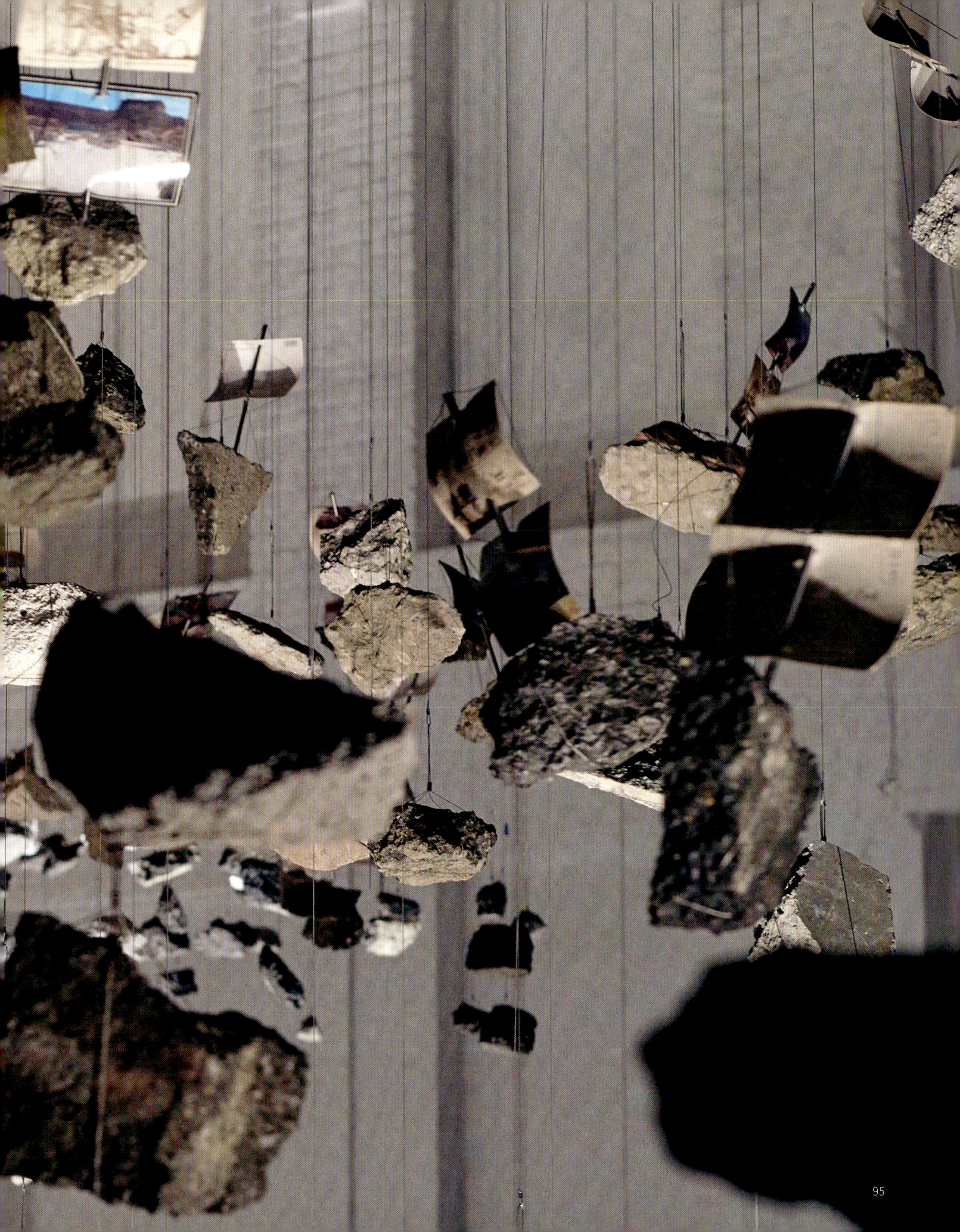

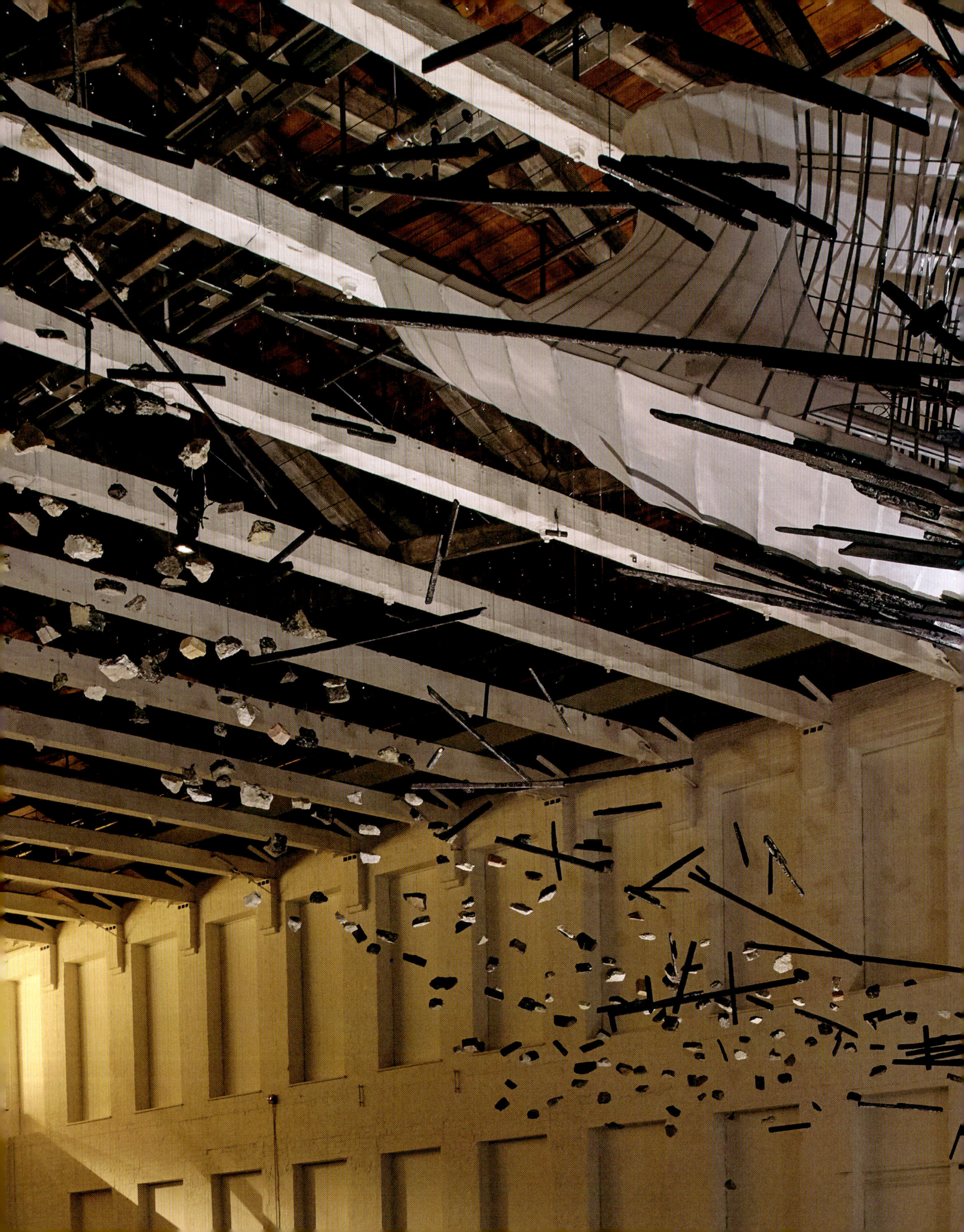

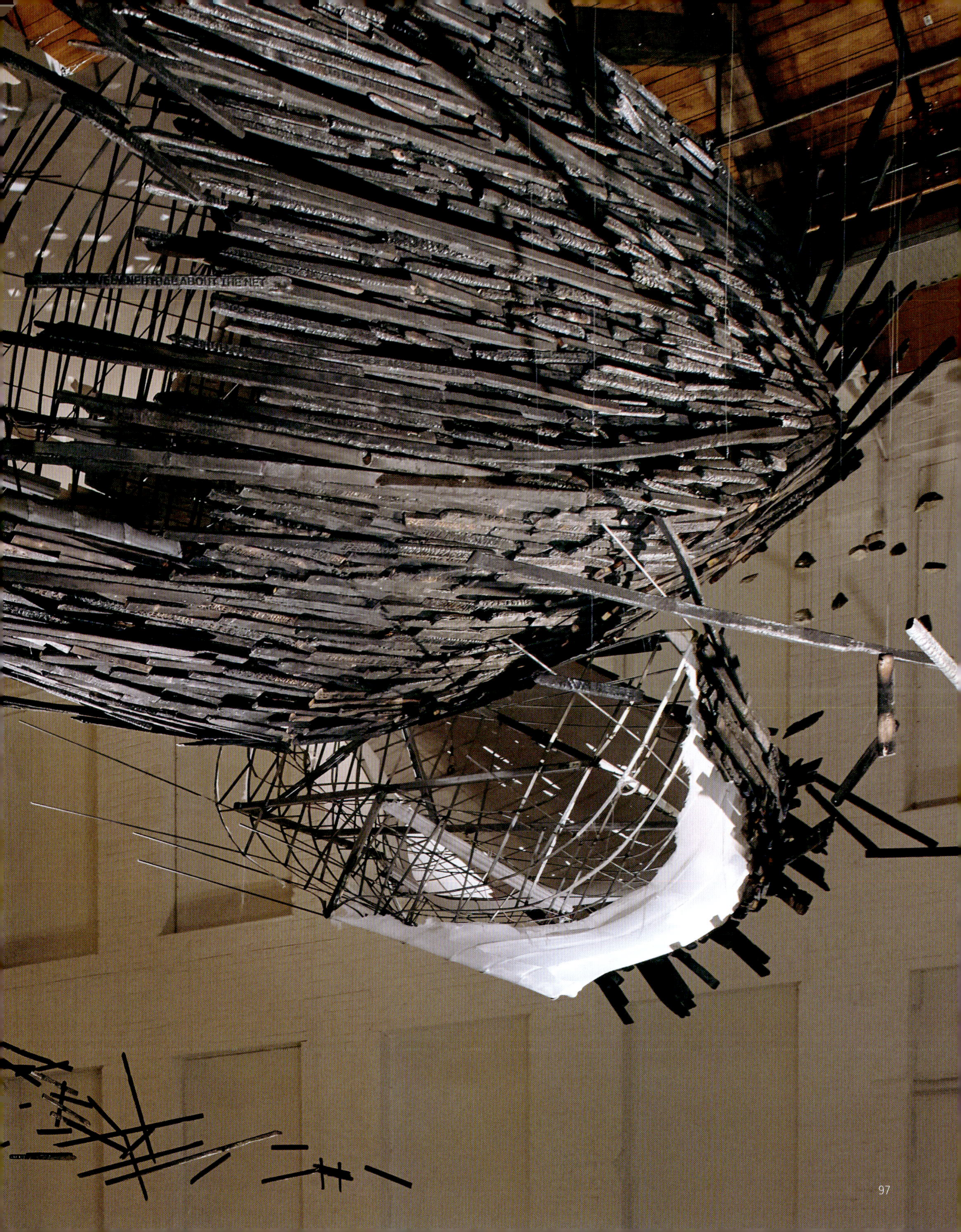
NEUTRAL ABOUT THE NET

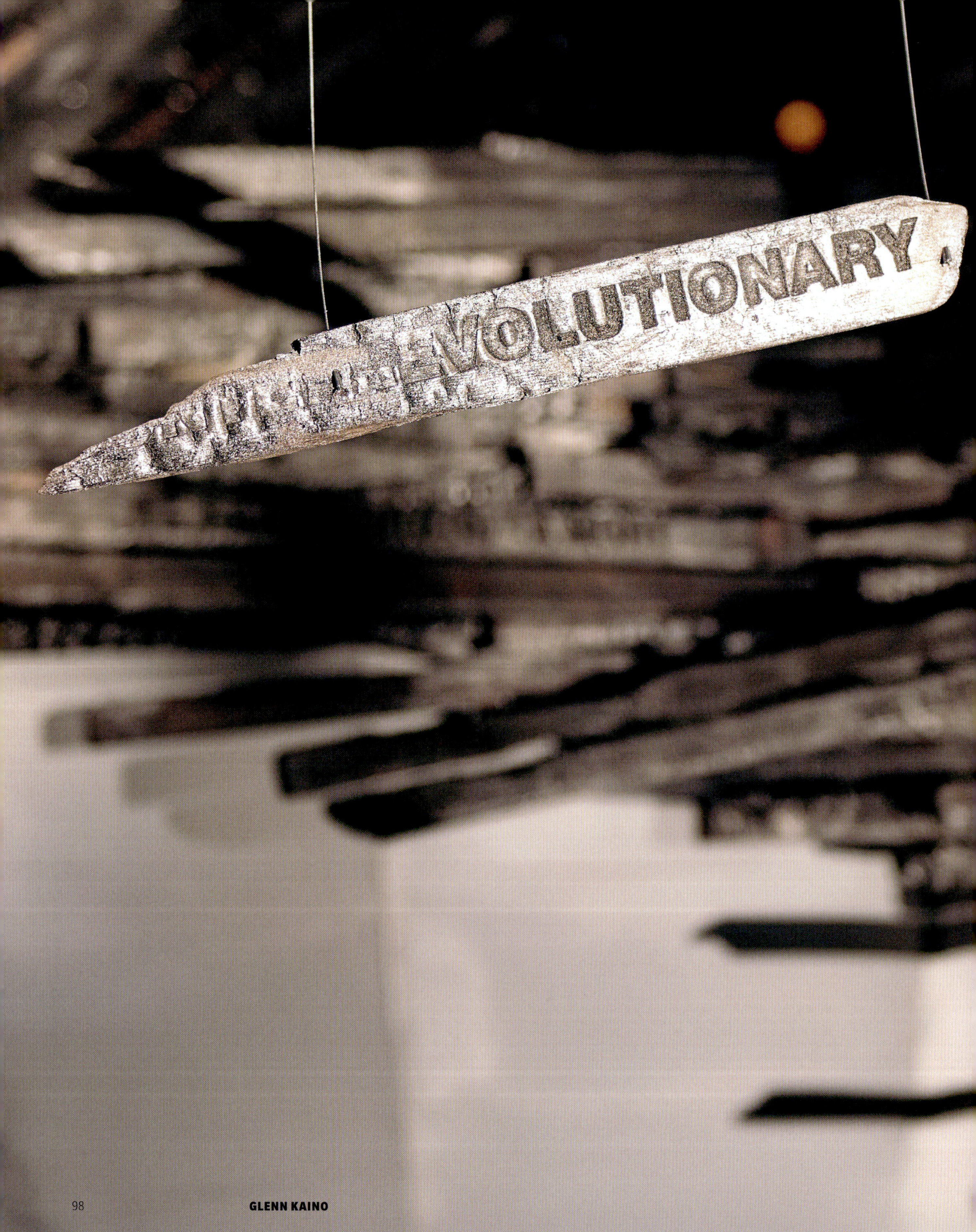
EVOLUTIONARY

# **Glenn Kaino** in conversation with **Deon Jones** and **Stacey Abrams**

When Deon Jones arrived at my studio door in 2016, I had no idea what to expect. What I did know, however, was that he wore his intentions on his sleeve and had an internal energy that I recognized as akin to my own. I also somehow knew we were going to work together on big things. What I didn't know was that he was old friends with Stacey Abrams and Congressman John Lewis, and that together Deon and I would collaborate to create some extremely compelling moments of social justice: connecting Tommie Smith to President Barack Obama and Colin Kaepernick; helping to support Fair Fight and numerous other causes; and reimagining one of the most powerful rock songs of all time as a ballad, with Deon singing the lead supported by an all-star group of musicians. Yet, somehow, I also know that this is just the beginning.

I recently had the privilege of catching up with both Deon and Stacey as we concluded the chapter of our work that culminated with *In the Light of a Shadow*. It was not surprising that, as we pivot to our next set of challenges, they had wonderful ideas to share. This exhibition was not meant to be a celebration of protest for protest's sake. It was intended to be a platform where knowledge production, inspiration, and tangible change-making ideas could be considered and even acted upon. The work in the museum is the result of years spent building toward these ideals and goals. And this dialogue is a part of that.

**— Glenn Kaino**

**Glenn Kaino: Deon, I usually tell this story, but why don't you tell it this time! How did we meet?**

**Deon Jones:** When I moved to LA, over five years ago now, I was looking to start a new creative chapter after spending time working in a political orbit. One of President and Mrs. Obama's closest friends, and an early mentor of mine, Mike Strautmanis, introduced me to you through one of your collaborators. His message to y'all was to "beat the DC out of me." I finally understand what he meant by that. And I'm grateful that you took that directive seriously. You agreed to meet with me at your old Hollywood studio, and I remember that I came pretty dressed up! You had a board meeting at the Hammer and you said that you could talk with me on the way. In the car on the ride over, you discussed the current projects the studio was working on. When we got to the meeting, you asked me to wait outside, so we could finish the conversation afterwards. While you were inside, I wrote down pages and pages of ways that I thought I could contribute to the collective work of the studio. And I remember you saying after I showed you, "I don't know who the hell you are or what the fuck you're going to do. But, let's do this!" And, the rest is history. We've been inseparable**!**

**GK:** You've grown so much since that first meeting, and now we've worked on new media projects with Oprah, a film with Tommie Smith, apps with Jesse Williams, but also in support of the relationship you have had for a long time with Stacey Abrams. How did that get started?

**DJ:** Stacey and I grew up in the same part of Mississippi, although Stacey moved from the area to Atlanta in the tenth grade while her parents pursued their master's degrees at Emory. Stacey would go on to Spelman, and her parents moved back to Mississippi. Her mother became my family's pastor. To have a congregation and lead a church as a Black woman in South Mississippi, even in the 1990s and 2000s, was something that was not happening. Stacey's mom baptized me, instilled in me the same values of education and the love of God that she instilled in Stacey and her siblings, and I just remember how her eyes lit up when I did something well.

It was Stacey's mom who gave me my first platform to sing every Sunday and, OMG, at the time I thought I wanted to be a preacher and that she was gonna let me preach! It was a whole family intervention because I was singing "Falling in Love with Jesus" on Sundays, but also loved rapping "Tip Drill" on Saturdays! Everyone there knew I wasn't ready. It was actually in that church that I felt the hand of God setting in motion something bigger in my life. I would move to Atlanta in middle school, but would spend every summer until college in Mississippi. It was in Atlanta where I re-connected with Stacey (essentially, I cold called her out of the phone book!) and through the years she has been a constant support for me personally and professionally; our great care for humanity and love of justice has continued to bring us together in the work toward building political power and fighting for collective liberation.

**GK:** What does it mean for you to live with intention, while balancing work that is both very political and also creative?

**DJ:** Intention is my favorite word and it is how I rule every action in my life. I think it is what has allowed me to move through the world in the way I have been able to. As Gary Zukav has said, it is what helps us unlock our "authentic power" and purpose, allowing our "personality to align with the energy of our soul." Intention has always allowed me to ask myself the following questions, regardless of the space I occupy: What is my real motivation? How do I wish to serve? How do I wish to use these gifts that God has given me, this intellect that I have gained? How do I wish to use this for something bigger than myself? Because that Newton's Law thing is real, baby! Whatever you put into the world is destined to return back to you. So, when I was working in politics, I was interested in how policy could transform the outcomes of people's lives through the decisions of folks in rooms on Capitol Hill, at the White House, and through the work of nonprofits at the state and local level. As a creative and, now, working musician, from my songs to the stories we've been able to tell via film and technology, I think about how art is enlightening, moving, and liberating folks. God gave me a voice. He blessed me with intellect. I have to use it.

**GK:** The late Congressman John Lewis played a very important role in inspiring *In the Light of a Shadow*. When did you first meet him?

**DJ:** Hilarious story! When I met John Lewis, he was wearing a two-piece Under Armour bodysuit. You're not used to seeing icons and heroes dressed like that, right? I was sixteen and in high school, and some of my classmates and I got invited to participate in Jane Fonda's workout/health event at the Georgia Dome.

**GK:** That's hilarious. It reminds me of the time I was invited to SoulCycle for Oprah's birthday, but Oprah wasn't there. Everyone was wondering why we were all gathered around and then the instructor (Angela Davis, not that Angela Davis) called out "Happy Birthday, Oprah!" and sure enough, on the bike right behind me, there was Oprah! Somehow, she snuck in and was riding behind me and none of us knew she was there! And both of us were able to continue our relationships with these folks despite seeing them sweat.

**DJ:** Yes! So, from that encounter of us working out together and then talking about my future, John became a mentor and someone that I could count on for wisdom and advice. He was one of the first people I went to see when I moved to DC for college. I called him when I was in Georgia fighting against voter suppression, and, as you know, he was super supportive of the work we had been doing in the studio with Jesse and Tommie.

**GK:** We spoke about him coming to the opening at MASS MoCA and walking the show with us as our first guest, and then tragically he passed away. We found out about his passing when we were editing the video of you singing "Sunday Bloody Sunday." How do you think we can keep his memory alive and pay his work forward?

**DJ:** I think we keep his memory alive by passing federal legislation to protect the right to vote for every American. We also need to slash the suppression bills that state legislatures are passing that are clear in their intention to make voting harder for people of color and young folks. He gave me a mandate long ago that I've lived by since: when you see something wrong, you can't be silent. Get up, say something, do something. We pay his work forward by not choking on silence when injustice is in our faces, racism is spewed in our presence, and discrimination of any kind rears its head. I've been asked why I chose to go back out to protest on Saturday—which was the day I got shot in the face—when I had experienced brutality and had even been arrested on the preceding Friday night. I reminded them that John Lewis went back to Brown Chapel after he almost died on the Edmund Pettus Bridge. The same day! He prayed and rallied the people. That is the example we need to continue to follow in these times, because instead of looking at how far we have come, I would rather look at how close we are.

**GK:** What are you working on now?

**DJ:** I'm currently working on my freshman album, *REVIVAL*, after the release of the single "Sunday Bloody Sunday" last year. *REVIVAL* is a combination of the sounds of soul, rock, funk, and gospel, and is inspired by many of the events from when I was growing up to the present. The concept for the album was actually birthed two years ago from a conversation between you, me, and our friend, the producer Zack Sekoff. And, like many things, we believe in finding the right moment to give to the world what has been placed in us. *REVIVAL*'s moment finally seemed ready. I always tell the story of how when I was younger, the images of catching the holy ghost at church revivals and gyrating to secular music at a club looked the same to me. So, this album is about what revival means for people—that ability to get your fix in order to feel renewed, set free, and delivered. For some folks it's a religious experience; for others it's a sexual encounter; for some, it's letting something or somebody go; but in the end, they are determined to get their fix, and they shout, "I feel revived!" A great team of collaborators has come together to make it something special.

**Glenn Kaino: Stacey, I'd like to start with understanding your thoughts on some historic voting rights problems. Gerrymandering is over two hundred years old and seems as undemocratic as any type of activity, but with it having been a tactic of manipulation in service for so long, what's the most effective argument to abolish it?**

**Stacey Abrams:** Voters should choose their leaders; politicians should not game the system to select their preferred voters. In that way, gerrymandering not only usurps the voters' constitutional rights to elect their representatives, but also triggers complacency among lawmakers. When lawmakers control who can elect or fire them, they face less pressure to represent the will of their constituents. Opponents of redistricting reform likely stand to gain from the status quo—politicians who care more about holding on to power than serving the needs of the people they represent. Given recent Supreme Court decisions, partisan gerrymandering can only be thwarted by congressional action with legislation like H.R. 1, the For the People Act, which would end partisan gerrymandering at the federal level, require states to use independent commissions to draw congressional districts, standardize rules for map-drawing nationwide, and guarantee the public's right to review maps and provide input.

**GK:** There is a lot of dialogue right now about who gets to tell stories and it seems to me that there is a growing essentialist concern that is in opposition to ideas about intersectionality and allyship. As an artist who frequently collaborates with partners across culture, gender, and several other social issues, I think it's important for us to work together to find ourselves in each other's stories, so we can fight for each other in new, collective stories.

For *In the Light of a Shadow*, we present historic moments of unexpected international collaboration. Just prior to the murder of protesters in Northern Ireland during their Bloody Sunday in 1972, the crowd was singing "We Shall Overcome," and many of the children were unaware that the song came from the American South. After the Northern Ireland peace process, several countries learned what compromise and progress looked like. How can we foster these moments of cross-cultural exchange to learn from each other? Are there instances where you learned something from studying a movement or cause in another community or part of the world?

**SA:** Every citizen has a role in the fight to protect our democracy. Our ability to tackle the challenges that threaten our communities depends on participation in the process. We must elect leaders and vote for policies that will end systemic injustice, address climate change, and ensure economic opportunity for all. Throughout my career, I have intentionally engaged people across a variety of spaces and platforms to ensure I understand their needs and their ambitions. Indeed, my first international travel focused on working with other young people from across the globe to discuss youth civic engagement. What we had in common—from Colombia to Liberia to Germany—was the core obligation to meet in their place, rather than expecting them to come to us, to listen to their needs, and to provide them with the tools necessary to build internal resilience. Intersectionality—be it across identity, demography or geography—operates as a convener of communities that can share knowledge, strategize for mutual upliftment, and, when most powerful, challenge narratives and policies that pit one against the other. When intersectionality and democracy collide, the result is typically jarring and, inevitably, progress for all.

**GK:** We respect you so much for everything you do, but it is your resilience that is one of your most impressive attributes. After the 2018 Georgia gubernatorial race, you continued to fight even harder for the rights of voters, and two years later helped to win a presidential and senate election. And that is after fighting for justice your entire life. I fear that people often have a hard time worrying about long-term issues because they have severe short-term issues. Your leadership is an inspiration, how do you keep perspective when fighting such long-term fights?

**SA:** Fighting for progress is hard; it can often feel slow, and winning sometimes means losing better. The task of transforming Georgia into a battleground state was the result of a ten-year plan that involved planning, testing, innovating, sustained investment, and organizing. We know Georgians deserve much better than current leadership provides: they deserve economic security, affordable healthcare, educational opportunity, and access to justice. For example, Georgians struggling with food insecurity may rely on food banks in the short term, but permanent change requires economic policies

that deliver a living wage. My work is designed to focus on the short term, the medium term, and the long term, always communicating with stakeholders to maintain their engagement and their faith. Regardless of the scale of need, each victory and every moment of progress is worthy of celebration. More importantly, recognizing what we should expect at each stage serves as a building block for the long-term goal of sustainable change and as a reminder that the work is worth the effort.

**GK:** There have been some setbacks in response to the 2020 election, and recently a new set of laws, Jim Crow 2.0 as you put it, is upon us and we must fight against it. You have put together a world-class example of fair fighting and brute-force work to counteract an unfair set of rules and campaigns from a deceptive set of politicians. Oprah has said, "There's no dirt on the high road," but do you think you can win fairly when the other side is cheating? How do you scale your efforts to account for an opponent who doesn't play fairly?

**SA:** The right to vote is under attack in Georgia and across the nation due to Republicans being more interested in preserving their power versus doing the work necessary to create policies that benefit the communities they represent. Lawmakers in Georgia, Arizona, Florida, New Hampshire, and Texas are pushing problematic legislation that will make it harder to vote—especially for communities of color. It is critical that we push back against these dangerous anti-voting bills at the state and local level by reaching out to lawmakers, corporate leaders, and communities under attack. We must also demand that leaders in Congress protect our democracy at the federal level by passing the For the People Act and the John Lewis Voting Rights Advancement Act. The passage of this legislation will ensure that a voter's access to our democracy does not depend on the state in which they live.

**GK: Thank you. You have done so much for this country and the world on many levels, from your on-the-ground organizing to your overall leadership and commitment. We appreciate you and I am so grateful for this conversation. We can all learn from these examples of intergenerational commitment and I'm now more hopeful than ever about the next generation of leaders who are fighting across intersectional lines for a more equitable world.**

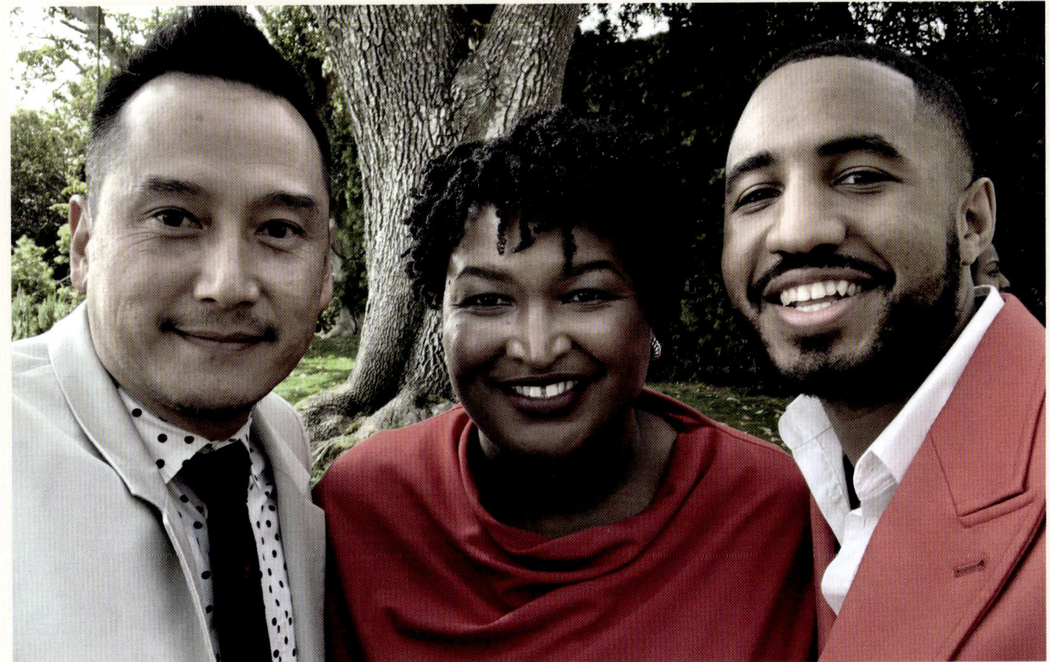

**Kaino, Abrams, and Jones, 2019**

*Photo: Glenn Kaino*

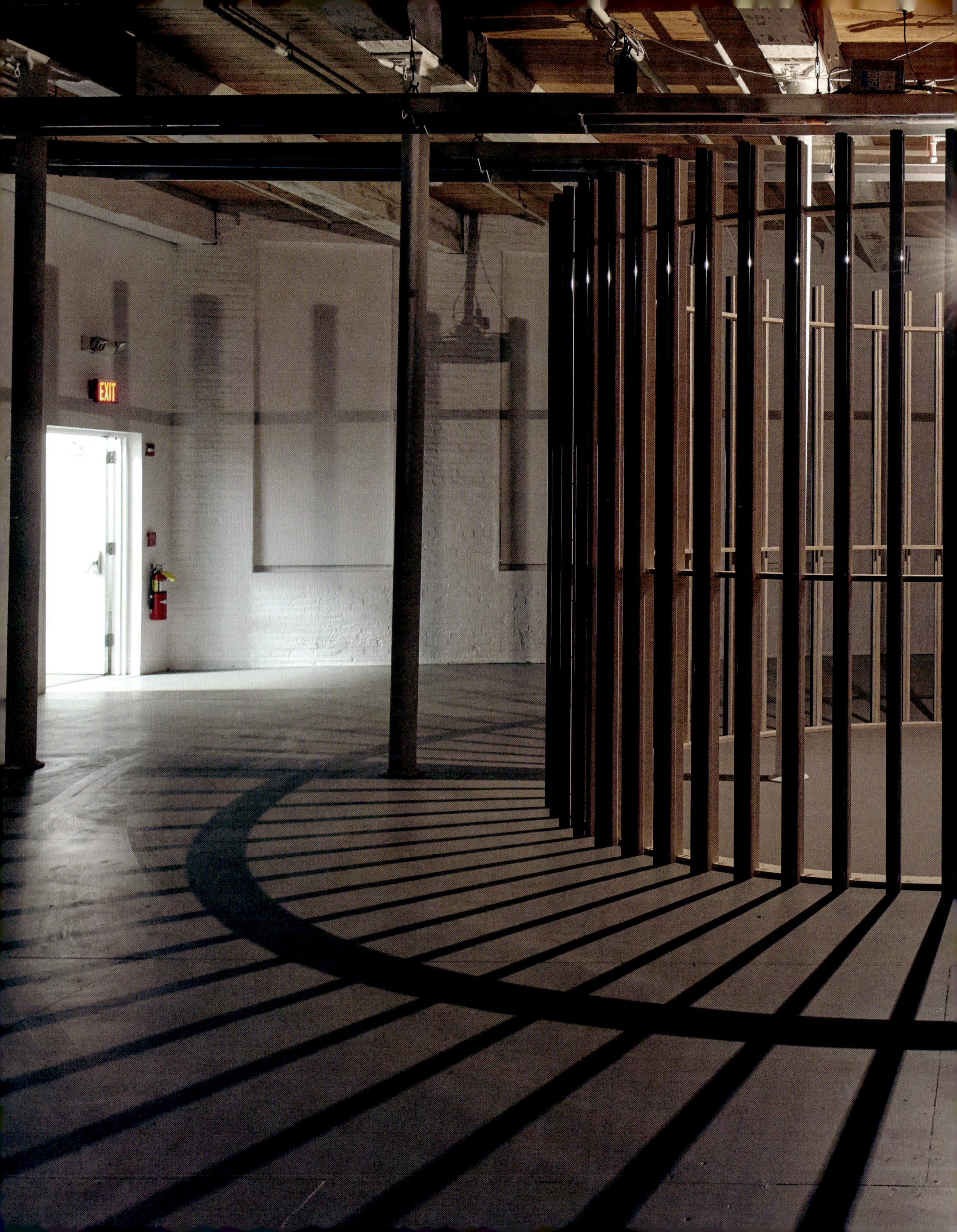
EXIT

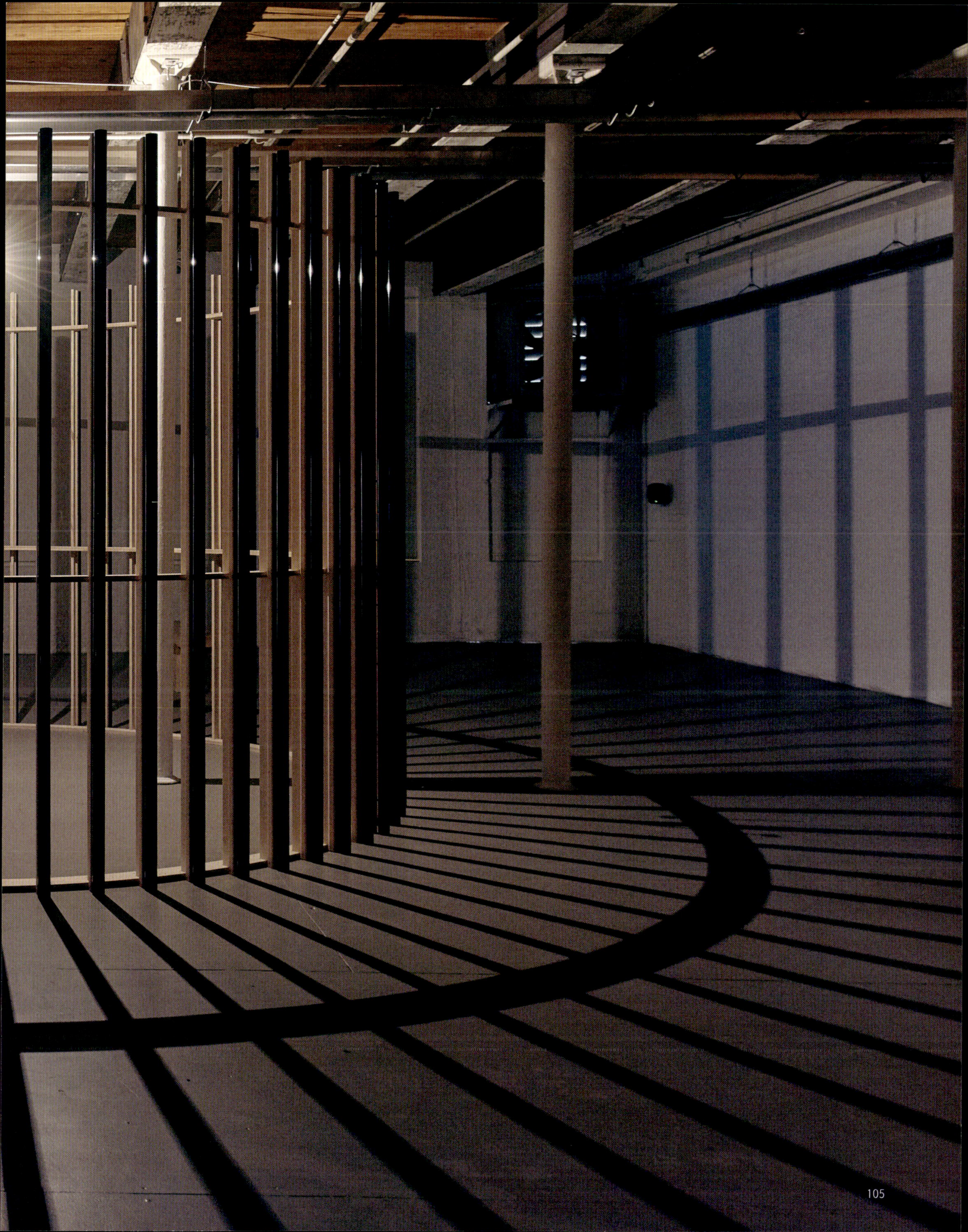

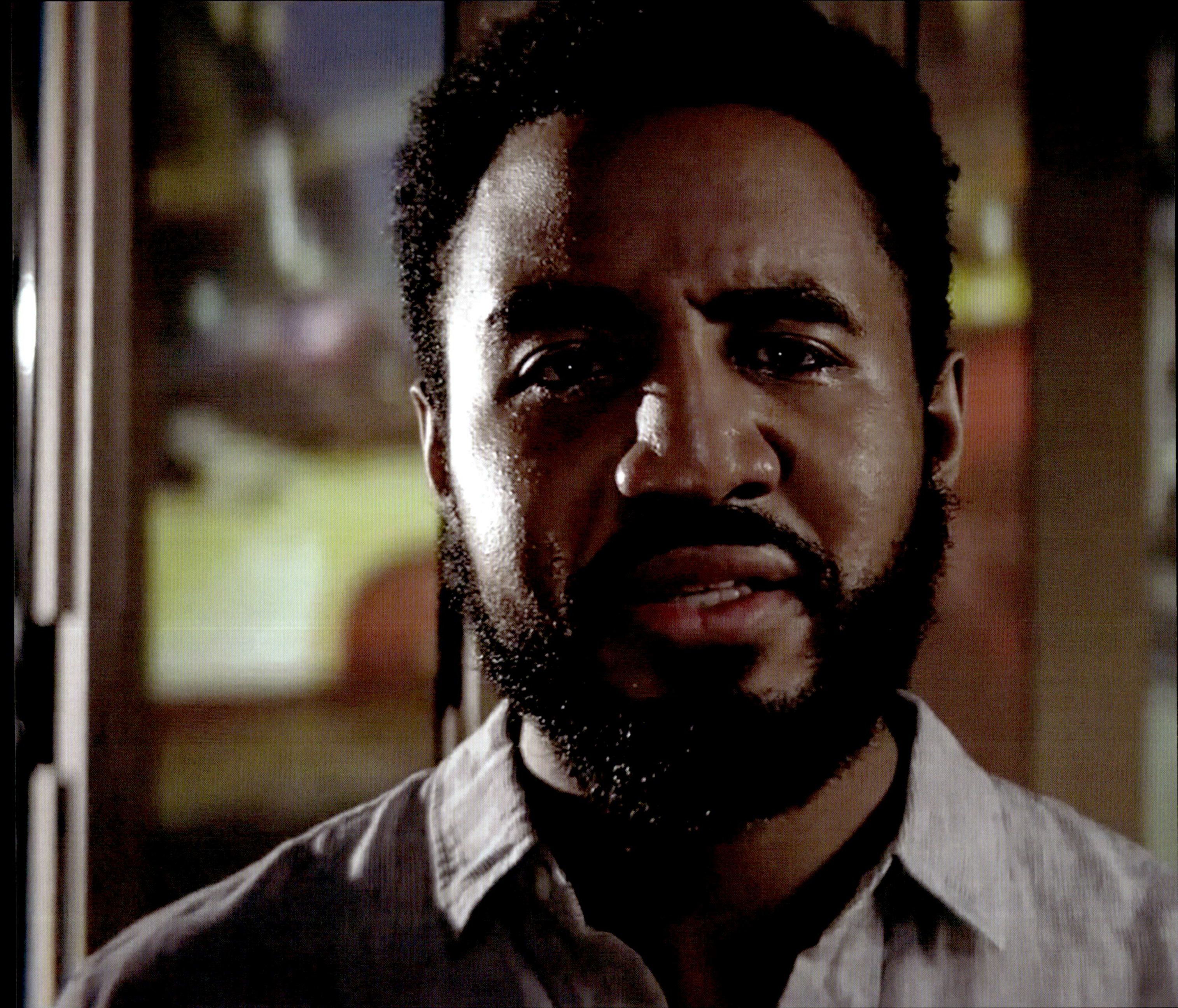

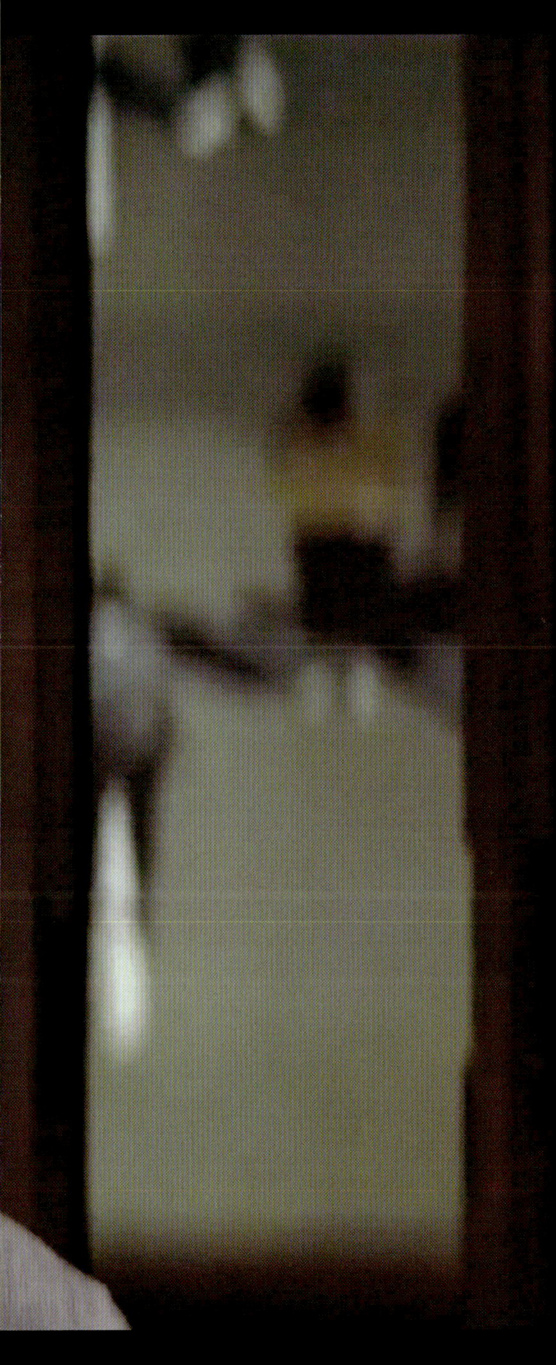

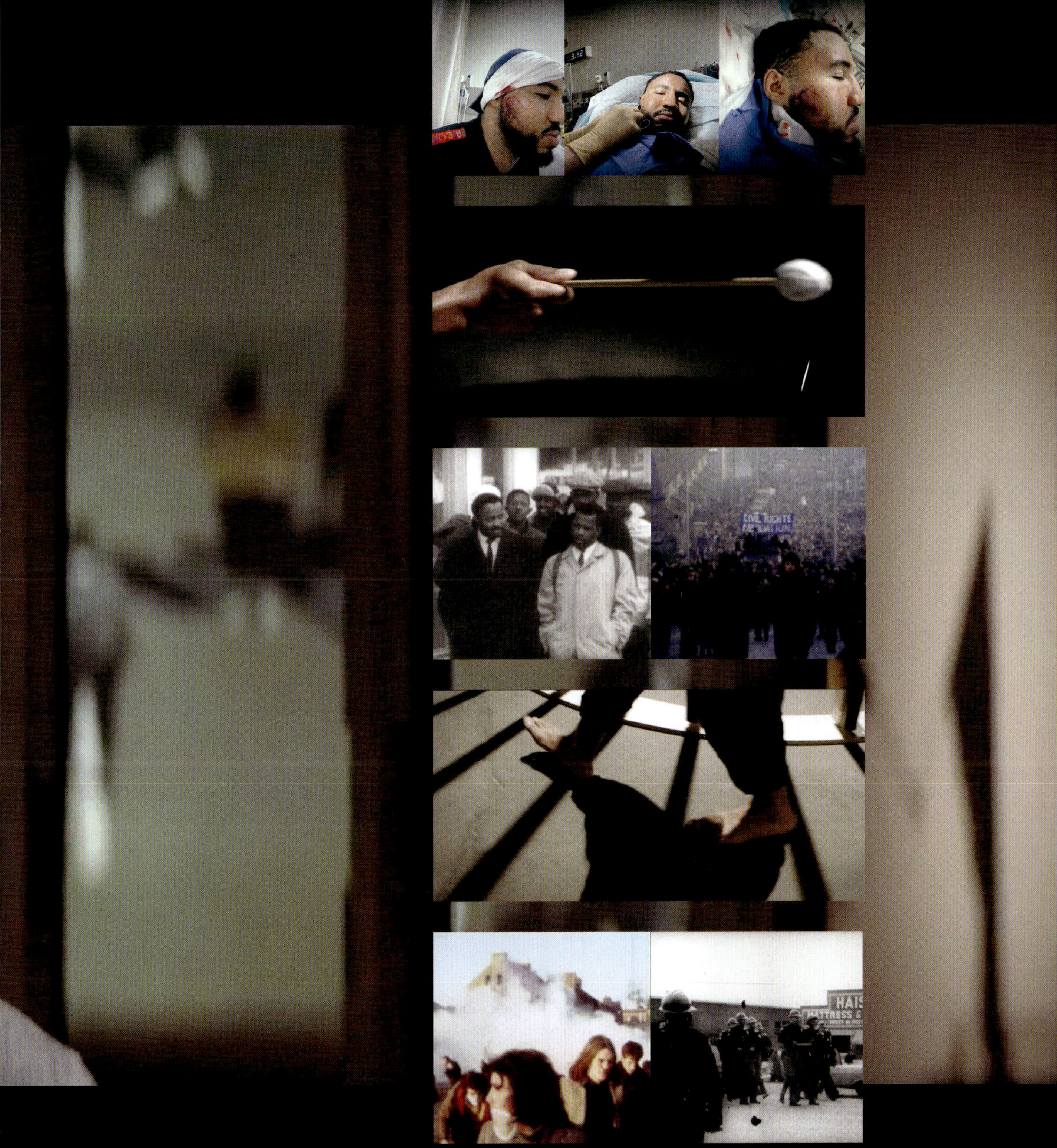

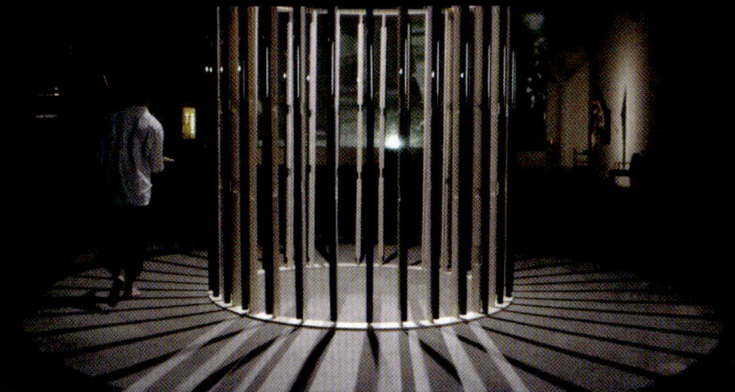

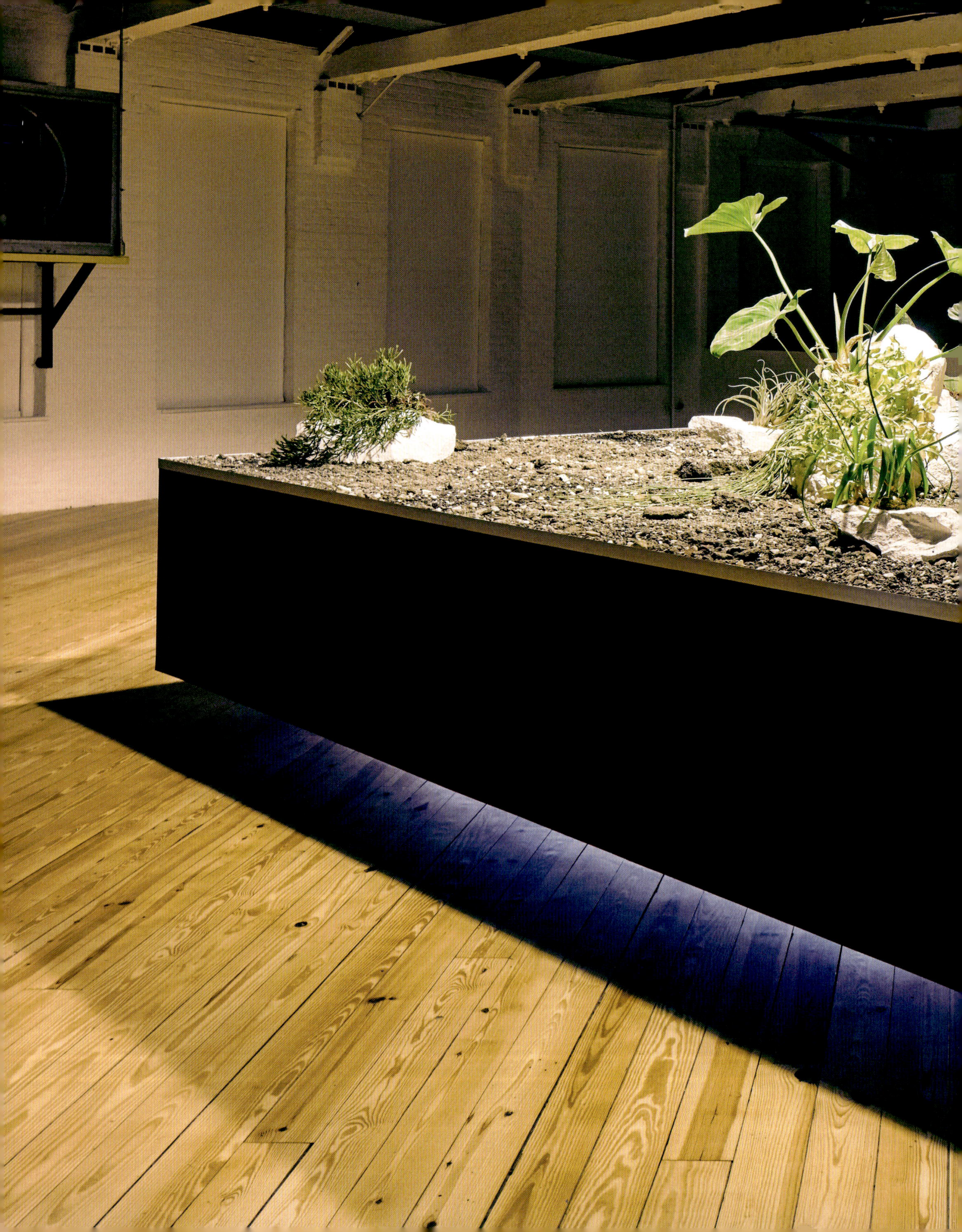

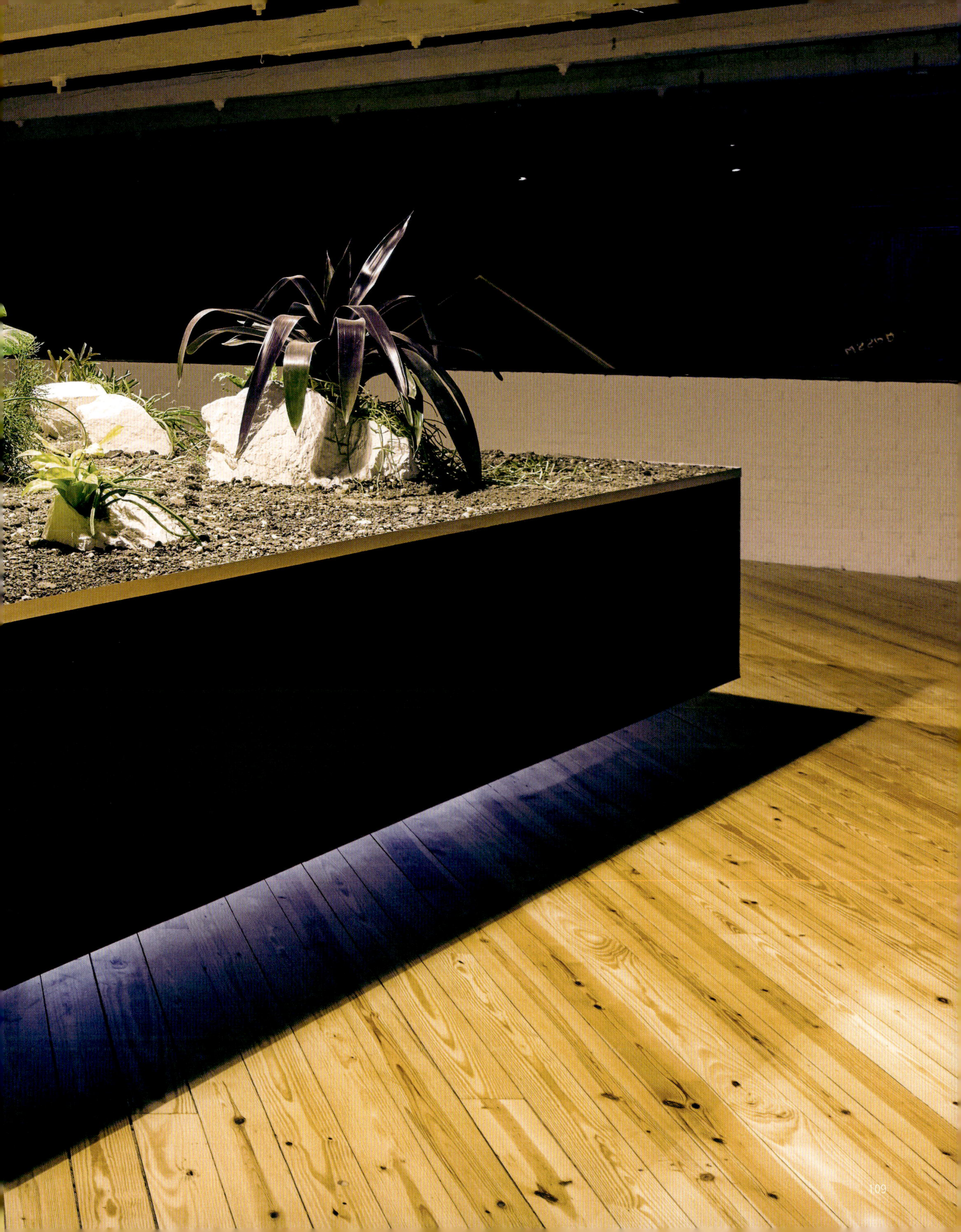

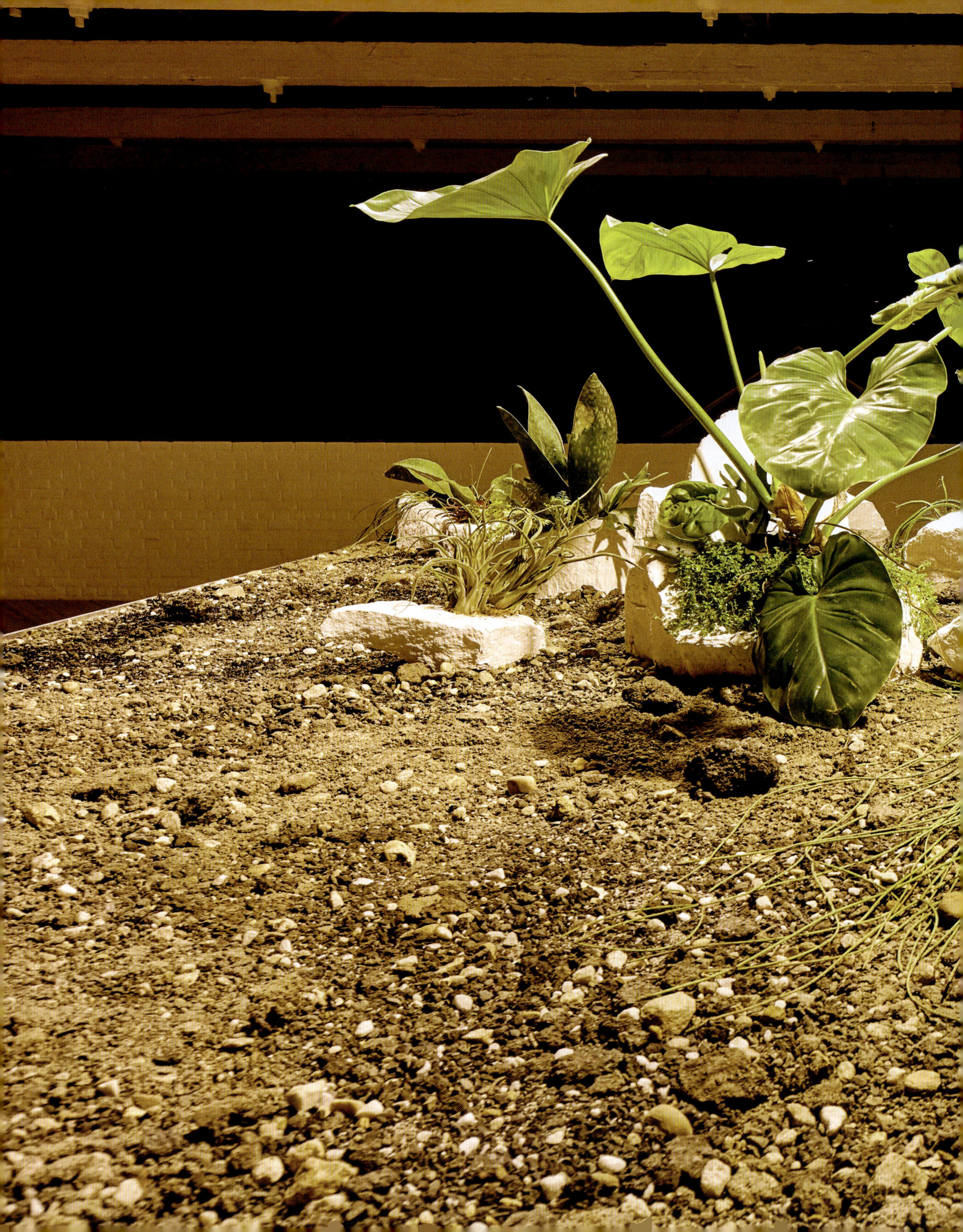

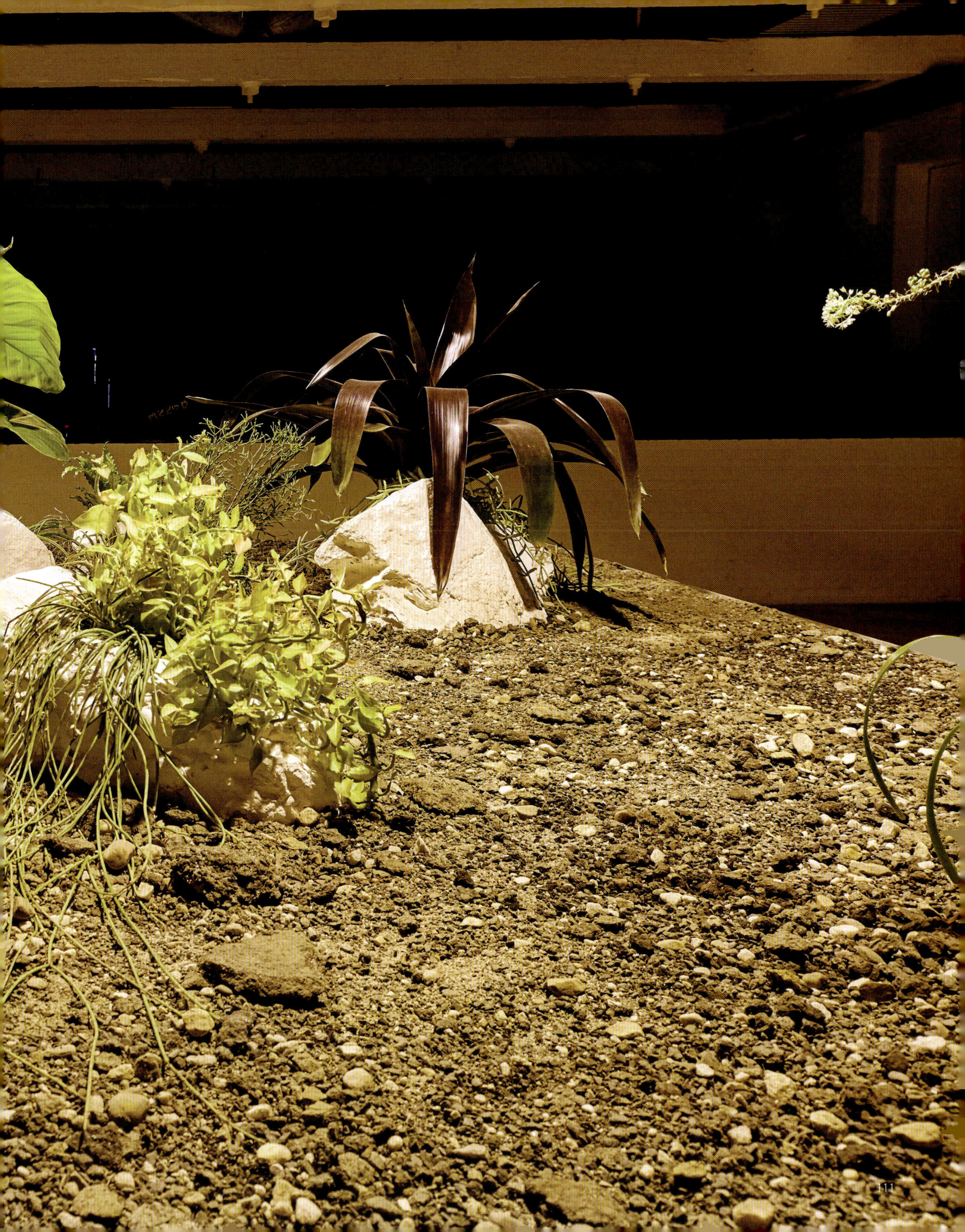

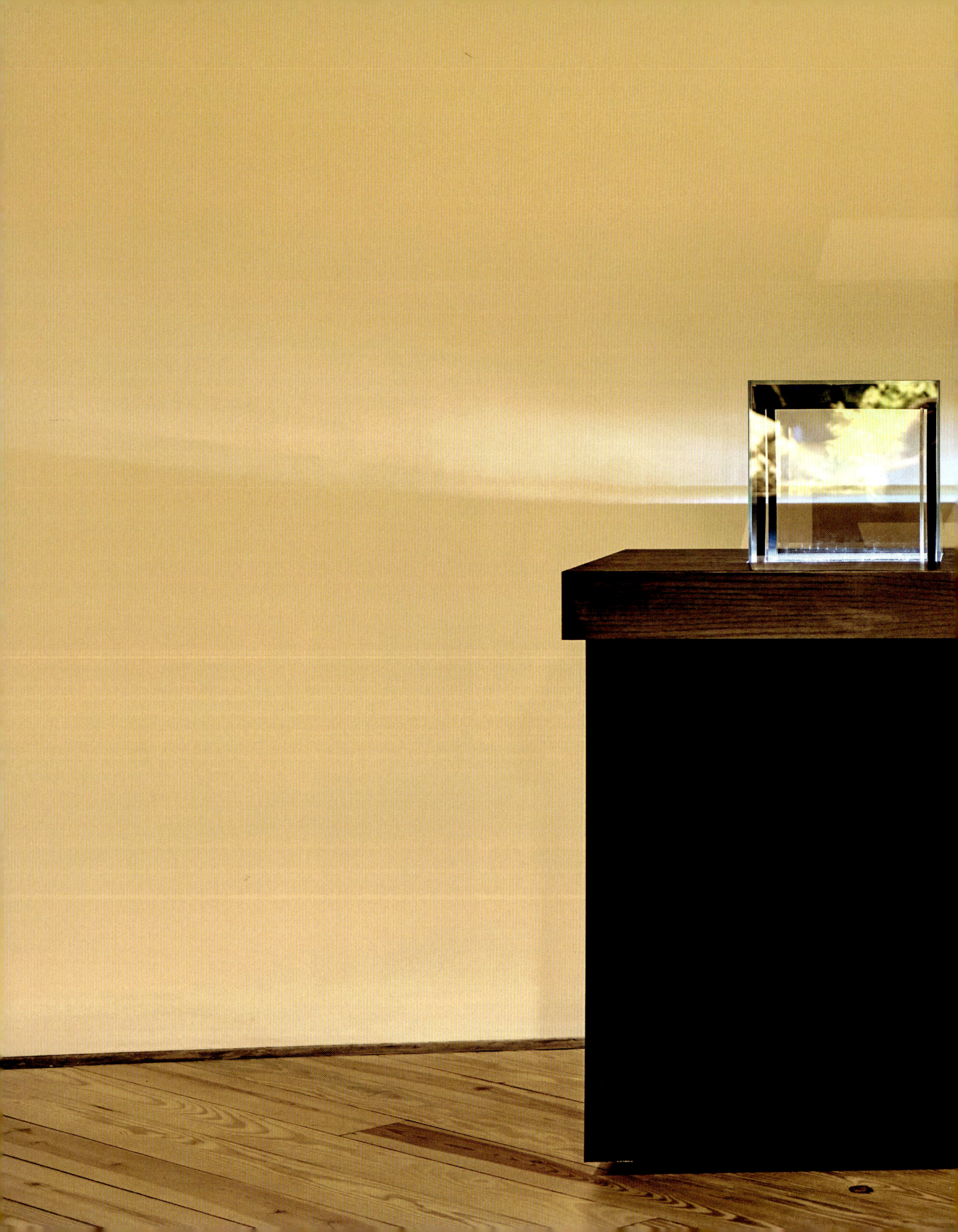

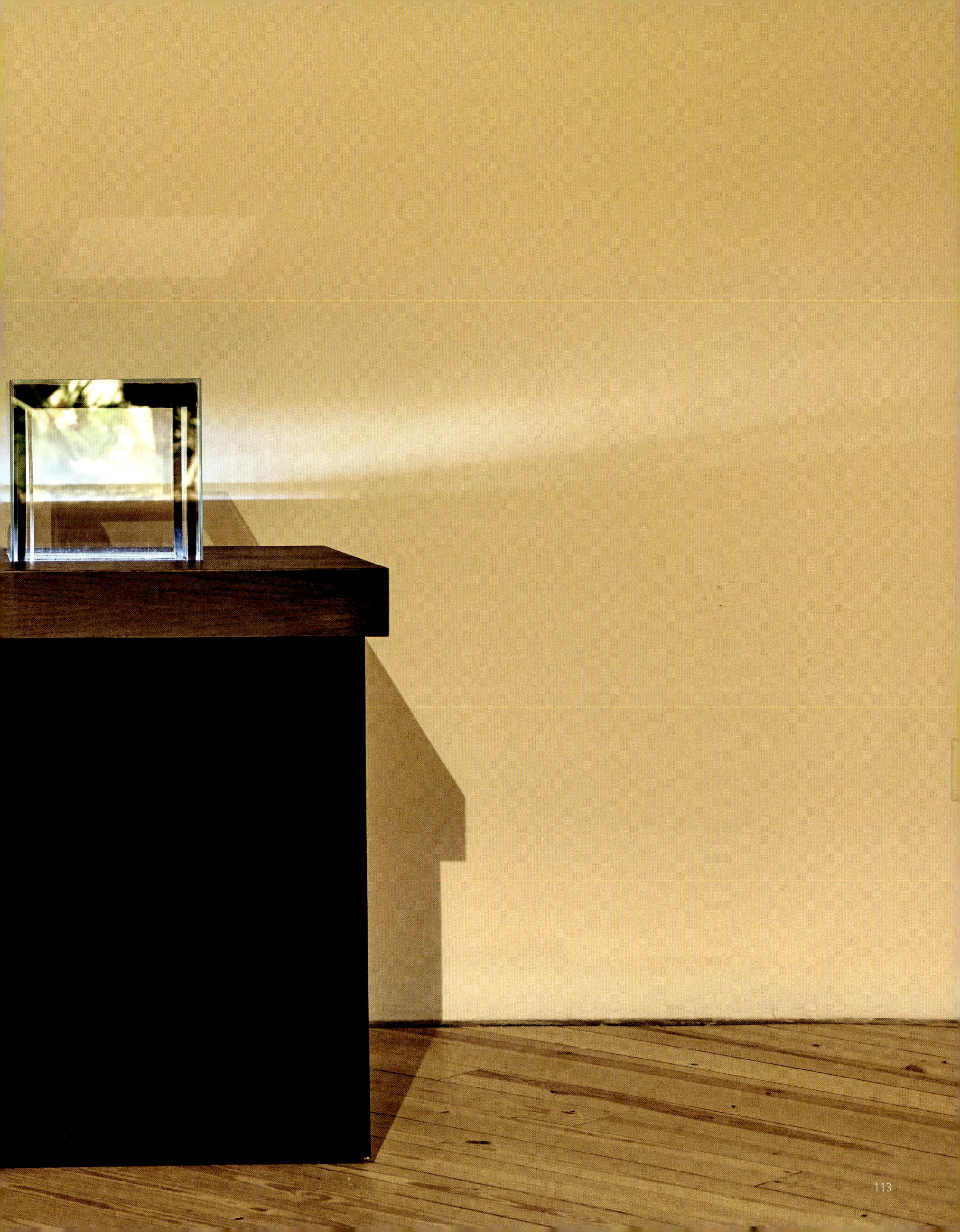

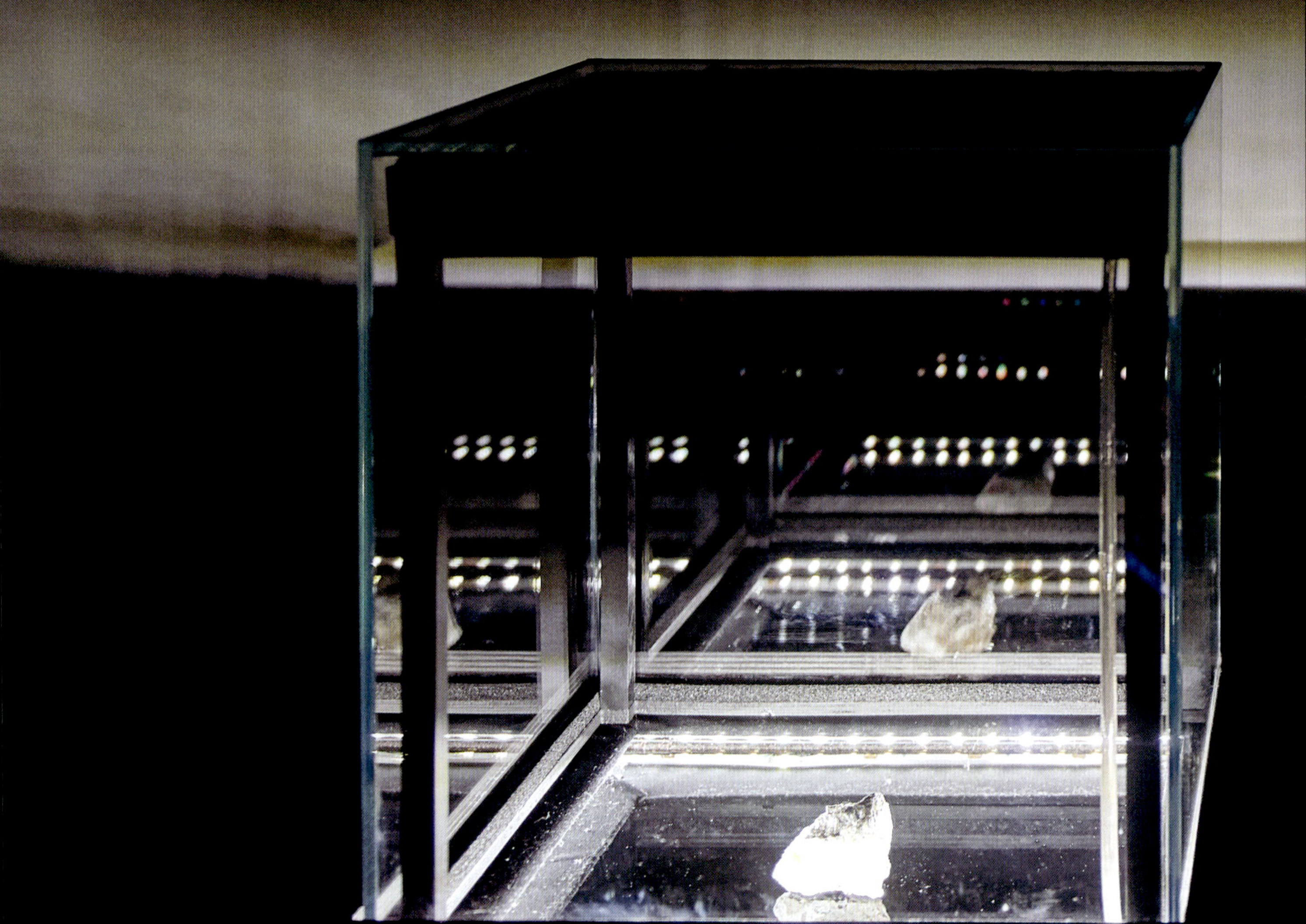

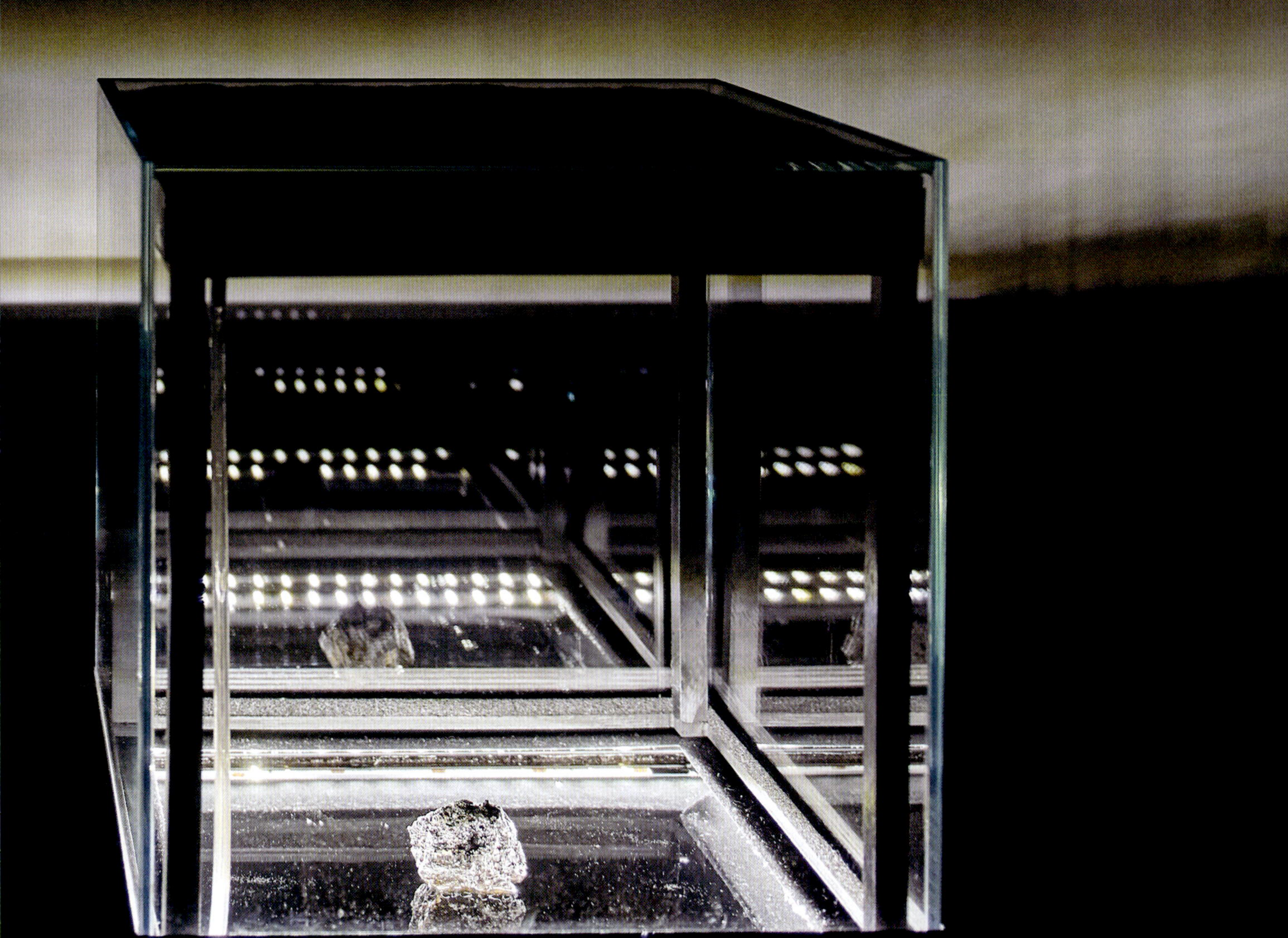

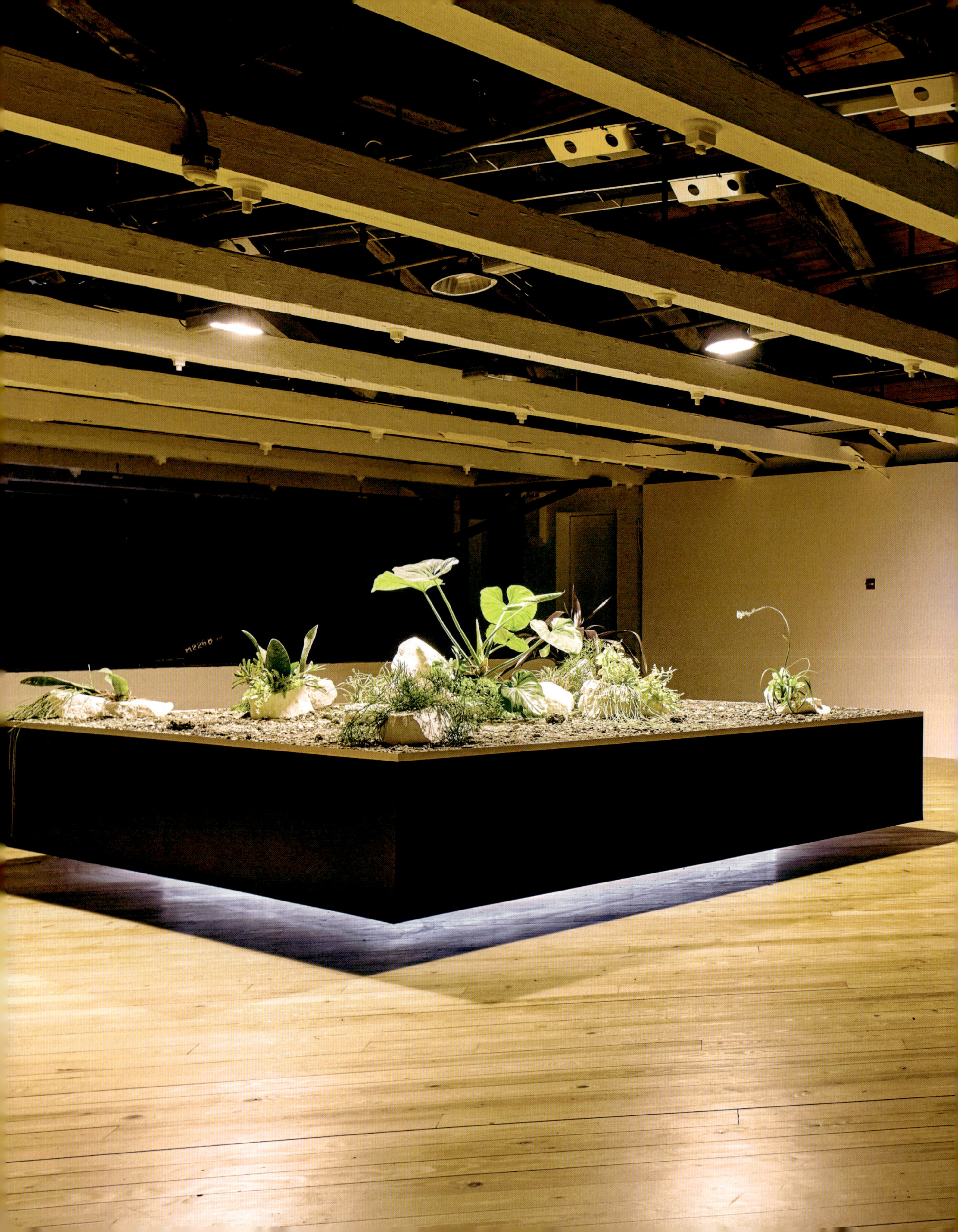

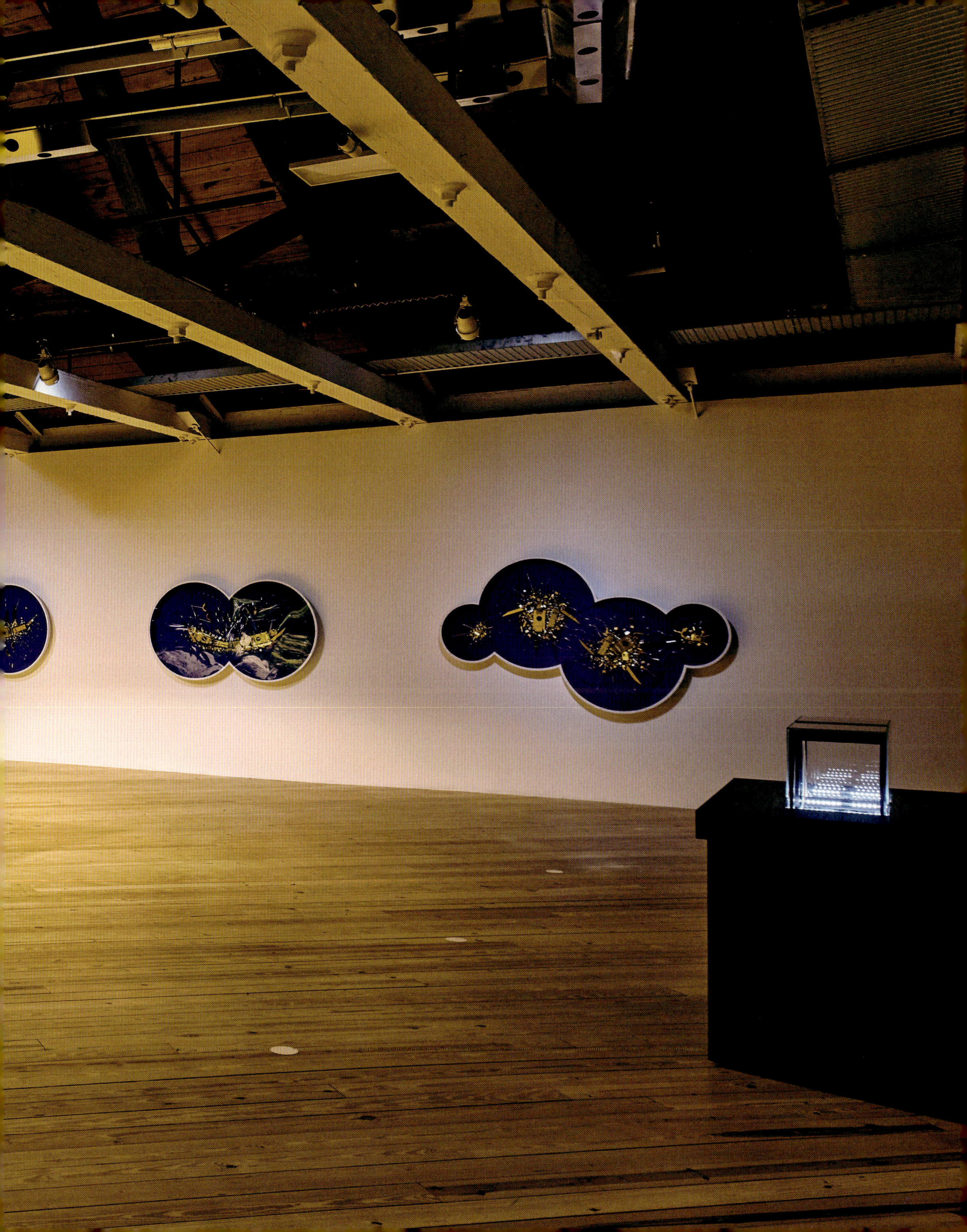

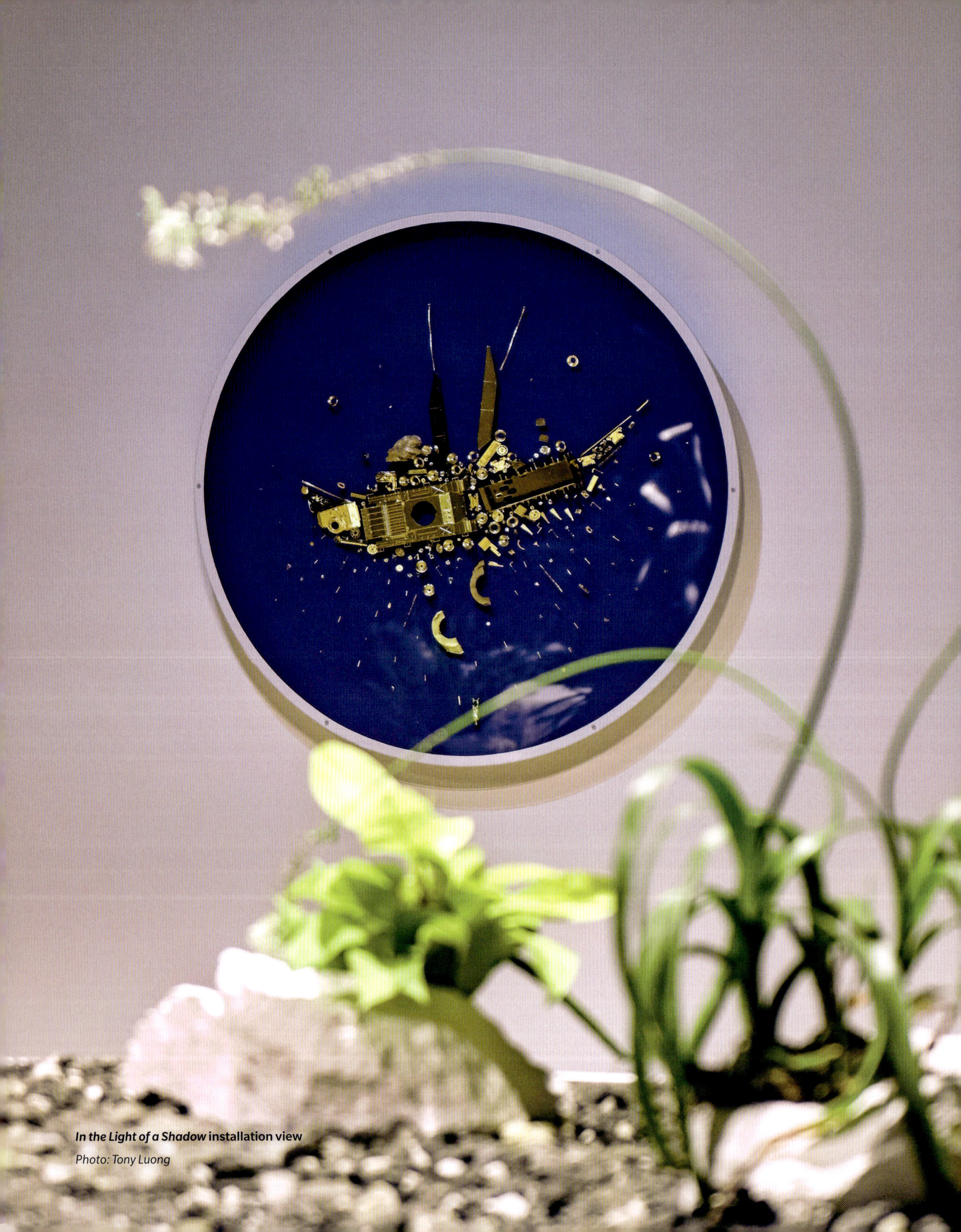

***In the Light of a Shadow*** **installation view**

*Photo: Tony Luong*

# Hopeful Objects

An arm once raised in protest, now leveled and multiplied to build a bridge; submerged and eroded weapons of past wars becoming platforms to grow living cartographies that negotiate between contested terrains; the tragic explosion of a ship, stretched into the form of an ouroboros, converting an image of death into a symbol of life; a posture of fear transformed into a poetic moment of reflectivity. These moments resonate with a quality not often attributed to contemporary art: hope.

The world is ending, always. Things fall apart. Matter is never truly destroyed. We can take the next step. Things can be reassembled; repurposed; reimagined. This is day one of the next world. The way forward is open, undiscovered. The long-term and seemingly paradoxical projects engaged by my studio ask questions—and do not assume answers—about a constellation of concerns held together by the gravity of our intentions.

What meaning is carried in a pirate ship after the pirates have been exiled, or by a castle made of sand that aspires to be permanent? We know where we have been and we know what we think we have learned. But what does history tell us, or a map really show us? They can lead us to certain destinations, but in this new model, where the poetic collides with the epistemic, there are other ways. Borders are obscured, eliminated, becoming ephemeral. In this world view, we must change our relationship to power. We must reject the colonial framework upon which our entire way of knowing has been established. This was someone else's place and these were someone else's tools, but now they are in our hands. We must consider, What is our place here? What could these tools do? What is our vision? What is the new way of knowing?

Hopefulness; possibilities; resurrection.

I have often invoked the term kitbashing in regard to my work: the act of putting disparate and broken parts together without instruction, or constructing new ways of seeing the future. But, it is more than that. Kitbashing is about linking together in the present people and things that may never have realized they had the potential to connect. It is about the leap of faith one must take in order for art to have value, for a magic trick to astonish us, and for the symbolic to have influence over the real.

Strangers sit across from one another at a would-be chessboard. The expected symbols of war and privilege are replaced by ethereal lights. Maneuvering burning candles, the players connect over the uncanniness of the experience—a game both ancient and novel, its meaning dancing as enigmatically as the flames. Then, the pieces dissolve. One reality ends, while new possibilities take shape, based on a new memory shared with an unexpected collaborator.

Art is an ambassador, a harbinger of the emergent present—the imagination age—where creativity surpasses information as the driver of human experience. It is material transformed. Icons transfigured. Opportunity made manifest. Possibilities that inspire us not to quit. To continue to be in service. To each other, to the planet—and to the idea that we can and will find a new way to believe.

# Contributors

## STACEY ABRAMS

Stacey Abrams is a *New York Times* bestselling author, serial entrepreneur, nonprofit CEO, and political leader. After serving for eleven years in the Georgia House of Representatives, seven as Democratic Leader, in 2018 Abrams became her party's nominee for Governor of Georgia, winning more votes than any other Democrat in the state's history. Abrams was the first Black woman to become the gubernatorial nominee for a major party in the United States, and the first Black woman and first Georgian to deliver the response to a State of the Union address. After witnessing the gross mismanagement of the 2018 election by the Secretary of State's office, Abrams launched Fair Fight to ensure every American has a voice in their election system through programs such as Fair Fight 2020, an initiative that funded and trained voter protection teams in twenty battleground states. Over the course of her career, Abrams has founded multiple organizations devoted to voting rights, training and hiring young people of color, and tackling social issues at both the state and national levels.

## AMIR AHMADI ARIAN

Amir Ahmadi Arian started his writing career as a journalist in Iran in 2000, while an undergrad engineering student at the University of Tehran. From 2002, he began writing fiction and translating books. He has published hundreds of articles and essays in Iranian newspapers and magazines on literature and politics, two novels, a collection of stories, and a book of nonfiction. He also translated from English to Persian novels by E. L. Doctorow, Paul Auster, P. D. James, and Cormac McCarthy. Arian left Iran in 2011 to undertake a PhD in comparative literature at the University of Queensland, Australia. He has published short stories and essays in the *New York Times*, *New York Review of Books*, *Paris Review*, *LRB*, *Lithub*, *Massachusetts Review*, *Michigan Quarterly Review*, etc. His first novel in English, *Then The Fish Swallowed Him*, was published by HarperVia/HarperCollins in March 2020.

## KIMBERLY JUANITA BROWN

Kimberly Juanita Brown is associate professor of English and creative writing at Dartmouth College. Her research engages the site of the visual to negotiate the parameters of race, gender, and belonging. Her book, *The Repeating Body: Slavery's Visual Resonance in the Contemporary* (Duke University Press) examines slavery's profound ocular construction, the presence and absence of seeing in relation to the plantation space and the women represented there. She is currently at work on her second book, tentatively titled *Mortevivum: Photography and the Politics of the Visual*. This project examines images of the dead in the *New York Times* in 1994 from four overlapping geographies: South Africa, Rwanda, Sudan, and Haiti.

## MIKE CAVENEY

Mike Caveney's magic skills have, over the last fifty years, taken him from Japan to Russia, from Monte Carlo to Borneo, Australia, and China, throughout Europe, and to most of the fifty States. He is a member of the most prestigious group of magicians in the world, The Inner Magic Circle of London, England, and was twice voted Stage Magician of the Year by Hollywood's Magic Castle. He has appeared on A&E's *Story of Magic*, NBC's *The World's Greatest Magic* special, *The Tonight Show with Jay Leno*, and *The Late Late Show with James Corden*. He has written more than a dozen books on the history, practice, and theory of magic.

## BRIAN DOOLEY

Brian Dooley is an Irish human rights activist, senior advisor at Human Rights First, and the United Nations' Special Rapporteur on Human Rights Defenders. He is the author of several books about the Troubles in Ireland, and about US politics, including *Black and Green: The Fight For Civil Rights in Northern Ireland and Black America*. He worked for Amnesty International for sixteen years in a variety of roles in London and Dublin. In the 1980s, Dooley worked in a Black township in South Africa in defiance of apartheid's racial segregation laws, and researched the 1986 Anti-Apartheid Act for Senator Ted Kennedy. He is a prominent voice on human rights on social media @dooley_dooley.

## LAURA FRIED

Laura Fried is a Los Angeles-based curator and a co-founder and director of Active Cultures, a nonprofit organization that explores the convergence of food and art in contemporary life. Through collaborative projects by cooks and artists, the programming of Active Cultures takes a multitude of forms, such as performances, workshops, meals, public art, and free programs. Throughout her career, Fried has advocated for artists and institutions while pushing forward new models for engagement and exhibition making. In 2016, she served as founding artistic director of the Seattle Art Fair, for which she organized a comprehensive program of large-scale installations, performances, talks, and projects. Fried was previously on the curatorial staff of MASS MoCA in North Adams, as well as a curator at the Contemporary Art Museum St. Louis. She received her MA in the History of Art from Williams College and the Clark Art Institute.

## DAVID GRUBER

David Gruber is Presidential Professor of Biology and Environmental Science at Baruch College, City University of New York, and research associate in invertebrate zoology at the American Museum of Natural History. His interdisciplinary research builds bridges between marine biology, biophysics, climate science, and animal communication, and his inventions deploy groundbreaking technology to help humans view the underwater world from the perspective of those who call it home. In 2019, he was awarded the Lagrange Prize, recognizing scientific research in the field of complexity sciences, for advancements "focused on the conservation of biodiversity, protection of resources, and the safeguarding of ecosystems." He assembled the scientific team for Project CETI, a nonprofit organization and 2020 TED Audacious Project. Gruber has collaborated on various artists' projects, including Janaina Tschäpe, *Fictionary of Corals and Jellies* (2017; commissioned by TBA21) and Joan Jonas, *Moving off the Land II* (2019; Ocean Space, Chiesa di San Lorenzo, Venice).

## DEON JONES

Deon Jones is a musician, entrepreneur, and longtime creative collaborator of Glenn Kaino. His activities range from managing projects at the Oprah Winfrey Network, mounting exhibitions at the High Museum of Art, and associate producing a documentary selected for the Tribeca Film Festival, to developing Webby Award-winning apps with actor Jesse Williams. A staunch advocate for the right to vote without barriers, Jones serves on the Creative Council at Fair Fight, the organization created by Stacey Abrams to end voter suppression and ensure fair elections. He is also a key proponent of abolishing youth jails, once serving as the National Spokesperson for the Campaign for Youth Justice. Jones attended American University in Washington, DC, which named him a 2020 Changemaker of the Year. During and after his studies, Jones worked in the office of Vice President Joe Biden at the White House, and on President Barack Obama's TechHire Initiative at Opportunity@Work. He is currently recording his first album, titled *REVIVAL*.

## JANNA LEVIN

Janna Levin is the Claire Tow Professor of Physics and Astronomy at Barnard College of Columbia University. She is also the chair and founding director of the Science Studios at Pioneer Works. A Guggenheim Fellow, Levin has contributed to an understanding of black holes, the cosmology of extra dimensions, and gravitational waves in the shape of spacetime. She is the presenter of the NOVA feature *Black Hole Apocalypse*, aired on PBS—the first female presenter for NOVA in thirty-five years. Her previous books include *How the Universe Got Its Spots*, *Black Hole Blues*, and a novel, *A Madman Dreams of Turing Machines*, which won the PEN/Bingham Prize. Her most recent book is *Black Hole Survival Guide*.

## DENISE MARKONISH

Denise Markonish is the senior curator and director of exhibitions at MASS MoCA. Her exhibitions include *Suffering from Realness*; *Trenton Doyle Hancock, Mind of the Mound: Critical Mass*; *Nick Cave: Until*; *Explode Every Day: An Inquiry into the Phenomena of Wonder*; *Teresita Fernández: As Above So Below*; *Oh, Canada*; *Nari Ward: Sub Mirage Lignum*; *These Days: Elegies for Modern Times*; and *Badlands: New Horizons in Landscape*. She edited the books *Teresita Fernández: Wayfinding* (DelMonico/Prestel) and *Wonder: 50 Years of RISD Glass*, and co-edited *Sol LeWitt: 100 Views* (Yale University Press). Markonish has taught at Williams College and the Rhode Island School of Design, was a visiting curator at Artpace, San Antonio, and Haystack School of Craft, Deer Isle, Maine.

## CHUS MARTÍNEZ

Chus Martínez is head of the Art Institute at the FHNW Academy of Arts and Design in Basel, Switzerland. She was the expedition leader of The Current, a project initiated by TBA21–Academy (2018–2020) and led a research project on enhancing women's equity in the arts in 2018 at the Art Institute, supported by Muzeum Susch. Martínez previously worked as chief curator at El Museo del Barrio, New York. For dOCUMENTA(13) (2012) she was head of department, and a member of the Core Agent Group. Other past positions include chief curator at MACBA, Barcelona (2008–2011), director of the Frankfurter Kunstverein (2005–2008), and artistic director of Sala Rekalde, Bilbao (2002–2005). She also curated the National Pavilion of Catalonia at the 56th La Biennale di Venezia (2015) as well as the National Pavilion of Cyprus in 2005. She collaborated with Istanbul Biennial (2015), Carnegie International (2010) and the Bienal de São Paulo (2010).

## JOSEPH C. THOMPSON

Joseph C. Thompson is the founding director of MASS MoCA, where for thirty-three years he helped grow the institution into one of the nation's leading centers for making and showing new visual and performing arts, while also positioning the museum as a force for community redevelopment.

# Glenn Kaino

Born 1972, Los Angeles, CA

Lives in Los Angeles, CA

## EDUCATION

1996 MFA, University of California, San Diego, CA

1993 BA, University of California, Irvine, CA

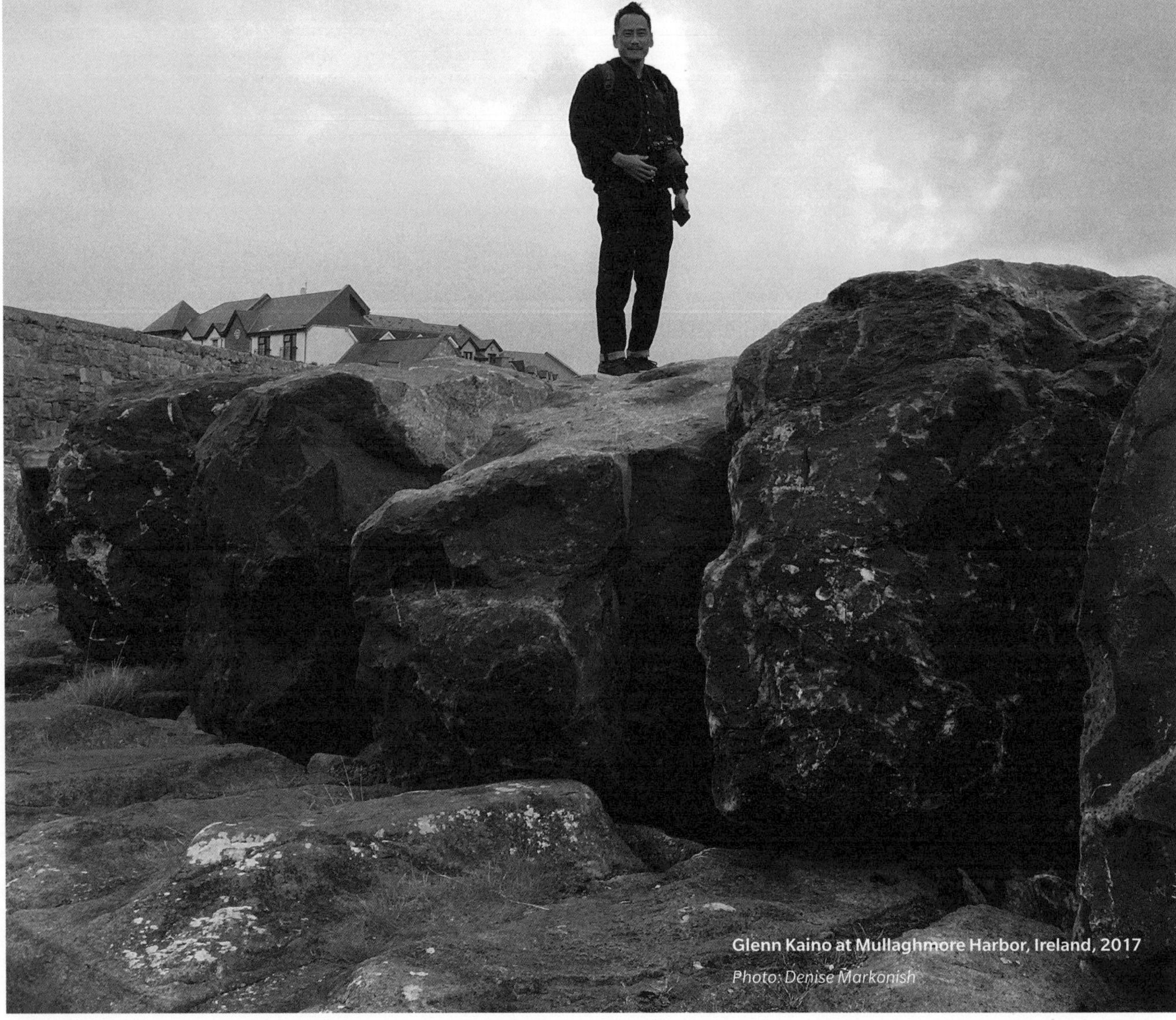

Glenn Kaino at Mullaghmore Harbor, Ireland, 2017
*Photo: Denise Markonish*

## SOLO EXHIBITIONS

2021 *In the Light of a Shadow*, MASS MoCA, North Adams, MA

*Tidepools*, Compound, Long Beach, CA

2020 *With Drawn Arms*, San Jose Museum of Art, CA

2019 *When a Pot Finds Its Purpose*, Brooklyn Academy of Music, NY

2018 *With Drawn Arms*, High Museum of Art, Atlanta, GA

2017 *Glenn Kaino: A Shout Within a Storm*, Contemporary Arts Center, Cincinnati, OH

*Sign*, Kavi Gupta, Chicago, IL

2016 *FOCUS: Glenn Kaino*, Modern Art Museum of Fort Worth, TX

2015 *Labyrinths*, Honor Fraser, Los Angeles

*Tank*, Grand Arts, Kansas City, MO

2014 *Leviathan*, Kavi Gupta, Chicago, IL

*19.83*, The Studio Museum in Harlem, New York

2013 *In Every Grain*, US Pavilion, 13th International Cairo Biennale, Egypt

2012 *Bring Me the Hands of Piri Reis*, Honor Fraser, Los Angeles

2011 *Levitating the Fair (The Flying Merchant Ship)*, Art Basel Miami Beach Public 2011, The Bass Museum of Art, FL

*Ready To Be Made*, as A.Bandit, LAXART Annex, Los Angeles

2010 *Safe/Vanish*, LAXART, Los Angeles

2009 *Honor Among Thieves*, Creative Time for Performa 2009, New York

2008 *Transformer: The Work of Glenn Kaino*, The Andy Warhol Museum, Pittsburgh, PA

*Arch*, Public Sculpture for City of Pittsburgh, PA

2007 *International Artist-In-Residence New Works: 07.1*, ArtPace, San Antonio, TX

*The Burning Boards*, Whitney Museum of American Art at Altria, New York

2006 *Laws Were Made For Rogues*, Cerca Series, Museum of Contemporary Art San Diego, CA

2005 *Of Passed Pawns and Communicating Rooks*, The Project, New York

2004 *Bounce: Glenn Kaino and Mark Bradford*, Gallery at REDCAT, Los Angeles

2003 *Simple Systems for Dimensional Transformation*, The Project, New York

*Glenn Kaino*, The Project, New York

2001 *Style Telegraphiqúe*, Rosamund Felsen Gallery, Santa Monica, CA

2000 *Blue*, Venetia Kapernekas Fine Art, New York

*Chasing Perfect*, Three Rivers Gallery, Pittsburgh, PA

1999 *Scratch*, Rosamund Felsen Gallery, Santa Monica, CA

## SELECTED GROUP EXHIBITIONS

2021 *Manif D'art*, Musée national des beaux-arts du Québec, Québec City, Canada

*Stories of Resistance*, Contemporary Art Museum St. Louis, MO

2020 *Emergency on Planet Earth*, UTA Artist Space, Beverly Hills, CA

2018 *Parallel Lives*, Kavi Gupta, Chicago, IL

2017 *Observatories*, Center for the Arts, Jackson Hole, WY

*Desert X*, Coachella Valley, CA

*Third Space/Shifting Conversations about Contemporary Art*, Birmingham Museum of Art, AL

*Paper*, Kavi Gupta, Chicago IL

2016 *March Madness*, Fort Gansevoort Gallery, New York

*Ground Control*, Art Public, Art Basel Miami Beach 2016, The Bass Museum of Art, FL

*L.A. Exuberance: New Gifts by Artists*, Los Angeles County Museum of Art

*For Freedoms*, Jack Shainman Gallery, New York

*Gold Rush*, de Saisset Museum at Santa Clara University, CA

2015 *Art In The Age Of...Asymmetrical Warfare*, Witte de With Center for Contemporary Art, Rotterdam, Netherlands

*Piece by Piece: Building a Collection*, Kemper Museum of Contemporary Art, Kansas City, MO

*Come As You Are: Art of the 1990s*, Telfair Museums, Savannah, GA; University of Michigan Museum of Art, Ann Arbor; Blanton Museum of Art, University of Texas, Austin

2014 *Prospect.3: Notes for Now*, New Orleans, LA

*Art on Paper 2014*, Weatherspoon Art Museum, Greensboro, NC

*The Avant-Garde Collection*, Orange County Museum of Art, Newport Beach, CA

*ALTER/ABOLISH/ADDRESS*, Los Angeles Nomadic Division, Washington, DC

*GOLD*, The Bass Museum of Art, Miami Beach, FL

*Come As You Are: Art of the 1990s*, Montclair Art Museum, NJ

*Cage & Kaino*: Pieces and Performances, World Chess Hall of Fame, St. Louis, MO

2013 *Kiss Me Deadly: A Group Show of Contemporary Neo-Noir from Los Angeles*, Paradise Row, London, UK

*Meanwhile...Suddenly, and Then*, 12th Biennale de Lyon, France

*The Voyage, or Three Years at Sea Part VI*, Charles H. Scott Gallery, Vancouver, BC, Canada

2011 *Selections from the Hammer Contemporary Collection*, Hammer Museum, Los Angeles

*Trespass*, West of Rome Public Art, Los Angeles

*Role ImagesIRole Playing*, Museum der Moderne Mönchsberg, Salzburg, Austria

2010 *The Artists' Museum*, Museum of Contemporary Art, Los Angeles

*New Art for a New Century: Contemporary Acquisitions 2000-2010*, Orange County Museum of Art, Newport Beach, CA

*Mapping Identity*, Cantor Fitzgerald Gallery, Haverford College, PA

2009 *We Are Time: Seven Installations*, Impakt Festival, Utrecht, Netherlands

2008 *Southern Exposure: Works from the Collection of the Museum of Contemporary Art San Diego*, Museum of Contemporary Art, Sydney, Australia

*Disorderly Conduct: Recent Art in Tumultuous Times*, Orange County Museum of Art, Newport Beach, CA

2006 *One Way or Another: Asian American Art Now*, Asia Society, New York

2005 *Only Make-Believe: Ways of Playing*, Compton Verney, Warwickshire, UK

2004 *Blackbelt*, Santa Monica Museum of Art, CA

*Whitney Gala*, Whitney Museum of American Art, New York

*Dreamscape*, University Art Gallery, University of California, Irvine

*California Biennial*, Orange County Museum of Art, Newport Beach, CA

*Whitney Biennial*, Whitney Museum of American Art, New York

2003 *Blackbelt*, The Studio Museum in Harlem, New York

*Mine*, Lombard+Freid Fine Arts, New York

2001 *One Planet Under a Groove*, Bronx Museum, NY

2000 *Surf Trip*, Track 16 Gallery, Santa Monica, CA

1999 International Film Festival Rotterdam, Netherlands

1998 *Xtrascape*, Los Angeles Municipal Art Gallery

*i Candy*, Rosamund Felsen Gallery, Santa Monica, CA

*Access All Areas*, Fellows of Contemporary Art, Japanese American Cultural and Community Center, Los Angeles

1995 *Finding Family Stories*, Japanese American National Museum, Los Angeles

1993 *Computer Influence*, Downey Museum of Art, CA

## FILM AND VIDEO

2021 *In & Of Itself*, feature-length documentary, producer

2020 *With Drawn Arms*, feature-length documentary, director, producer

*Sunday Bloody Sunday*, music video, director

2012 *The Linking Rings*, short film

2010 *The Grand Finale*, short film

2004 *2.1 Billion Seconds (Do The Math)*, intervention into Super Bowl XXXVIII

## PERFORMANCES

2019 *The MSG Club*, in collaboration with Niki Nakayama, Active Cultures, Mexico City; Los Angeles; New York

2017 *Cabaret Series: Old Methods for New Wars*, Storefront for Art and Architecture, New York

2016 *Aspiration*, Seattle Art Fair, WA

2015 *The Burning Boards*, Rose Art Museum, Waltham, MA

2014 *The Burning Boards*, World Chess Hall of Fame, Saint Louis, MO

2012 *The Trials of Slydini*, LACMA Collector's Weekend, Los Angeles

2011 *A.Bandit: Experiments from The [Space] Between*, The Kitchen, New York

*A.Bandit: A Walk Through China*, LAXART Annex, Los Angeles

*A.Bandit: The Space Between*, Soho House, West Hollywood, CA

*A.Bandit: Ready To Be Made*, LAXART Annex, Los Angeles

*A.Bandit: The Mistake Room*, LAXART Annex, Los Angeles

*A.Bandit: My House Will Be Called a House of Art*, Art Los Angeles Contemporary, Santa Monica, CA

2008 *The Burning Boards*, Haudenschild Garage, La Jolla, CA

2007 *The Burning Boards*, Whitney Museum of American Art at Altria, New York

## PUBLIC PROJECTS, RESIDENCIES AND COMMISSIONS

2018 *In & Of Itself*, Geffen Playhouse, Los Angeles

*In & Of Itself*, Daryl Roth Theatre, New York

Artist in Residence, Anderson Ranch, Snowmass, CO

Airport Metro Connector Station Artist, LAX, Los Angeles

2017 *Untrained Eyes, The Engadget Experience: Alternate Realities*, Los Angeles

2014 Artist Commission, Sixth Street Viaduct Replacement Project, Los Angeles

2013 Lead Artist Commission, Glow Festival, Santa Monica, CA

*Nothing to Hide*, Pershing Square Signature Center, New York

2008 *Arch*, Public Sculpture for City of Pittsburgh, Commission of the Heinz Endowment and The Andy Warhol Museum, Pittsburgh, PA

## ACADEMIC APPOINTMENTS

1997–99 Adjunct faculty, School of the Visual Arts, University of Southern California, Los Angeles

1995–96 Visiting assistant professor, Film and Television Laboratory for New Media, University of California, Los Angeles

## PROFESSIONAL ORGANIZATIONS

2019– Co-founder, board member, Active Cultures, Los Angeles

2017– Board of Overseers, Hammer Museum, Westwood, CA

2016– Board of Directors, Los Angeles Music Center

2015–19 Board of Directors, Fathomers, Los Angeles

2014–16 Artist Council, Hammer Museum, Westwood, CA

2012–16 Co-founder, founding board member, The Mistake Room, Los Angeles

2005–8 Founding board member, LAXART, Los Angeles

1997–2002 Co-founder, co-director, Deep River Gallery, Los Angeles

1997–2000 President, Board of Directors, Los Angeles Center for Photographic Studies (LACPS)

1994 Society for Photographic Education, Western Region board member, Los Angeles

## FELLOWSHIPS AND AWARDS

2011 Mid-Career Artist Fellowship, California Community Foundation, Los Angeles

2008 Heinz Endowment Commission Award, Heinz Endowment with The Andy Warhol Museum, Pittsburgh, PA

1998 Artist Fellowship, Fellows of Contemporary Art, Los Angeles

## PUBLICATIONS

2017 Matijcio, Steven. *Glenn Kaino: A Shout Within a Storm*. Cincinnati: Contemporary Arts Center

A.Bandit, Markonish, D., *A Secret Has Two Faces*. New York: DelMonico Books-Prestel

2014 Bell Yank, Sue, and Kaino, Glenn, *Cipher #1*.

2009 Firstenberg, L., Fang H., Kaino, G., List, L., Sokolowski, T., Strauss, D. A. *Communicating Rooks: The Work of Glenn Kaino*. Ostfildern: Hatje Cantz.

2004 Joo, Eugene. *Bounce: Mark Bradford & Glenn Kaino*. Valencia: California Institute of the Arts.

1995 Higa, Karin. *Finding Family Stories*. Los Angeles: Japanese American National Museum

## PUBLIC COLLECTIONS

Birmingham Museum of Art, AL

Hammer Museum, Los Angeles

High Museum of Art, Atlanta, GA

JP Morgan Chase Art Collection, New York

Los Angeles County Museum of Art

Museum Folkwang, Essen, Germany

Museum of Contemporary Art San Diego, CA

Norton Family Collection, Los Angeles

Orange County Museum of Art, Newport Beach, CA

Pittsburgh International Airport, PA

San Jose Museum of Art, CA

Studio Museum in Harlem, New York

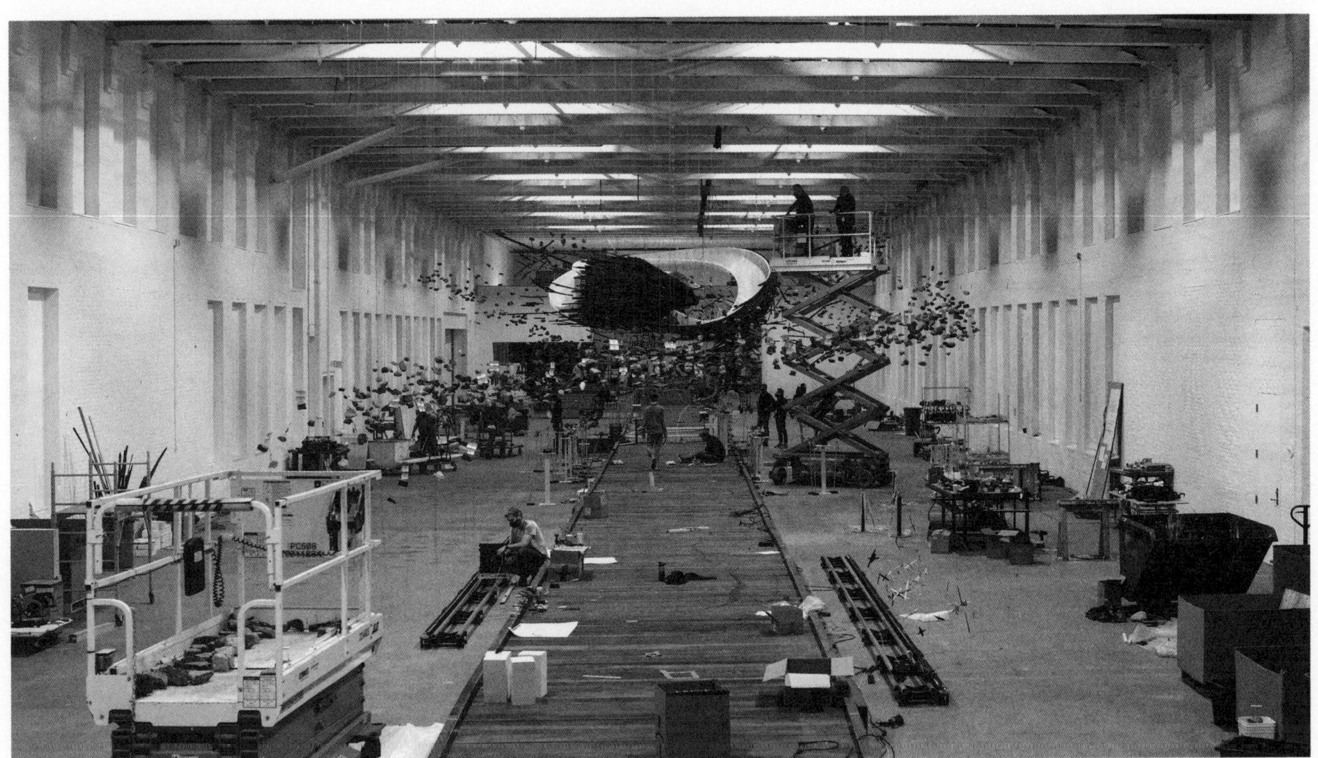

**Installing *In the Light of a Shadow* in Building 5 at MASS MoCA, 2021**

*Photo: Will McLaughlin*

# Acknowledgments

I first met Glenn Kaino in the spring of 2015. He was at Brandeis University (my alma mater) doing a performance of his work *The Burning Boards*, which consisted of about a dozen chess matches being played simultaneously with pieces made of lit candles. In a truly New England moment, the mid-April weather turned on us, and the wind swept through the courtyard in front of the Rose Art Museum, blowing out all the flames. Glenn immediately choreographed the audience to form a protective barrier between the wind and the players so the game could commence. Little did I know, but creating a moment of care and solidarity was far from unusual for Glenn.

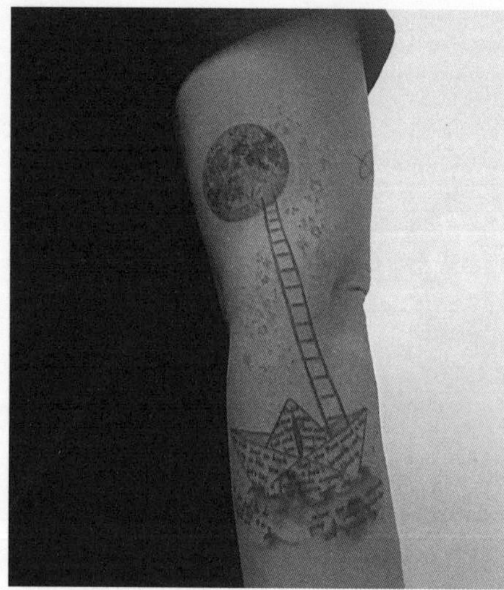

**Denise Markonish's tattoo illustrating Italo Calvino's "The Distance of the Moon," 2017**

*Photo: Denise Markonish*

In January of 2016, I visited his Hollywood studio for the first time. I still remember leaving the conversation elated, as if I had visited another universe. We talked about social justice, magic, coral, the creation of language, chess, and so much more. At the end of that meeting I said, "We should do something together in the biggest gallery at MASS MoCA, but it's not available for at least four years." He replied, "Perfect, I have a project that will take four years to make." And we were off. I remember excitedly coming back from LA and telling MASS MoCA's director, Joe Thompson, about the visit, and he recalled Glenn visiting the museum and proposing past projects, none of which panned out. So, it seemed as if the timing was finally right (a nod to the great magician, Slydini). The project that became *In the Light of a Shadow* took many forms over the years, but what never wavered was Glenn's commitment to thinking with me, to pushing the boundaries of what art can be, and to being one of the most generous artists a curator and a museum could ever work with. We have had so many adventures over the years—from a trip to Northern Ireland in the summer of 2017 (it started with crashing a car and ended with staying in a castle); to meetings with magicians like Derek DelGaudio and Ricky Jay; and time spent with Olympian Tommie Smith.

But what is most remarkable about Glenn is that his brain never stops. Not only did he create a show for MASS MoCA, he played the music of N.W.A. at one of our board meetings, helped us "Do the Right Thing" for our virtual gala, and sent ice cream to our installation crew, mid-pandemic, to lift their spirits. Glenn, I know you spend most of your career making other people's dreams come true (as you have mine); so, this book, this show, is my gift to you, to make some of yours come true as well.

None of this making, community-building, and dreaming takes place in a vacuum. So, for those who joined us on this journey I offer my sincerest thanks.

From MASS MoCA: Richard Criddle, Megan Tamás , Tavish Costello, Peter Mahoney, Chris Nelson, Az Acker, Richelle Soper, Deb Coombs, Odiase Williamson, Brad Dilger, Kathryn Carter, Andy Slemenda, Mike Kurpiel, Jenny Wright, Amy Chen, Hannah Fiske, Paulette Wein, Meg Hagyard, and Laura Thompson. With special thanks to Joe Thompson—this is your last show at MASS MoCA as you step down as our fearless leader; thank you for making me the curator I am today and for not accepting Glenn's earlier proposals. And to Sue Killam and Tracy Moore,

my appreciation for taking on the leadership role so seamlessly in this transitional moment, and for always offering supportive shoulders through everything.

From Glenn's studio: Gideon Webster, Joe Fellows, Riley Ogden, Alison Klein, and Brooke Baker, with special assistance from Chris Gabriel, Dylan Lukes, and Adam Blumenthal. You are a dream team, who were always there to answer any question (even when the answer was that you had no answer). I have never before worked on a show where I worried less that things wouldn't get done, and that says a lot given this show was built in the midst of a global pandemic.

Special thanks to the Metabolic Studio, especially Lauren Bon, Rich Nielsen, and Tristan Duke, for always hosting me in LA, for being great friends and art adventure buddies, and for coming to the Magic Castle with Glenn and me. And to Haystack Mountain School of Crafts in Deer Isle, Maine, for the space, time, and lovely landscape in which to start my research.

Thank you to all those involved in making this book happen. The writers: Amir Ahmadi Arian, Kimberly Juanita Brown, Janna Levin, David Gruber, Chus Martínez , Mike Caveney, Laura Fried, Brian Dooley, Deon Jones, and Stacey Abrams. Glenn is not an easy artist to categorize, and I thank you all for providing context to the practice (and the human) without sticking him in a box. Special thanks to Hunter Braithwaite from Cultural Counsel for advising on the book, and also to Robert Grand and Adam Abdalla for working with us on press. Jane Calverley and Paulette Wein, you always make our words better with your careful copy edits and proofreading; Mary Delmonico, thank you for your love of books; and Bob Faust—what can I say, you are a true friend and graphic designer extraordinaire, and I am so honored to work with you on making this promise come true.

This exhibition would not be possible without support from the trustees of MASS MoCA, Nicole Deller and Matthew Bliwise, the National Endowment for the Arts, the Director's Advisory Council of MASS MoCA, the Barr Foundation, Horace W. Goldsmith Foundation, and Mass Cultural Council, with additional support provided by Parsons Audio LLC and Genelec Inc., and by Crystalle Lacouture and Scott Stedman. Glenn, along with all these fine people, I thank you again, for being one of the best co-conspirators I could ever dream of—I believe in you, your magic is real.

— Denise Markonish

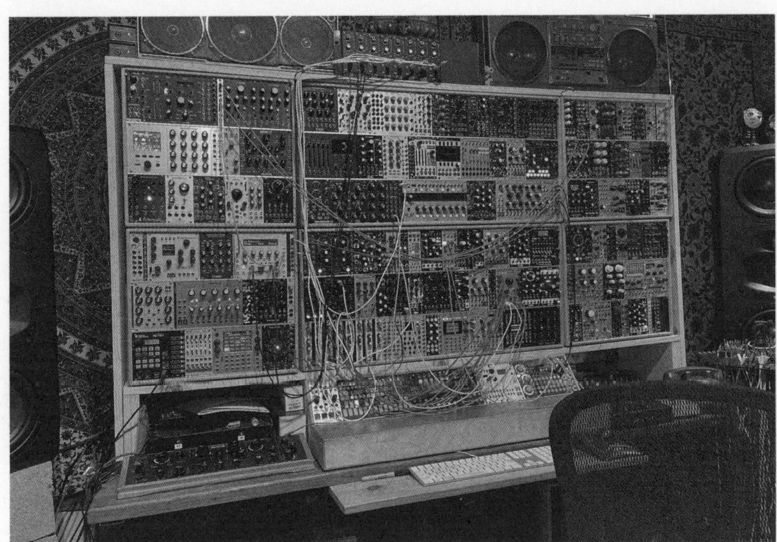

**Artificial Intelligence driven synthesizer by Dave Sitek used to create the soundscape for *In the Light of a Shadow*, 2021**

# Thank You

**MUSIC BY**
David Sitek

**LEAD FABRICATORS**
Gideon Webster
Riley Ogden

**VISUALIZATION AND DIGITAL OUTPUT**
Joseph Fellows

**TECHNICAL ADVISOR**
Chris Gabriel

**STUDIO FABRICATION**
Alison Klein
Derek Albeck
Lyndon J. Barrois Sr.
Daniel James Lorraine

**LIGHTING DESIGN**
Adam Blumenthal

**SUNDAY BLOODY SUNDAY**

***Performed by***
Deon Jones
Jon Batiste
Glenn Kotche

***Produced by***
Butch Vig

***Production***
Matthew Selby
Brian Vasquez
Landon J. Thomas, IV

***Cinematography***
Larry Fong

***Color***
Dave Cole
José Parra

***Additional Music***
Todd Simon

***Members of Silverlake Conservatory Youth Chorale***
Stella Kaino
Sadie Kaino
Isla Ferrier
Eleanor Dalton
Charlie Kreilkamp
Isla Farris
Maeve Rodriguez
Shanti Hubbard
Morgan Hubbard
Zaiel Felix
Anika Felix
Alani Kai
Laidy Silverman
Kaeliana Littlejohn
Pippa Mahmood
Tessa Kennedy
SJ Hasman

**HORTICULTURE**
Dennis Schrader
Landcraft Environments

**LIGHTING TECHNICIAN/ PROGRAMMER**
Dylan Lukes

**3D MODELING**
Hao Cui

**MASS MoCA ART FABRICATION**
Azariah Acker
Brad Dilger
Kathryn Carter
Richard Criddle
Debora Coombs
Tavish Costello
Chris Nelson
Andy Slemenda
Richelle Soper
Megan Tamas
Jon Verney
Ben Westbrook

**MASS MoCA CONSTRUCTION**
Arthur Bentley
Gregorio Chavez
Mike Kurpiel
Kristy Morris
Josh Provost
Alton Wright Jr.
Steve Ziaja

**MASS MOCA PERFORMING ARTS**
Sue Killam
Chris Lynch
Mike Martin
Tim McEvoy
Jill Strazzere

**_SHIPS & CATALOGUE DESIGN**
Bob Faust

**MASS MOCA DESIGN**
Amy Chen

**COPYEDITING**
L. Jane Calverley

**PROOFREADING**
Paulette Wein

**GLENN KAINO STUDIO**
Brian Kaino
Sanjay Kumar
Brooke Baker
Ming-Gih Lam
Quan Dong
David Kwong
Kemdah Stroud
Dianne Starzyk
Greg Pedersen
Randy Ky
George Domantay
Sean Hupe
Rick Dias

**ADDITIONAL ASSISTANCE**
Lola Selby
Charlie Reynolds

**JOHN & LILIAN MILES LEWIS FOUNDATION**
Michael Collins

**BLOODY SUNDAY TRUST/ MUSEUM OF FREE DERRY**
Tony Doherty
Adrian Kerr
Maeve McLaughlin

**CATALOGUE AUTHORS**
Stacey Abrams
Amir Ahmadi Arian
Kimberly Juanita Brown
Mike Caveney
Brian Dooley
Laura Fried
David Gruber
Deon Jones
Janna Levin
Denise Markonish
Chus Martínez
Joseph C. Thompson

**VERY SPECIAL THANKS**
Corey Lynn Calter
Sadie Jane Kaino
Stella Rose Kaino
Denise Markonish
Bob Faust
Joe Thompson
Paul Barnett
Michele Fleischli
U2
*Bono*
*Adam Clayton*
*The Edge*
*Larry Mullen Jr.*

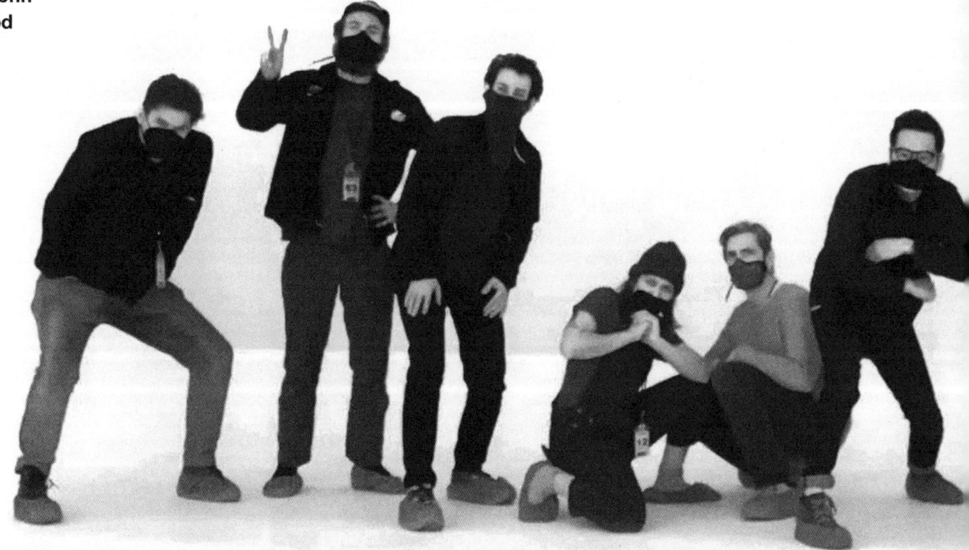

# MASS MoCA FOUNDATION

**SPECIAL THANKS**

Michael Maltzan
Tim Williams
Natasha Ryan
Jordan C. Brown
Sara Jacinto
Phil Lord
Annie Lord
Nelson George
Arthur Lewis
Derek DelGaudio
Kathleen Forde
Tommie Smith
Delois Smith
Mike Caveney
Tina Lenert
Jules Fischer

**PLEASE DONATE TO:**

John & Lilian Miles Lewis Foundation

Bloody Sunday Trust/ Museum of Free Derry

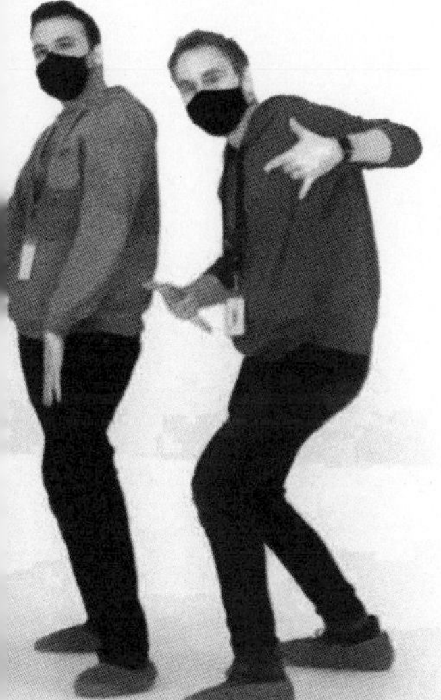

**Kaino Studio**

*Photo: Denise Markonish*

This book was published on the occasion of the exhibition *Glenn Kaino: In the Light of a Shadow*. Curated by Denise Markonish. Organized by the Massachusetts Museum of Contemporary Art, North Adams, MA. April 5, 2021 – September 5, 2022

Generous support for *In the Light of a Shadow* is provided by Nicole Deller and Matthew Bliwise, the National Endowment for the Arts, and the Director's Advisory Council of MASS MoCA. Additional support is provided by Parsons Audio LLC and Genelec Inc., and by Crystalle Lacouture and Scott Stedman.

Programming at MASS MoCA is made possible in part by the Barr Foundation, Horace W. Goldsmith Foundation, and Mass Cultural Council.



Editor: Denise Markonish

Copy editing: L. Jane Calverley

Proofreading: Paulette Wein

Production: Karen Farquhar, DelMonico Books

Design: Faust

Printed and bound in China

*In the Light of a Shadow*
Photography: Dylan Lukes: 48, 54, 60, 64, 66, 74-82, 92;
Tony Luong: 44-46, 50, 56-58, 100-104, 114-124;
Will McLaughlin: 70, 76, 84, 94-96

Other major photography: Glenn Kaino Studio

Published in 2021 by MASS MoCA and DelMonico Books • D.A.P.

MASS MoCA
1040 MASS MoCA Way
North Adams, MA 01247
413.662.2111
massmoca.org

DelMonico Books
available through
ARTBOOK | D.A.P.
75 Broad Street, Suite 630
New York, NY 10004
artbook.com
delmonicobooks.com

ISBN: 978-1-63681-011-9

Library of Congress Control Number: 2021939458

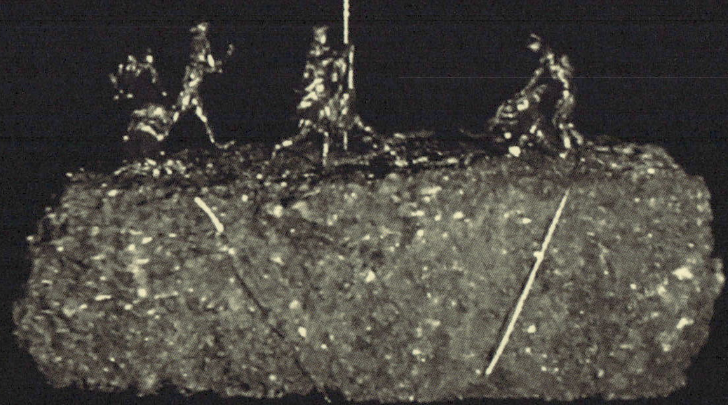

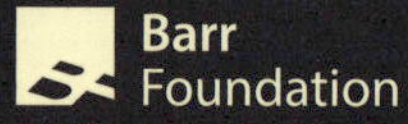


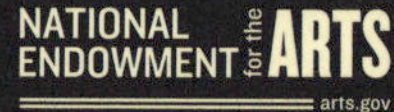


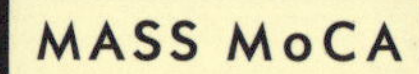


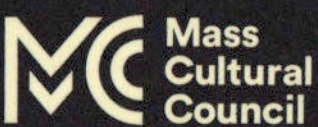

TRANSFORMATION

MAGIC

INTENTION

ELIEF

*bjects*

VISIBILITY

VOICE

LITY

LANGUAGE

AESTHETICS

OF CONCERNS

# Glenn Kaino

# This Book Is A **Memory**

DelMonico Books • D.A.P. New York | Massachusetts Museum of Contemporary Art

This Book

Is A

**Memory**

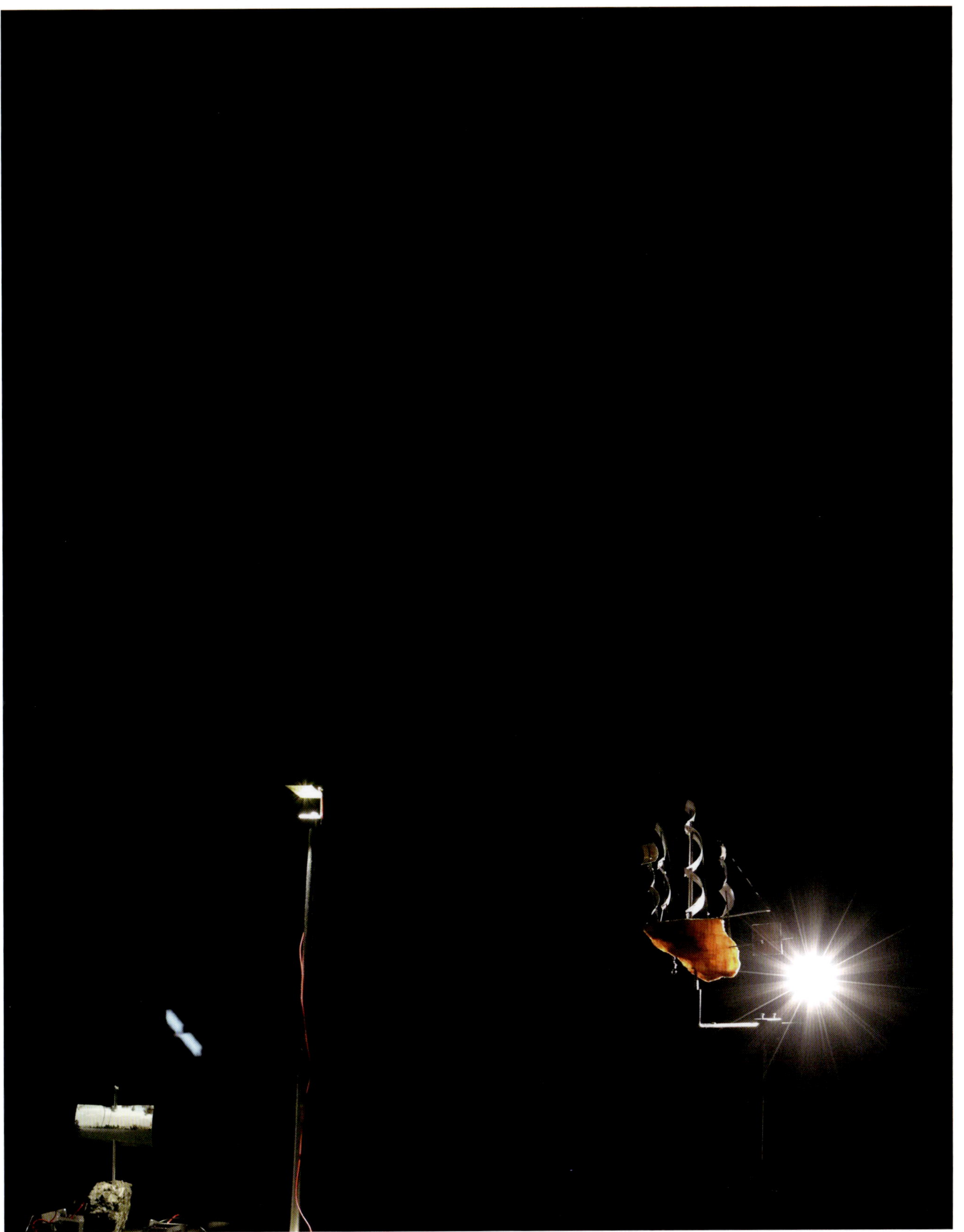

INTRODUCTION

# Notes on _SHIPS

## Glenn Kaino

X marks the spot.

We will never be here again.

Sailing away from home, we're entering uncharted waters. Everything we know, everything we thought we knew, is rapidly fading into the horizon and getting smaller. We fear this unknown. We fear that not only our lifestyle, but also our very survival is linked to the old world that is fading away.

And we feel threatened. And we threaten each other. Because we are each other.

But if we look out into the darkness, we can see others, on other ships. Looking back at us. We are alone, together. They have always been there, because we have always been here.

This is an adventure, not an exile. When we reach our destination, it will be the exact same space from which we departed, but the landscape of meaning beneath us will have shifted, changing under our feet in mid-stride.

Time is of the essence. The Essence of time. It stretches and compresses and is no longer linear. Time can now go sideways. Kairos Time.

On this journey, we are both the destination and the traveler. We see ourselves as we once were at the same time as we are now, and also as we want to be. We carry with us the scars of our past, the self-inflicted wounds of selfishness and colonialism that have been ingrained inside of us, alongside our best intentions for a new equitable world. We are living contradictions.

Ships are powered by the energy created between a promise and a memory. Between love and loss. Our ships are powered by potential energy, they are restorative, and generous.

With ships we will map our new world, with anchor points of intention but without trajectories. Old methods for new wars.

This crisis of knowing is not the end of the truth, it's the birth of a subjective and sensitive way of knowing. Truth is no longer singular, they are Ships. They are collective, and they are connected.

Connected truths. Connected.

_SHIPS

***In the Light of a Shadow* fabrication detail**

*Photo: Will McLaughlin*

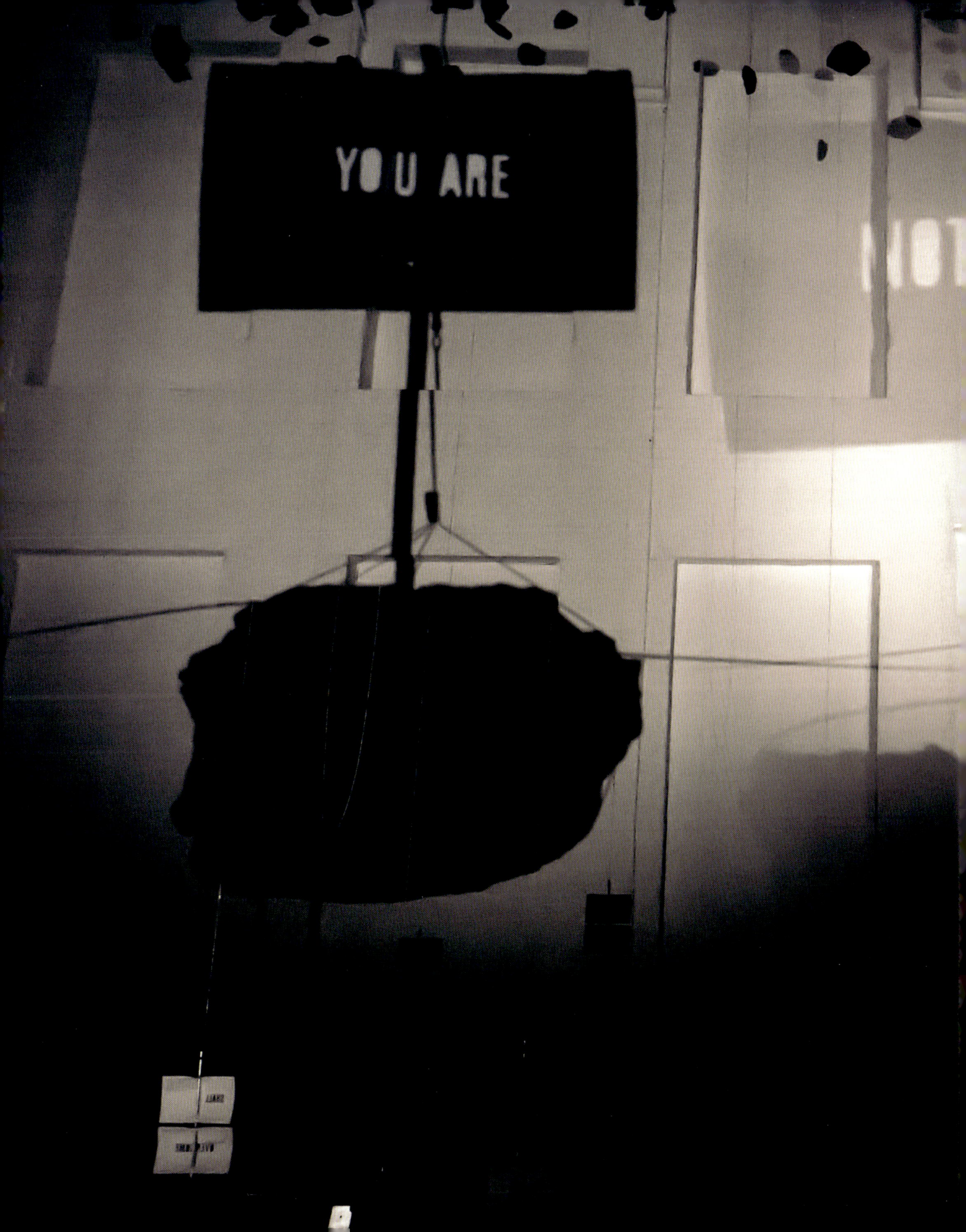

YOU ARE

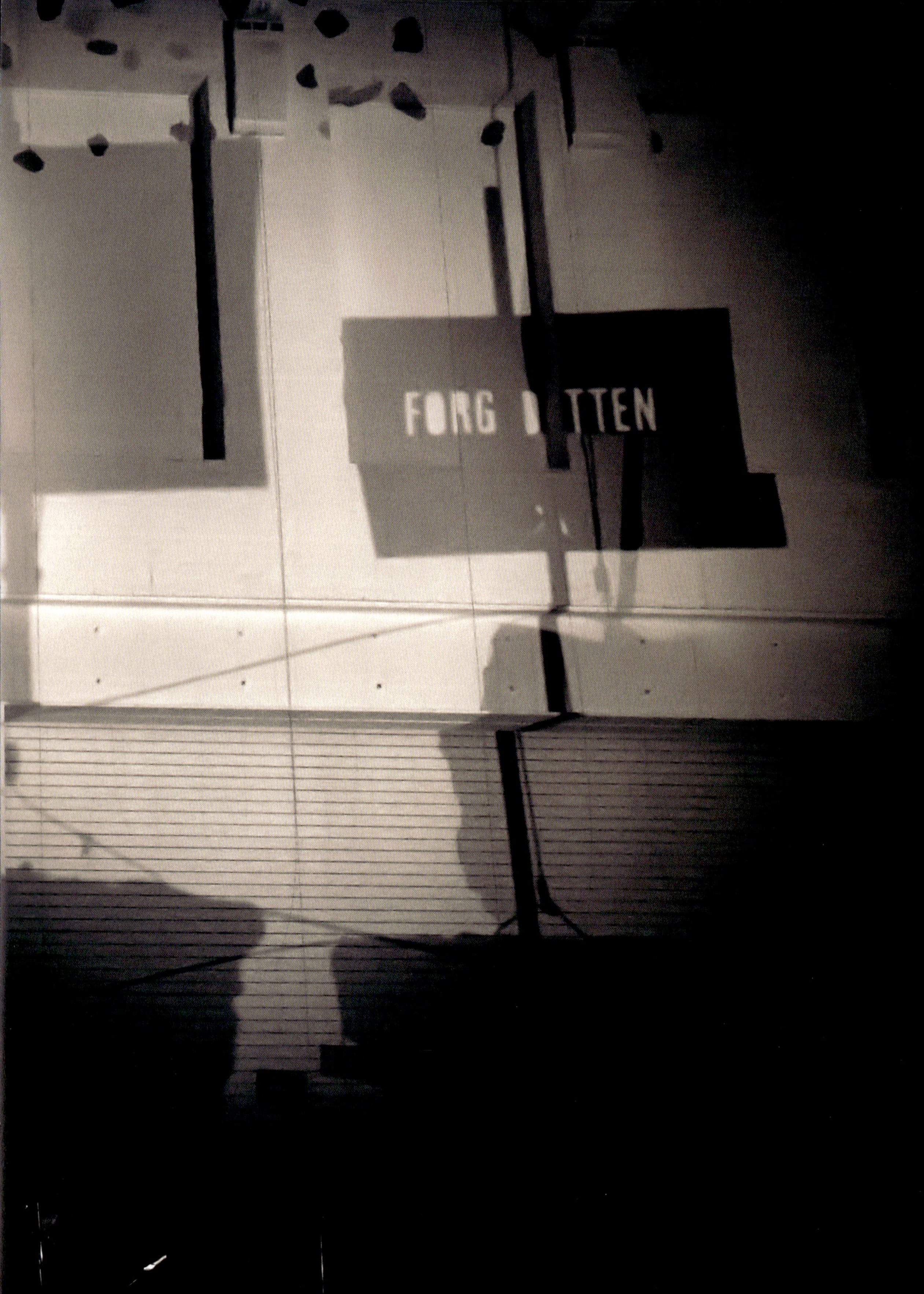
FORG TTEN

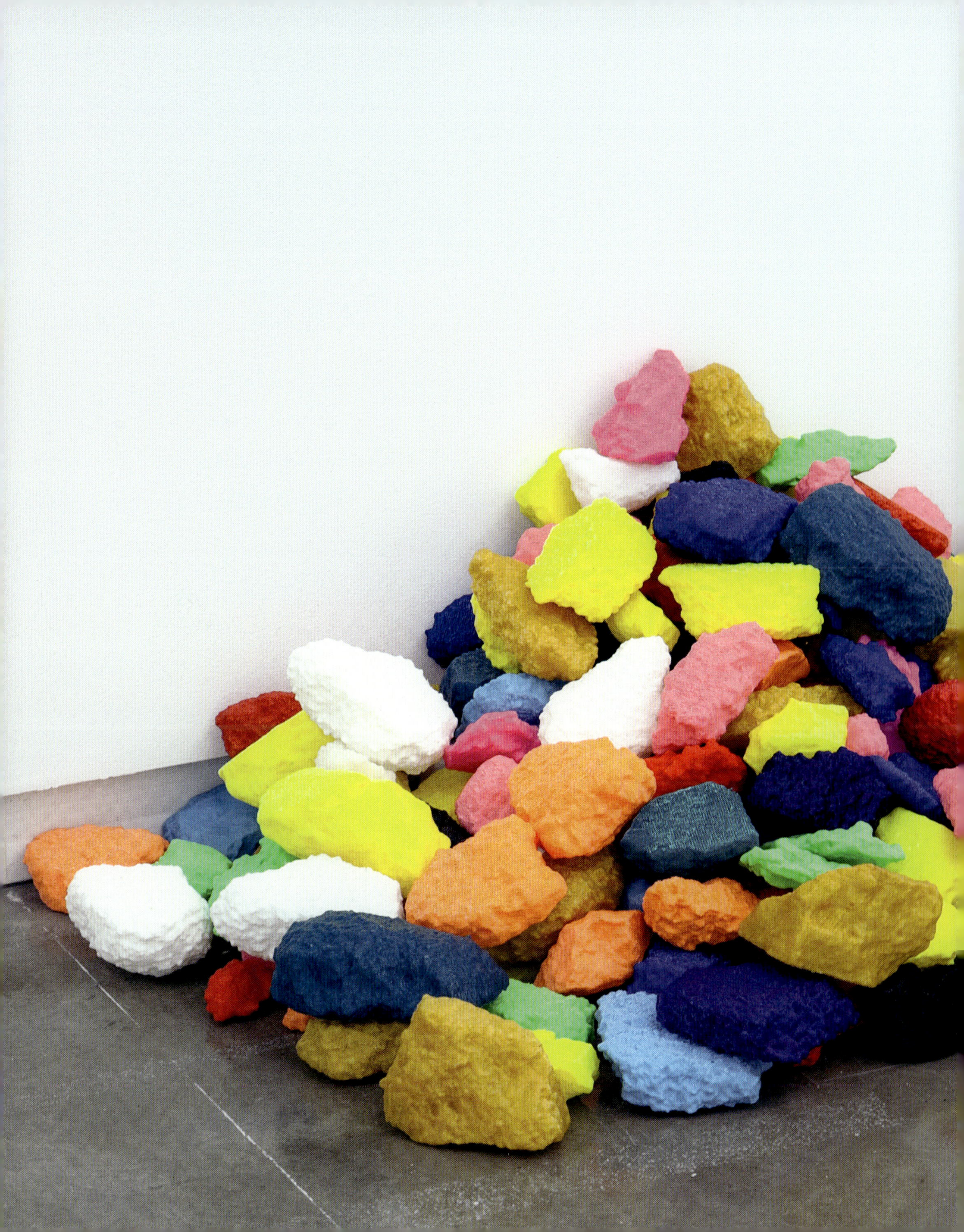

## Don't Bring a Gameboy to a Gunfight

*2014,PLA printed rocks, dimensions variable*

The pieces in this pile of 3D-printed multi-colored plastic rocks are facsimiles of actual rocks collected by a worldwide network of Kaino's agents from sites of protest and extremist oppression like Benghazi, Tahrir Square, and Yemen. The originals were scanned and sent out again to yet another network of renegade, underground 3D printers, and then returned to the artist. The absurdity of printing these "weapons" via digital file and reassembling them is underscored by a yet more sinister reference. The poster accompanying the rocks displays an illegal printable 3D digital-gun file that was outlawed by the US State Department. In creating the possibility of an unlimited multiple, an inexhaustible cache of ammunition, and in igniting a process that connects revolutionary spirit across the globe, this work raises questions about how object value, functional utility, and symbolic agency become entangled in social and sculptural practice.

*Photo: Tony Walsh*

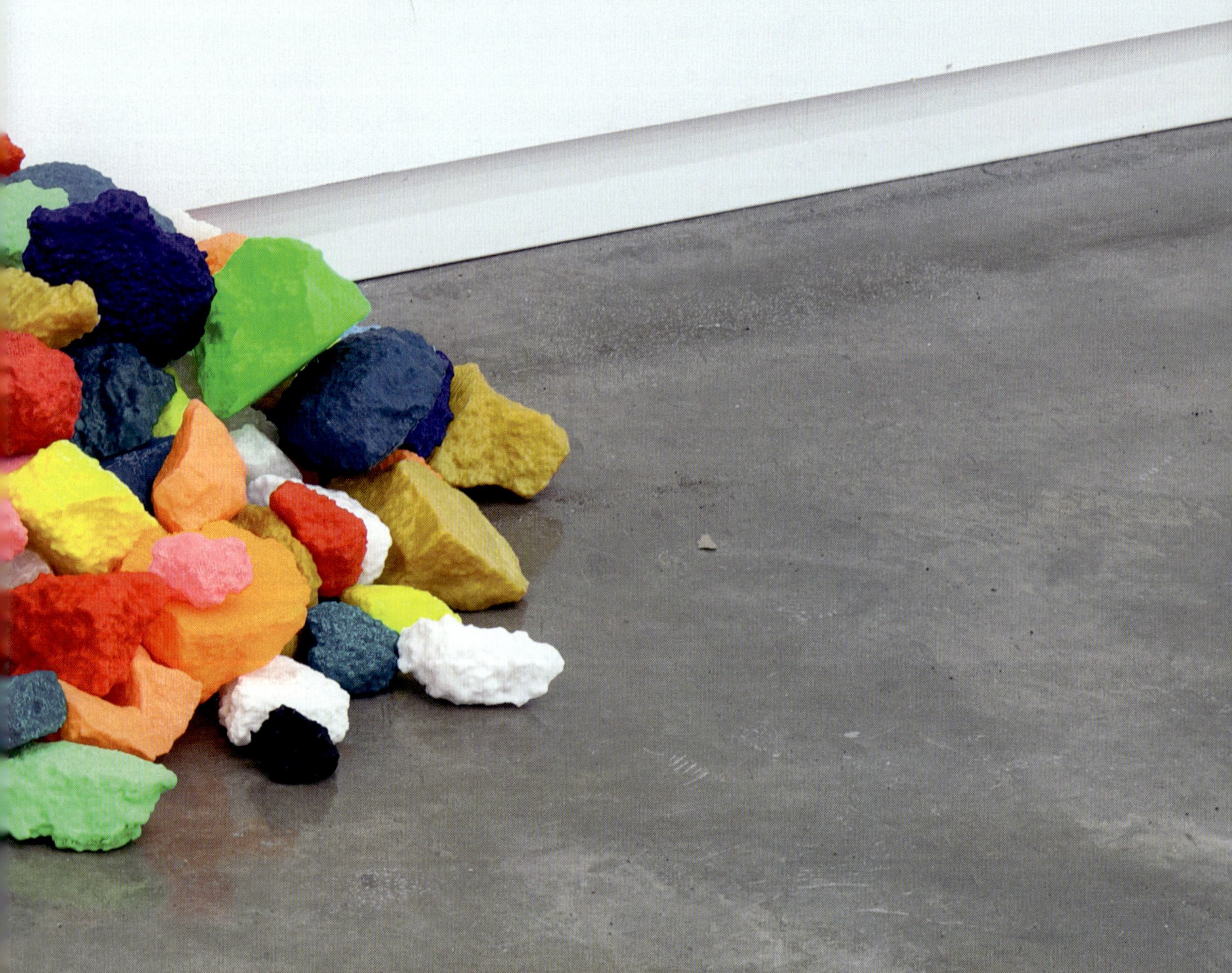

# Paradoxes of Hope

Amir Ahmadi Arian

## ON *IN THE LIGHT OF A SHADOW*

Standing before Glenn Kaino's exhibition *In the Light of a Shadow*, one beholds a metaphorically Janus-faced installation. It is a hanging head with two countenances, one looking into the past, the other into the future.

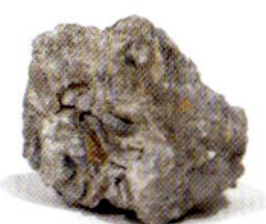

What can a work of art teach us about the past? In one view of history, the past is the business of historians and archaeologists. They arrive after the collapse, when the edifice of a historical moment is annihilated into countless little pieces. Historians walk through the ruins and observe the remaining scraps. After poring over the archives, examining the broken bricks and the glass shards and the twisted metal and charred wood, they go back to their desks and, through the magic of words, piece the fragments together, extrapolating what they saw into the building to which these pieces supposedly belonged.

Kaino subscribes to a different view of history. Like the historians, he wanders amid the ruins, but he refuses to try to reassemble the detritus into an imagined coherent whole. To him, the ruin is not the evidence of history. It *is* history. For his MASS MoCA exhibition *In the Light of a Shadow*, Kaino uses this detritus—rocks and chunks of asphalt—to conjure the history of revolution. However, the simple rocks, which take the form of a galaxy orbiting around a sun/blackhole, do not merely indicate a past. They embody that past.

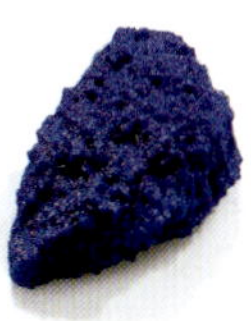

By putting these rocks on display in this fashion, Kaino takes his audience into the ruins of history. Historians conjure the past into a narrative and organize it into a book or a film that tells a familiar story with a beginning, middle, and end. Kaino, on the other hand, takes pains to reconstruct the immediate aftermath of the explosion, when the rocks are still hot and the ghosts of the dead still lurk around on the walls.

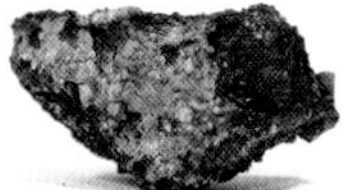

The other side of this Janus head is looking ahead into the future. In his own words, Kaino gives us a clue as to what this second gaze is seeking, when in writing about the exhibition he describes his work as a "celebration of the spirit of hopefulness." Elsewhere, in a text titled "Hopeful Objects," Kaino and writer Phillip Barcio go into more details, stating his work "tangibly materializes hopefulness, possibilities, and connections . . . it is also about linking people and things in the present that may never have realized the potential that they had for connection."[1] This implies that signs of hope abound in this work of art; but we need some effort to find them.

Crucial as it is to human survival, hope is especially hard to define. As usual, the ancients give us great hints. In Hesiod's version of the tale of Pandora, when the jar is opened all the evils leave, and the only thing that remains at the bottom is hope. To Hesiod, hope might be found in the space from which evils are expelled. The evils Hesiod jettisons are uncontroversial: disease, war, poverty, vice. To get closer to this space, we need to take one more step and detect the fake hopes, the pseudo-hopes, and get them out of the jar as well.

One of the concepts often confused with hope is optimism. Hope and optimism are fundamentally different. Optimism relies on probability. You can be optimistic when your desired outcome is likely. Hope, on the other hand, offers no guarantee. It is by no means rare to hope for an unlikely outcome. Hope entails risk, which makes it the opposite of naivete. In his celebration of hope, Kaino cautions us to remain wary of optimism.

The strange structure at the center of Kaino's galaxy—the black hole/sun—is in fact a representation of Earl Mountbatten of Burma's boat, the *Shadow V*. In bombing the *Shadow V*, the Irish Republican Army carried out the assassination of one of its highest profile targets, someone who was, ironically, at the same time one of its rare sympathizers in the British aristocracy. The operation was initially touted as a big success, yet in hindsight it marked the beginning of the organization's downfall, as public sentiment turned against the group in response to its bloody and indiscriminate attacks. In this instance, the remotely detonated bomb killed not only Lord Mountbatten, but also three other people, including two teenagers. This incident neatly encapsulates the paradox of the revolutionary act, its messiness, and its inevitable ethical complications.

To represent this dilemma, Kaino twists the replica of the exploded boat into the shape of an ouroboros, the snake that eats its tail, suggesting that the revolution is not always in opposition to oppression. It can be parallel to it—sometimes at the same time. He shows us that revolutions don't just eat their children. They engage in self-cannibalism as well.

The lighting of the piece highlights this inherent contradiction. The luminous center illuminates rocks and postcards, giving life to the galaxy, rendering the text and images on the cards visible and legible. But the darkness at the core conveys an opposite effect. It looks as though it has the potential to swallow the other objects, even the light itself, into a pool of oblivion. The same source that allows us to see the ruins of history threatens to swallow it out of memory. The rocks are subject to these dual, contradictory effects. Hope and despair emanate from the same place, just as they do in history.

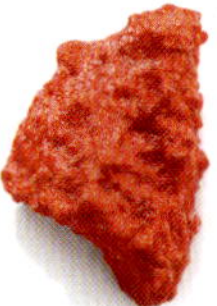

To approach hopefulness from a different angle, let us reflect on the boat as an idea. In his famous essay *Of Other Spaces*, Michel Foucault calls on his fellow philosophers to abandon their perennial obsession with history and pay attention to geography. He preaches a shift of focus from time to space, from linearity to simultaneity, to juxtapositions and networks. In this essay, he introduces the concept of *heterotopia*, which he defines as "an effectively enacted utopia in which the real sites, all the other real sites that can be found within the culture, are simultaneously represented, contested, and inverted."[2] Heterotopias are places with outsider status and otherness, yet they can be located in reality. They offer a joint experience of utopia (from the Greek "ou" and "topos," literally meaning "nowhere") and existing places. Foucault offers a list of examples of heterotopia, which includes mirrors, cemeteries, airplanes, museums, and boats.

For Foucault, boats exemplify heterotopia the best. Each is a roaming slice of place, a meeting point of specificity and "nowhere," a small world unto itself set afloat upon the infinity of the ocean. "In civilizations without boats, dreams dry up," he writes, "espionage takes the place of adventure, and the police take the place of pirates."[3]

In Kaino's galaxy, the black hole/sun is an exploded boat, and thousands of hanging little boats, comprised of rocks and postcards, are orbiting it. The shadows have a doubling effect: they are locations that can be spotted in reality, but at the same time are also insubstantial, utopic. The rocks are on a journey from the real places to utopia, and we have caught them somewhere midway, frozen in time and space.

On the opening pages of Kaino's selected project catalogue[4] there is a graph that represents the themes of his work (see endpapers). They range widely, from the Anthropocene to magic, from the public sphere to ethics, from maps to language. All of these concepts are arranged around a central motif, similar to the way the rocks are organized around the exploded boat. In the graph, this hub is called the "hopeful object."

The term "hopeful object" brings to mind what the philosopher Timothy Morton calls "hyperobjects." In Morton's conceptualization, a hyperobject is an entity of vast scale in time and space that the human mind has no way of apprehending in its entirety. It is everywhere and nowhere. It sticks to everything, becomes present in all aspects of our lives, and yet remains stubbornly incomprehensible. Hyperobjects are the main antagonists in the story of human life in the twenty-first century. The COVID pandemic is only one example. Big data is a hyperobject specific to our time. So is global warming, caused by the enormous and thickening cloud of carbon dioxide in the atmosphere, leaving its mark on every aspect of life on the planet.

Kaino's hopeful objects, both conceptually and functionally, counter and combat hyperobjects. As opposed to the abstract, threatening omnipresence of hyperobjects, he creates material, tangible, hopeful objects, by imbuing everyday objects, through kitbashing and reassembling and reconfiguration, with hope. The hand of Tommie Smith, who raised his defiant fist on the podium of the 1968 Olympics to protest racial injustice, is multiplied hundreds of times, and assembled into a bridge that connects the past and the future. *In the Lightof a Shadow* falls into the same category, except that here the hopeful objects explode in number.

Against the hyperobject of infinitely complex algorithms, which annihilate memory by hooking users to clickbait headlines and cause endless doomscrolling, the postcards that make up the sails of the hanging rocks exist as simple, tangible scraps of paper that bring alive a lost moment in the past. Against the abstract calls for a total shakeup of everything, thereby rendering the world susceptible to myriad disasters, his replica of *Shadow V* brings political idealism down to the ground and materializes it into the remains of a ship that embodies the inherent contradiction of revolutionary practice. Against the doomsayers and downplayers of the unfolding climate horror, the little sprouts that emerge every day from a dead rock give us a clear indication of the resilience of life on our planet, reminding us of the time we still have in which to turn things around.

In an age fraught with hyperobjects so large and terrifying that they invoke a sense of paralysis and doom, Kaino's hopeful objects provide us with small, temporary shelters, opening doors to more liberatory mental and emotional spaces.

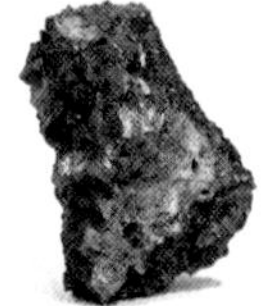

[1] www.glennkainostudio.com/writings/hopeful-objects.

[2] https://web.mit.edu/allanmc/www/foucault1.pdf.

[3] Ibid.

[4] This catalogue is a pdf Kaino prepared for the author to describe his studio practice.

## Escala-

*2014, Found scales, various objects, 120 x 72 x 11 inches*

**A multi-tiered monumental work with multivalent implications, *Escala-* is comprised of many precisely weighted and balanced vintage scales arranged in a tree-like mobile, each filled with diverse objects. The form, reminiscent of Boolean analytical reasoning, creates a complicated physical and conceptual chain of causal relationships. The title of the sculpture, the Spanish word for "scale," also prefaces the word "escalation," confusing and complicating our notions of appropriately scaled threat and punishment. The objects counterweighting the scales must be carefully placed or removed in coordination with the entire network, requiring several people to act in unison rather than an impulsive individual act that would throw the system out of parity. On a theoretical level, the work asks us to reconsider the relevancy and viability of analyzing deterministic dependencies as the basis of our system of logic—uprooting the foundations of Western epistemology and how we can even begin to rationally understand and remediate the causes of societal breakdown.**

*Photo: Tony Walsh*

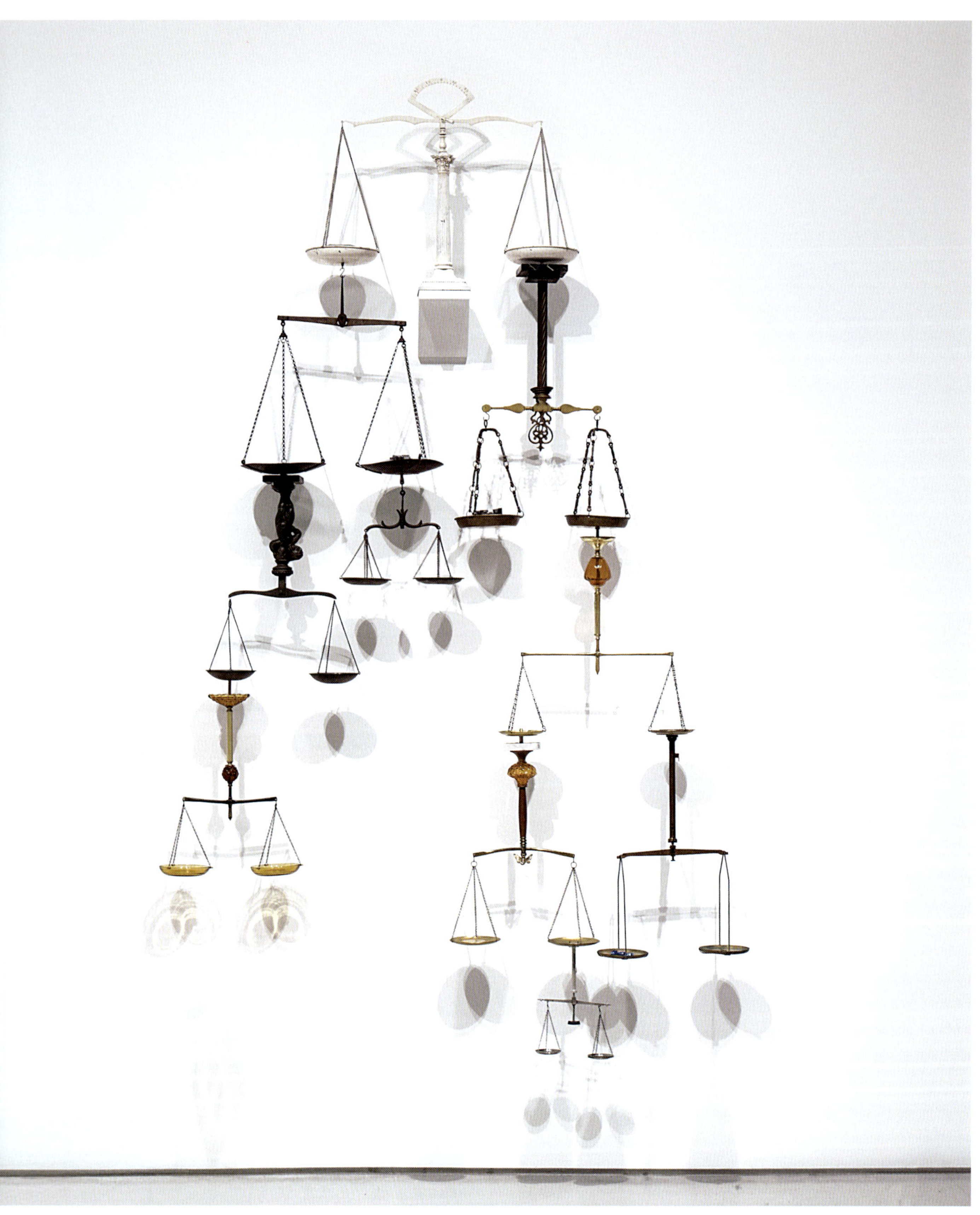

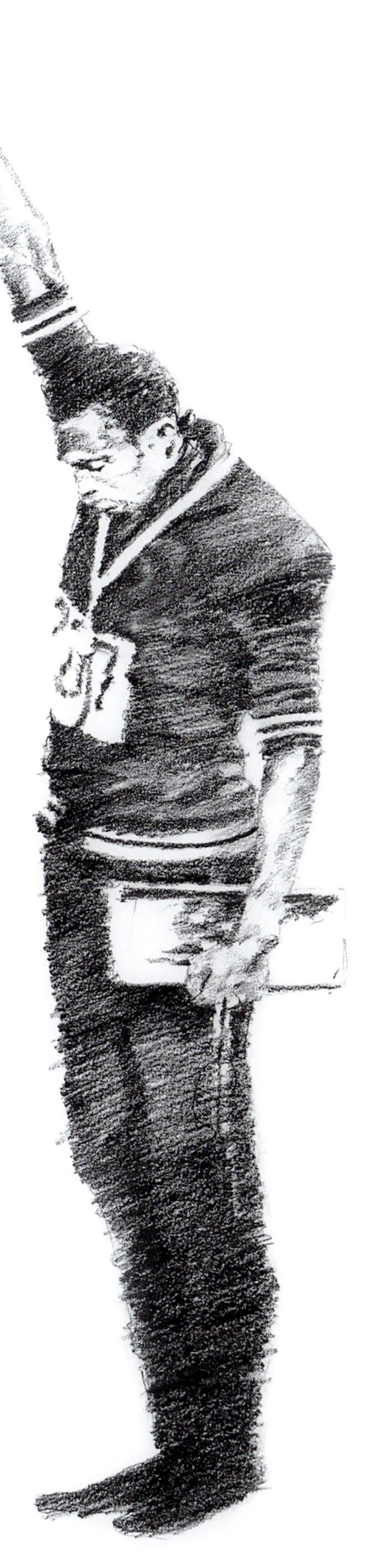

Sketch for *With Drawn Arms*, 2017, Graphite on paper

# Glenn Kaino's Sculptural Vision

Kimberly Juanita Brown

Glenn Kaino is interested in history, not just to reflect on the past, but to bring it alive in the present. In recent projects, he has done this by stressing the significance, as well as the complicated use, of photographs from the civil rights era, particularly those that have captured the visual imagination of a global audience. In this, he connects his work to a larger ethical impulse that orients his line of sight toward correcting and resurrecting the images of the past, providing new context for the future. Kaino follows this line of sight to its aesthetic and humanistic conclusion, as was evident in the work in his exhibition *With Drawn Arms*. Central to this series is Kaino's 100-foot installation, *Bridge* (2013), which negotiates the territory between suspension and space, using the duplication of the famous image of Olympian Tommie Smith's iconic arm, raised in protest and resistance at the 1968 Olympic Games in Mexico City.

Let us back up a moment to that XIX Olympiad. Amid racial turmoil in the United States after the assassination of Martin Luther King Jr., Smith and fellow track and field athlete John Carlos mount the stand during the medal ceremony after they take gold and bronze prizes respectively in the 200-meter race. Smith and Carlos each raise a fist, covered in a matching leather glove, during the national anthem. (They were joined on the podium by Australian Peter Norman, who received the silver medal.)

The visual image that came to be known across the globe was one that held the moment of the protest in space and time. In this holding, though, the limitations of representation are also present. How does one figure move beyond the enclosure of history when this enclosure is a part of the process of becoming? To grapple with what is possible in the arena of the visual is to peel back the layers of history and memory to see what lies beneath. It is an investment of the will, driven by purpose and creative desire. *Bridge*, which consists of two hundred replicas of Smith's raised fist, hovers like a haunting, a vessel and a tunnel, bringing an aesthetic view of the history of social justice to bear on open space. Kaino's installation expands and extends Smith's iconic gesture, inviting viewers to metaphorically bridge the space between concept and intention by reckoning with both the historical significance of Smith's gesture and the figurative reference point the sculpture highlights through its multiplication and disembodiment of the raised fist.

Kaino's 2021 exhibition at MASS MoCA, *In the Light of a Shadow*, complements the *With Drawn Arms* work by illustrating Kaino's investment in an unyielding quest for social justice. The exhibition brings together images of disparate protests for equality from Selma, Alabama; Derry, Northern Ireland; and 2020's Black Lives Matter marches. This latter category is made palpable in the figure of Deon Jones, a vocalist and member of Kaino's studio team. Jones was injured by a rubber bullet shot by police while at a protest over the police killing of George Floyd. As a result, Kaino created a circular wall made of metal bars and filmed Jones encased within the sculpture as he offered a rendition of the famous song "Sunday Bloody Sunday" by the band U2.[1] Threading together protests for civil rights and justice with the circular aesthetic of Jones's musical performance, Kaino enables a discourse of collective resistance into the visual realm.

The issue of visibility (of presence or absence) and images from the civil rights movement in the United States is fraught. Documentary images, still photographs in daily newspapers and film clips on the evening news, offer evidentiary proof of the struggle for citizenship and liberation for African Americans.[2] Embedded within this "evidence" is a photographic imperative—to document history as it is unfolding, with the key players presented on gelatin silver prints. These photographs, the iconic and unknown alike, occupy prime real estate in the landscape of racial progress. They show us how activists and allies, participants and witnesses organized themselves and envisioned the moment, which tells us something important about the power of the image over time.

Kaino's practice employs spatial fluidity with dense conceptual territories, allowing viewers to ponder the intricate details that make up a three-dimensional whole. Active in the art world since the early 2000s, the Los Angeles-based artist propels an aesthetic order into each installation space, one that conceptually retrieves humanity from the structures of dispossession. For example, Kaino's *Bridge* opens the space between artistry and intentionality, with its replication of Smith's protest pose visualized in the series of casts of his arm, extending the line of resistance from 1968 to 2013, and beyond the confines of history. The viewer is able to imagine each arm cinematically reproducing itself in an overflow of presence, creating a gold-inflected barrier that also resembles the contours of a harp. You are invited to take Smith's silent gesture and imbue it with sound: the flutters of a bird, the waves of the sea against the shore.

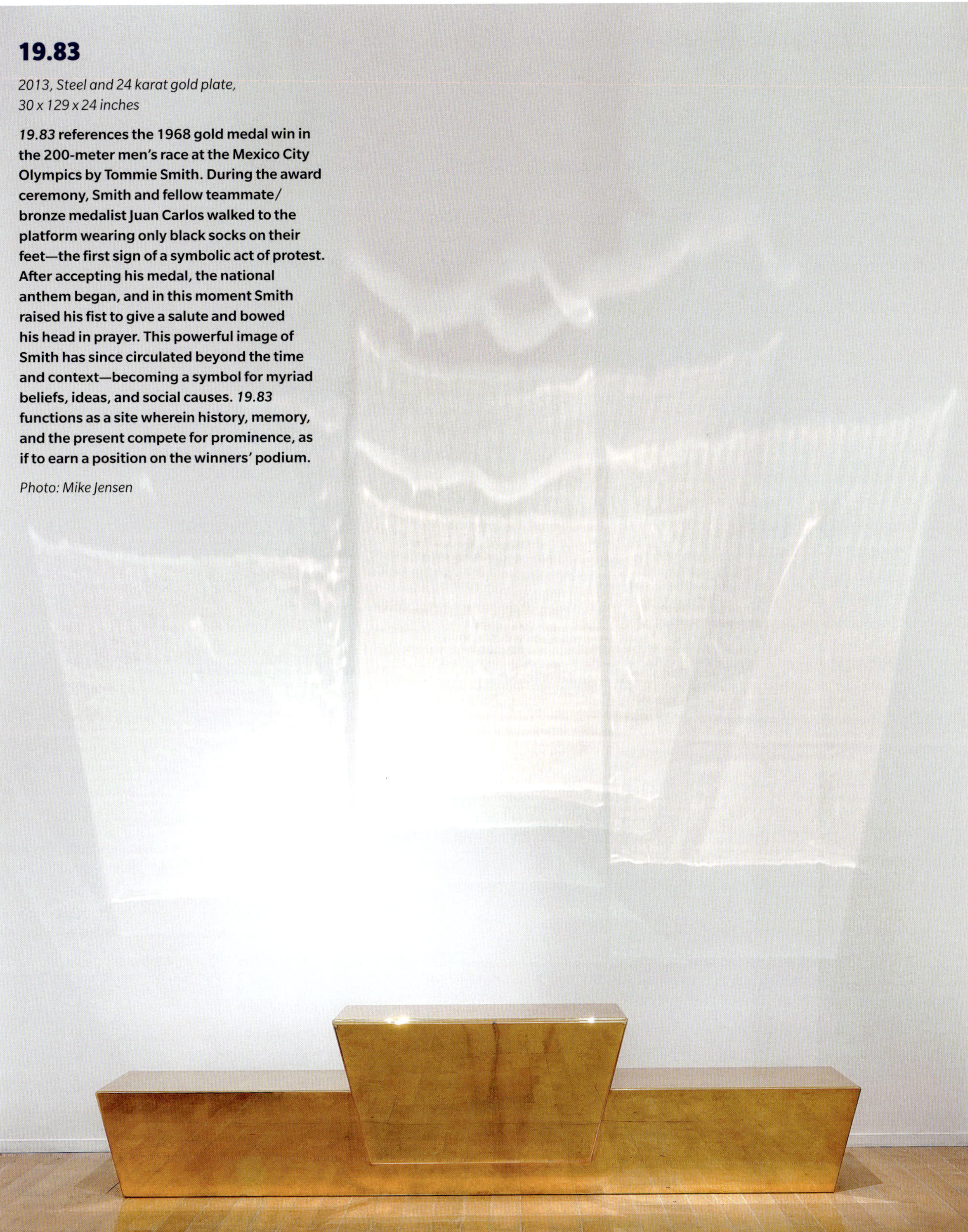

## 19.83

*2013, Steel and 24 karat gold plate, 30 x 129 x 24 inches*

***19.83* references the 1968 gold medal win in the 200-meter men's race at the Mexico City Olympics by Tommie Smith. During the award ceremony, Smith and fellow teammate/ bronze medalist Juan Carlos walked to the platform wearing only black socks on their feet—the first sign of a symbolic act of protest. After accepting his medal, the national anthem began, and in this moment Smith raised his fist to give a salute and bowed his head in prayer. This powerful image of Smith has since circulated beyond the time and context—becoming a symbol for myriad beliefs, ideas, and social causes. *19.83* functions as a site wherein history, memory, and the present compete for prominence, as if to earn a position on the winners' podium.**

*Photo: Mike Jensen*

In the wave-like duplication of Smith's resistant arm, public memory and public forgetting take central stage. What is held in memory or forgetting in the public imaginary is often dependent upon the whims of the moment, or the movement of the images associated with history. Of the famous photograph that inspired *Bridge*, Kaino has stated: "That image, it was one of the most powerful protest gestures of the twentieth century."[3] From this gesture, Kaino builds an entire world, one that takes the grandeur of Smith's resistance as the certainty of vision, and the promise of the will. Suspended from above by steel and wire, *Bridge* is the visual memory of a moment in history that has had a profound effect on the way we visualize resilience, race, citizenship, and representation.

The Black Power gesture, one with its own visual history and narrative, has always been a phenomenon of global significance. It connects Black people across the diaspora to the concept of freedom, autonomy, and sovereignty. It offers a silent mark of collective agreement in which members of the Black diaspora reproduce a corporeal signal that registers multiple meanings: power, grievance, strength, recognition, and engagement.

*Bridge* also showcases the shimmering gold that signified Smith's medal in the 200-meter race. Obscured by the runners' heroic gesture, little is said about the ceremony's other spectacular achievement: that two of the three medal recipients in the 200-meter track and field category were African Americans. Kaino's sculpture embeds the force of Black Power with the gestural elegance of gold. He tells the story of the moment Black excellence and Black grievance were combined. "Something very sinister happens to people of a country when they begin to distrust their own reactions as deeply as they do here," James Baldwin writes in *The Fire Next Time*. "It is this individual uncertainty on the part of white American men and women, this inability to renew themselves at the fountain of their own lives, that makes the discussion, let alone elucidation, of any conundrum—that is, any reality—so supremely difficult." Baldwin continues: "The person who distrusts himself has no touchstone for reality—for this touchstone can only be oneself."[4]

Smith's visibility in the iconic image led to hyper-surveillance and retaliation afterward, as Olympic officials wrestled with how to control the fallout from the act. The backlash Smith experienced in the aftermath of the Olympic medal ceremony, and the psychic life of racism undergirding it, is something that the former athlete lives with to this day. In an interview with Ken Belson for the *New York Times*, Smith said: "All I did was stand there with a fist in the air. It was a cry for freedom. And now people are beginning to throw a right fist up and throw it up for different reasons, but now they have the freedom to do it. It was a small crack so all generations are moving through with a form of thanks in their hearts. That's the way I have to see it because so many people have died because they raised a fist in their hearts or took a knee in their souls to eradicate the knee to the neck."[5] There is, in Smith's pose and Kaino's extension of it, so much reflected certainty. An externalization of Smith's interiority. To put this in starker visual context, images from the US civil rights movement give us one perspective of the historical event and its significance. Artistic extensions/reinvisionings like Kaino's give us another perspective.

More than negotiating a space between documentary and artistic production or two-dimensional versus three-dimensional image making, Kaino blends disparate concepts into a cohesive whole. In Kaino's sculptural vision, Smith's gesture expands upwards and outwards, so that a circular history can form, one that is also echoed in the cell-like structure from which Deon Jones sings. If we imagine *Bridge* as an optics of the spatial imagination, Kaino presents this in its most vibrant form, like musical notes set against a reverberating enclosure. "Ultimately," Blaire Zeiders writes, "Kaino seems to have no interest in deciphering his pieces for others: he is hoping to elicit a creative response in his viewer, not to reveal a fundamental truth about or official reading of his art."[6] *Bridge* has the ability to manage multiple visual possibilities: replication and response, public and private, power and resistance. Kaino tethers Smith's raised arm to a larger visual narrative of racial progress that slowly unfurls over time.

[1] *https://massmoca.org/event/glenn-kaino-in-the-light-of-a-shadow/.*

[2] *In her essay, "'Come Let Us Build a New World Together': SNCC and Photography of the Civil Rights Movement," Leigh Raiford writes, "It is my belief that photography is essential to understanding the civil rights movement and its participants on the ground." Her article details the importance of the Student Nonviolent Coordinating Committee and its leadership, who understood the power of the photographic image in the context of Black liberation.* American Quarterly, *vol. 59, no. 4 (December 2007), pp. 1129-1157, 1131.*

[3] *Deborah Vankin, "Science + Social Justice + Magic. The Spellbinding Formula of Artist Glenn Kaino,"* Los Angeles Times, *November 9, 2020.*

[4] *James Baldwin,* The Fire Next Time *(1963; Vintage Books, 1993), p. 43.*

[5] *Ken Belson, "Tommie Smith's Fist is Still Raised: 'We Still Need to Fight,'"* New York Times, *June 13, 2020.*

[6] *Blaire Zeiders, "The Artist and the Exegete: Decoding Visions in Glenn Kaino's 'The Siege Perilous,'"* Arthuriana, *vol. 24, no. 1 (Spring 2014), pp. 86-110, 103.*

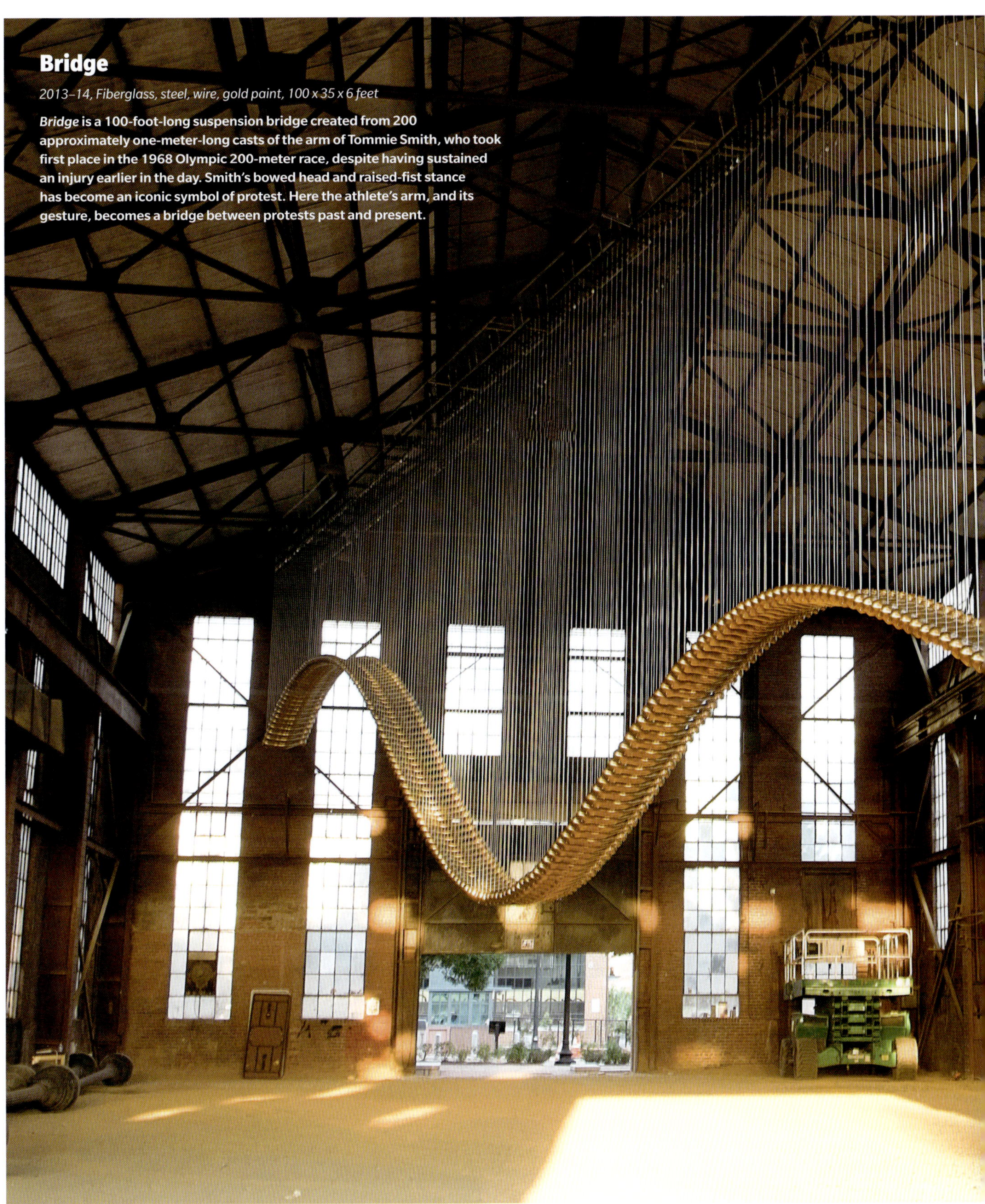

## Bridge

*2013–14, Fiberglass, steel, wire, gold paint, 100 x 35 x 6 feet*

**_Bridge_ is a 100-foot-long suspension bridge created from 200 approximately one-meter-long casts of the arm of Tommie Smith, who took first place in the 1968 Olympic 200-meter race, despite having sustained an injury earlier in the day. Smith's bowed head and raised-fist stance has become an iconic symbol of protest. Here the athlete's arm, and its gesture, becomes a bridge between protests past and present.**

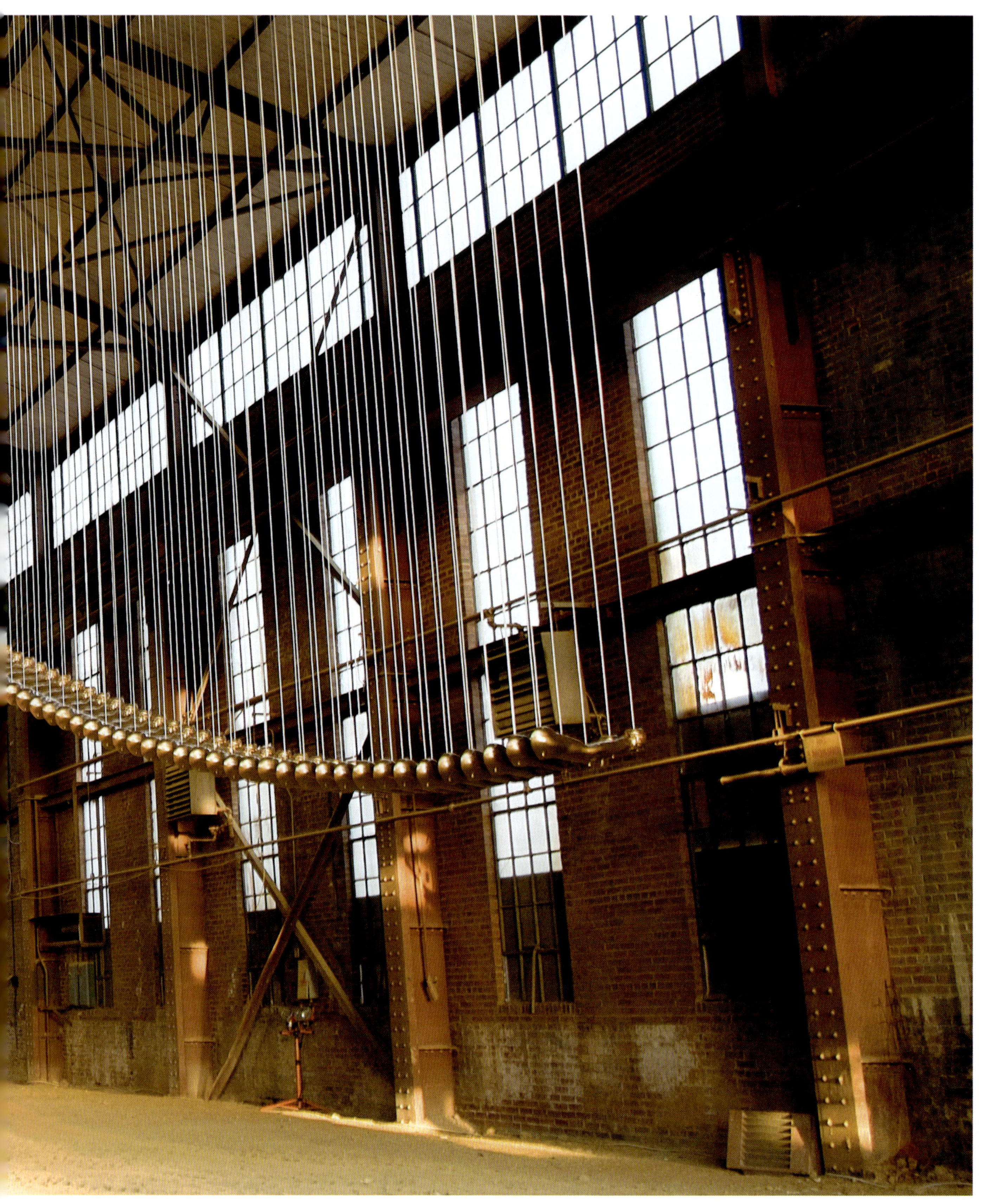

## Champion

*Paper, ink, time, 2.64 x 7.65 x 11.81 inches*

**Champion is a large-scale multiple created in collaboration with General Mills, the makers of the cereal Wheaties. Appearing on a Wheaties box is widely considered to be one of the highest signifiers of success as a professional athlete, primarily rooted in the fact that during the heyday of the brand there were limited outlets for mainstream America to connect to sporting figures in everyday ways. Tommie Smith was never featured on the box due to the controversy surrounding his salute on the medal stand at the 1968 Mexico City Olympics, after he had taken the gold in the 200-meter race. As part of his ongoing collaboration with Smith, Kaino convinced General Mills to create a box, as an artwork, and release it to the public.**

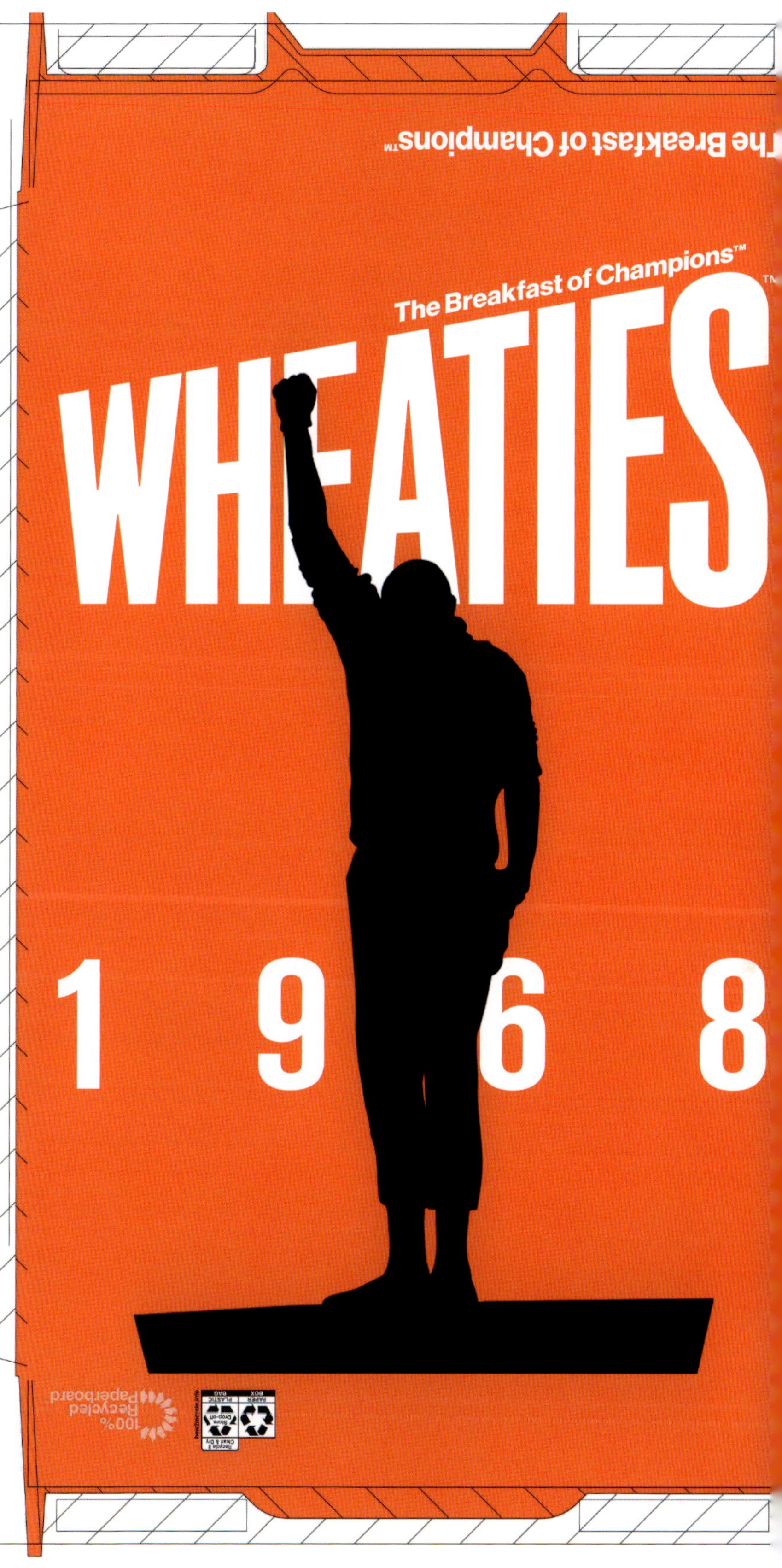

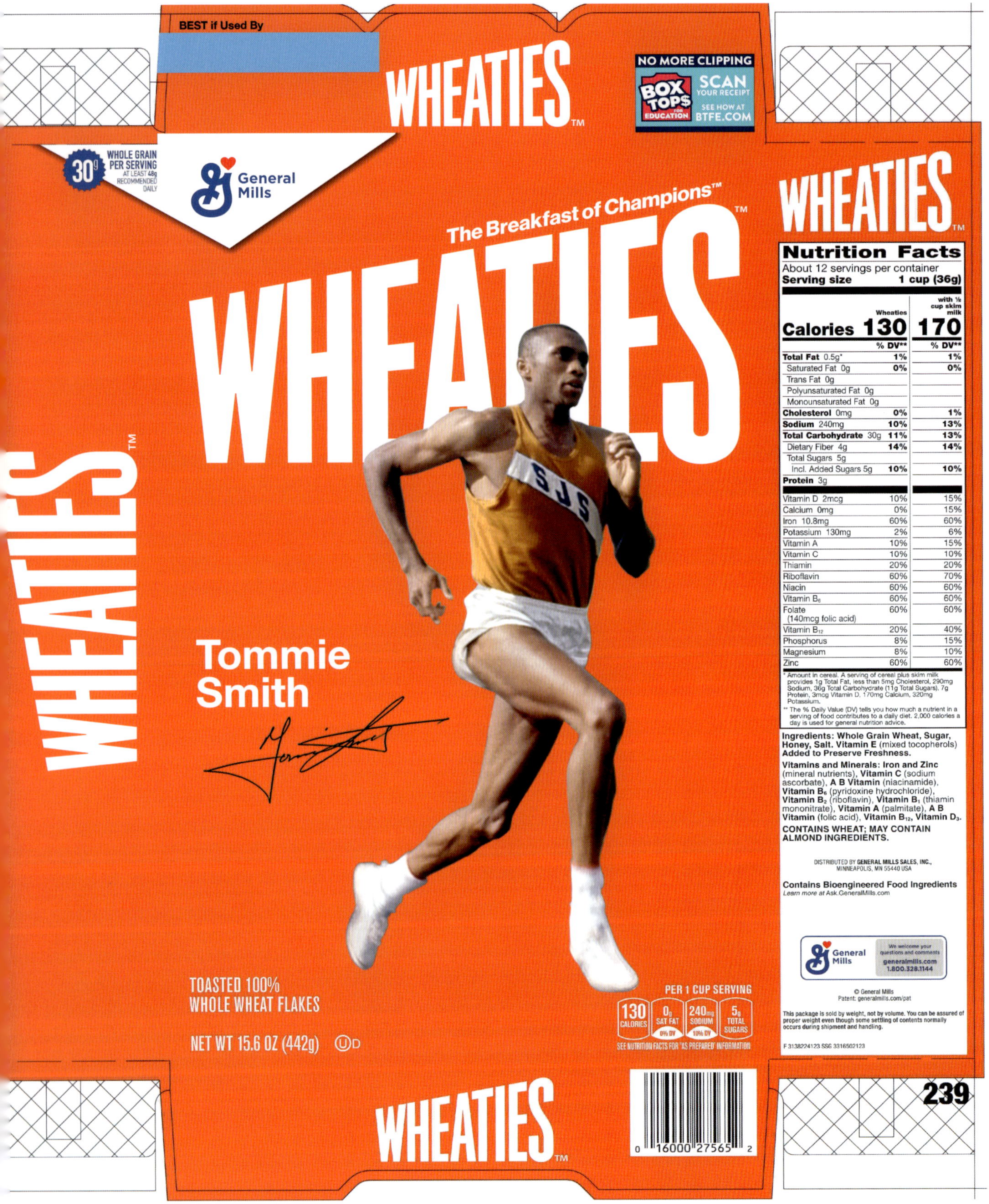

BEST if Used By

WHEATIES™

NO MORE CLIPPING
BOX TOP$ FOR EDUCATION
SCAN YOUR RECEIPT
SEE HOW AT BTFE.COM

30g WHOLE GRAIN PER SERVING
AT LEAST 48g RECOMMENDED DAILY

General Mills

The Breakfast of Champions™

WHEATIES™

Tommie Smith

SJS

TOASTED 100% WHOLE WHEAT FLAKES

NET WT 15.6 OZ (442g) ⓊD

PER 1 CUP SERVING

130 CALORIES | 0g SAT FAT 0% DV | 240mg SODIUM 10% DV | 5g TOTAL SUGARS

SEE NUTRITION FACTS FOR "AS PREPARED" INFORMATION

WHEATIES™

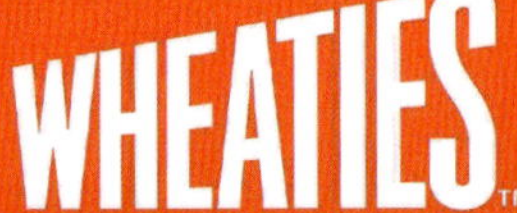


**Nutrition Facts**

About 12 servings per container
**Serving size** **1 cup (36g)**

| | Wheaties | with ½ cup skim milk |
|---|---|---|
| **Calories** | **130** | **170** |
| | **% DV**** | **% DV**** |
| **Total Fat** 0.5g* | **1%** | **1%** |
| Saturated Fat 0g | **0%** | **0%** |
| Trans Fat 0g | | |
| Polyunsaturated Fat 0g | | |
| Monounsaturated Fat 0g | | |
| **Cholesterol** 0mg | **0%** | **1%** |
| **Sodium** 240mg | **10%** | **13%** |
| **Total Carbohydrate** 30g | **11%** | **13%** |
| Dietary Fiber 4g | **14%** | **14%** |
| Total Sugars 5g | | |
| Incl. Added Sugars 5g | **10%** | **10%** |
| **Protein** 3g | | |
| Vitamin D 2mcg | 10% | 15% |
| Calcium 0mg | 0% | 15% |
| Iron 10.8mg | 60% | 60% |
| Potassium 130mg | 2% | 6% |
| Vitamin A | 10% | 15% |
| Vitamin C | 10% | 10% |
| Thiamin | 20% | 20% |
| Riboflavin | 60% | 70% |
| Niacin | 60% | 60% |
| Vitamin $B_6$ | 60% | 60% |
| Folate (140mcg folic acid) | 60% | 60% |
| Vitamin $B_{12}$ | 20% | 40% |
| Phosphorus | 8% | 15% |
| Magnesium | 8% | 10% |
| Zinc | 60% | 60% |

* Amount in cereal. A serving of cereal plus skim milk provides 1g Total Fat, less than 5mg Cholesterol, 290mg Sodium, 36g Total Carbohydrate (11g Total Sugars), 7g Protein, 3mcg Vitamin D, 170mg Calcium, 320mg Potassium.

** The % Daily Value (DV) tells you how much a nutrient in a serving of food contributes to a daily diet. 2,000 calories a day is used for general nutrition advice.

**Ingredients: Whole Grain Wheat, Sugar, Honey, Salt. Vitamin E** (mixed tocopherols) **Added to Preserve Freshness.**

**Vitamins and Minerals: Iron and Zinc** (mineral nutrients), **Vitamin C** (sodium ascorbate), **A B Vitamin** (niacinamide), **Vitamin $B_6$** (pyridoxine hydrochloride), **Vitamin $B_2$** (riboflavin), **Vitamin $B_1$** (thiamin mononitrate), **Vitamin A** (palmitate), **A B Vitamin** (folic acid), **Vitamin $B_{12}$, Vitamin $D_3$.**

**CONTAINS WHEAT; MAY CONTAIN ALMOND INGREDIENTS.**

DISTRIBUTED BY **GENERAL MILLS SALES, INC.,** MINNEAPOLIS, MN 55440 USA

**Contains Bioengineered Food Ingredients**
*Learn more at* Ask.GeneralMills.com

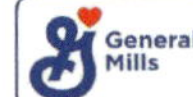



Patent: generalmills.com/pat

**This package is sold by weight, not by volume. You can be assured of proper weight even though some settling of contents normally occurs during shipment and handling.**

F 3138224123 SSG 3316502123

WHEATIES™

0 16000 27565 2

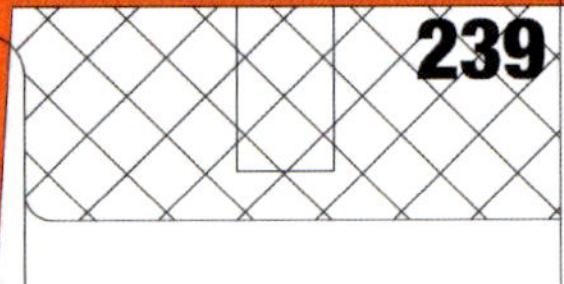

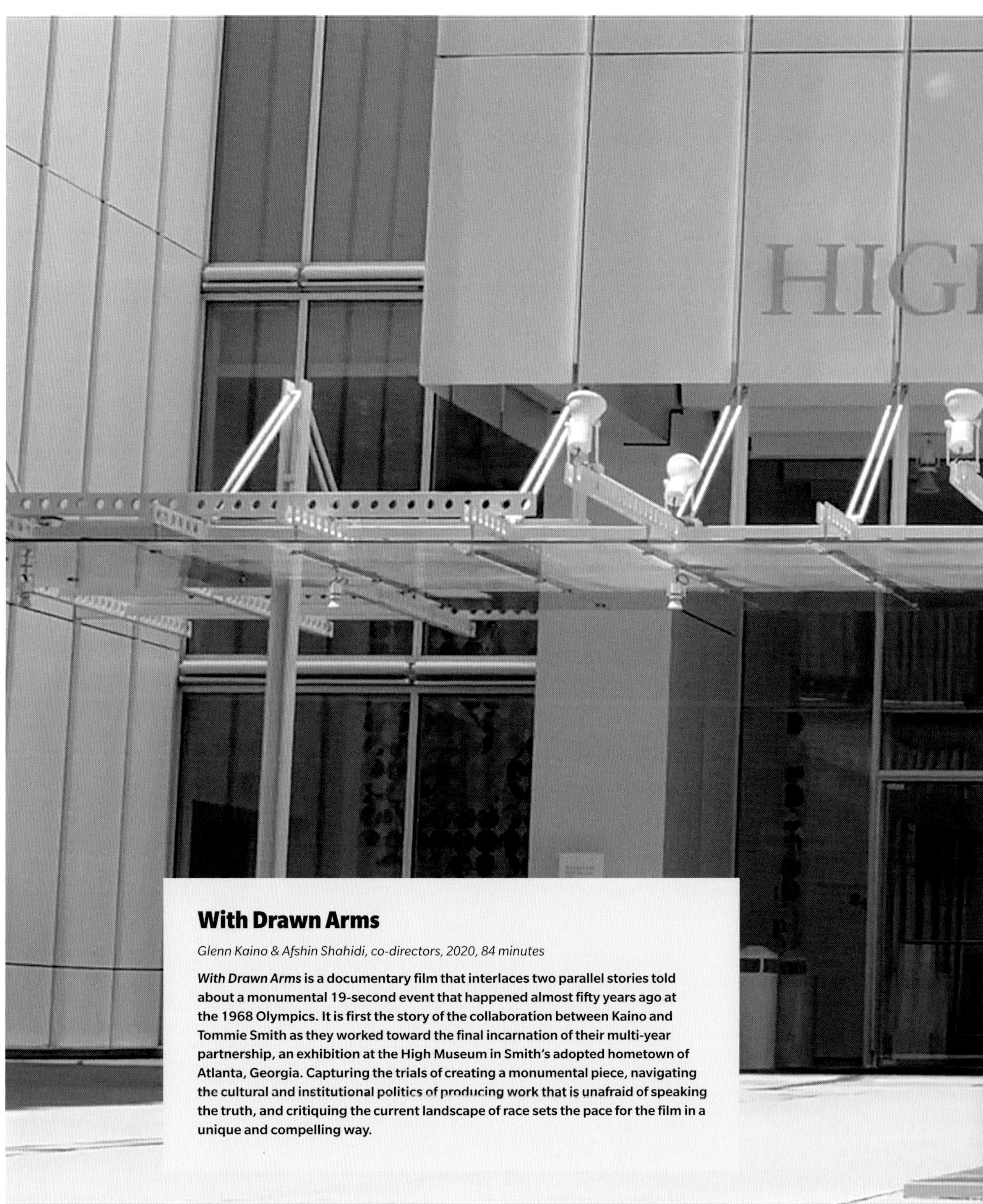


## With Drawn Arms

*Glenn Kaino & Afshin Shahidi, co-directors, 2020, 84 minutes*

***With Drawn Arms*** **is a documentary film that interlaces two parallel stories told about a monumental 19-second event that happened almost fifty years ago at the 1968 Olympics. It is first the story of the collaboration between Kaino and Tommie Smith as they worked toward the final incarnation of their multi-year partnership, an exhibition at the High Museum in Smith's adopted hometown of Atlanta, Georgia. Capturing the trials of creating a monumental piece, navigating the cultural and institutional politics of producing work that is unafraid of speaking the truth, and critiquing the current landscape of race sets the pace for the film in a unique and compelling way.**

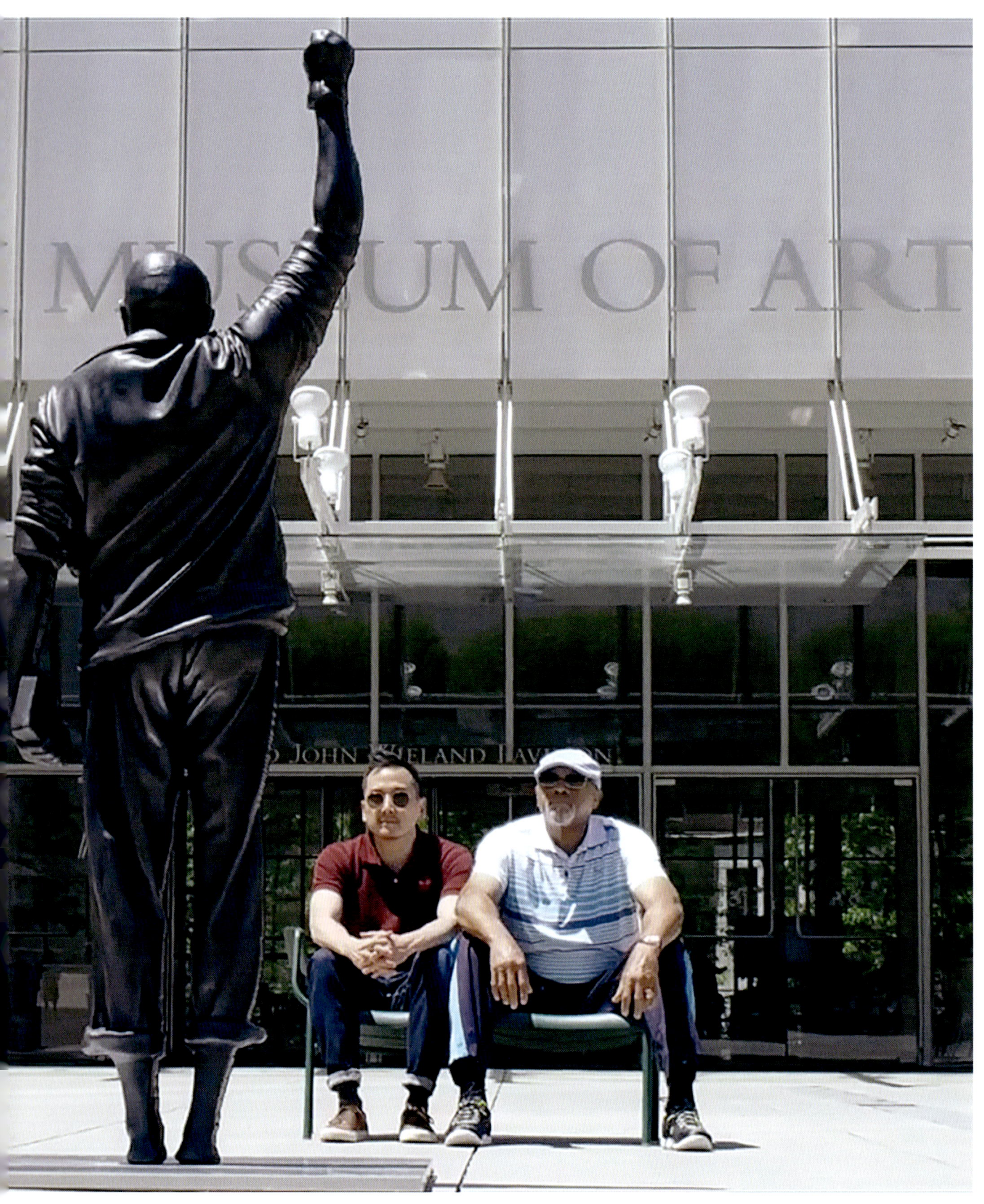
OF
JOHN

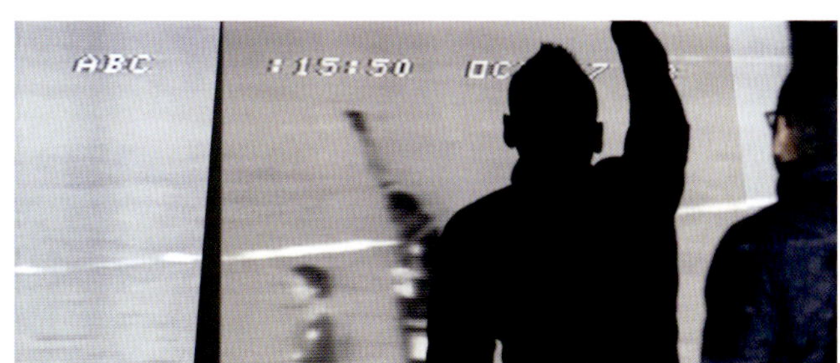


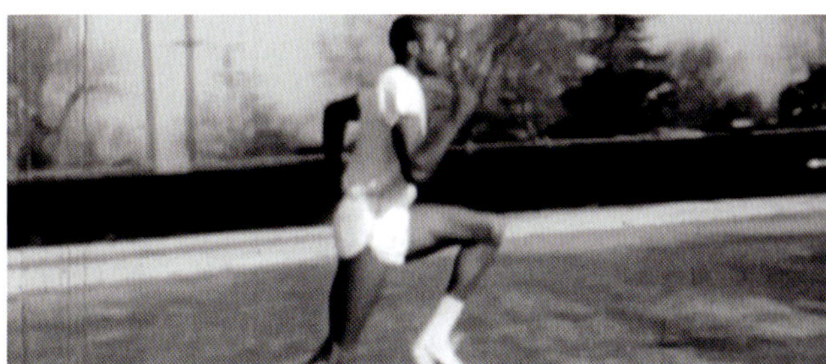

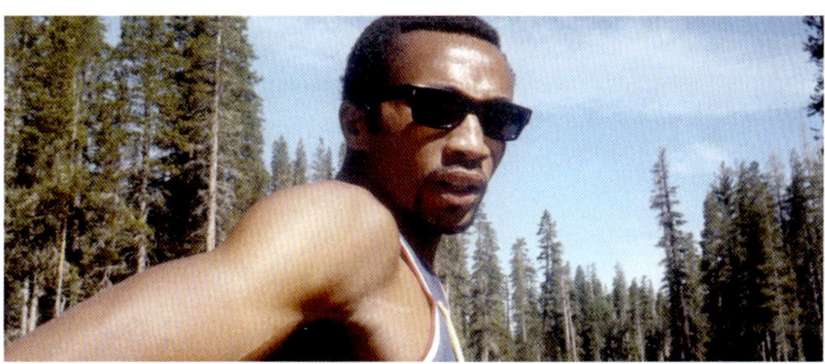

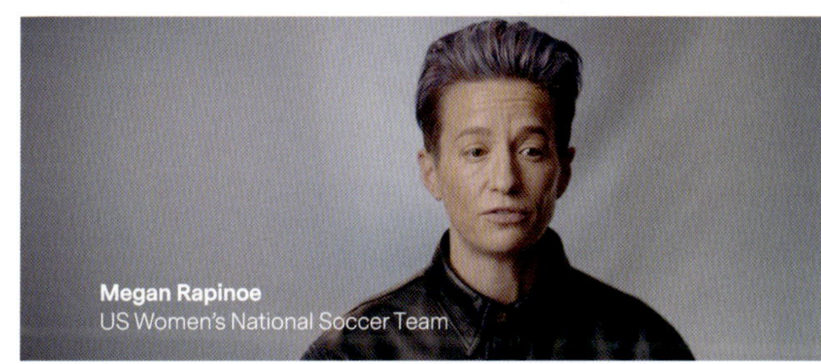


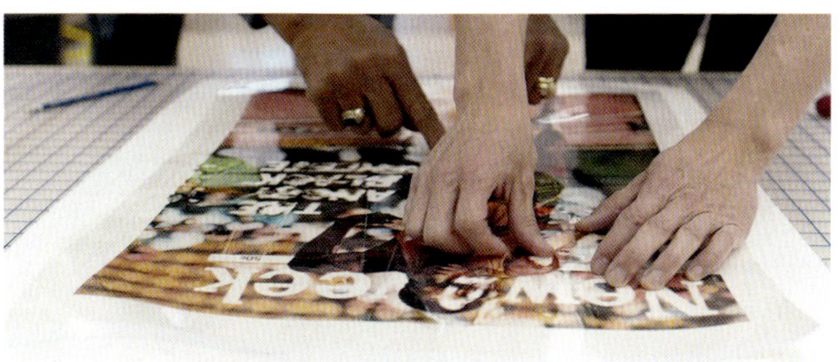

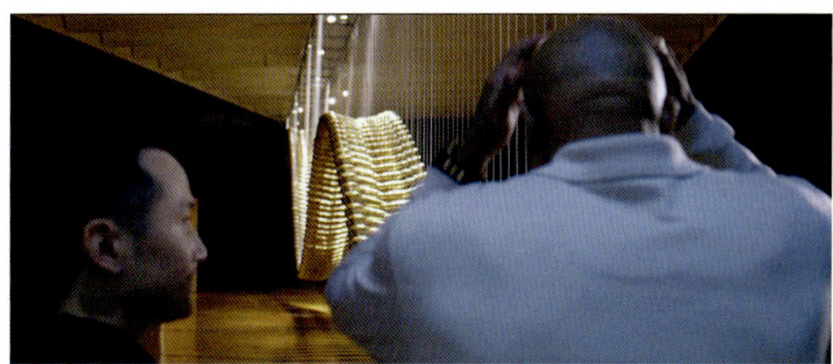

*With Drawn Arms* film stills

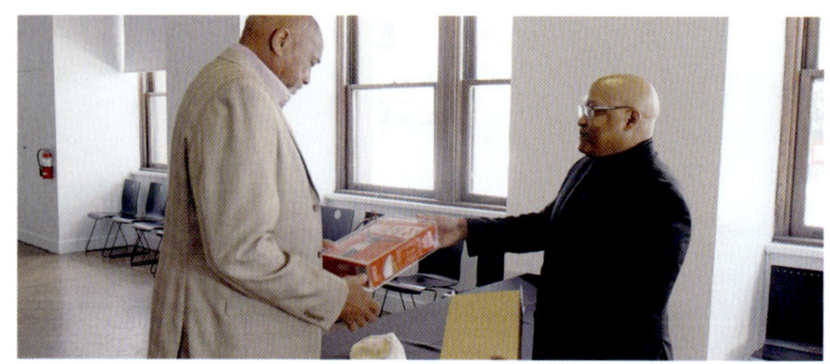

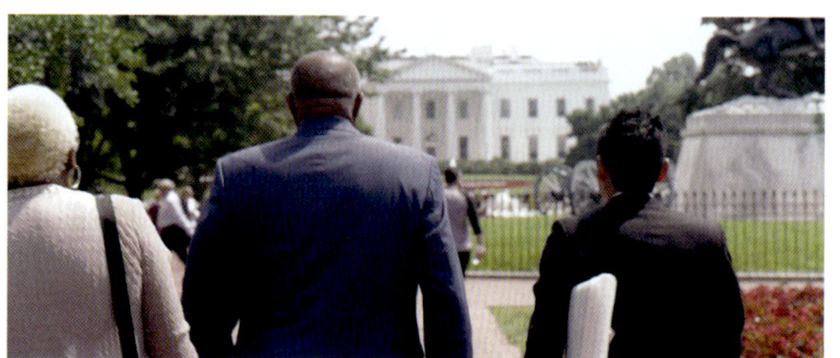

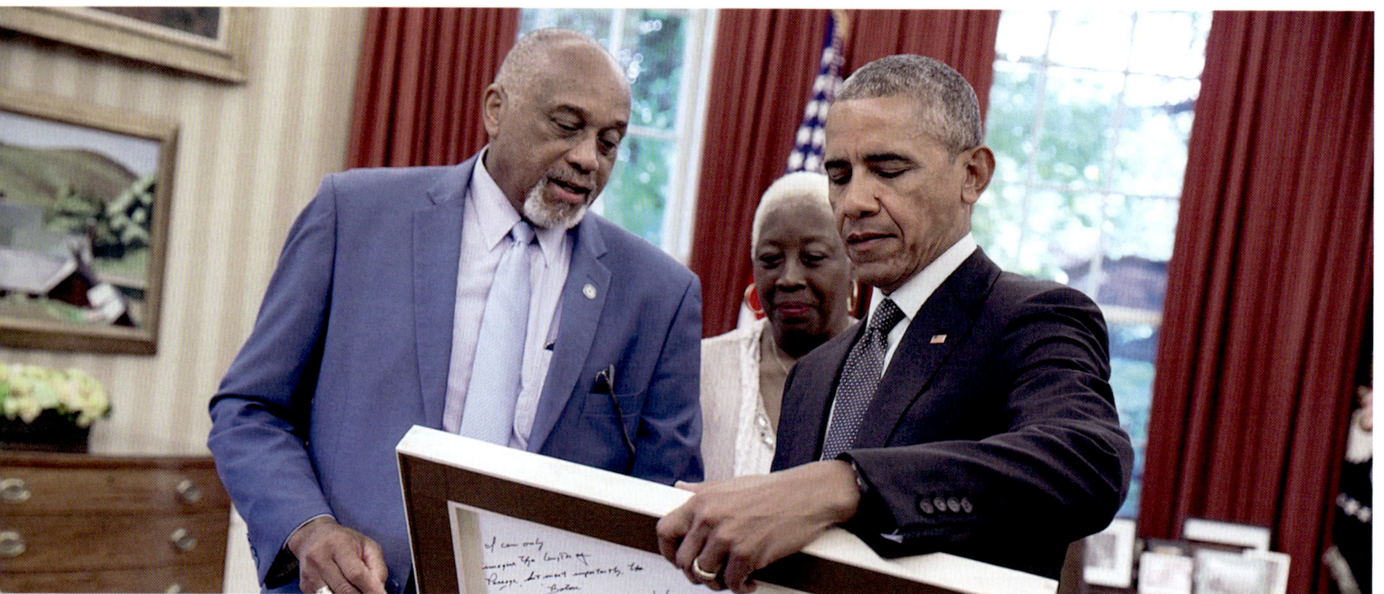

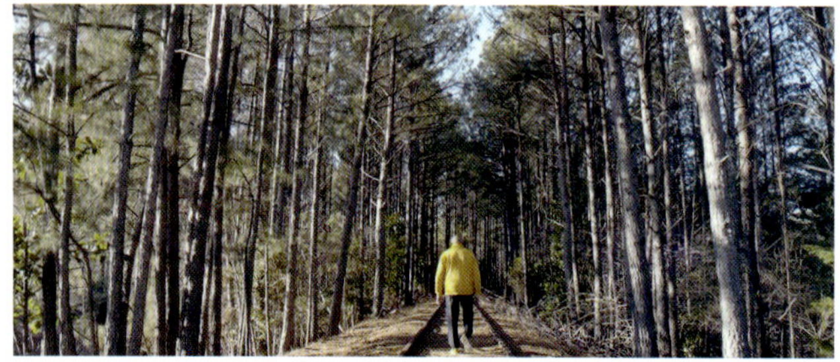

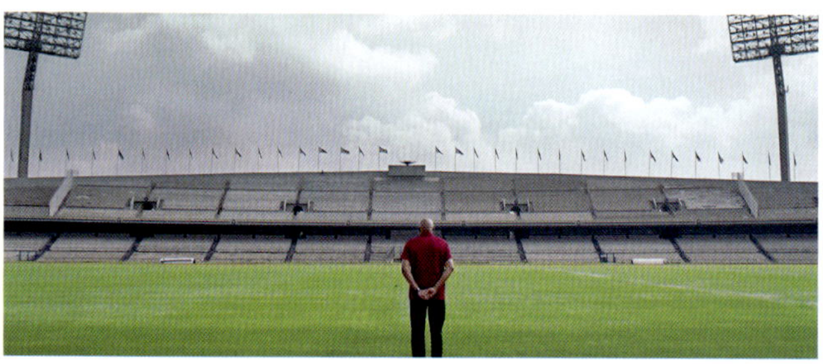

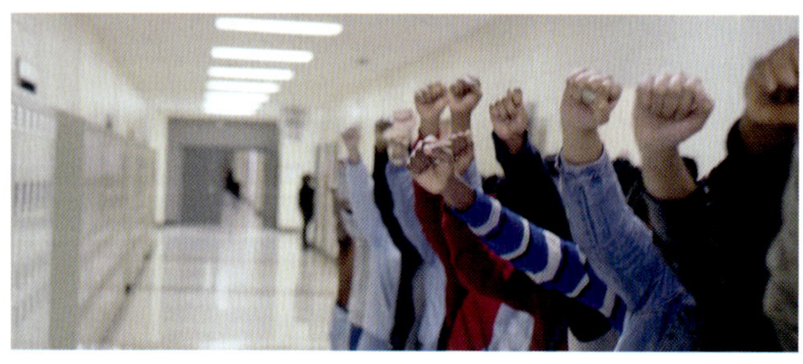

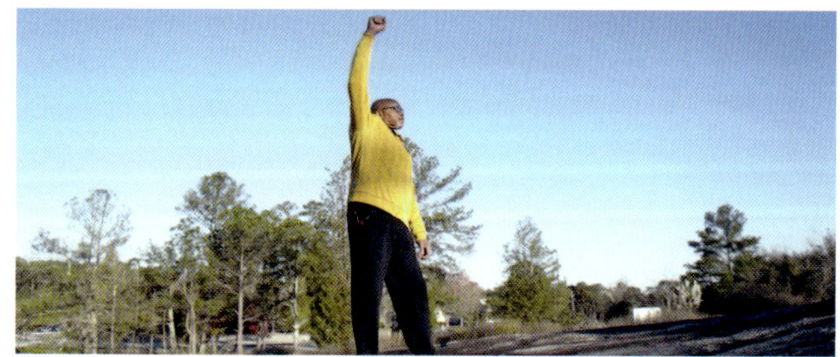

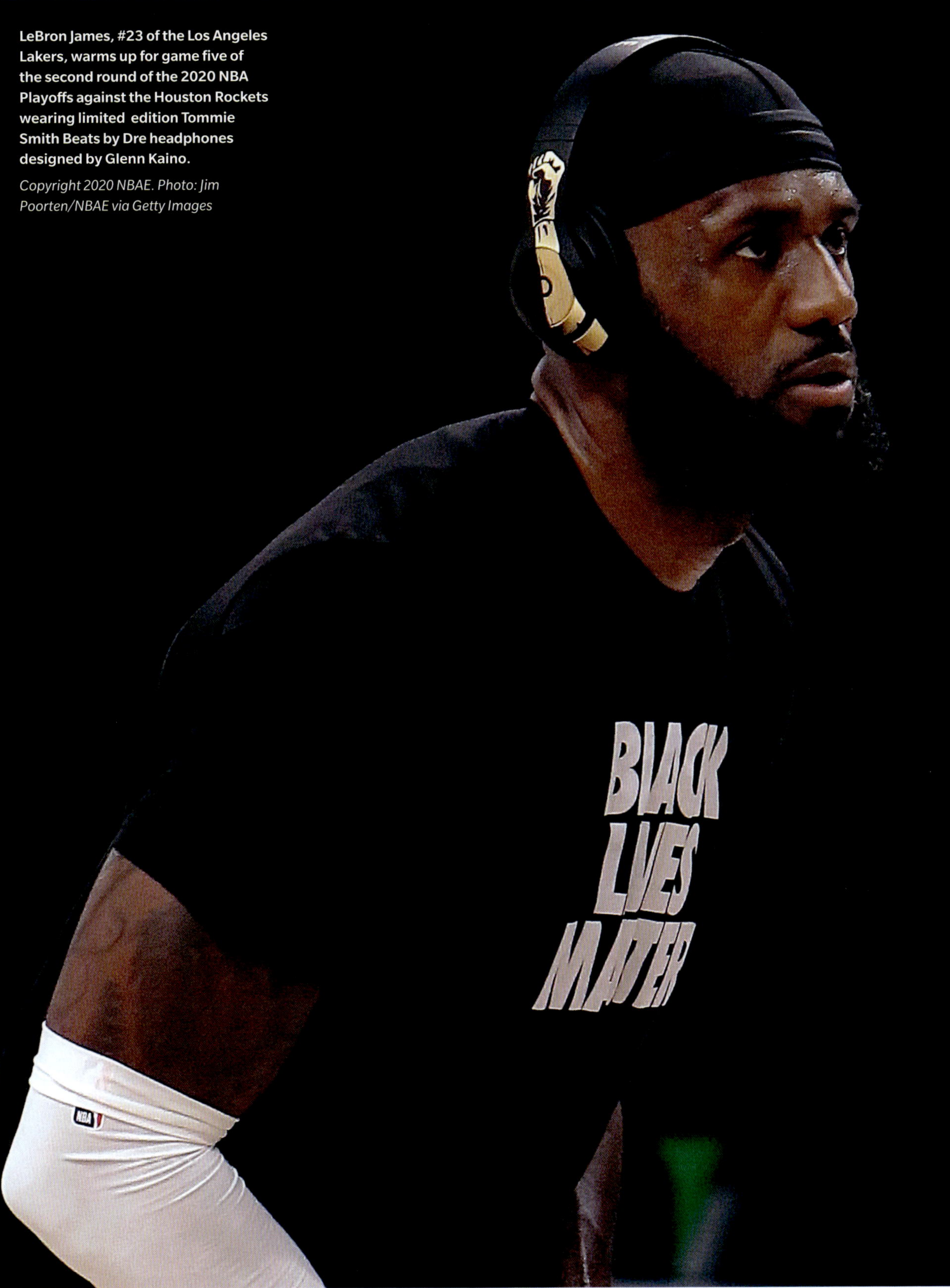


**LeBron James, #23 of the Los Angeles Lakers, warms up for game five of the second round of the 2020 NBA Playoffs against the Houston Rockets wearing limited edition Tommie Smith Beats by Dre headphones designed by Glenn Kaino.**

*Copyright 2020 NBAE. Photo: Jim Poorten/NBAE via Getty Images*

## Unite

*Ongoing, Multimedia*

**UNITE is a multifarious project centered on a holistic strategy to widely disseminate the ideological position unearthed by Kaino and Tommie Smith during their years-long collaboration. The two agreed that "Unite" was the appropriate word to describe how Smith would like his legacy to be memorialized, and the Glenn Kaino Studio created a design that was applied across various implementations—first executed as a series of silkscreen prints at Anderson Ranch Arts Center in Snowmass Village, Colorado. The posters were distributed to March for Our Lives protestors, who used them for their own messages, connecting Smith's historic salute to a new generation of activists. Subsequently, t-shirts were designed and a custom set of headphones created by Kaino for Beats by Dre, which were distributed to professional athletes such as LeBron James, Jayson Tatum, Deshaun Watson, Odell Beckham Jr., and more.**

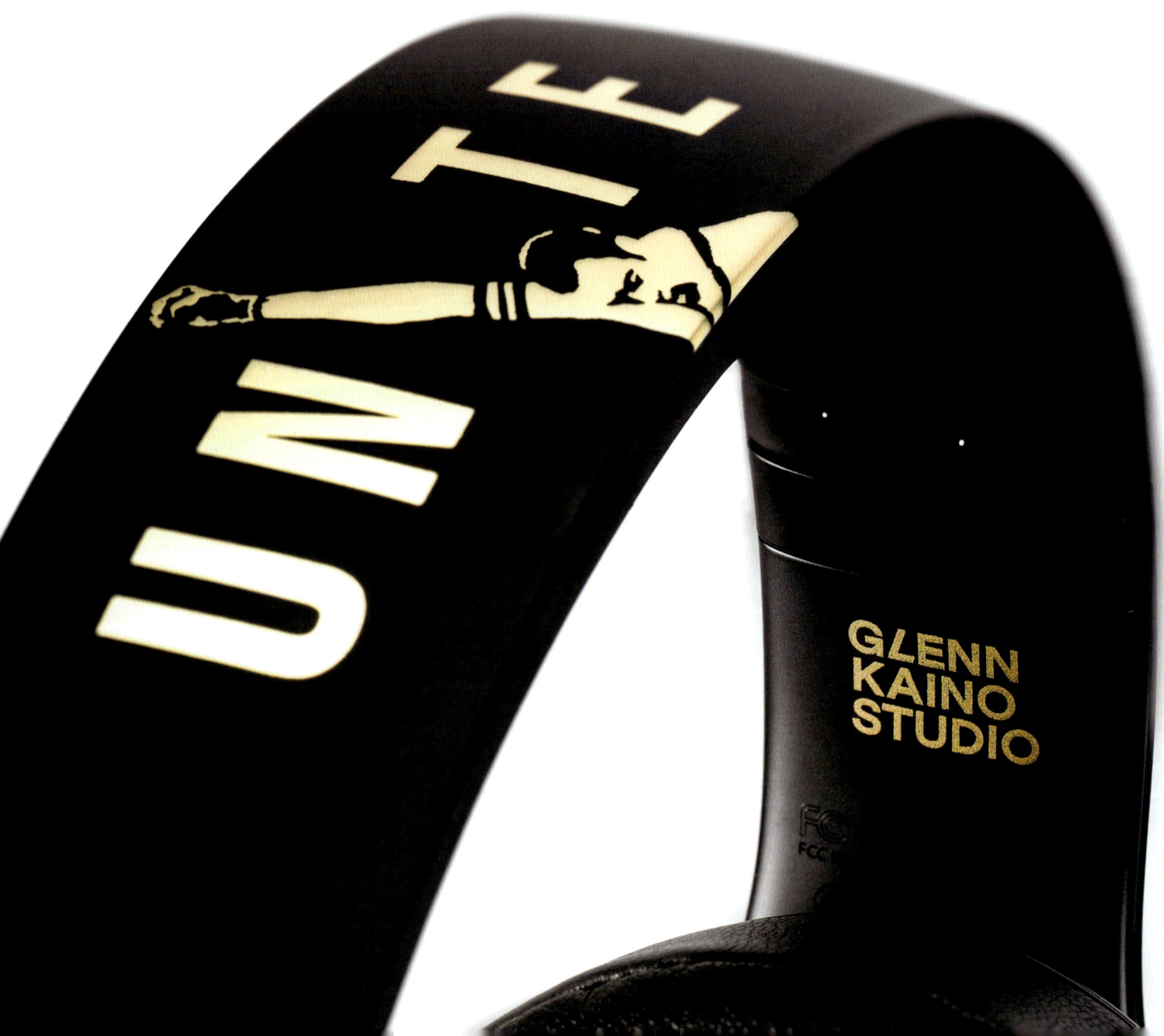

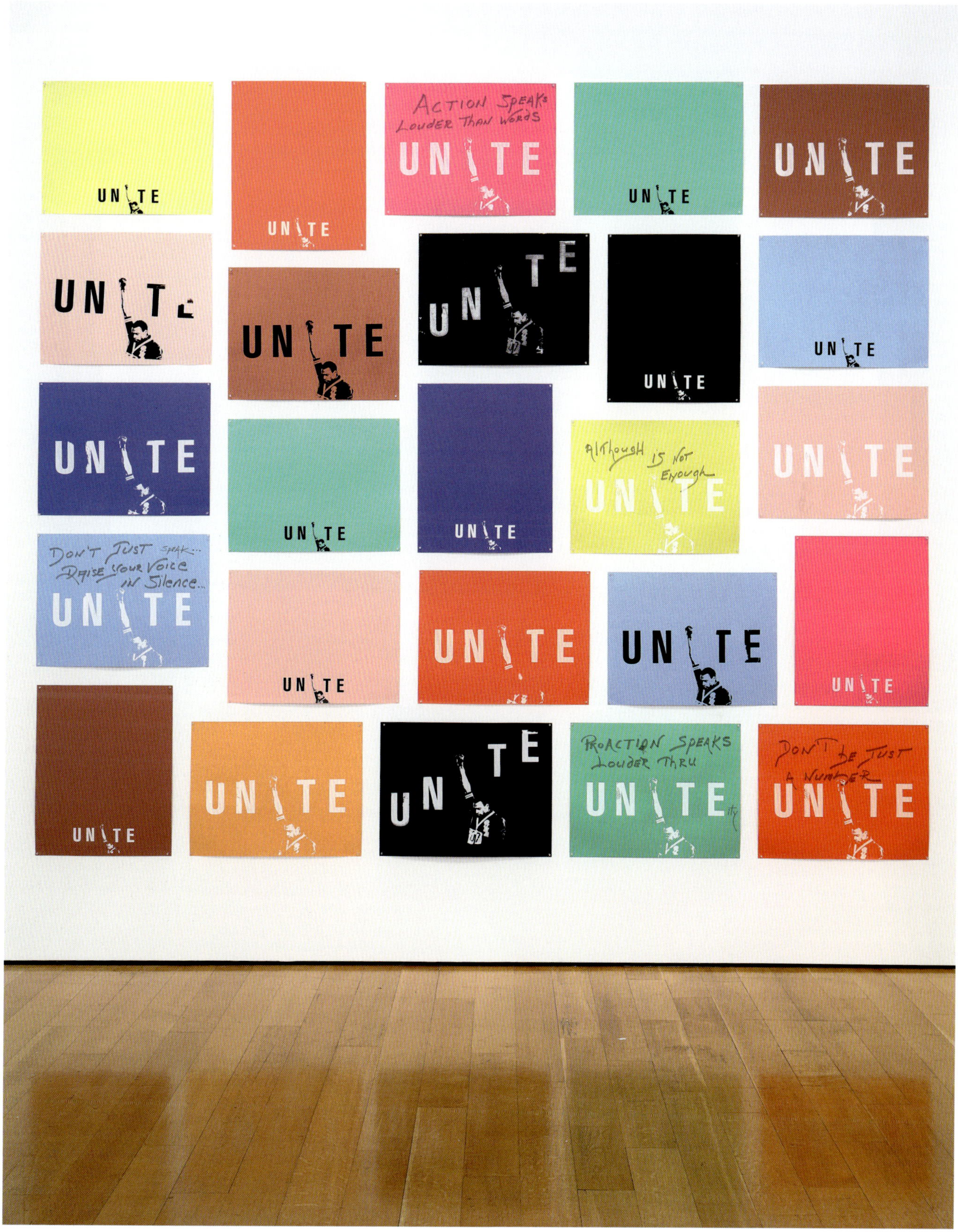

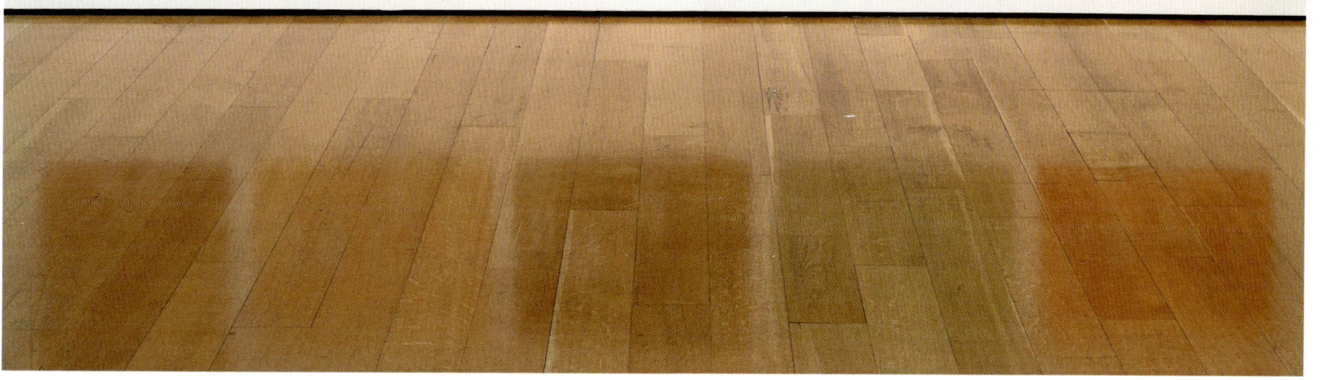
ACTION SPEAKS LOUDER THAN WORDS
UNITE
Although is not Enough
UNITE
DON'T JUST speak... RAISE YOUR VOICE IN Silence...
UNITE
PROACTION SPEAKS LOUDER THRU
UNITE ity
DON'T BE JUST A NUMBER
UNITE

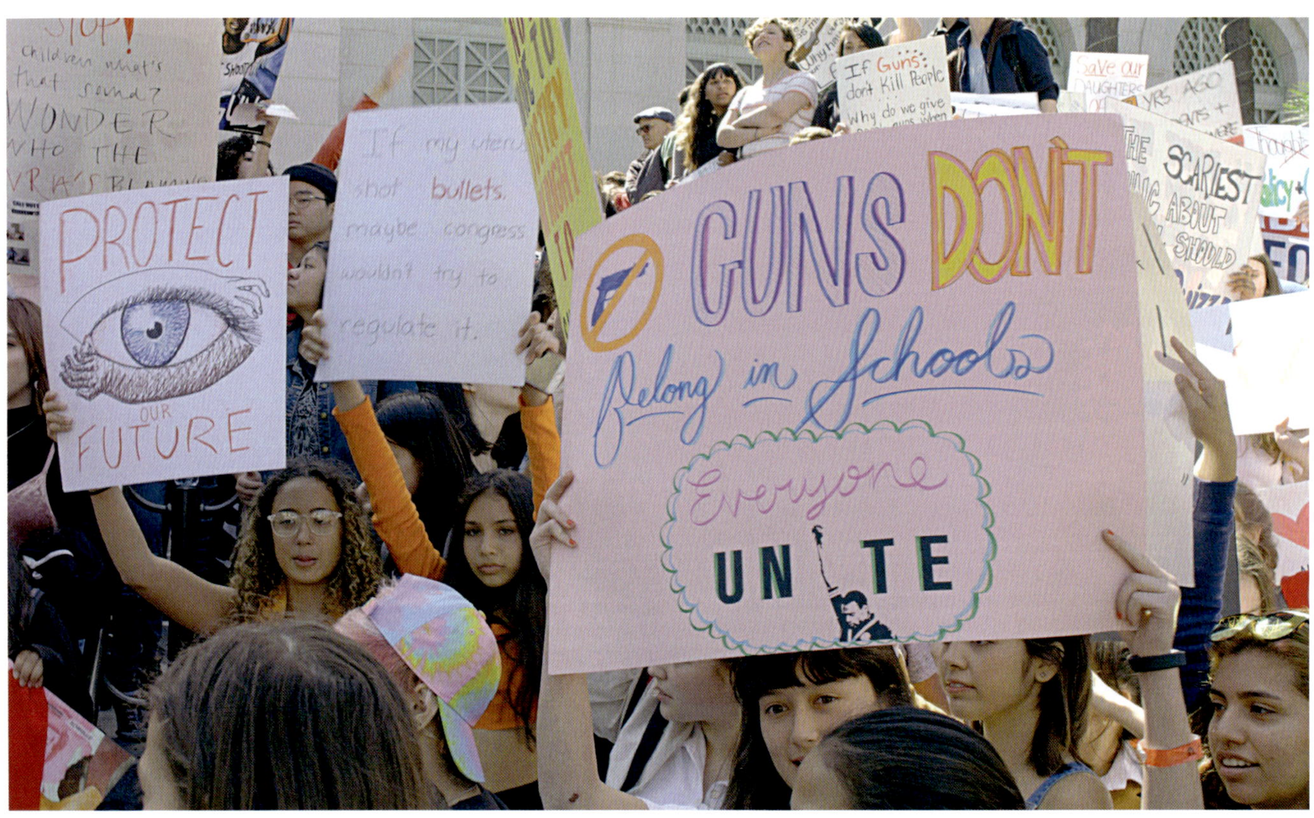


**(Above) Film still from *With Drawn Arms***

**(Left) Unite posters, 2018, Ink on paper, created at Anderson Ranch Visiting Artists Program**

*Photo: Mike Jensen*

Unwittingly, we inhabit an imperceptible, complex, astronomical weather system. The earth is awash in perpetual storms of invisible particles. Hot fat plumes of solar plasma erupt and spray winds over the rocky planets. Exploding stars launch cosmic rays, bare nuclei, into our atmosphere from across the galaxy, initiating cascading showers of nuclear reactions. An impalpable halo of dark matter envelops our galaxy as we orbit the shadow of a black hole 26,000 light-years away. We are insensible to these invisible tempests. We meander through a parallel atmosphere, distracted by the flickering bright shiny objects of the visible world, though they amount to less than 5 percent of the entire universe.

Glenn Kaino wants to remind you of the teeming reality of the unseen with the illuminated tracks of particle sprays in his *Cloud Chamber* (2020), or the childlike delight of glistening aquamarine plankton in *Wish* (2020), or a riveting statue titled *Invisible Man* (2016) that depicts iconic athlete and activist Tommie Smith as a mirrored silhouette that disappears and reappears with a shift in perspective. These reminders of the invisible also provoke us to question our presumptions of visibility. True, we are unable to viscerally perceive much of the phenomena that surround us. True, we are limited to our direct perception of familiar experience. And it is also true that our perception of familiar experience falsely represents reality. Nothing is as it seems.

We are not universally visible.

I stand in the sunlight and the rays that have traveled to me for eight minutes from that roiling nuclear furnace scatter off my hand to create the illusion that my flesh is solid. But I know that the atoms in my body are mostly empty space. Atoms are composed of tiny nuclei on the order of a thousandth of a trillionth of a meter, surrounded by elusive electron clouds. Comparatively, the spacing between nuclei is vast, hundreds of thousands of times bigger than the nuclei themselves. If I could perceive the world without light negotiating the information, I would be cognizant that I am a tenuous collection of a thousand trillion minute particles moving as an ensemble like subatomic insects in a swarm. The walls of my building would vanish, and the floor, and the very earth—all exposed as the predominance of near emptiness they hide behind their reflective facades. On a deeper level, all of the matter and energy in the cosmos may be reducible to a symphony of fundamental strings. Regardless, we are assured that our familiar material world is essentially porous and scant.

The solidity of the world that we navigate, that we see and touch, is an illusion imparted to us through our electromagnetic interactions. Eyes are a glorious mechanism for collecting an accordioned bandwidth of light, oscillating electromagnetic fields. Our eyes are intricately, astronomically sculpted, tuned to a specific star. Our sun's radiance peaks in yellow light and, consequently, so does our vision, quickly falling off for hotter blue light and cooler red light. The rest of the electromagnetic spectrum is invisible to us, and we are invisible to any ocular mechanism tuned to a vastly different bandwidth. High-energy light, like X-rays, notices that we are mostly empty space and passes right through our skin and muscles. Our bones are dense enough to scatter X-rays, hence their medical use for inspecting our internal workings. The higher-energy gamma-rays are undeterred even by bone and pass right through our marrow, transiting our skeletons right now with only occasional damage to our cells.

If I could dial the human eye's sensitivity to a different range of frequencies, like tuning a radio to catch a particular frequency, my hand would be rendered invisible, a collection of sparsely distributed nuclei and their quantum clouds of electrons. A radio itself is a light detector. We cannot see a radio wave, which is just the name for a bandwidth of light used historically to encode the data transmitted by radios, because our eyes were not designed for those frequencies. They are invisible to us and we to them. We inhabit an ocean of light that we simply cannot detect, a veritable storm of rays that we encode with a glut of information. We intentionally attach data to electromagnetic fields that do not stimulate our optic mechanism. These signals ping our phones and our computers and our televisions and our radios, but not our eyes. We do this precisely so that we are not blinded by the overwhelming chaos, so that we can move through this sea that is invisible to us, but not to our gadgets.

Visual perception is not merely the collection of light. The detection is converted through electromagnetic signals in the body to the ethereal consciousness. The light sensors that we have inherited absorb the narrow range of light, visible light, and translate that information to our minds. As a consequence of the qualia of perception, we are compelled to believe a myriad of untruths. I am compelled to believe the visible world that I observe is solid. I am compelled to believe my skin separates my insides from the outside, that the wood planks on the thirtieth floor of a building are unremitting and substantial as opposed to transparent voids. Our perception of corporeality is an absurdly distorted simulation that may exist solely in the minds of terrestrial animals.

We are only visible to creatures with light detectors similar to ours. We should expect to be invisible to aliens. If creatures evolve eyes on exoplanets around different suns, undoubtedly they will be tuned to a completely different range of light, possibly a frequency of light that we do not reflect efficiently. An alien might only see the storm of wifi and not us. Eyes themselves may not evolve. Imagine a planet around a faint dead star or a black hole. There will be no evolutionary pressure to detect light and sentient life in those solar systems will have never known sight. They may map their terrain with different senses, exploiting echolocation or smell or a magnetic sense. Perhaps they too have evolved consciousness and qualia and their internal experience of their non-visual sensory data is rich with analogues to color, depth, beauty, ugliness, dimness, shadow, and luminosity.

Most spectacular in the roster of evasive phenomena is the dark sector of the universe. By definition, dark matter does not interact electromagnetically. Dark matter cannot emit or reflect light. That's the essence of dark matter, perhaps better described as invisible matter. We see right through dark particles as they stream into and out of us unimpeded. We are as invisible to dark matter as it is to us. We could occupy the same location as a dark matter creature, effectively cohabitating each other's bodies, and remain blissfully unaware of the intrusion on our solitude. Dark energy is invisible, too, permeating every volume of the dark sky, the dominant source of energy in the universe, yet still we see only the proverbial twinkling of the smattering of stars.

Kaino's provocation, through his work, is intended to expose metaphorical invisibility, political and social invisibility. By destabilizing confidence in our own discernment, in our basic mundane observations, we are rendered more vulnerable, humbled by the awareness of our own unawareness. If we can be so misled, so fooled about the essentials of the physicality of our most convincing experiences, then we must accept the limitations of our beliefs in the far muddier terrain of human values and principles, of morality and ethics and civics. The moment Kaino disarms us with a seemingly bottomless tunnel, a wish rendered bright, sparks trailing unseen debris through a cloud, he simultaneously arms us with an altered consciousness. We are primed to imagine new perspectives on reality, on nature, on power and protest, culture and identity. Kaino instigates that openness. Beyond the gallery, elongating that moment, maintaining the apprehension that the world is not as we see it, earnestly challenging our own presumptions of certitude, allowing ourselves to imagine a different cultural reality . . . that part is on us.

# Eyes and I's

## Janna Levin

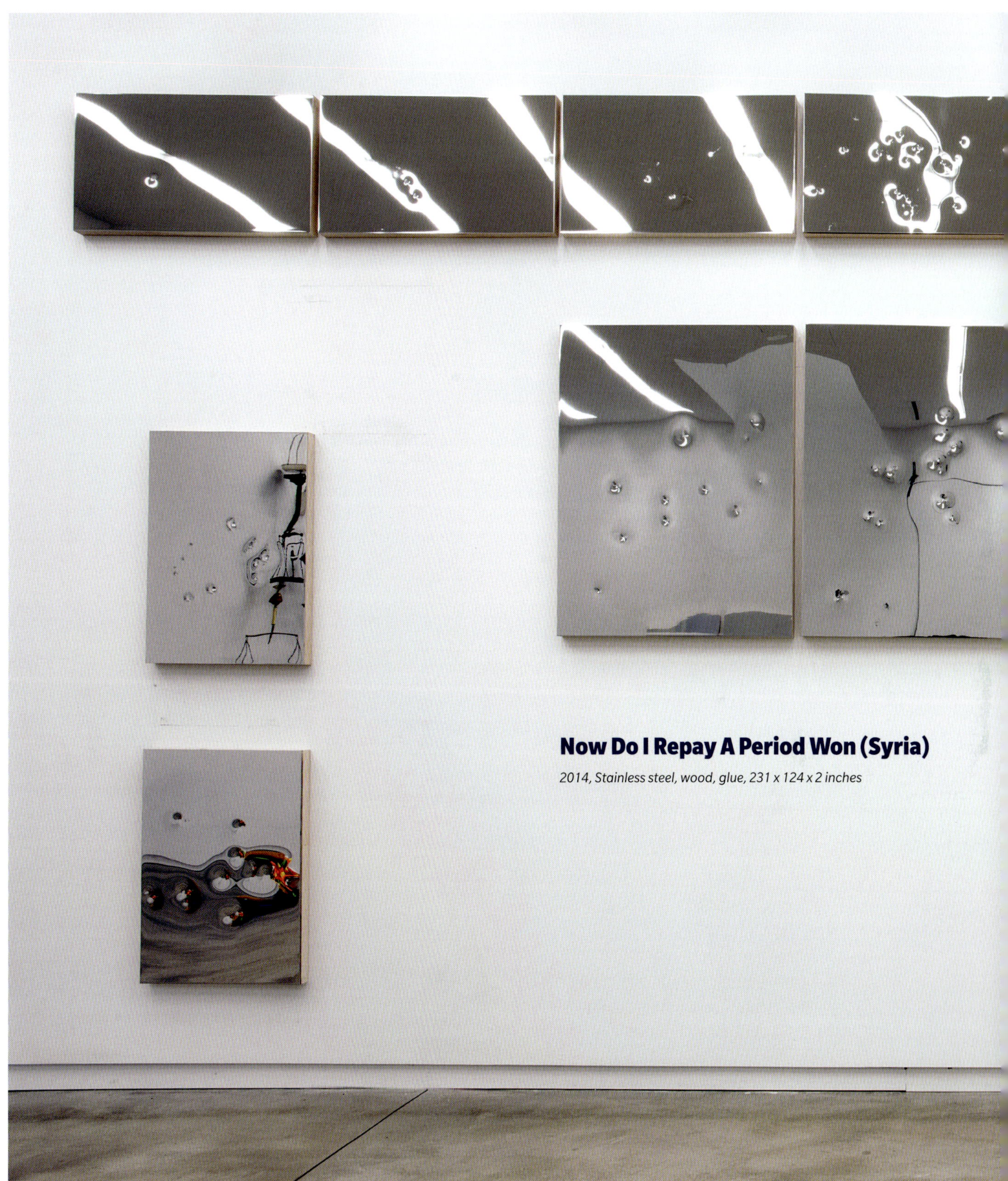

**Now Do I Repay A Period Won (Syria)**

*2014, Stainless steel, wood, glue, 231 x 124 x 2 inches*

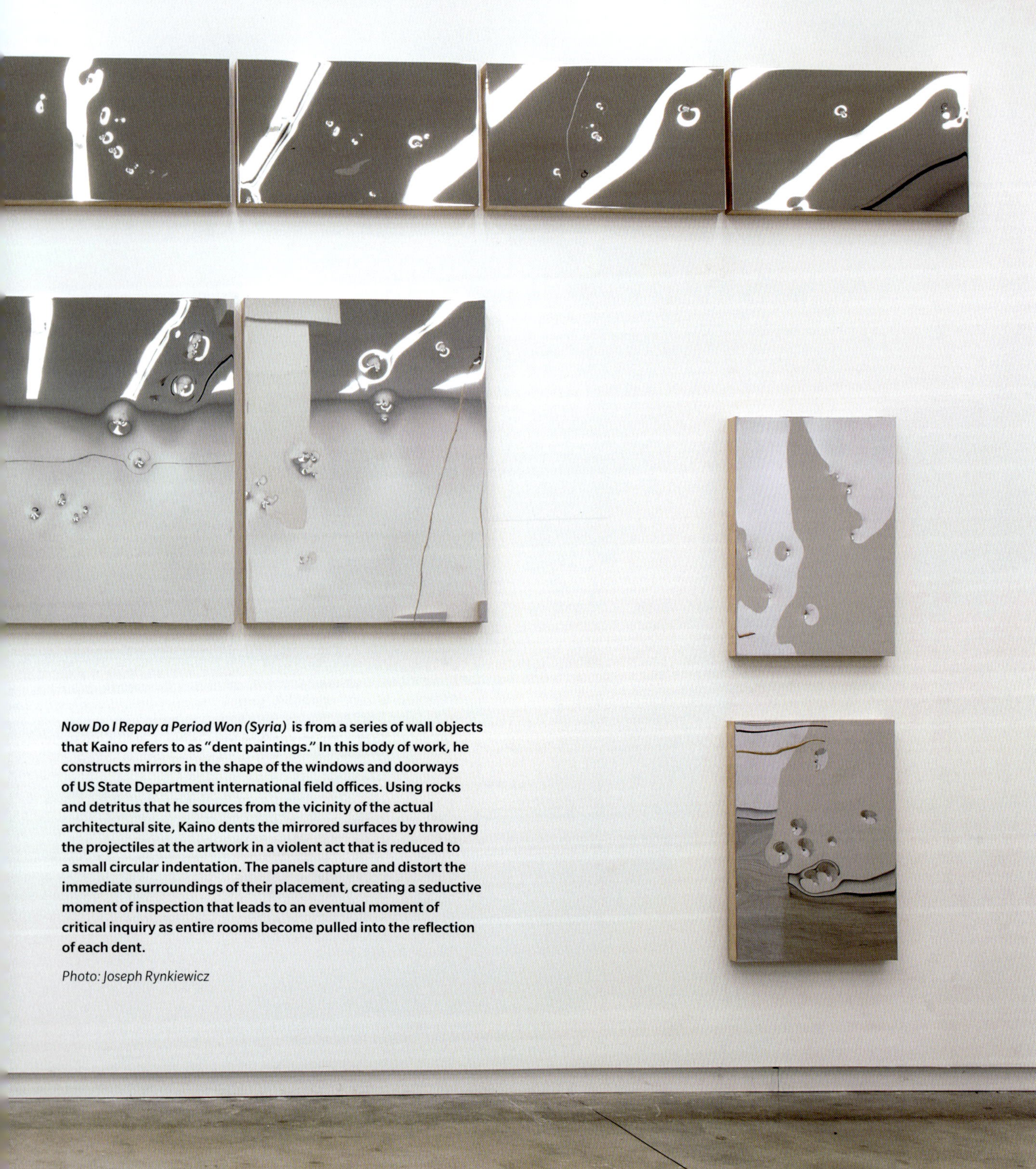

*Now Do I Repay a Period Won (Syria)* is from a series of wall objects that Kaino refers to as "dent paintings." In this body of work, he constructs mirrors in the shape of the windows and doorways of US State Department international field offices. Using rocks and detritus that he sources from the vicinity of the actual architectural site, Kaino dents the mirrored surfaces by throwing the projectiles at the artwork in a violent act that is reduced to a small circular indentation. The panels capture and distort the immediate surroundings of their placement, creating a seductive moment of inspection that leads to an eventual moment of critical inquiry as entire rooms become pulled into the reflection of each dent.

*Photo: Joseph Rynkiewicz*

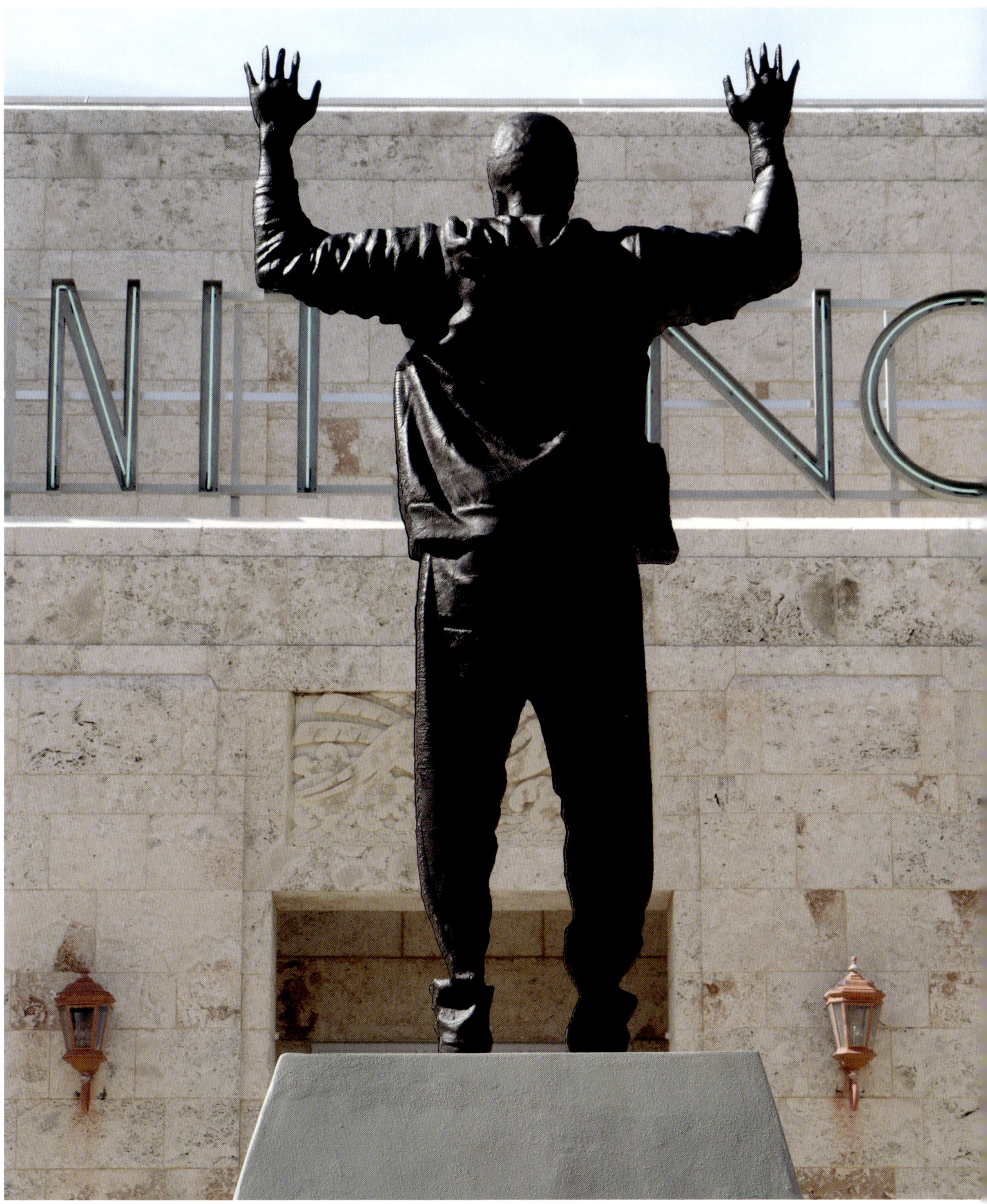

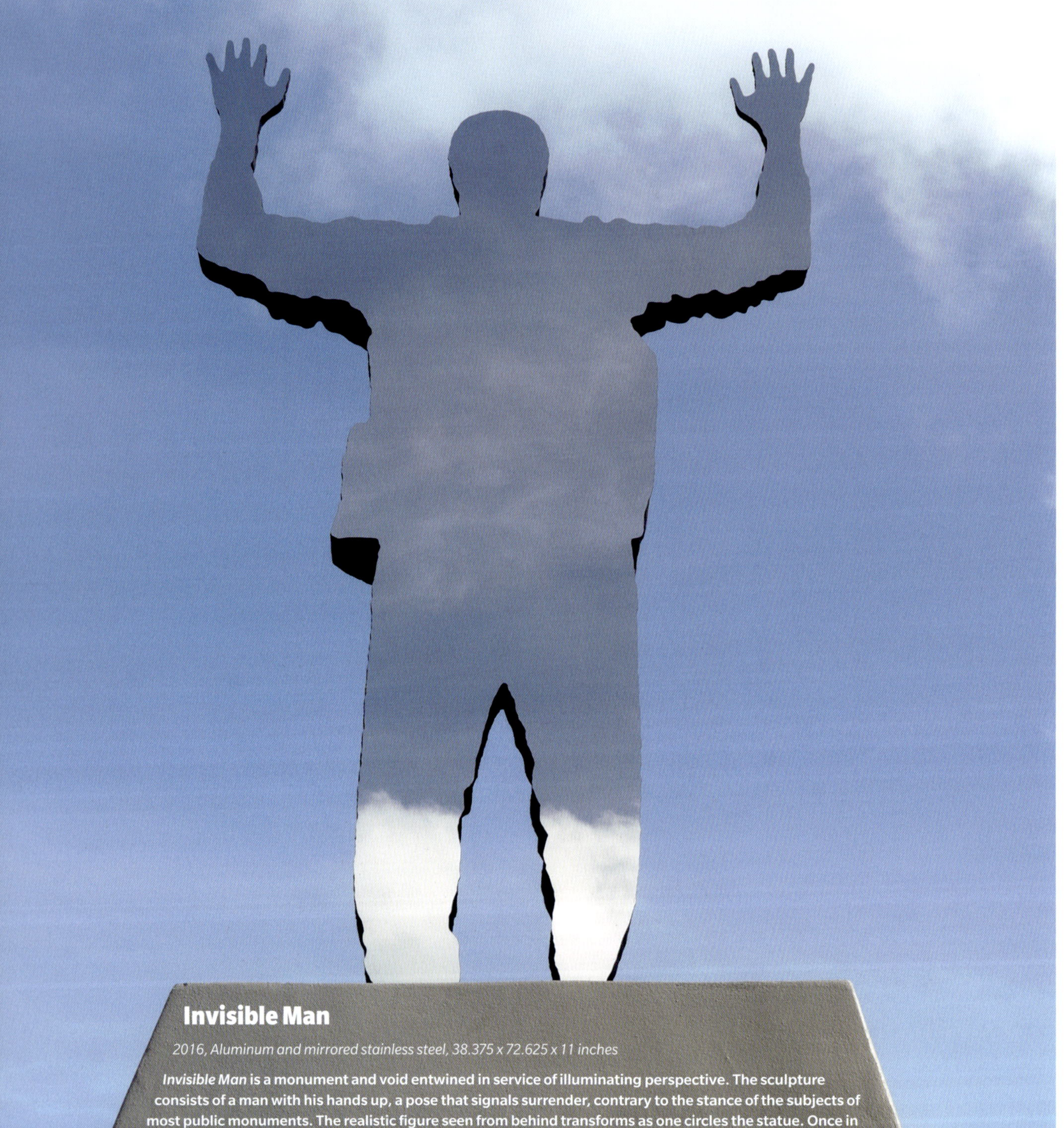

## Invisible Man

*2016, Aluminum and mirrored stainless steel, 38.375 x 72.625 x 11 inches*

***Invisible Man*** **is a monument and void entwined in service of illuminating perspective. The sculpture consists of a man with his hands up, a pose that signals surrender, contrary to the stance of the subjects of most public monuments. The realistic figure seen from behind transforms as one circles the statue. Once in front the figure disappears leaving a seemingly empty pedestal. In fact, this surface is mirrored creating either absence or reflection depending on the viewer's vantage point. The title, referencing Ralph Ellison's classic novel about visibility and race,** ***Invisible Man*** **(1952), serves as a monument to the forgotten and ignored, an interrogation of the purpose of artistic commemoration as a means toward cultural catharsis, and the political implications of canonizing figures in public spaces. Though it is said that a memorial immortalizes its subjects, memorials are ultimately objects that can be destroyed. By way of this conviction, the symbol of surrender instead emerges as an icon of defiance.**

## V|S|B|L|T|Y

*Glenn Kaino & Jesse Williams*
*2015–ongoing, Mixed-media experiential organization*

**V|S|B|L|T|Y is an organization with the mission to create interventions into a larger media landscape in order to prove that diversity can be both popular and profitable, so as to make significant positive change in our world. V|S|B|L|T|Y has consistently demonstrated the power of inclusion for products and experiences, including game-changing apps, shows, movies, and other forms of creative production. V|S|B|L|T|Y is also an experiment in scalability; ideas are expanded to the level of spectacle as a form of mass disruption and pedagogy. V|S|B|L|T|Y is behind the Webby Award-winning game BLeBRiTY, a multiple-time number-one app in the Apple Store, which has been played over five million times and been featured in numerous television and internet shows.**

*Photo: Ismail "Calligrafist" Sayeed*

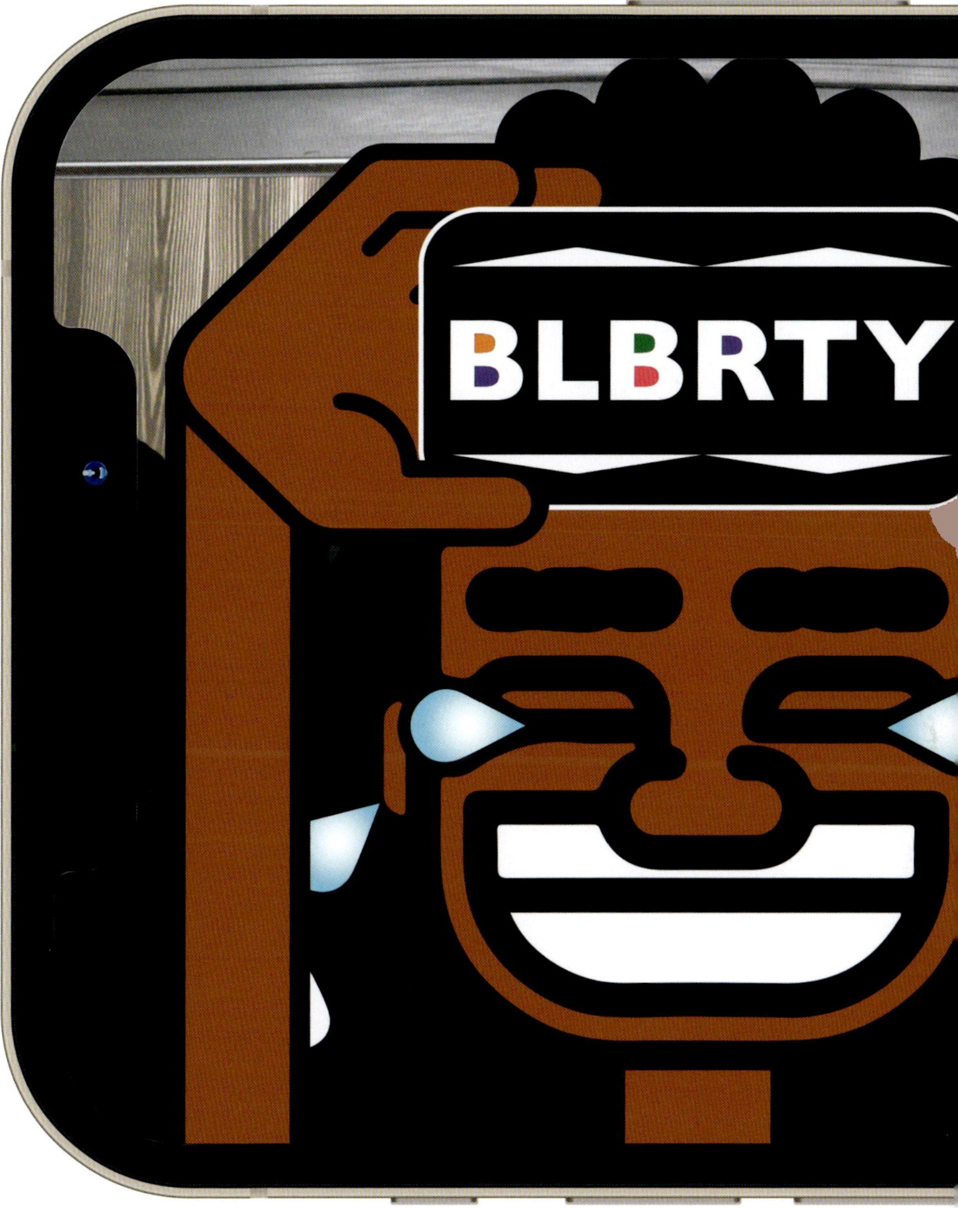

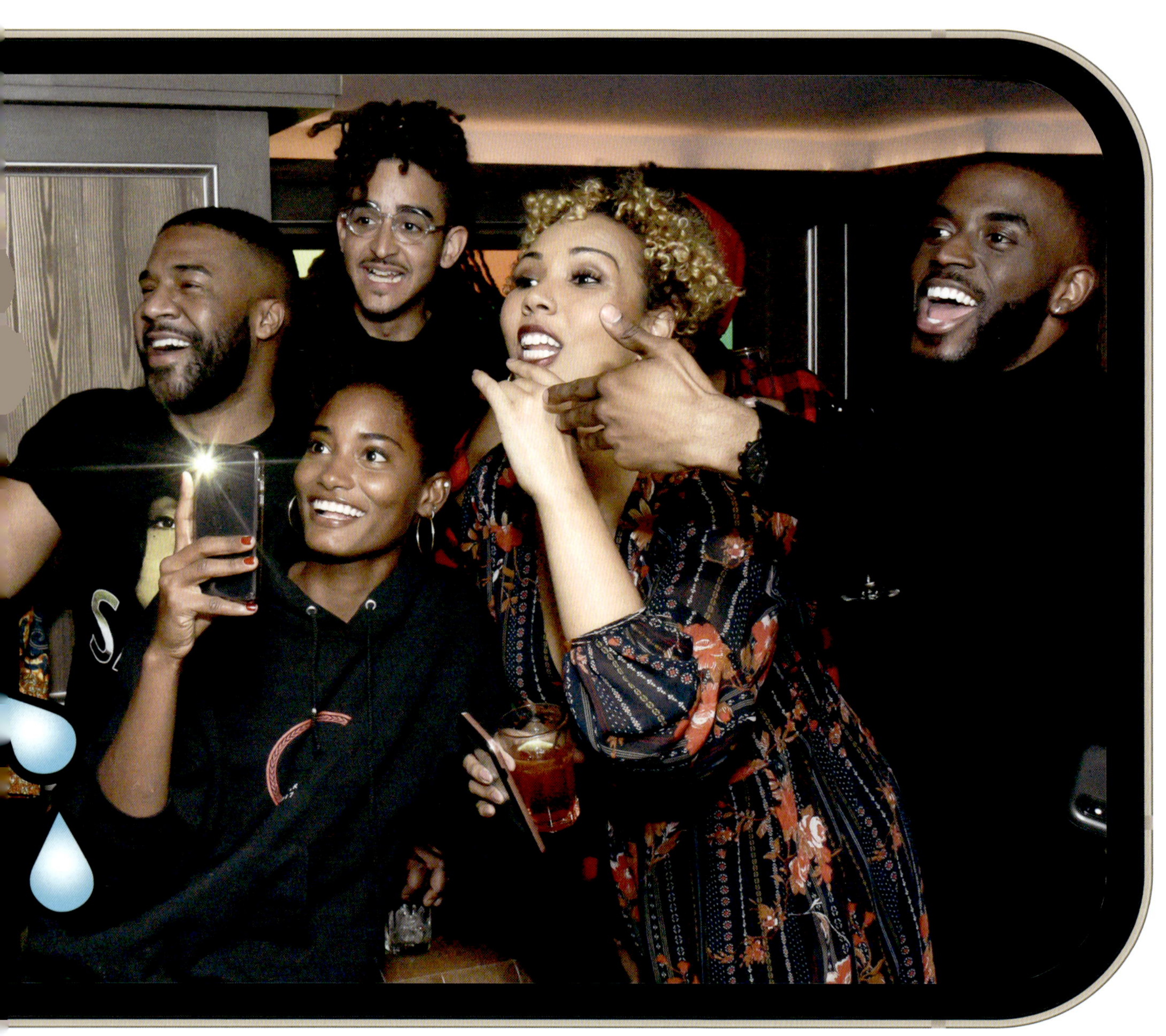

## L’ènetènafionale

*2016 , Mixed media, dimensions variable*

***L’ènetènafionale*** **is a re-creation of a nineteenth-century “Pierrot and the Moon” automaton. Upon entering the room where the sculpture is installed, the visitor’s depth perception is impaired inside the illusion of an infinite darkness. A slight mechanical sound is audible as the Moon sculpture’s eye follows the visitors’ steps. The Pierrot character is dressed in his familiar clown outfit and holds a mandolin, but his face is a smooth robotic mask, crafted to resemble the image of writer Frantz Fanon. The Moon’s eye continues to track visitors when two people are present in the room. When three or more people enter the space, the Moon’s eye closes, Pierrot begins to generate music, represented by a glowing choreography of lights in his head, and the Moon begins to sing “The Internationale,” the classic nineteenth-century French anthem of the socialist movement. When the song is finished, Pierrot and the Moon rest in silence, awaiting new visitors.**

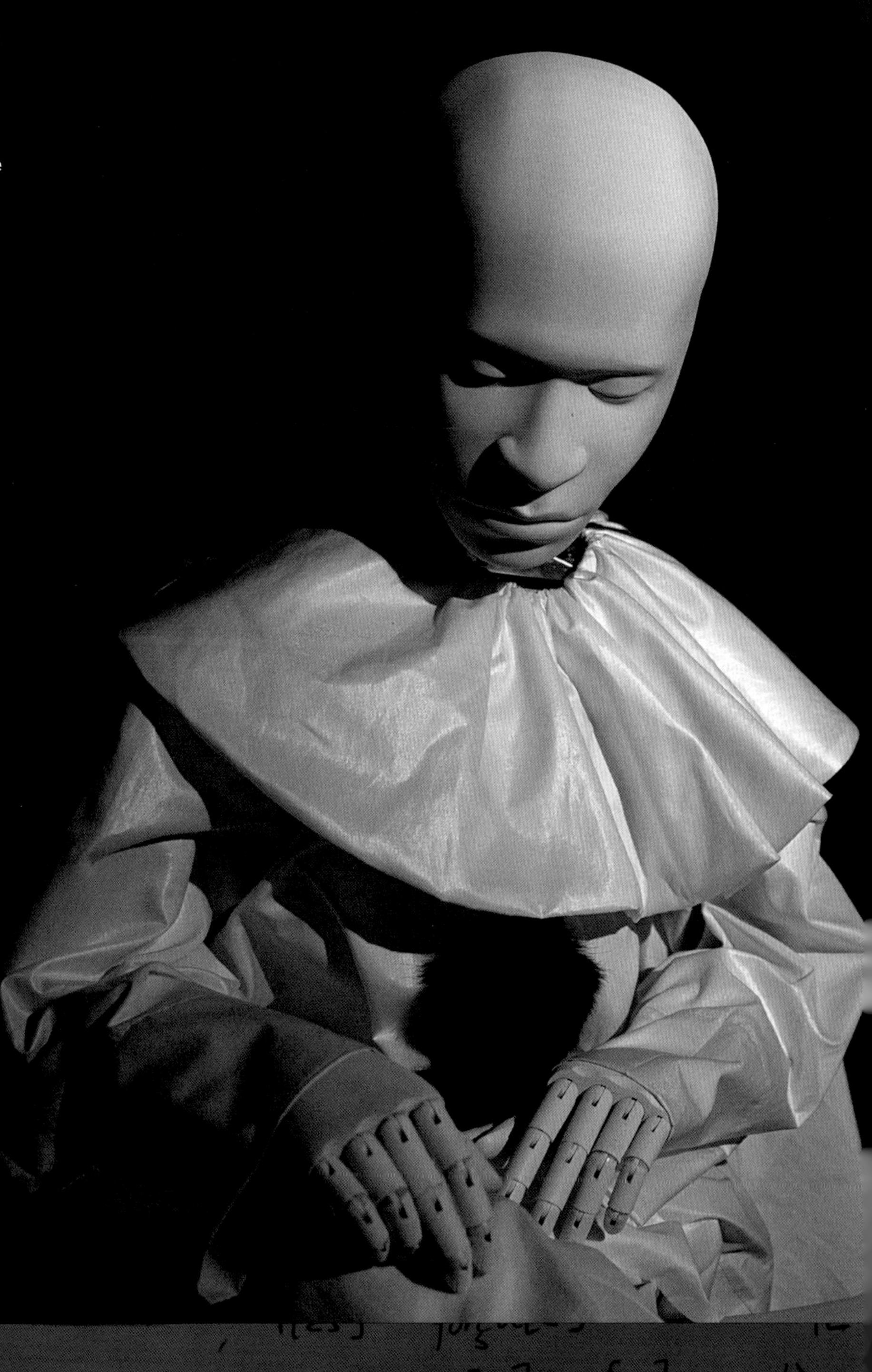

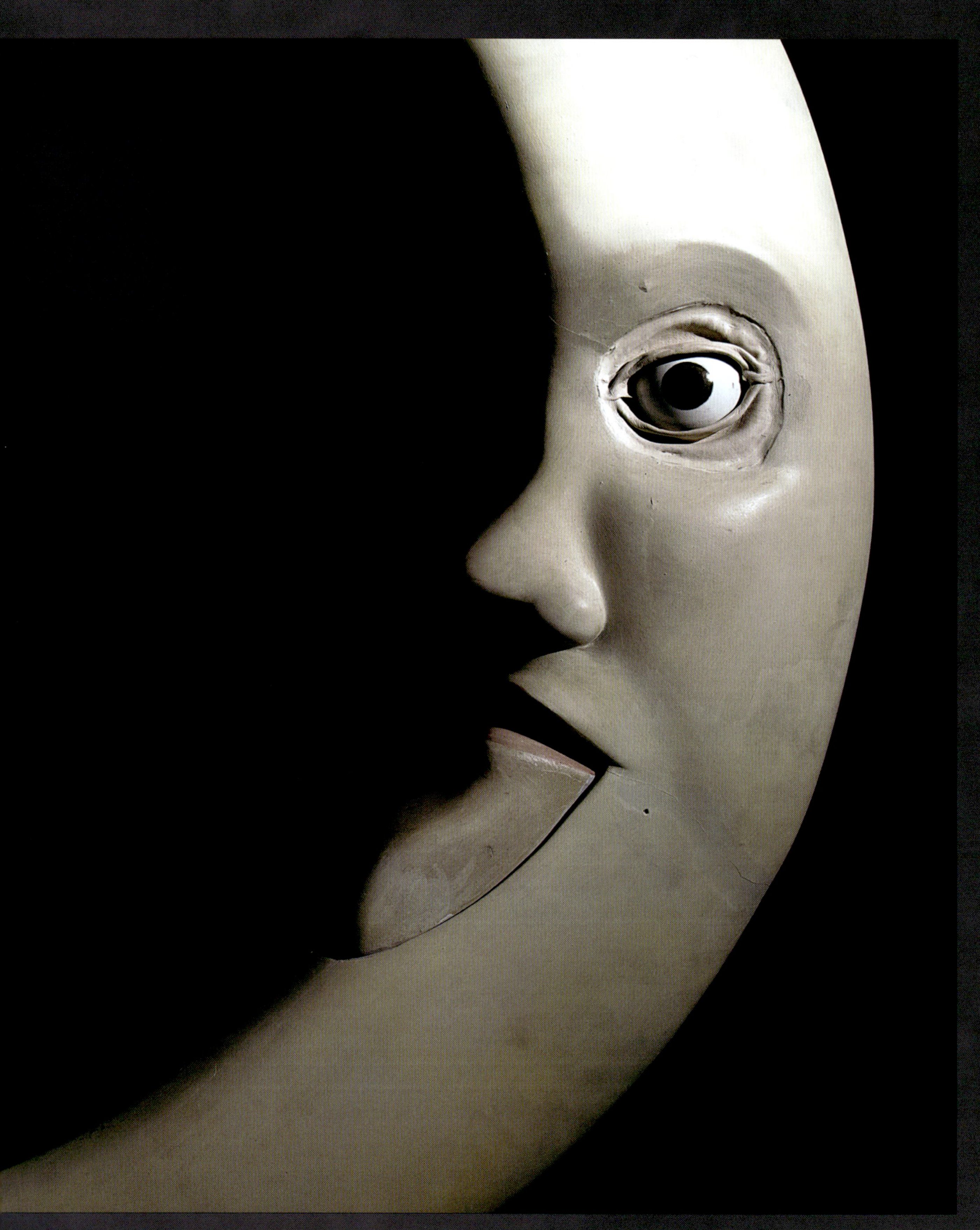

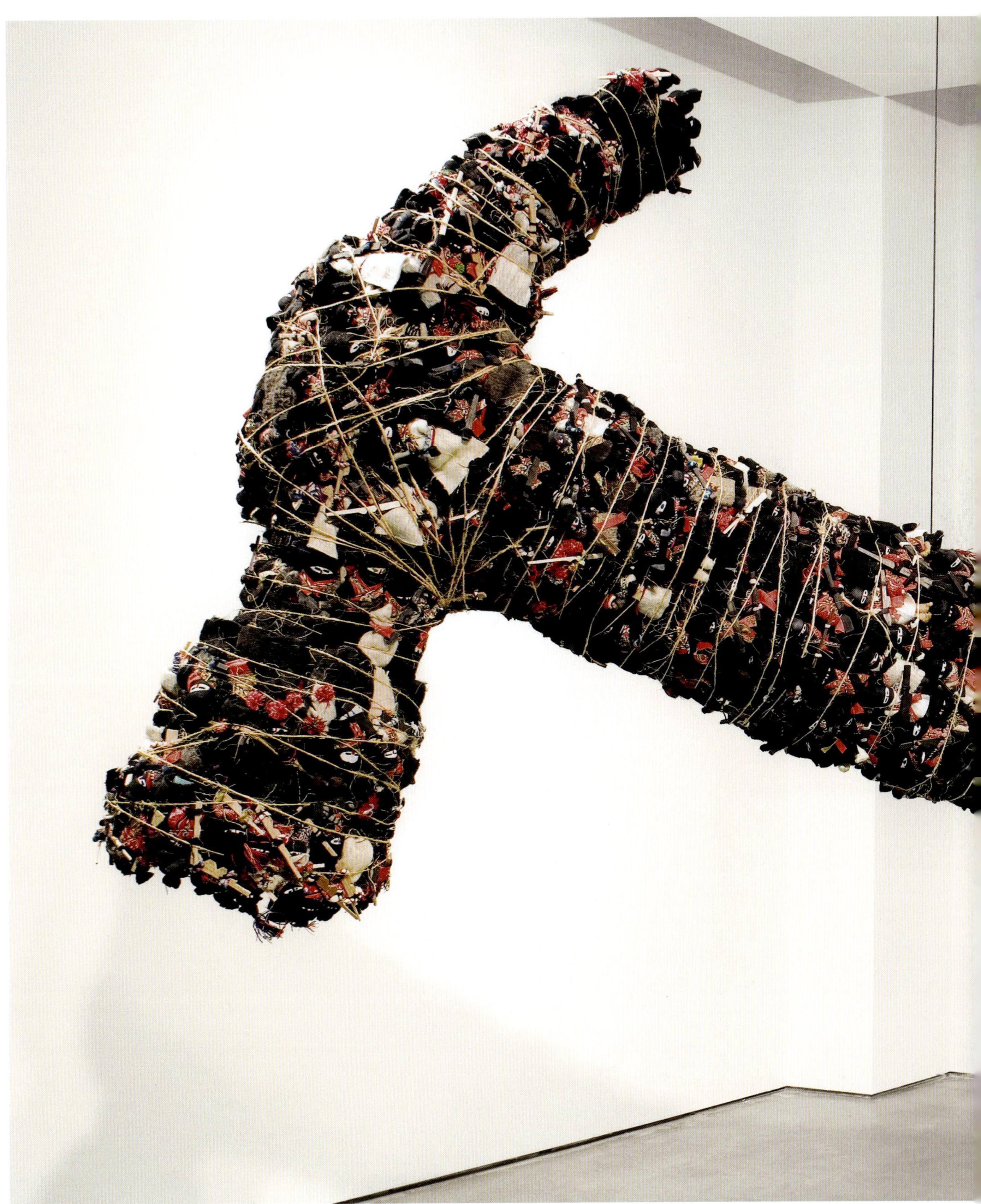

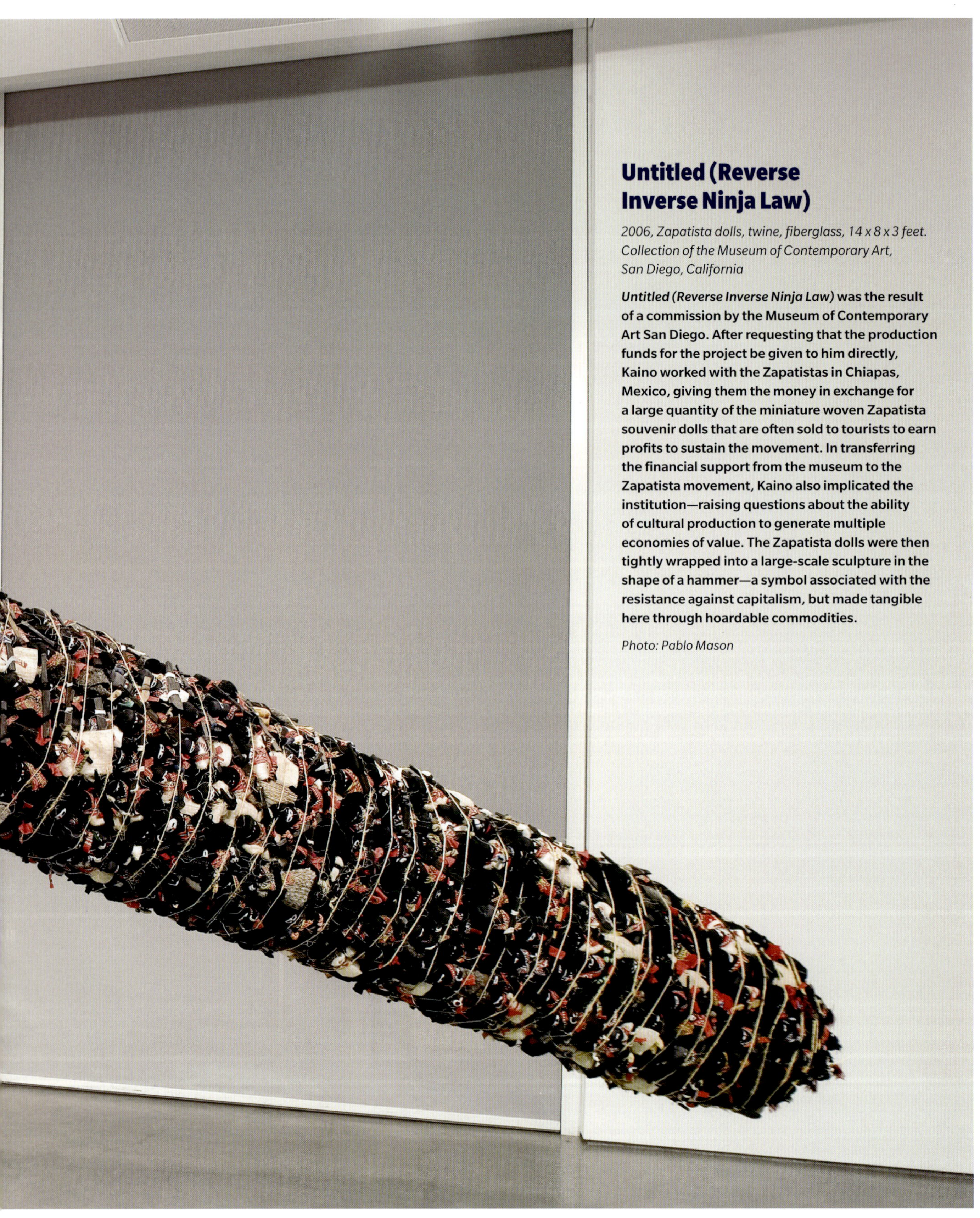

## Untitled (Reverse Inverse Ninja Law)

*2006, Zapatista dolls, twine, fiberglass, 14 x 8 x 3 feet. Collection of the Museum of Contemporary Art, San Diego, California*

***Untitled (Reverse Inverse Ninja Law)*** **was the result of a commission by the Museum of Contemporary Art San Diego. After requesting that the production funds for the project be given to him directly, Kaino worked with the Zapatistas in Chiapas, Mexico, giving them the money in exchange for a large quantity of the miniature woven Zapatista souvenir dolls that are often sold to tourists to earn profits to sustain the movement. In transferring the financial support from the museum to the Zapatista movement, Kaino also implicated the institution—raising questions about the ability of cultural production to generate multiple economies of value. The Zapatista dolls were then tightly wrapped into a large-scale sculpture in the shape of a hammer—a symbol associated with the resistance against capitalism, but made tangible here through hoardable commodities.**

*Photo: Pablo Mason*

# Don't Let Him Fool You

## Mike Caveney

We magicians tend to be very secretive. We can spend hours talking about magic principles and how an impossible effect might be accomplished. We do this only with each other, because other magicians are the only ones who speak the language. A layperson eavesdropping on our conversation wouldn't have a clue as to what we were talking about. And if we notice an outsider listening in, the conversation stops. Ours is a closed society and we prefer it that way. Visitors are not welcome. It's not that we don't like you, in fact we need you, but not just yet. After all of our work is completed, and the impossibility has become reality, then we need your virgin eyes to validate our effort with a genuine and sincere "WOW!" It is then that we know our effort was not in vain.

*Wands Bygone*, 2010, detail of John Baldessari wand. **"Pointing was the gesture, meaning was the result"** *Photo: Kelly Barrie*

One outsider has managed to breach our fortress. Glenn Kaino may not think of himself as a magician, but we know better. He is as passionate about creating wonder and making people think as anyone I've ever met. He has enjoyed a long and remarkable career, but every so often he likes to get nudged in a direction he didn't even know existed. And that's when he'll call. I'm never sure what he is looking for, but then, neither is he. He just knows that surrounding himself with magic and opening up his mind is a powerful combination.

I have a collection of antique magic wands. No two are alike, each one belonged to a famous magician of the past, and each one has a wonderful story attached to it. Most people who see these wands are fascinated by them, but one person was inspired by them. The names of the magicians meant nothing to Glenn, but the idea that each wizard had his own unique object that facilitated his magic, he found mind blowing. That little nudge caused Glenn to create his own magic wand collection and each of his wands also had a story. The difference was that each of Glenn's wands had the ability to tell its own story. When the viewer saw the name that was attached to each wand, the story became instantly clear and made perfect sense.

On another visit, Glenn said one word, "Shadows." My library contains many books on the art of shadowgraphy, and in my travels I have befriended a number of hand-shadow artists. As I described performances I had seen, Glenn paged through hundred-year-old books on the subject. I never know what, if anything, is hitting the target, but the conversation continues. Then, months later, when I see the result of our meeting, it's my turn to be a layman, "WOW!"

It is worth noting that Glenn is more interested in magical effects than he is in how they are accomplished. Magicians spend their entire lives making you think something happened, when in fact, it didn't happen at all. For hundreds of years we have published our secrets in books, but these books rarely make it into the real world. Oh, we put a few into bookshops, but that's basically just to throw you off the scent. If you're so inclined, you are welcome to those secrets. The others we keep to ourselves.

A better way to learn the craft is through a mentor. Secrets are easy to come by, but turning those secrets into a polished performance that can entertain and deceive a sophisticated audience, that's something else. Years of struggle can be minimized when an experienced magician takes a young conjurer under his wing and shares what he has learned through decades of performing.

In 1900, when W. W. Denslow was hired to illustrate L. Frank Baum's children's book, *The Wonderful Wizard of Oz*, he used magician Harry Kellar as inspiration. At that time, when people thought of a magician, it was Kellar's familiar face that came to mind. Late in life, Kellar took a young, enthusiastic magician under his wing. Howard Thurston was already an accomplished magician, but Kellar knew that he could be more than that. They traveled together for one season, each presenting half of the evening's performance. Then, in 1908, Kellar gave the final performance of his storied career. At the conclusion of the show, Kellar draped a cloak over Thurston's shoulders and handed him the sacred magic wand. The mantle of magic had been passed. This moment was captured in a stunning poster that declares, "Thurston will be the greatest magician the world has ever known." The magic wand, and all that it represents, had passed from one generation to the next. When Glenn saw this poster, I could see that it made an impression on him, but it wasn't until years later that I realized just how big of an impression.

Watching Glenn Kaino and Afshin Shahidi's film, *With Drawn Arms*, about the great American sprinter Tommie Smith, moved me to tears. In 1968, everyone on my high school track team looked up to Tommie and we were all watching when he and John Carlos made that simple yet powerful gesture of raising their fists atop the medal stand at the Olympic Games. The whole world condemned their action, but today we know that it was we who were wrong, and they who were right. Forty-odd years later, seeing Tommie at the White House, handing President Barack Obama the Olympic relay baton, reminded me of Kellar and Thurston—the wise veteran passing the baton to the next generation. Glenn confirmed that, as he filmed this historic meeting in the Oval Office, the image on that magic poster was in the back of his mind.

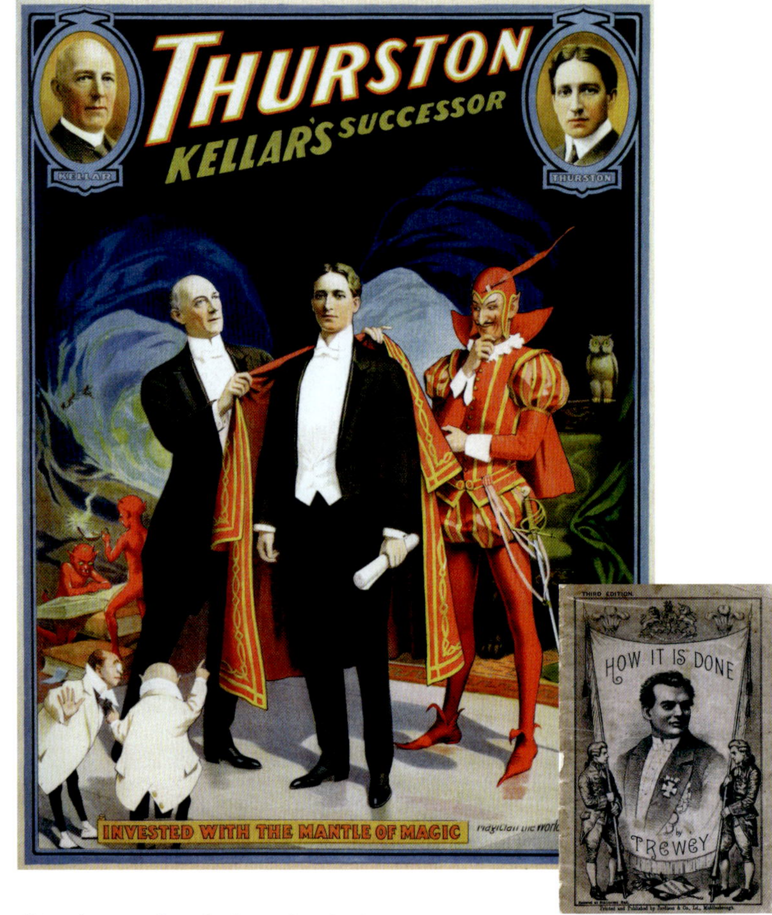


**Howard Thurston promoting the mantle being passed to him from Harry Kellar, 1908, lithograph**

***The Art of Shadowgraphy: How It Is Done* by Felicien Trewey, 1919. The great French variety artist, Trewey, helped popularize Shadowgraphs during the late nineteenth century**

*Photos: Mike Caveney's Egyptian Hall Museum*

Glenn's many fans believe that he is a great artist and there is certainly plenty of evidence to back up that opinion. Just one example is the Tommie Smith statue that today stands at the High Museum of Art in Atlanta. Approached from behind, it appears to be a dramatic statue of Tommie with his fist raised. Then you walk to the front of the statue and it transforms into one of two things. Either it vanishes completely, or you are staring at yourself. A flat, mirrored surface creates both of these illusions. Yes, for once it is all done with mirrors. When the angle is such that the mirror reflects the surrounding environment, the statue tends to disappear. But when you see yourself within the outline of Tommie Smith, it causes you to wonder if you would have had the courage that Tommie exhibited in 1968.

Yes, Glenn Kaino is a brilliant artist; but if you think that's all he is, you're missing the point. He also has the heart and soul of a magician.

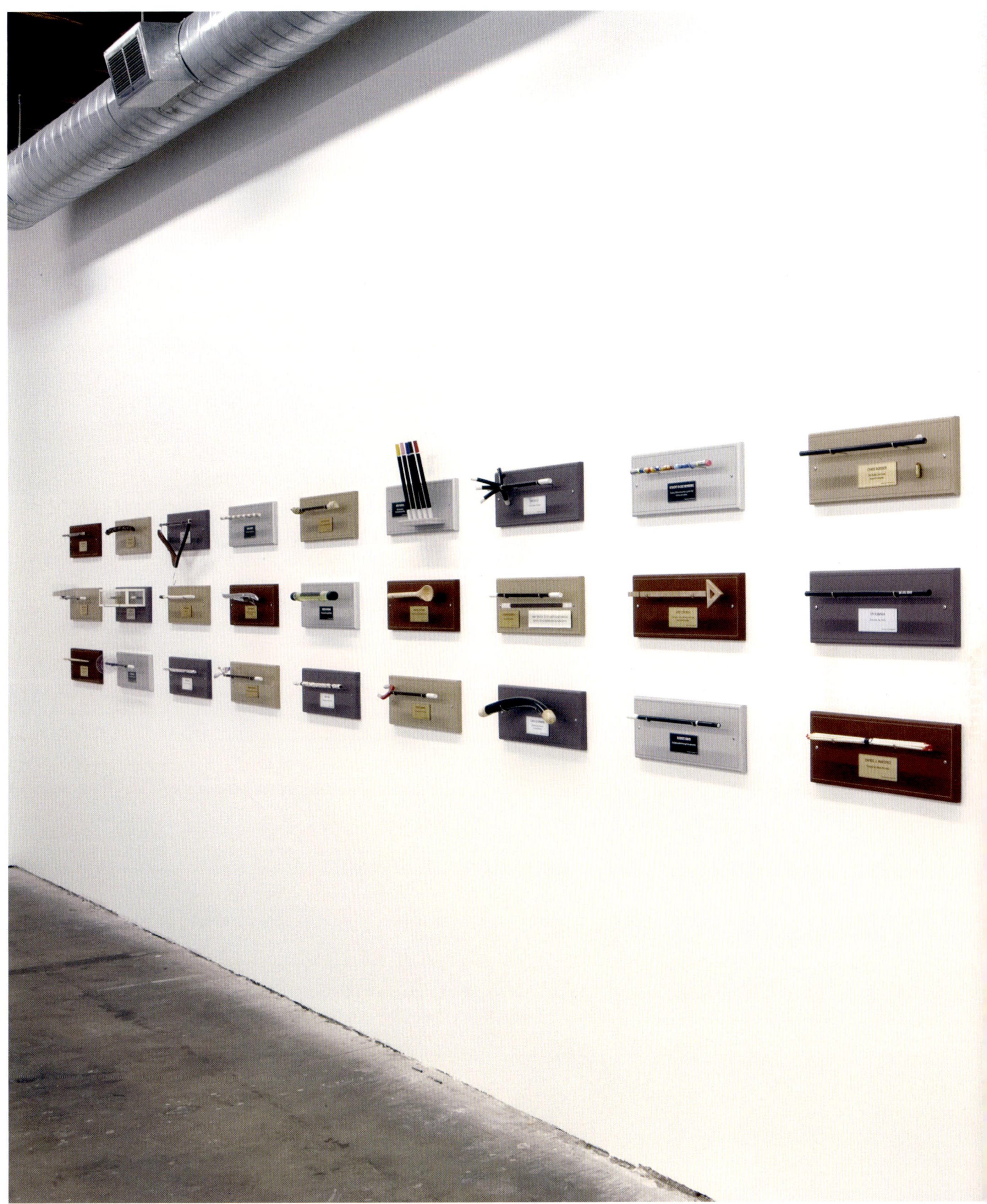

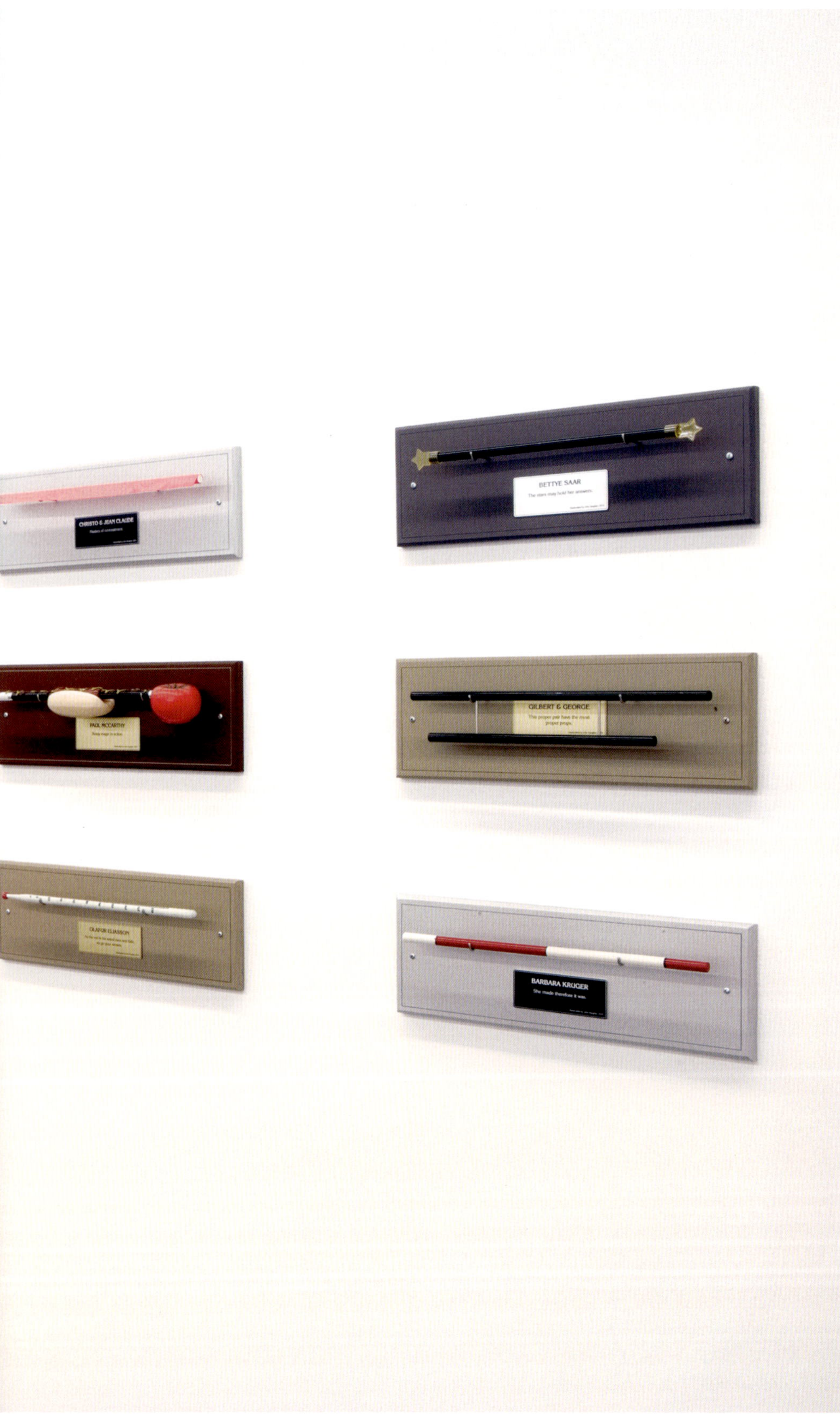


## Wands Bygone

*2010, Mixed media, dimensions variable*

**Kaino and magician Derek DelGaudio were driving to visit fellow magician John Gaughan with the intention of soaking up his aura. On the way to Gaughan's studio they talked about his magic wands. Gaughan makes the wands that are given out by Hollywood's Magic Castle for their "Magician of the Year" awards annually. These wands are not for sale, they must be earned, therefore making them priceless. Kaino and Gaughan then collaborated on a series of wands made for conceptual artists. The wands become symbolic tokens encapsulating the power of conceptual artists, just as they have historically been for magicians.**

*Photo: Kelly Barrie*

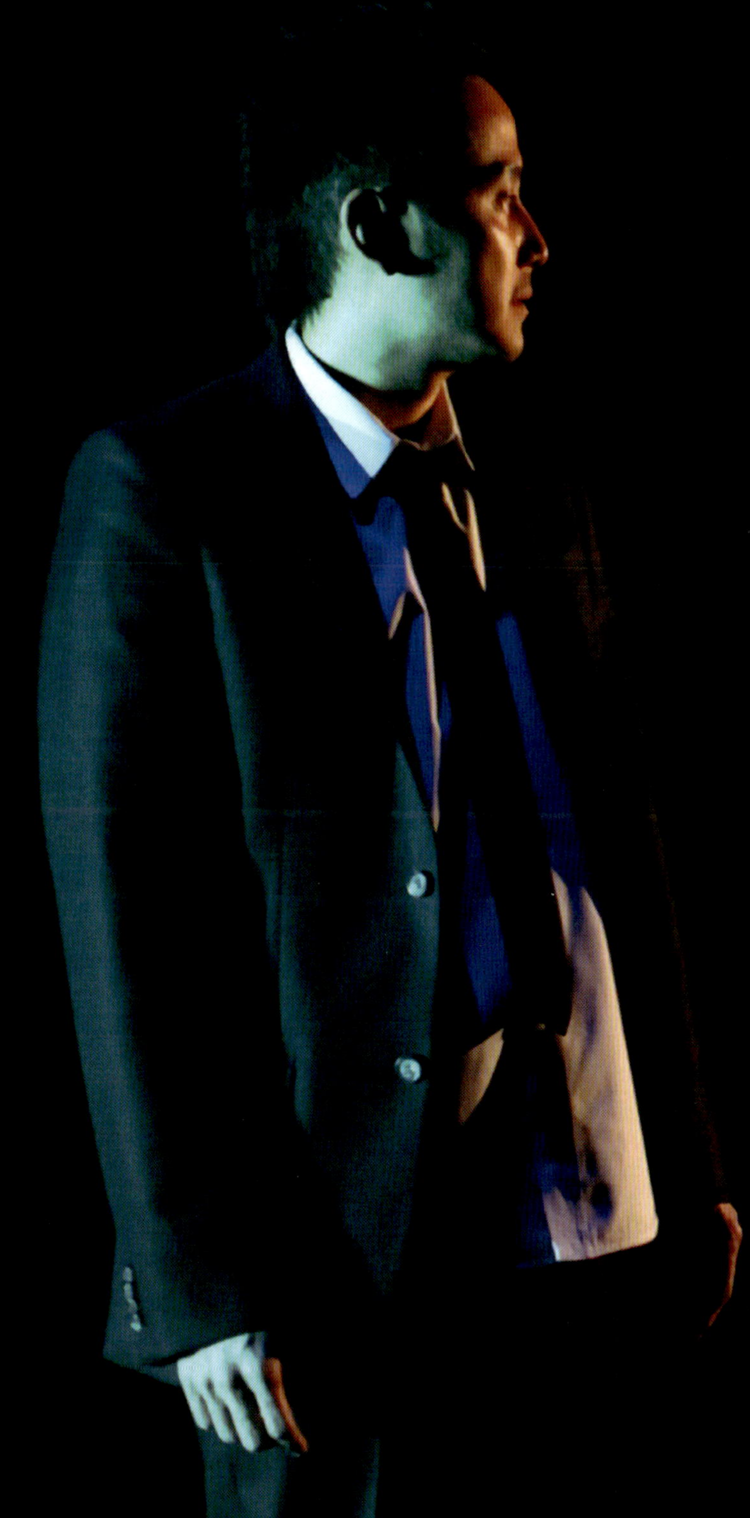

## A.Bandit

*The Mistake Room, 2011*

**A.Bandit is an experimental performance art group started by conceptual artist Kaino and conceptual magician Derek DelGaudio. Formed as an alliance with the intention of creating a new performative medium between the worlds of art and magic, A.Bandit has performed their spectacular psycho-spatial interventions at such venues as The Kitchen, New York; the Geffen Playhouse, Los Angeles; Pershing Square Signature Center, New York; Soho House, Los Angeles; Art LA Contemporary, Santa Monica, CA; and LAXART Annex, Hollywood, CA, where in 2011 they were in residence for six months to open a conceptual magic shop called "The Space Between." The duo published their first collaborative artist monograph, *A Secret Has Two Faces*, with Prestel/Delmonico in 2018, and created the hit off-Broadway show *In & Of Itself* the same year.**

*Photo: Pamela Court, courtesy of The Kitchen, New York*

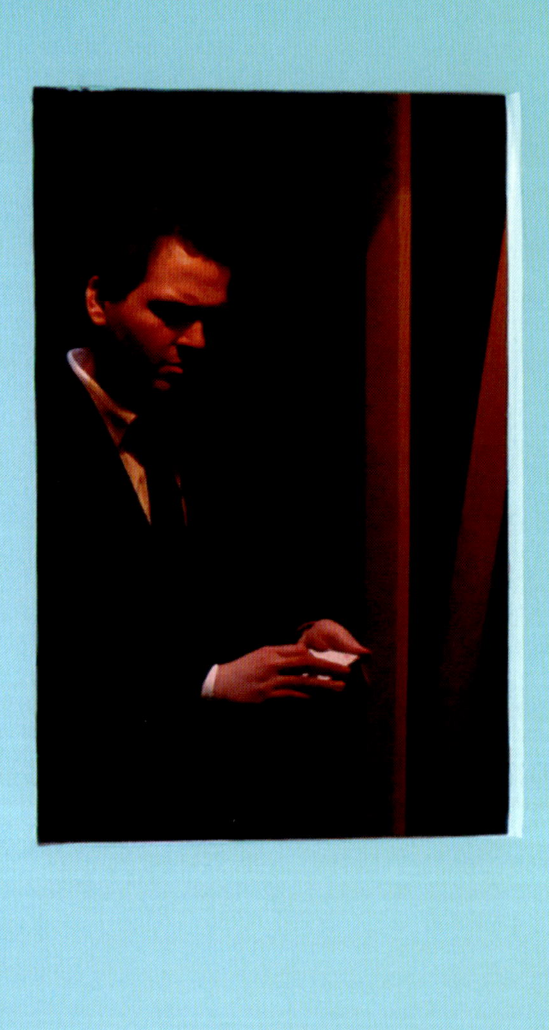

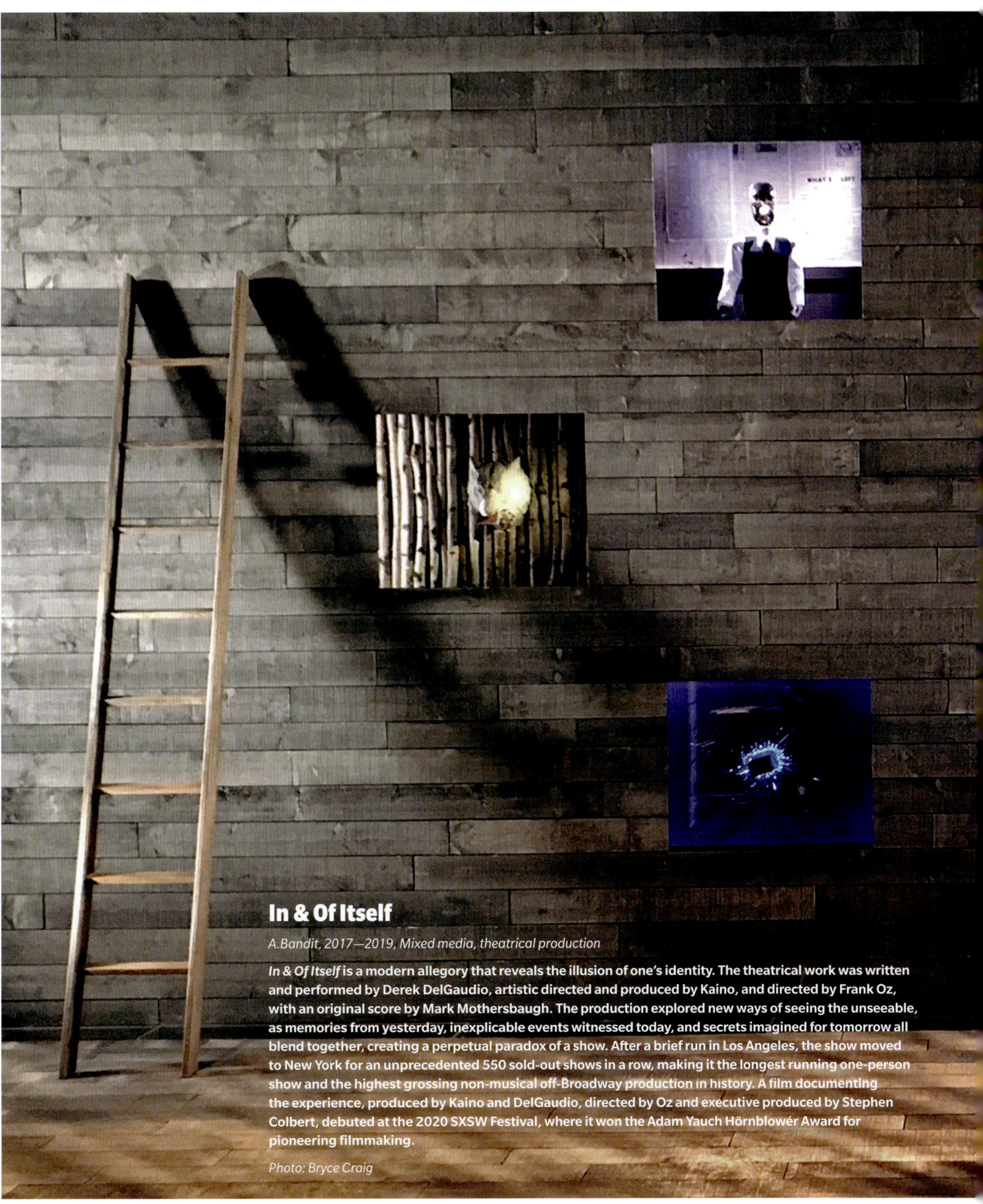

## In & Of Itself

*A.Bandit, 2017—2019, Mixed media, theatrical production*

***In & Of Itself*** **is a modern allegory that reveals the illusion of one's identity. The theatrical work was written and performed by Derek DelGaudio, artistic directed and produced by Kaino, and directed by Frank Oz, with an original score by Mark Mothersbaugh. The production explored new ways of seeing the unseeable, as memories from yesterday, inexplicable events witnessed today, and secrets imagined for tomorrow all blend together, creating a perpetual paradox of a show. After a brief run in Los Angeles, the show moved to New York for an unprecedented 550 sold-out shows in a row, making it the longest running one-person show and the highest grossing non-musical off-Broadway production in history. A film documenting the experience, produced by Kaino and DelGaudio, directed by Oz and executive produced by Stephen Colbert, debuted at the 2020 SXSW Festival, where it won the Adam Yauch Hörnblowér Award for pioneering filmmaking.**

*Photo: Bryce Craig*

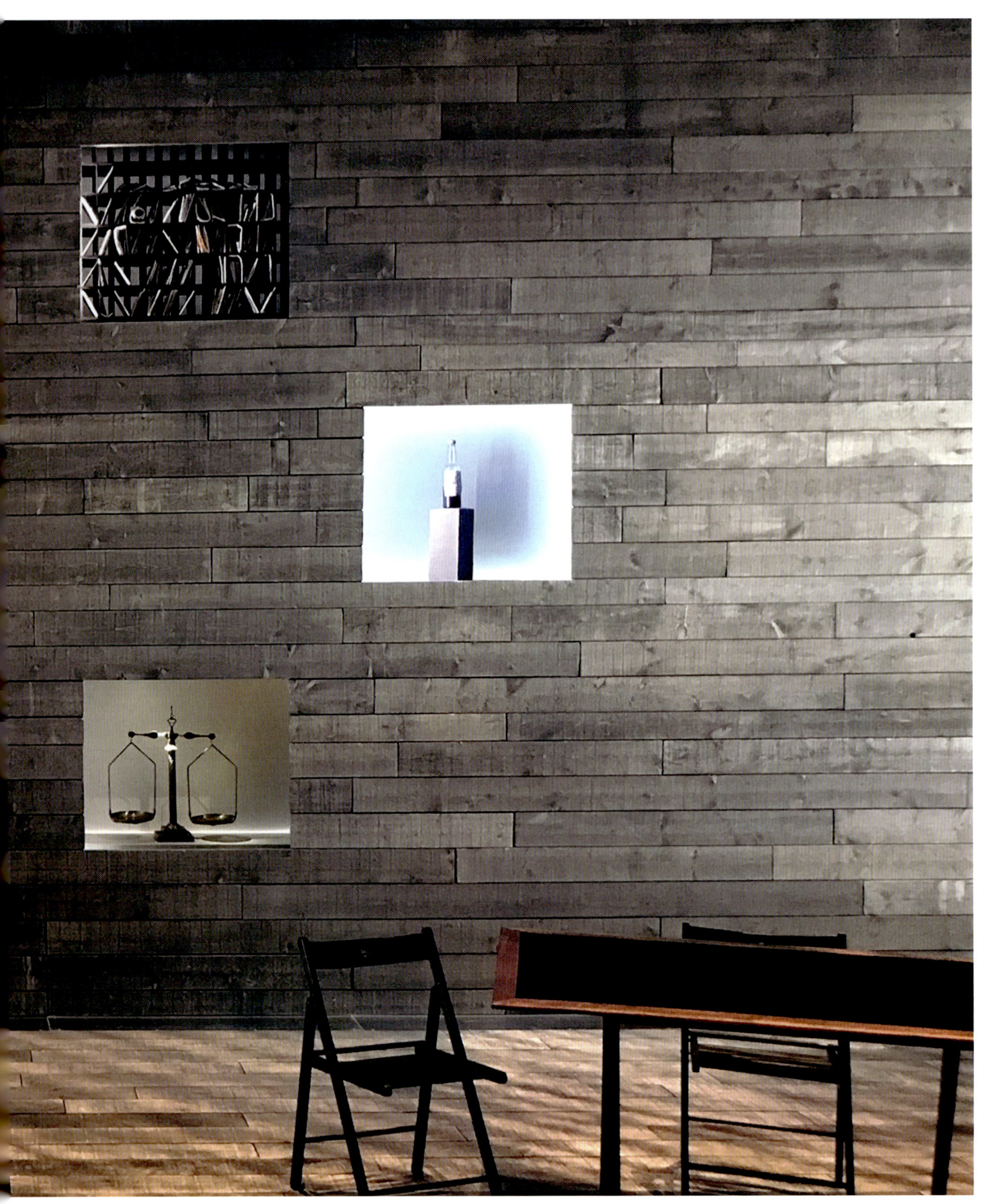

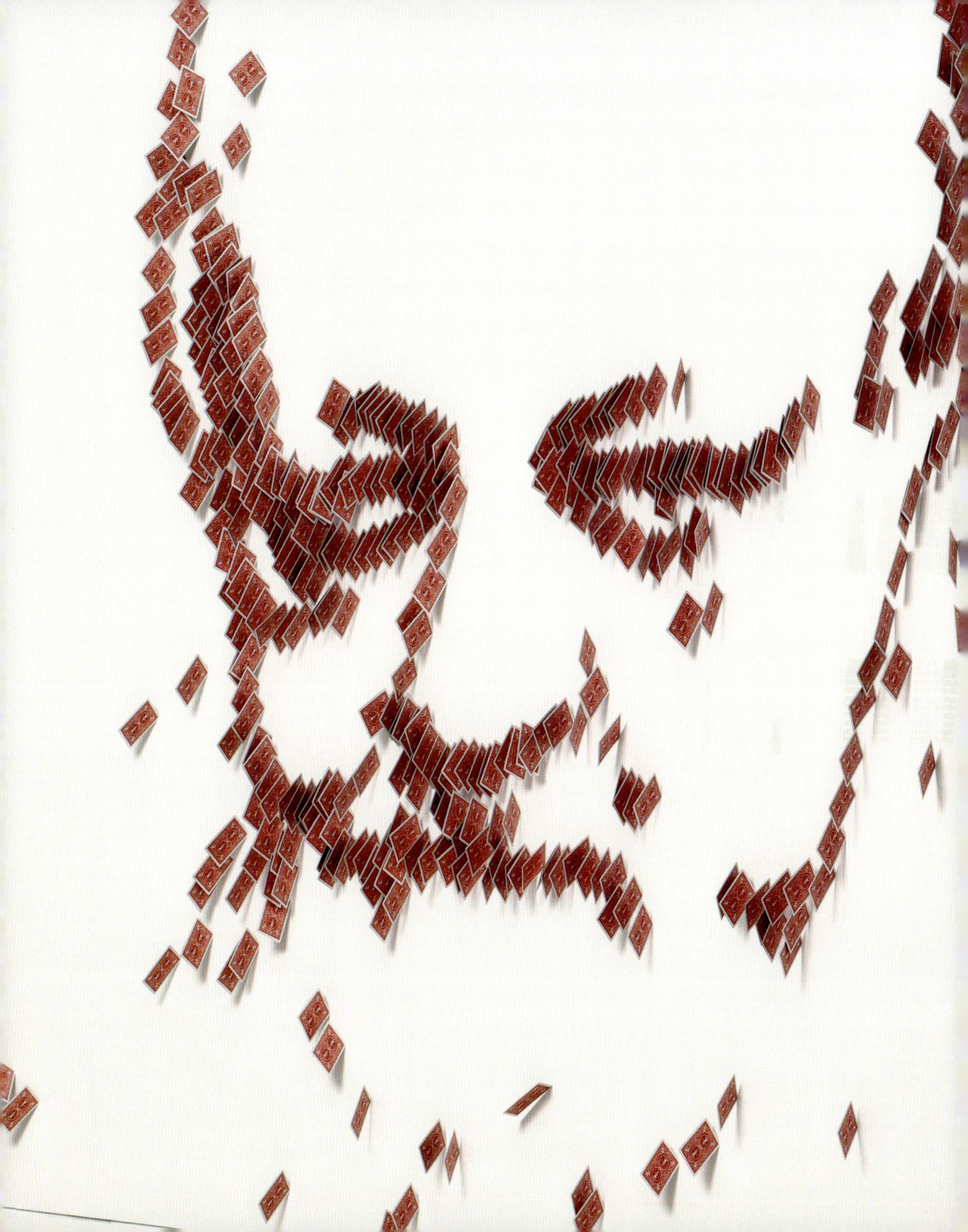

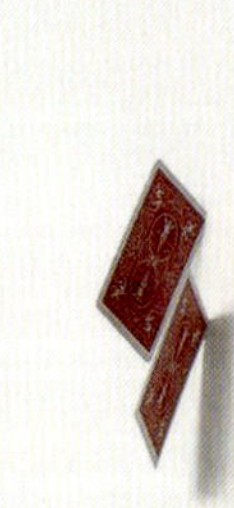

## Untitled (Ricky Jay)

*2010, Playing cards, dimensions variable.*
*Collection of the Hammer Museum, Los Angeles*

**A sculptural wall portrait of magician Ricky Jay is formed using a playing-card-throwing technique famously employed by Jay himself. Applying mechanisms used to create magical illusions to unconventional materials, an installation takes shape that at first glance appears to be a chaotic field of planes and colors. As viewers walk from left to right in front of the work, they eventually reach a vantage point from which the cards coalesce into a detailed portrait that ages and transforms.**

*Photo: Bryan Forrest*

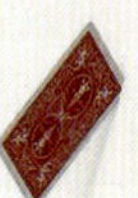

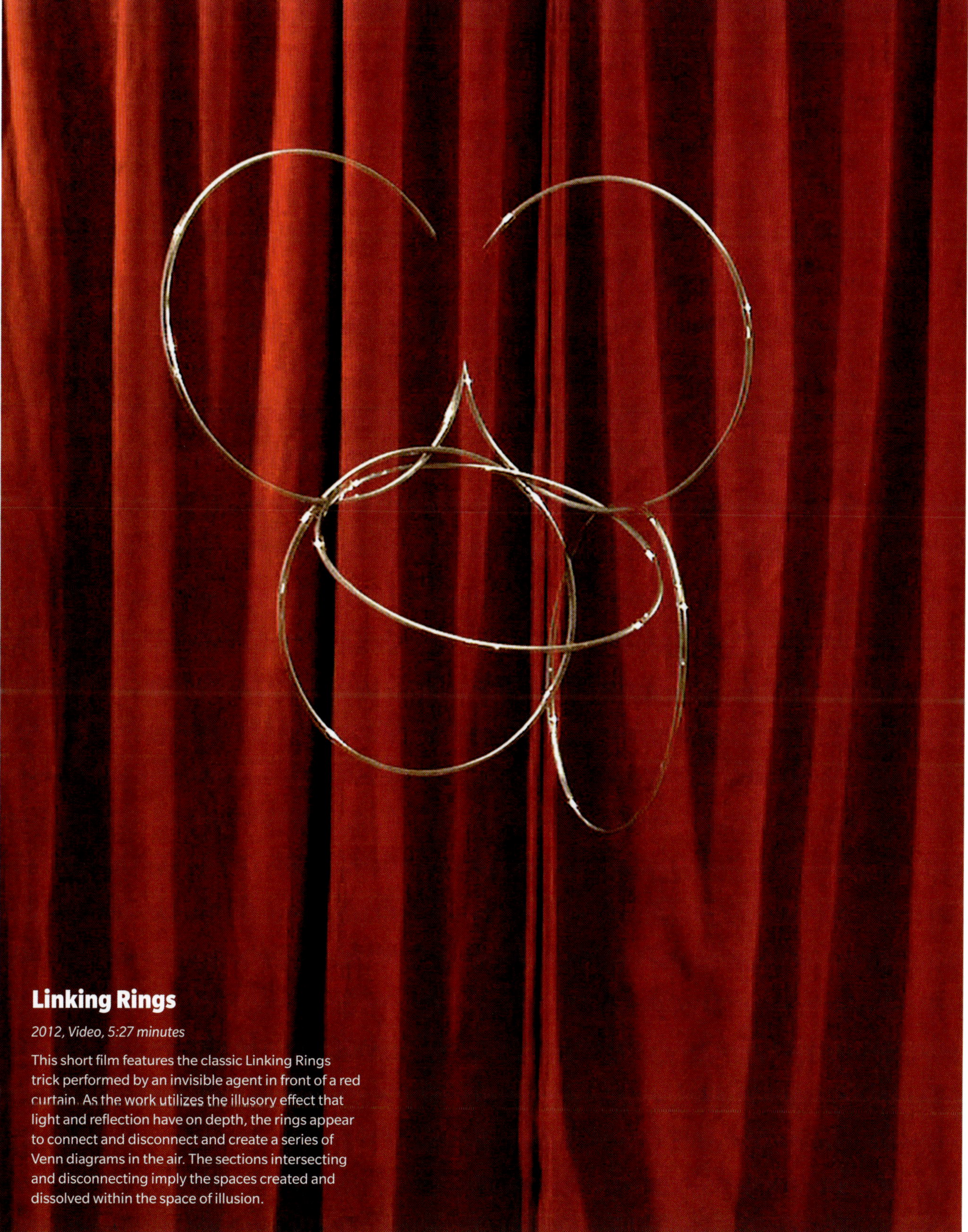

## Linking Rings

*2012, Video, 5:27 minutes*

This short film features the classic Linking Rings trick performed by an invisible agent in front of a red curtain. As the work utilizes the illusory effect that light and reflection have on depth, the rings appear to connect and disconnect and create a series of Venn diagrams in the air. The sections intersecting and disconnecting imply the spaces created and dissolved within the space of illusion.

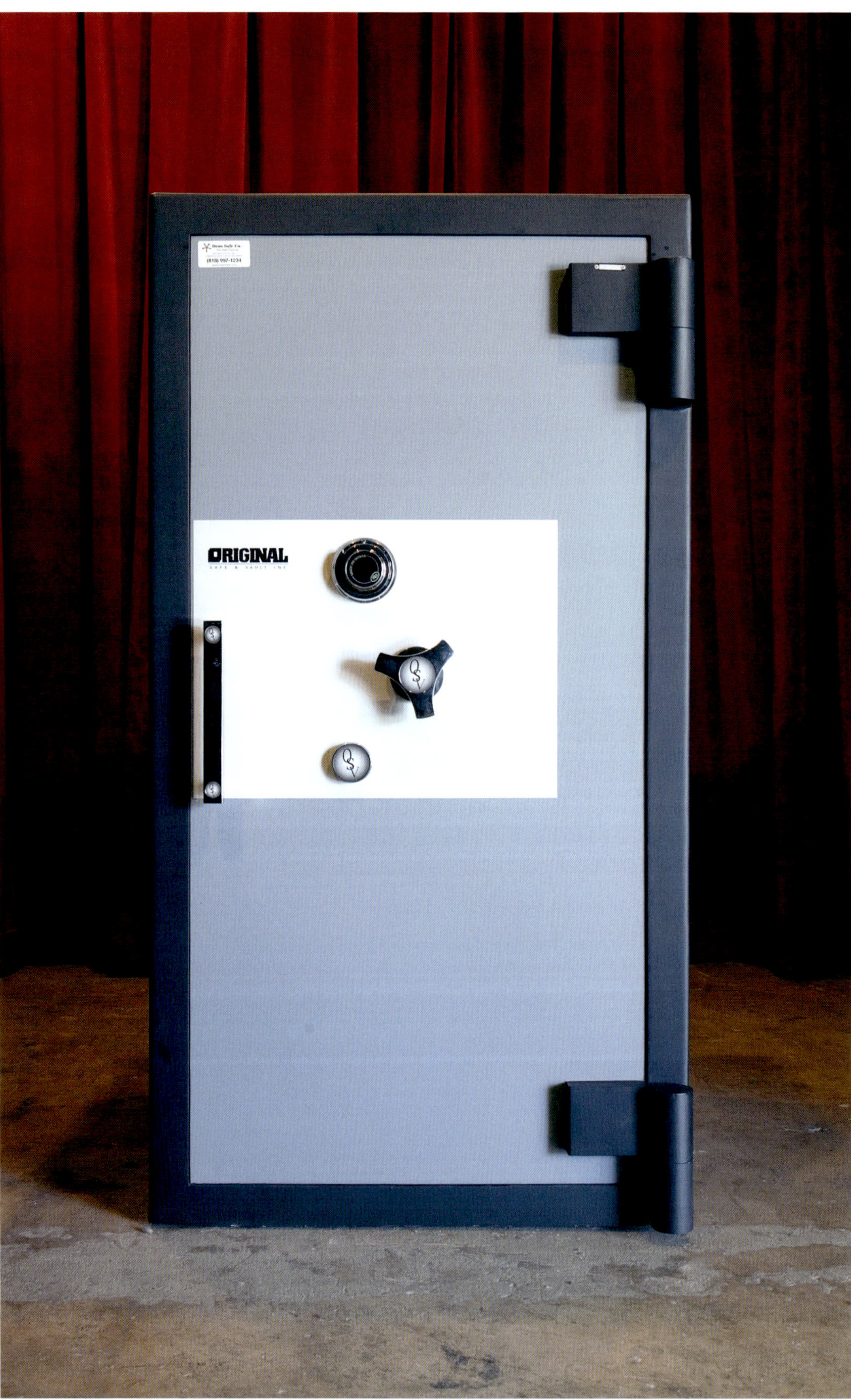


## Safe

*2010–ongoing, Secrets, safe deposit, dimensions variable*

**A sculpture made from secrets is held together by a safe deposit structure. Attempting to sculpt with invisible materials, over the course of a year Kaino gathered more than 220 secrets from a wide range of individuals involved in the business and art worlds, the entertainment and fashion industries, and politics. Participants were asked to record their secrets onto an audiocassette that was then stored inside a safe, never to be heard by anyone, not even the artist. They then wrote down a title for the secret that would be made public. The material of the work is simultaneously its content—charged with symbolic value, but with no physical or visible form—obscured by the vessel within which it resides, the safe. The work exists through a legally binding notification that states that the safe may never be opened, even if the work is purchased. If it is, the structure ceases to be an artwork.**

*Photo: Kelly Barrie*

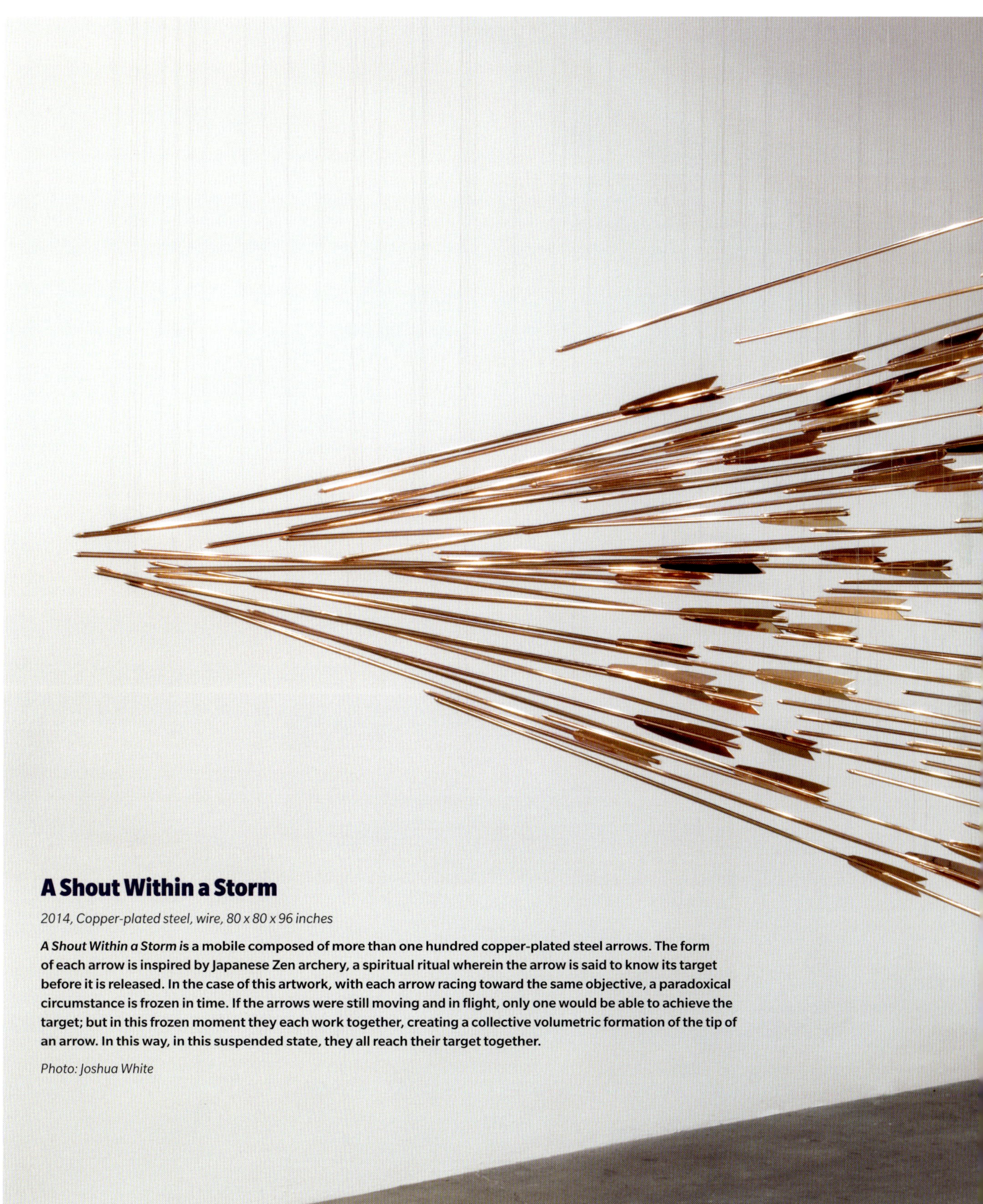

## A Shout Within a Storm

*2014, Copper-plated steel, wire, 80 x 80 x 96 inches*

***A Shout Within a Storm*** **is a mobile composed of more than one hundred copper-plated steel arrows. The form of each arrow is inspired by Japanese Zen archery, a spiritual ritual wherein the arrow is said to know its target before it is released. In the case of this artwork, with each arrow racing toward the same objective, a paradoxical circumstance is frozen in time. If the arrows were still moving and in flight, only one would be able to achieve the target; but in this frozen moment they each work together, creating a collective volumetric formation of the tip of an arrow. In this way, in this suspended state, they all reach their target together.**

*Photo: Joshua White*

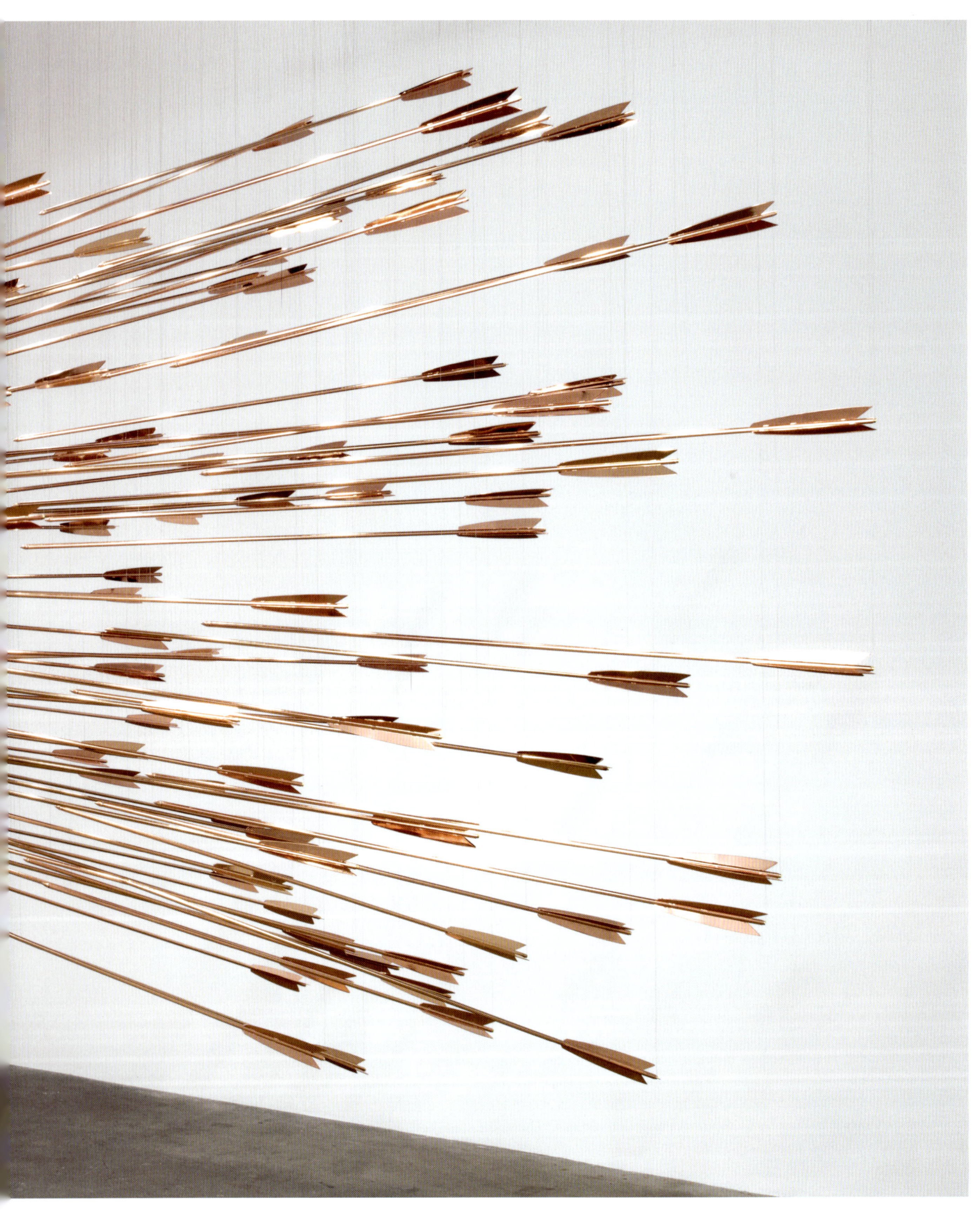

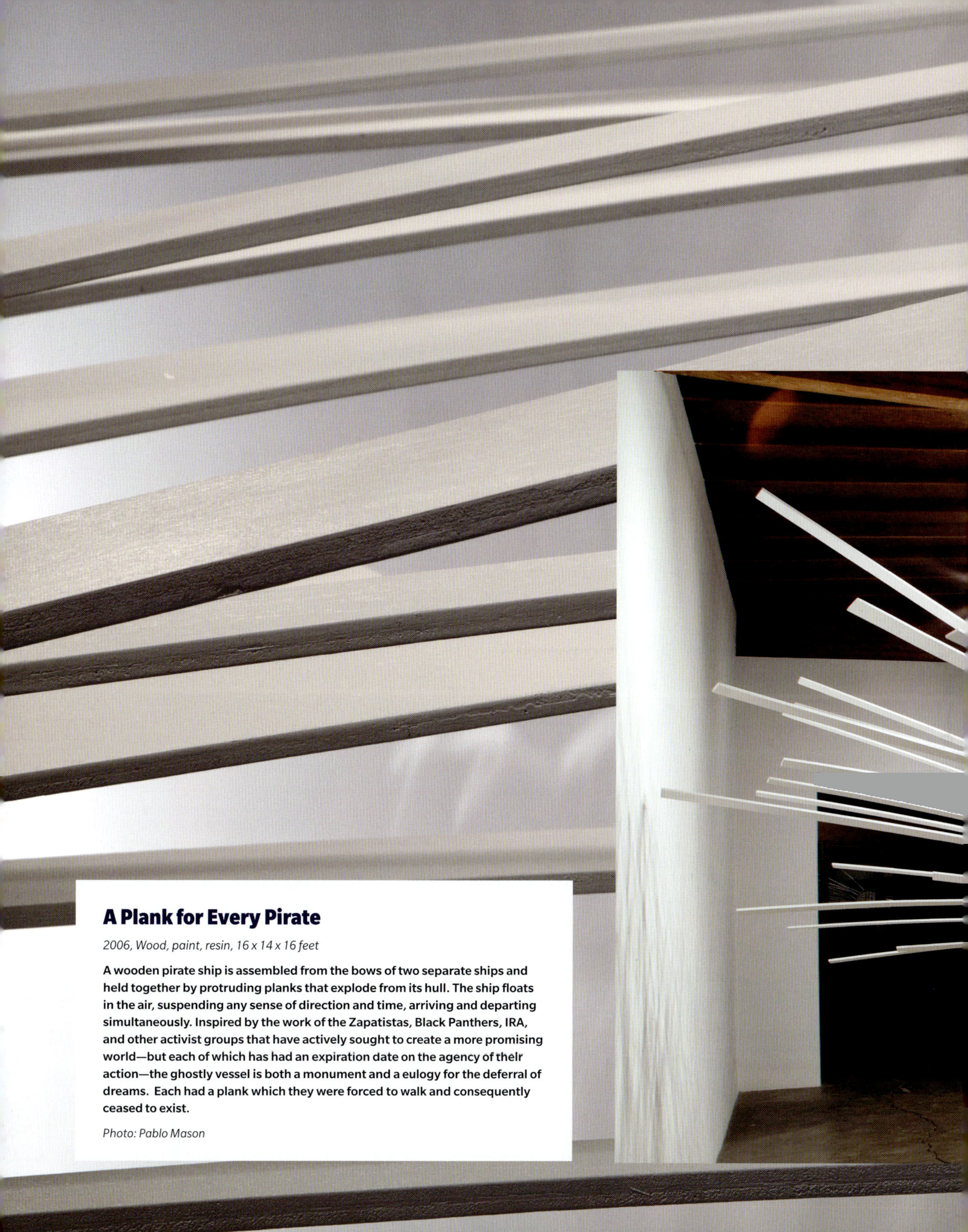

## A Plank for Every Pirate

*2006, Wood, paint, resin, 16 x 14 x 16 feet*

**A wooden pirate ship is assembled from the bows of two separate ships and held together by protruding planks that explode from its hull. The ship floats in the air, suspending any sense of direction and time, arriving and departing simultaneously. Inspired by the work of the Zapatistas, Black Panthers, IRA, and other activist groups that have actively sought to create a more promising world—but each of which has had an expiration date on the agency of thelr action—the ghostly vessel is both a monument and a eulogy for the deferral of dreams. Each had a plank which they were forced to walk and consequently ceased to exist.**

*Photo: Pablo Mason*

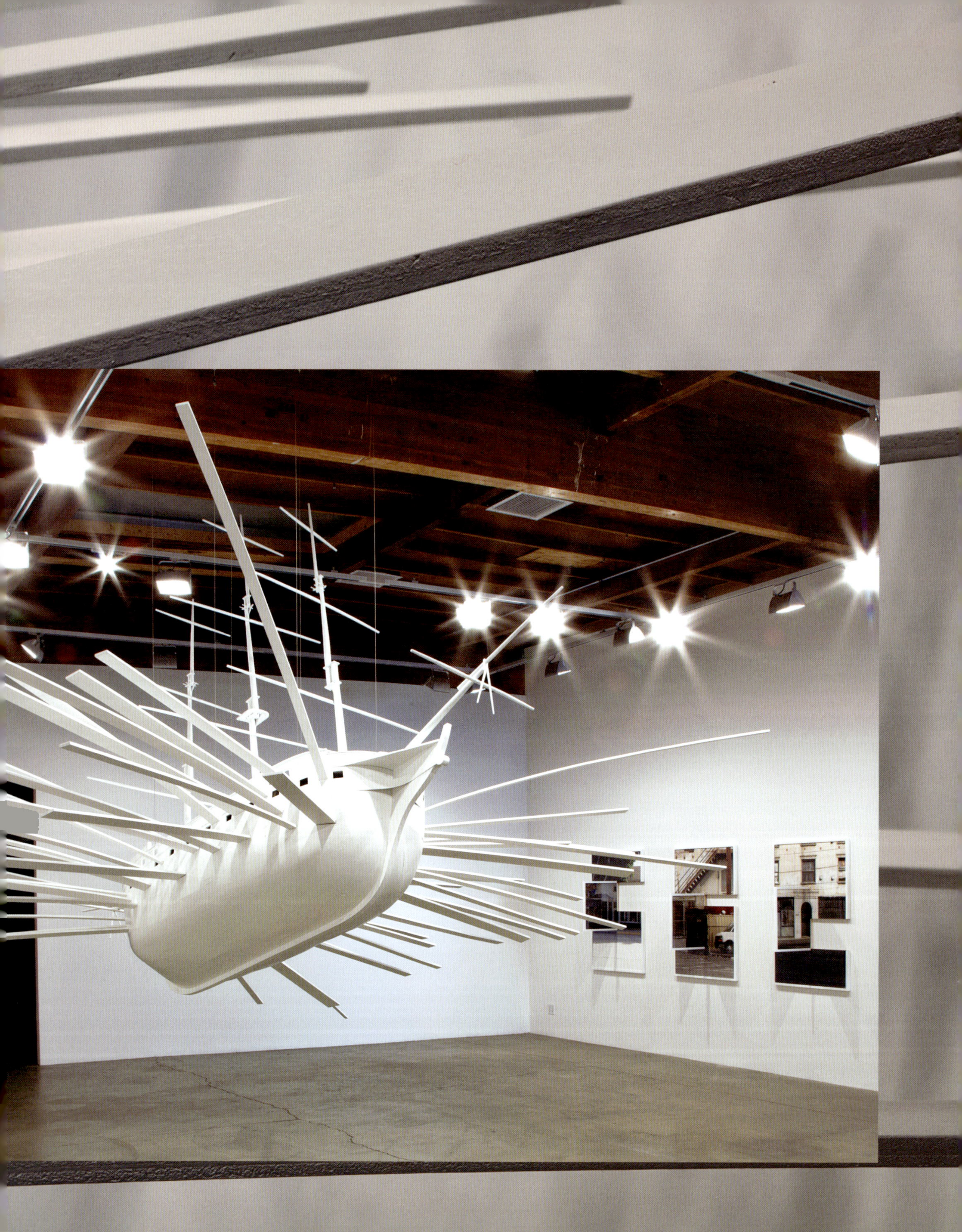

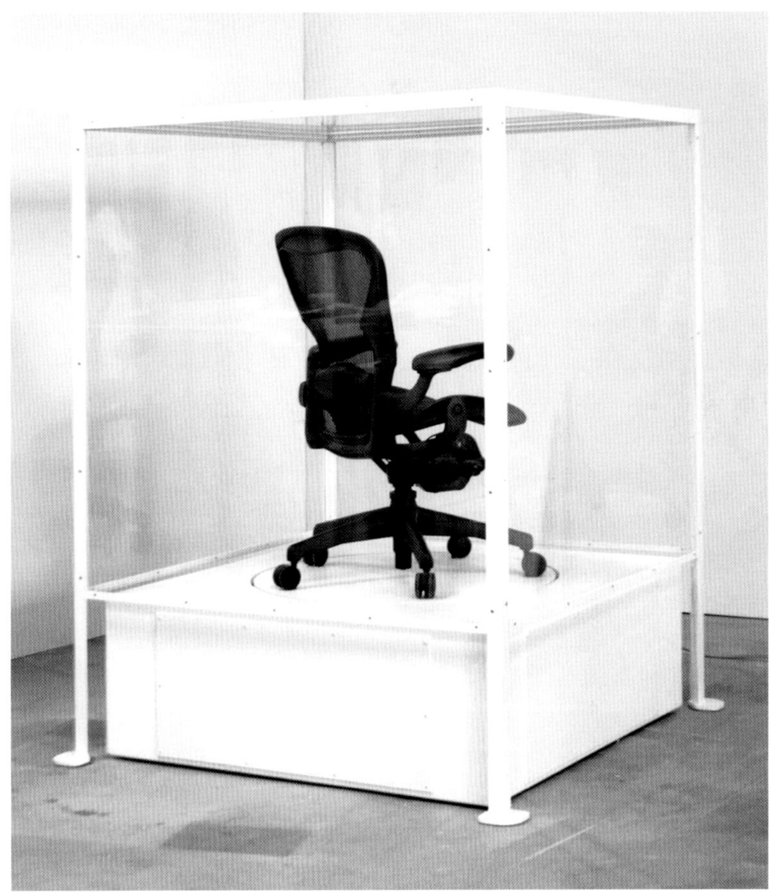

## The Siege Perilous

*2002, Aeron chair, Plexiglas, wood and steel base, mechanized component, 65 x 49 x 49 inches*
*Private Collection*

***The Siege Perilous*** **takes its name from the chair created by Merlin the magician for the one who locates the Holy Grail, the medieval icon of absolute power. A hidden motor spins an Aeron chair at extreme velocity. As it rotates within a steel and Plexiglas vitrine, the chair loses its distinguishing features to become a blurred form that resembles a chalice.** ***The Siege Perilous*** **is a disruption in the certainty of two objects—one real, the other imagined—now in a state of perpetual indeterminacy.**

*Photo: Erma Eastwick*

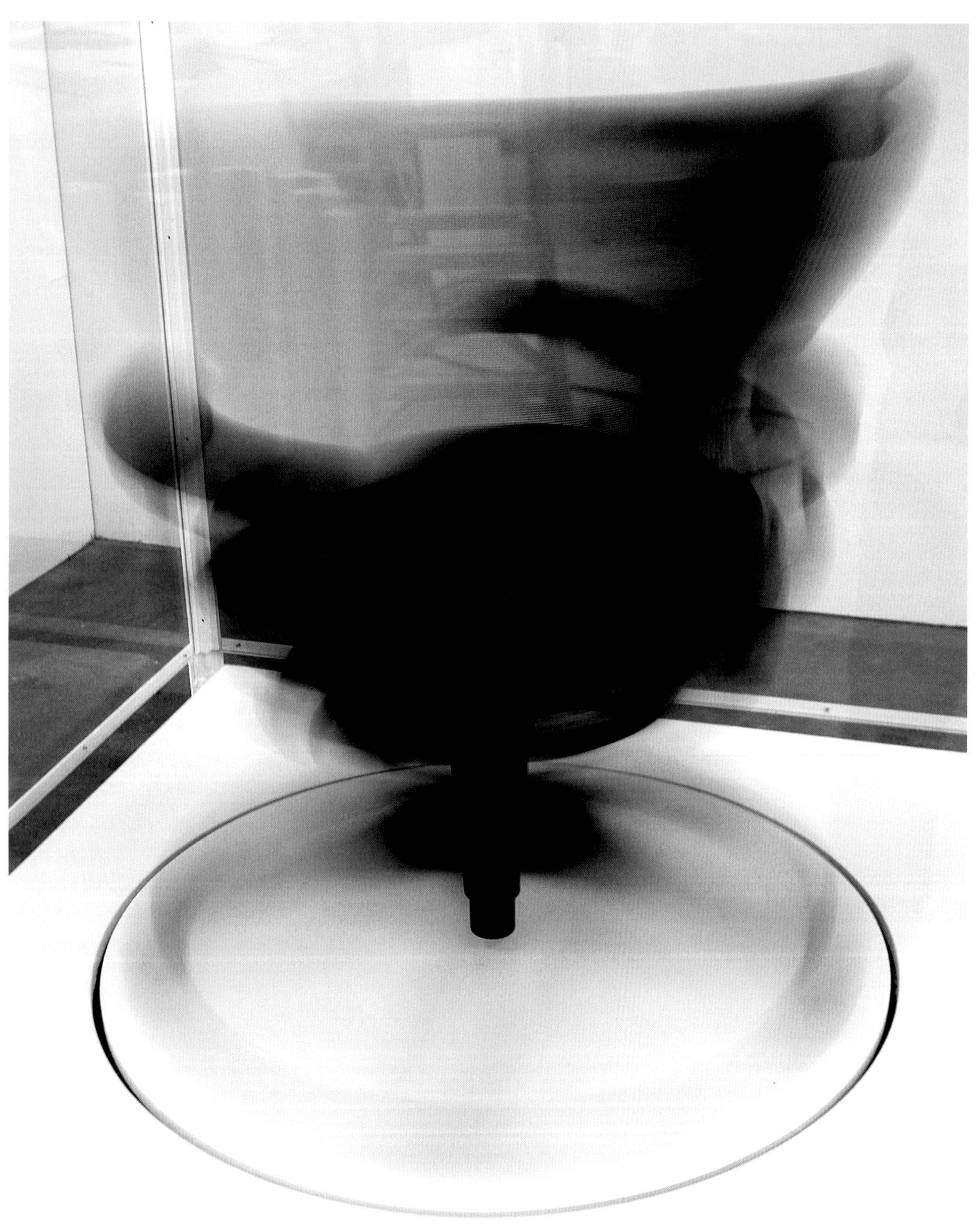

## The Burning Boards

*2007–ongoing, Chess game performance for 32 players with wood chessboards and wax chess pieces, dimensions variable*

**In an attempt to give form to the processes of thinking and negotiation, a chess tournament is staged between chess masters and artists, writers, and curators. Using wood boards and chess pieces made from different colored household candles, cut to varying sizes to differentiate between pieces, players engage in the game as the lit pieces add an invisible third opponent—time, which both must play against. As candle pieces melt during the game, the identity of the pieces themselves is erased, destabilizing the logic and rules of the game; this converts the encounter into a series of silent exchanges and rapid negotiations that are visualized on the boards through overlapping wax remnants that function as traces of vanishing thoughts and decisions. A performative and sculptural exercise in alchemy, the game itself becomes a poetic reflection on failure, as attaining the objective of winning becomes improbable, leaving only the waxy echoes of an encounter between two subjects and their spectral opponent.**

*Photo: Nhat Nguyen*

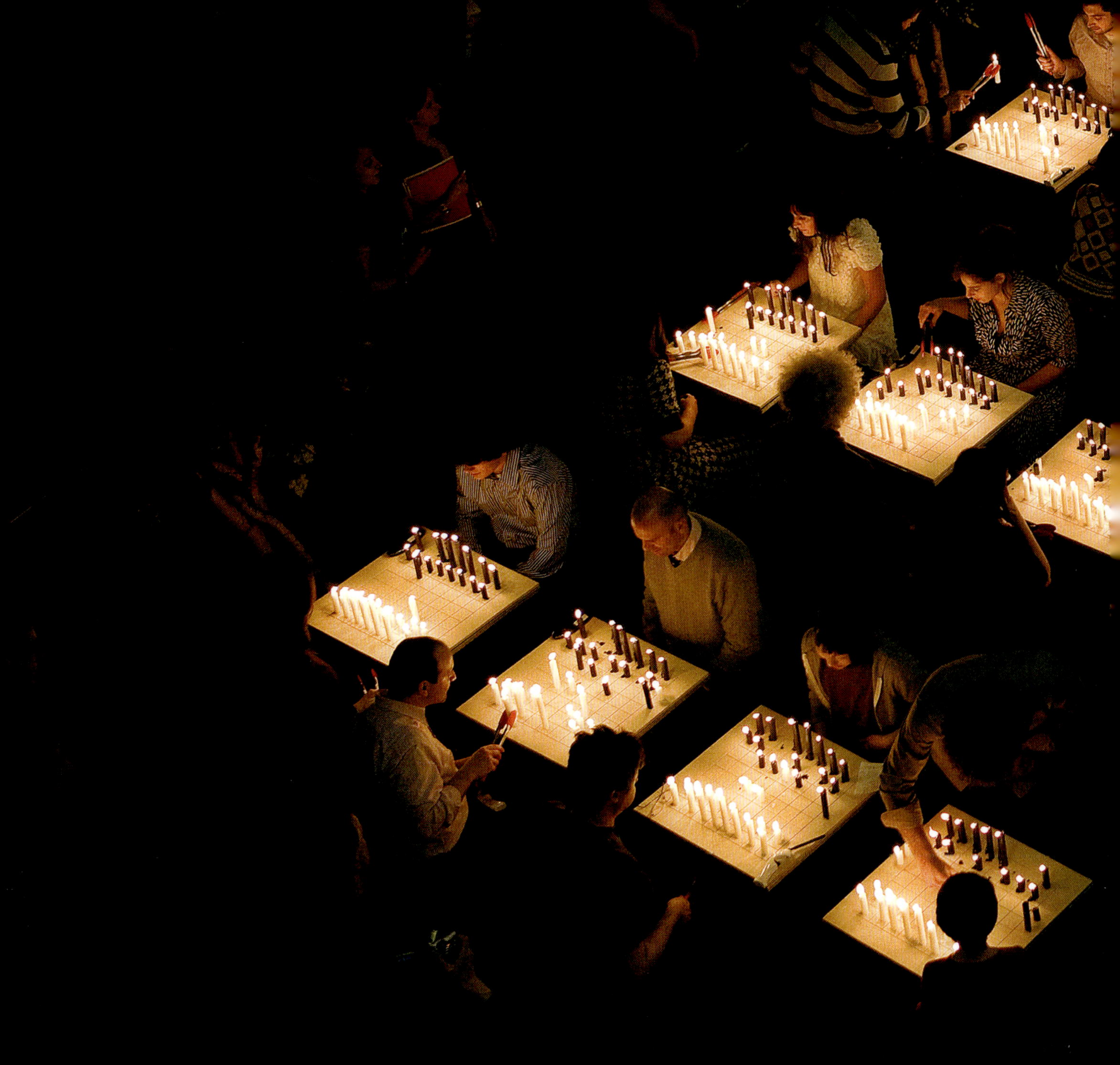

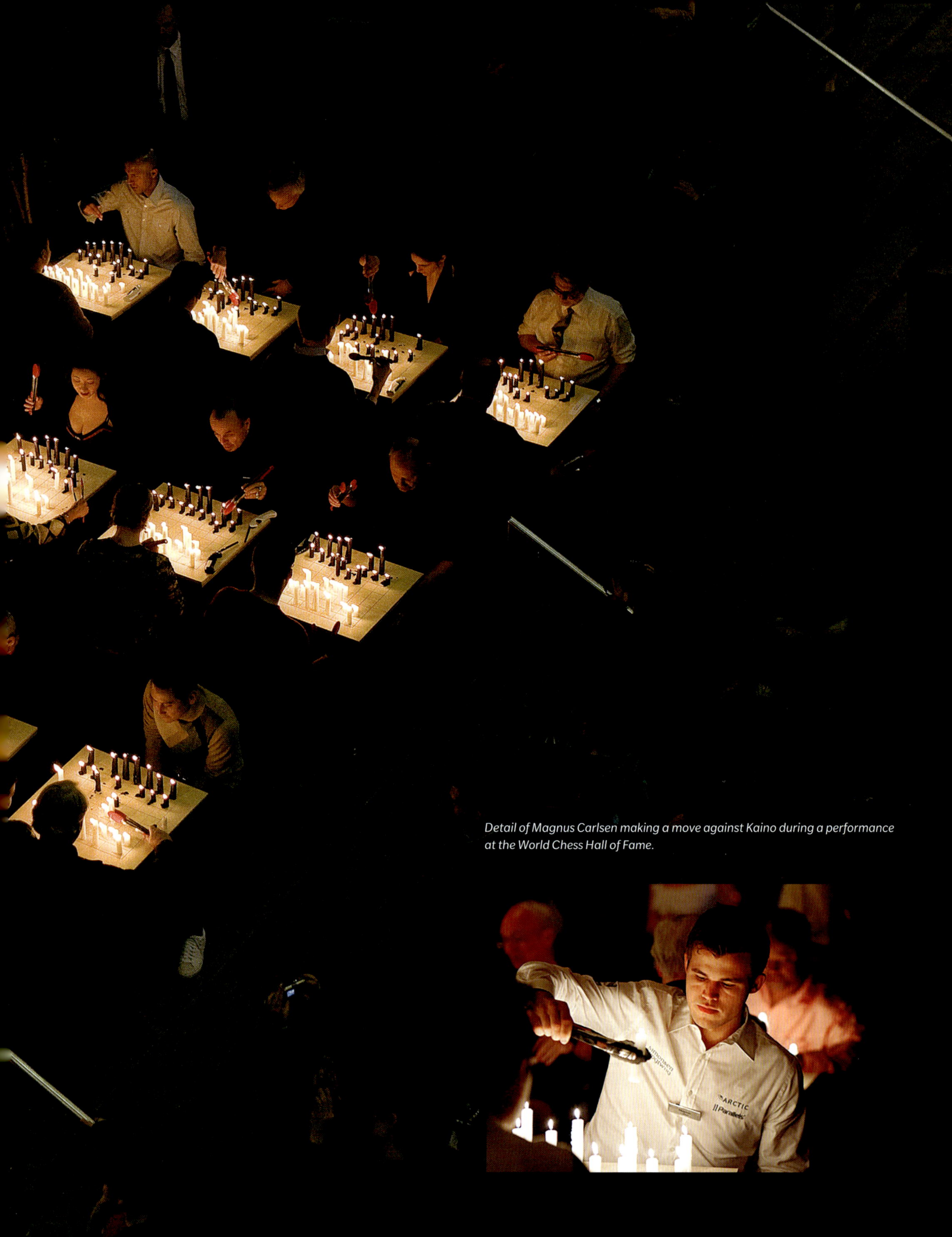


*Detail of Magnus Carlsen making a move against Kaino during a performance at the World Chess Hall of Fame.*

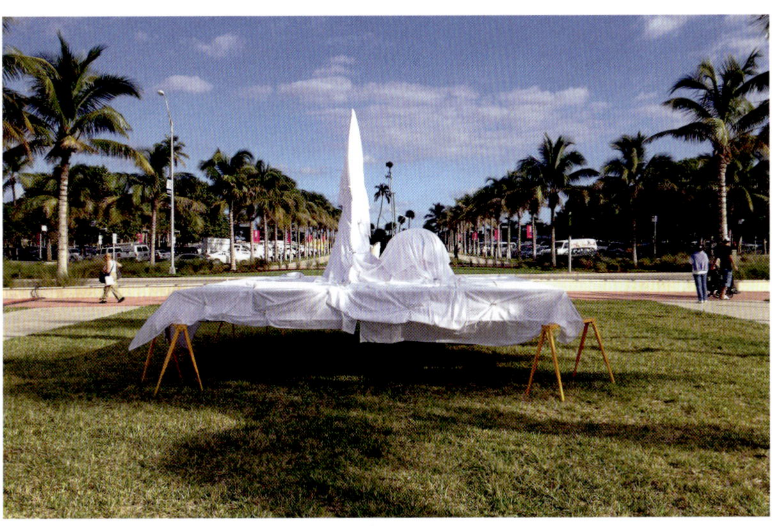

## Levitating the Fair

*2012, Performance, dimensions variable*

*Levitating the Fair* is an endurance performance and exercise in temporary world making. For the work, Kaino built a large-scale platform supporting two abstract forms referencing monuments of historical world's fairs. During Art Basel Miami Beach 2012, the artist launched a massive call for volunteers who were interested in helping produce a creative moment in the midst of the encounter between contemporary art and commerce. In front of the Bass Museum of Art, the artist, alongside a group of volunteers, lifted the platform off the ground. Volunteers swapped in and out and passersby briefly joined in at times, attempting to sustain the possibility of a creative encounter outside the realm of capital. A willing exchange of communal labor, the piece existed for over seven hours, later becoming a story disseminated by those who saw, those who participated, and those who chose not to.

*Photo: Afshin Shahidi*

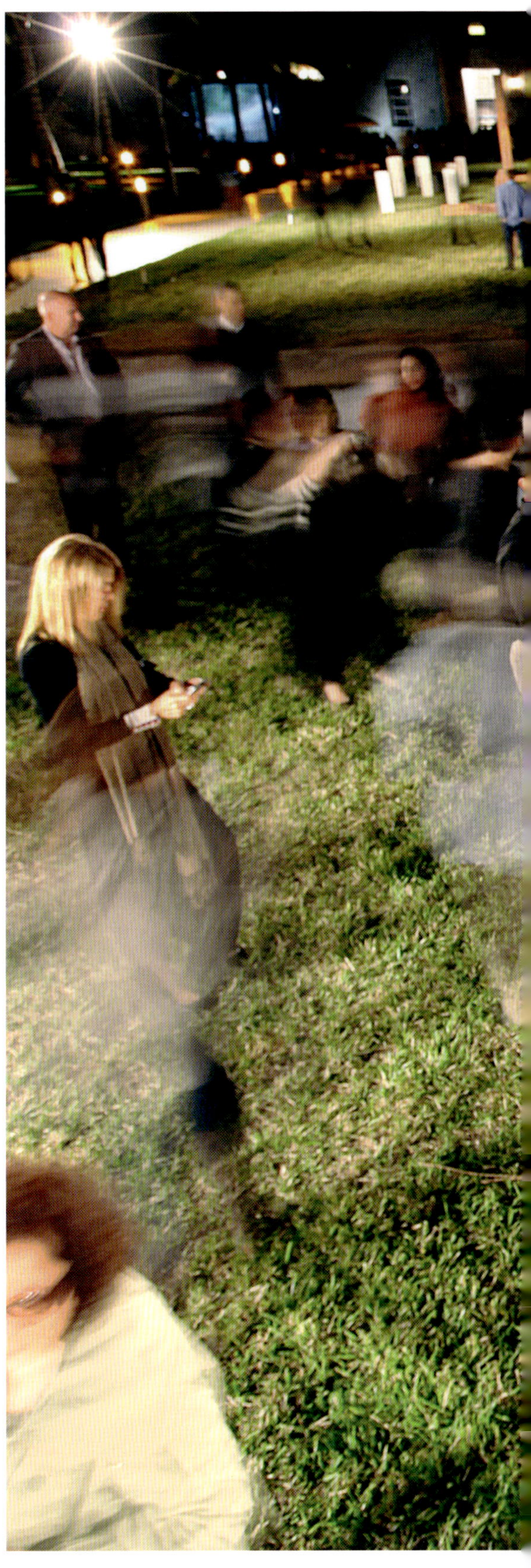

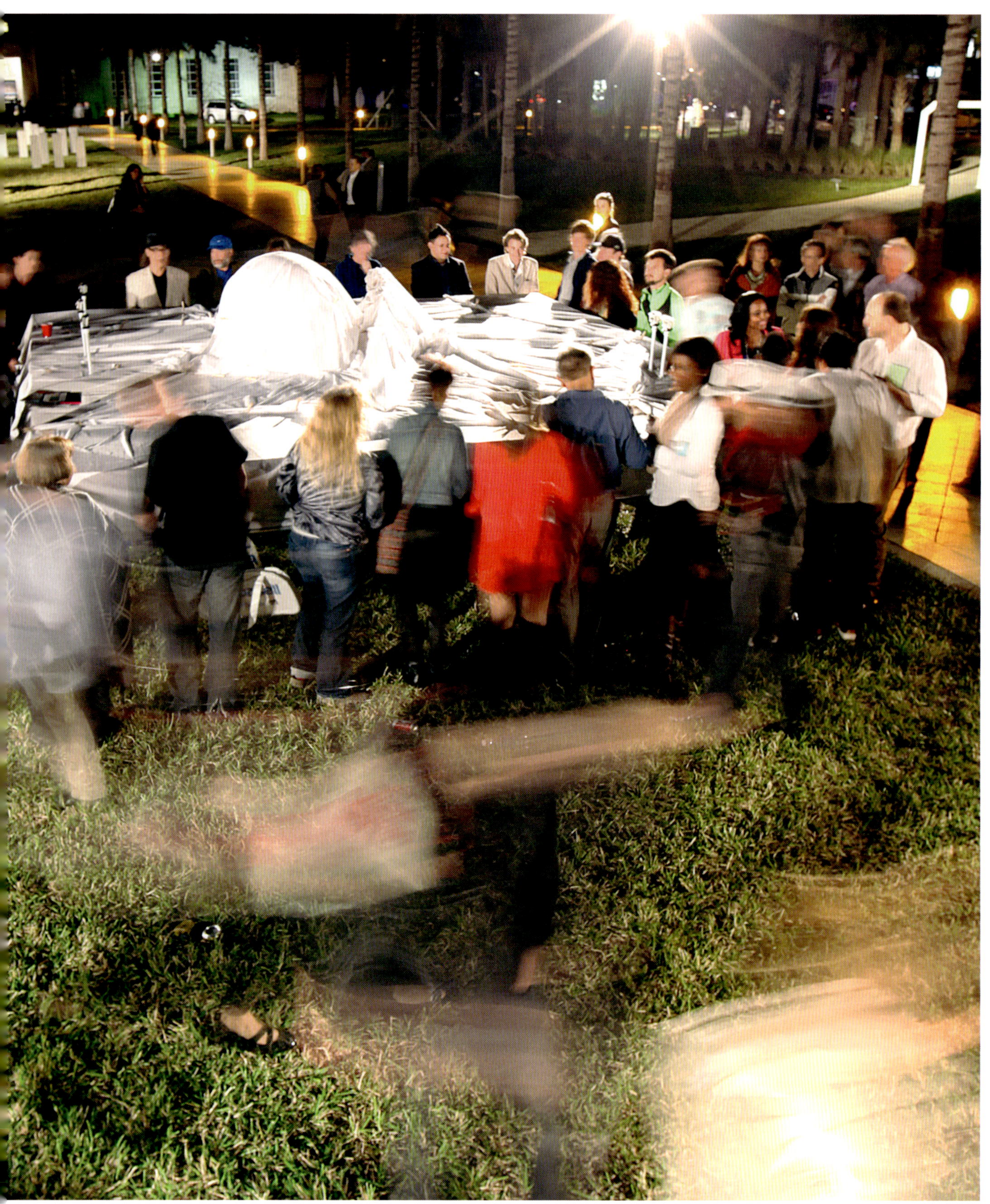

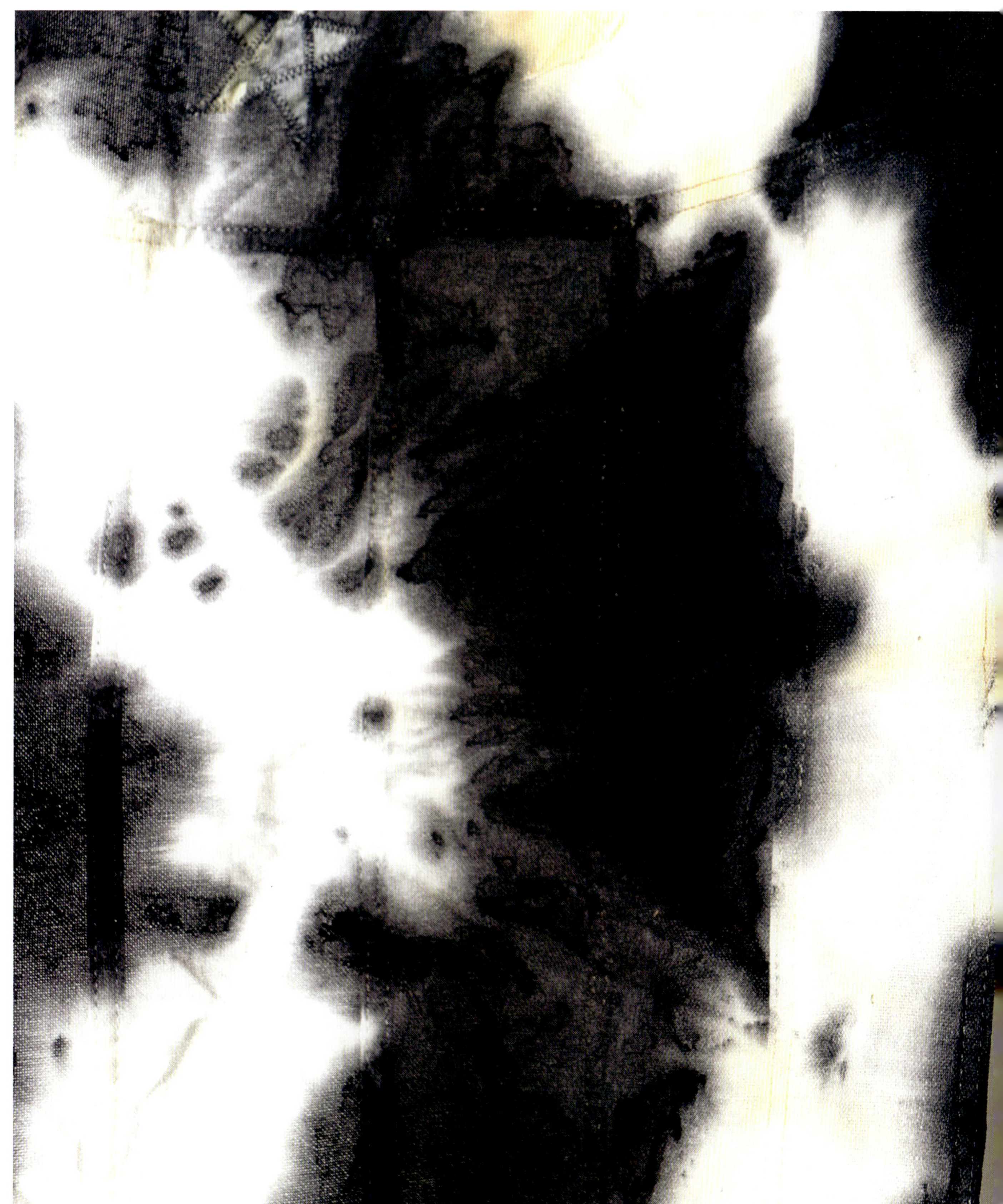

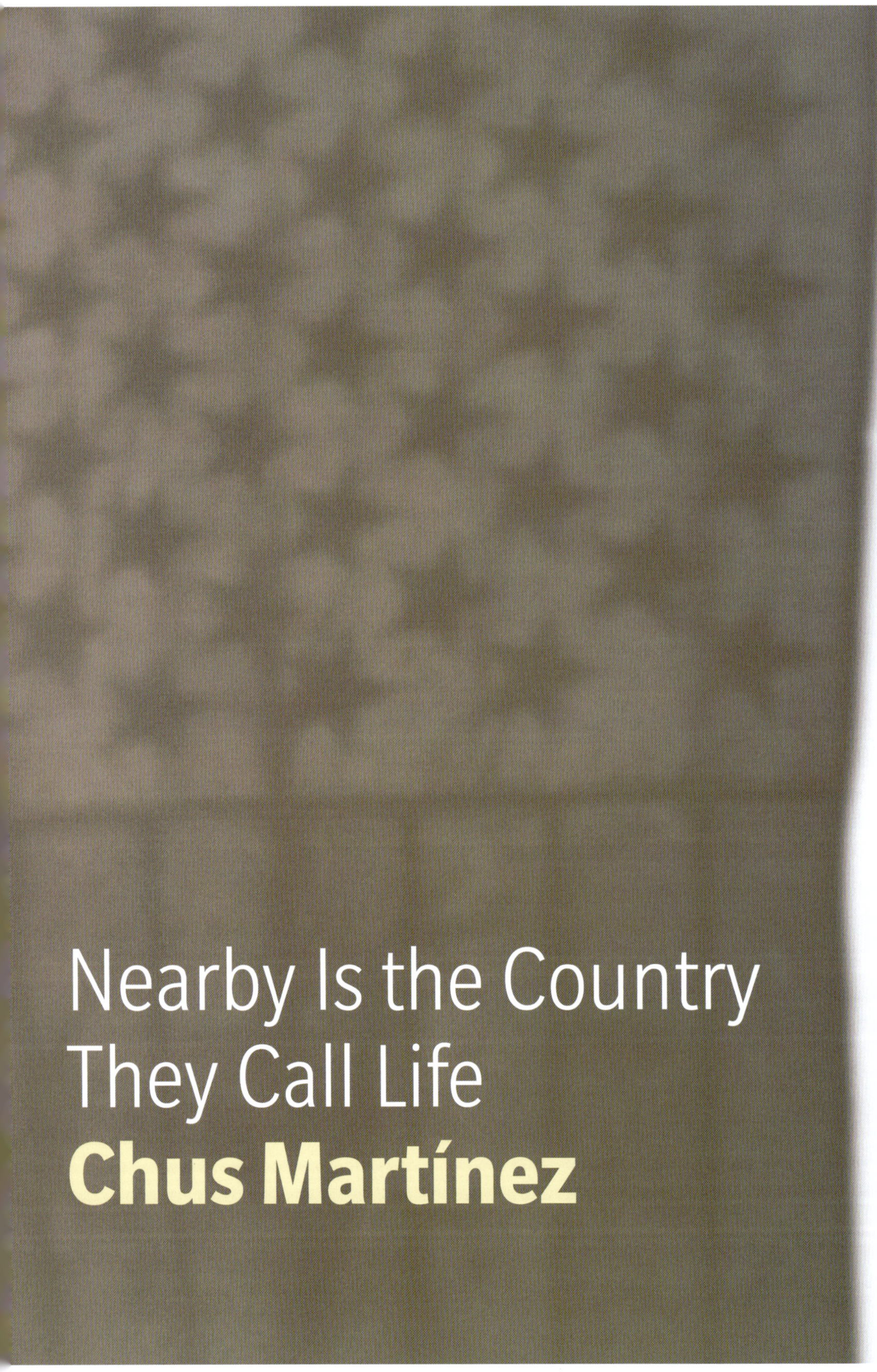

# Nearby Is the Country They Call Life

## Chus Martínez

## PART 1

Imagine a work that emerges and that, in doing so, discovers every time its own logic, its own structure, language, and form. Imagine the world from the point of view of a seed, and the surprise of discovering your own being, little by little, at different stages, through different relationships—to the ground, to water and light, and finally to all the other plants that are around you; then, imagine being mesmerized by the prairie. We are now in the mind of a seed, but we could try to be in the eye of a bird, in the substance of a tree or a coral. This exercise has existed for centuries—think of "animism," a word too often used to dismiss the possibility of comprehension of other forms of life from within. As humans, we have colonized the realm of intelligence, we have convinced ourselves that we are intelligent forms of life and that the intelligence of others is relative to ours. We have no problem in describing how, as in every patriarchal system of power, we may trespass upon this trait, but only via an inorganically programmed machine. Artificial intelligence is easy to imagine and it is becoming a familiar environment to many. We love to dream about the possibility of those machines being unchained from our ownership and discovering new worlds, as the colonial and imperial logic is still very much alive in this myth of creation, possession, and control.

But nothing speaks in opposition to a movement of liberation where the minds replicated in those programmed machines would not be ours, but the minds of the seeds at the beginning of my text. It is easy to imagine that the opening sentence of Donna Haraway's *When Species Meet*, "Whom and what do I touch when I touch my dog?"[1] would just as well apply one day to a computer seed or a computer bird or whale. Decolonizing intelligence, freeing the artificial world from the burden of human resemblance, acknowledging other forms of communication, would be crucial to finally adapting our minds and bodies to a mutuality so radical and beautiful that it would serve as the perfect ground for a new social.

Glenn Kaino's work acts in this manner already, and that's the reason why his work takes a different form with every project. There is no single artistic language, but multiple tongues able to adapt and embody the situation and the circumstances that the work inhabits. A decade or so ago, European discourse was possessed by the notion of artistic research. Since the question of production seemed inadequate to deal with the question of the "making of culture," research produced a needed fiction of depth and nearness to the subject matter. Research, though, is a concept so similar to the exploration by vessels that were dispatched from that very same continent, centuries back, to navigate, map, and take all the new territories at which they arrived. In research there strongly resonates the will to be civilized, to adapt the "discoveries" to the methods, norms, and rules drawn by prior researchers.

The differences among Kaino's works embody a thinking that is able to stray from a plot, from centrality principles, from a formal purpose that repeats itself through the works, from referencing something that could not be read or understood from the work itself. Why is this important? And what are the values and the dynamics that emanate from a work conceived this way?

In 1988, philosopher Vilém Flusser visited the Ars Electronica festival in Osnabrück, Germany. He gave an interesting interview for the occasion, in which he related simply how words can no longer describe the world.[2] Flusser explains how the alphabet was not only a radical invention that—more than 3,500 years ago—provided a code to describe reality; it was also the genesis of our notion of "historical time." The line of the text and the timeline are analogous, and over centuries, the logic of reading became the logic of the sequence of events. We are, says Flusser, in a revolution of thinking and communication, since neither text nor image alone can sufficiently describe reality. The "new" reality, or time, so to speak, needs a language that measures as well as maps, describes as well as depicts. There is no single language, discipline, or realm of knowledge that can alone handle the task of dealing with the world. Information technologies, he continues, have tried for years to produce synthetic codes that help us to define the tools of the near future.

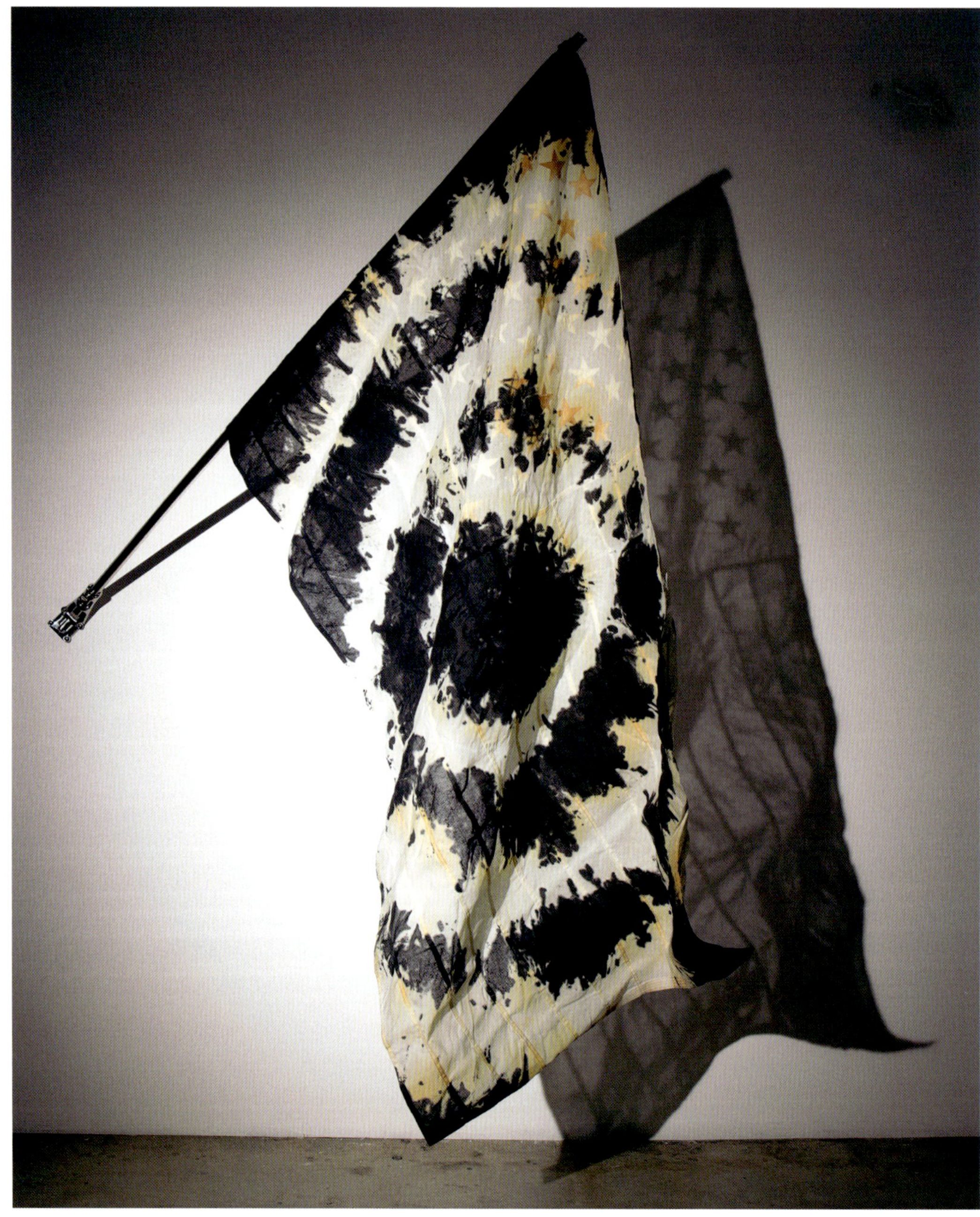

## Spontaneous Combustion

*2017, Cotton, tarring solution, time, 41 x 68 inches*

For this work, Kaino created a series of all-white flags in the pattern of the United States flag, each of which he wrapped and tie-dye painted using a historic Civil War-era recipe for tarring. Left alone, the fabric heats up to the point of spontaneous combustion, as the oxidation of the chemicals creates an exothermic reaction. The principal artistic gesture, the unwrapping of the flags, extinguishes the flame that has begun to scar the material. The self-igniting fire becomes a symbolic representation of the volatile nature of this time of crisis. The resulting pattern, a charred and stained surface of meandering territory, is a beautiful and simultaneously poignant image of a series of concentric circles: a target, alternating black, tan, and white. Under the light of display, the work transforms, and the object ceases to be the artwork, giving way for its shadow to be the primary visual signifier. Shadows, that defiantly and purposefully represent the Stars and Stripes as clearly and pristinely as a new flag might, provoke the poetic hope that even during our most unstable and explosive time, the ideals that lie within us and our nation might still be preserved.

*Photo: John Davis*

After Flusser, I would say that many artists—without knowing his theories—had the same instinct: to teach the nature of this new time and to develop the capacity to grasp its multiplication of synthetic realities. Already, in that interview, Flusser had mentioned a few positive examples of formulating the "good practice" of such a task: to address the complex architecture of today's forms of knowledge. And here lies the enormous importance of artistic practice, because as we see in the modus operandi of Kaino's works, the only way to address the diversity and the complexity of those architectures of knowledge is by trying, every single time, to adapt their language and to adopt their form. Only by leaving behind the linearity of art's presentation and explanation, its inside/outside logic, can we produce a collective way of exercising the needed nearness to many different forms of living, from the public realms of the social to the oceans.

This is, of course, very difficult, as it demands a completely new trust both in ways of making and in the discovery and performance of space under these different premises. Kaino's interest in different types of presentations (and also exhibitions) reflects a need unfulfilled in terms of figuring out how to de-formalize the production, presentation, and reception of art.

More than an "after form,"[3] our time demands a graspable method for an "un-form." It is known that we need to collapse the core premise of "aesthetics"—the distance that separates art from institutions, viewers, and artists themselves. However, this implies a nearness, or unprecedented fusion, of substances that have remained apart for so long that it would demand new organs; that is, a whole new theory of the relevance of the senses to an epistemology yet to come. It is for this reason that I believe in both a return to experimental conditions and an abandonment of the "middle class" as the universal *receiver* of our acts. The first is easy to name yet very difficult to put in place, because we are more interested in defining the steps that lead to results than the *educts*, the forces that motivate the experiment and make it possible. Art becomes the place for the continuous effort that creates these experimental conditions. And I am also positive that "presenting"—curating, if you will, which is an impulse very present in Kaino's work, with all its beauty and horror and rigor and humbleness—is the right way to challenge the way audiences encounter the works.

## PART 2

What is this all about? Regeneration.

This notion is central to Kaino's work, as is hope. A good example of how these principles operate is an installation entitled *Tank* (2014). A series of aquariums populated by corals are exhibited on different tables in a room, allowing the viewer to come close to the corals. Corals are the best example of our permanently distorted "cultural misunderstandings." They are often perceived as "plants" and as such they have suffered the same form of discrimination as the whole vegetable world. If we, the superior humans, occupy the top of the evolutionary pyramid, plants are at the bottom. Our perception of corals is mediated by their beauty. They are immobile and mesmerizing, so their appearance has created a sort of objectifying version of the "female problem" in the underwater world. Facts say, however, that corals are a community, a symbiotic collaboration between animals and plants to get nourishment. Oh well! We could say that science corrects our interpretation on the basis of research, but it also produces another one. It has been shown that corals are not only "beautiful," but also fundamental in the production of oxygen for earth. This shows their immense importance and has motivated great calls for action in recent years. Indeed, the bleaching of the coral reefs—due to pollution of the oceans caused by humans—has a devastating impact on marine life, and on the planet as a whole. However, the "rescue" impulses are motivated mainly by the usefulness of the corals. It is not out of deep respect, but out of convenience that we should not destroy our oxygen resources. I chose this example because it directly addresses the notion of regeneration in a direct way: the possibility of ending the damage to the coral reefs. But because it enables us to think about this notion in a wider and more open manner: as a value, as a practice.

What is it that would sustain this regeneration practice? Biotopism.

Biotopists consider that if this tree or this fish exists in a certain place, it is necessary to let it live where it is. There is no order to impose on the living beings. We should respect nature such as it is, and not such as it should be. I would say that this principle of coming close and exercising respect runs—each time in a different form—through all of Kaino's work. This way of thinking implies that life development is governed by a non-linear dynamic systems principle, and that the main task of artistic practice is to produce an experience that ensures we keep our awareness of this. We need art not for its aesthetic purposes, but because we remain fit, able, ready, elastic, and able to perceive how many worlds connect, and how perception helps us to grasp this reality. A reality that, without doubt, is going to shape the future of our relation with others, is the key to social justice, and promises a technology able to respect and care for all forms of life.

A new era demands a new human: a human capable of a depiction of the world without disaster, without the dualism between heaven and hell, human and nature. The exercise of adapting—our minds, our bodies, our cells—to an interpretation of life as a practice, the practice of the mutually productive relations of knowledge, thought, and care giving formed within shifting relationships of power, seems to me the biggest contribution of art and artists. Inventing and practicing new forms of inquiry reveals the inadequacy of our institutions, but more importantly the role the senses play in making language tell us about an epistemological transformation that entails an ethical metamorphosis of knowledge, thought, and care.

## PART 3

Kaino's *Wish* (2020) presents us with what we have done the most during these pandemic times: wishing. A fountain-like structure allows us three wishes. Complex in its design, with a tank where we can throw three objects that act as coins, it is simple in what it stands for. The work appeals, in another way, to the possibility of connecting our minds to the real—and to all the other minds wishing, too. There is a very long history of wishing wells. Offerings to wells are a tradition as people continue to offer pins, buttons, coins, as well as pieces of clothing to the fountain, so that they might be given good health in return. There is nothing more logical than to refer to and respect the source of water. Fountains are objects designed to teach us—through their prominent presence in public spaces—the importance of water; they refer to its origin underground, but they also allow for storytelling. And storytelling is another key element of Kaino's work.

One of the most difficult notions to come to terms with is freedom; we might assume that we know what it is, yet our experience of freedom is through the social norms and structures that are imposed upon us. While our laws guide us on freedom, art has historically offered a means of controlling the known, by bending it toward the unknown in such ways that freedom emerges. Within artistic discourse, the importance of the term "freedom is experimentation" lies not only in its relation to given norms and structures, but also in how it places nature at the core of art, almost without our noticing it. Historically, we have distinguished three understandings of nature: the Enlightenment's controlled nature; romantic nature, as in the creative-aesthetic nature of Romanticism; and motivated nature, the Hobbesian ideal of all against all. These are simultaneously present in our modern ideas of the subject and the social, with the experimental as the choreographic force that highlights their presence. Experimentation, then, is an announcement: a way of explaining how culture sees itself in opposition to the force of nature. Within the realm of art, the force of beauty and the terrifying force of nature coexist, containing and preventing these natures from penetrating the realms of organized life. And so, the task of an artist today is to break these dams and let the energies flood the world. But how?

By means of storytelling and love. Dissimilarly from argumentative and dialectical thinking, in storytelling there are no winners over ideas. The narrative—the artwork in this case—creates a ground where our emotions merge. We surpass the binary forces of separation in a realm where agreement is sublimated through empathy. All of Kaino's sculptural work is produced with the awareness that story telling is a collective practice that hopefully will re-emerge through the work. The Russian Structuralists dedicated time and effort to understanding what was needed to produce a tale: the elements that a story needs, the ingredients that add or twist the machine that narrates, as well as the actions needed to move us. Storytelling is grounded in the possibility of generating empathy for the story's characters in their relationship with the listeners/viewers. Storytelling drills in patterns and expectations that we solidify in the social—and therefore it has an enormous potential for changing old patterns—even before we have a chance to reach the level of politics.

And love? Love is the key experience that needs to be redefined, reinvented as a force that can transform Western, modern ways of framing political and social action. This is a fundamental thought in Kaino's work. Love as the notion that names a new political contract between human and all other forms of life. But, in addition, love as the force that enables an experience of this bond, replacing aesthetics by forms of experiential relation that open up a transformative future for the audience. His work is driven by the desire to provide a ground for many different ways of relating to the real, to the elements of nature, to the languages of science, to the dreams of a better world, to total inclusivity.

Which love is this? It is the power of becoming defined by differences. A force that aims to overcome liberal individualism through the production of commonality. A force that cannot be refused, it mutates into the collective effort to embrace indigenous epistemologies, the decolonization of science, a competent rescue of ethnological knowledges; love as the invention of new methods of transmission capable of producing eloquence on the future(s) to come. Love as the socio-political force that proposes life as radically different from violence.

Love is the key experience that needs to be redefined, reinvented as a force that can transform Western, modern ways of framing political and social action. This is a fundamental thought in Glenn Kaino's work.

Which love is this? It is the power of becoming defined by differences. A force that aims to overcome liberal individualism through a production of commonality. A force that cannot be refused, it mutates into the collective effort to embrace indigenous epistemologies, the decolonization of science, a competent rescue of ethnological knowledges, love as the invention of new forms of transmission capable of producing eloquence on the future(s) to come. Love as the socio-political force that proposes life as radically different from violence.

[1] *Donna Harraway,* When Species Meet *(Minneapolis: University of Minnesota Press, 2008).*

[2] *https://red-thread.org/en/about-technical-revolution/.*

[3] *Author's note: I believe that we are in a time where art does not need to fight existing or inherited forms or formats, but can engage in a morphing of that which has been inherited in order to see how this may provoke a different reality/artistic language.*

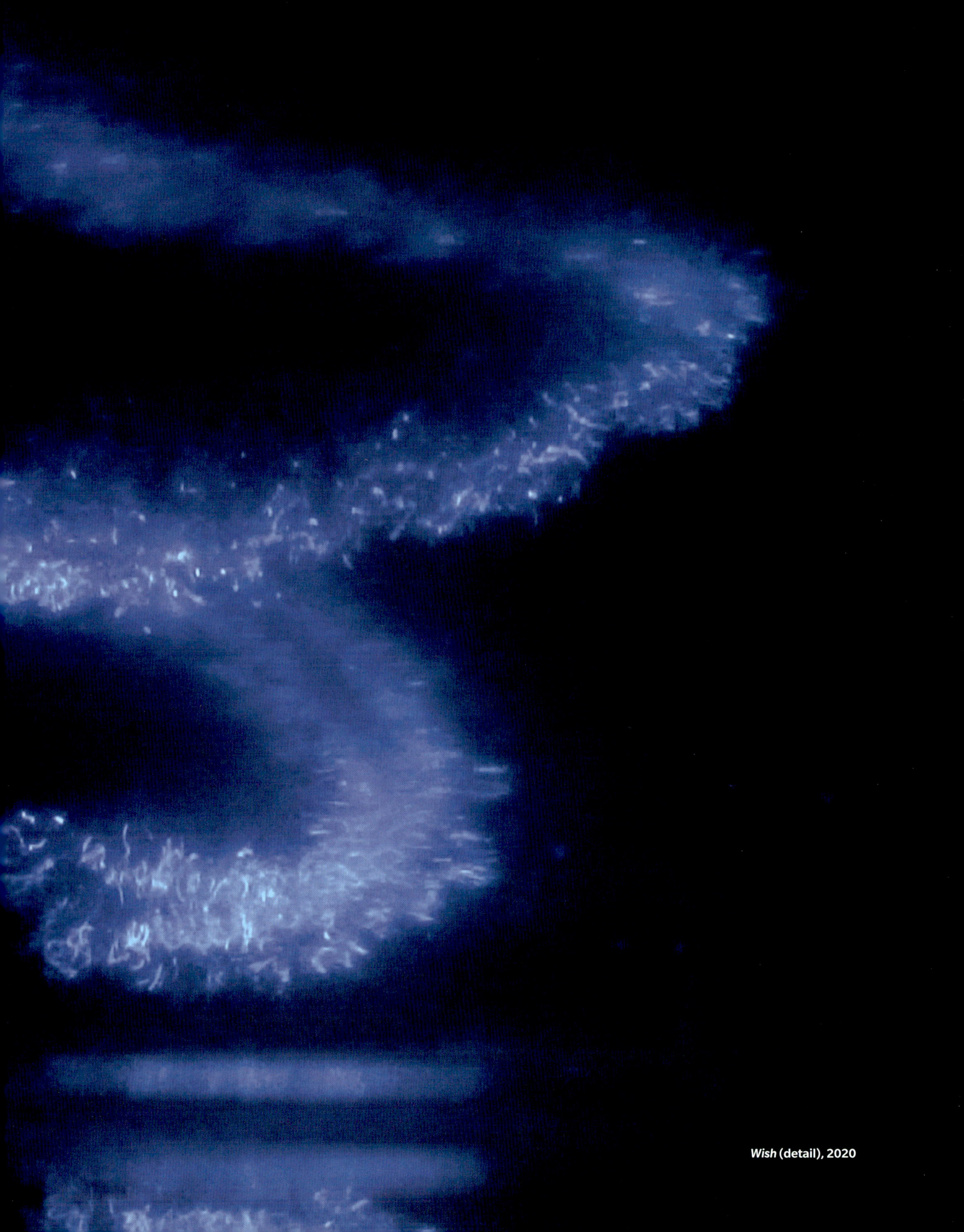

*Wish* (detail), 2020

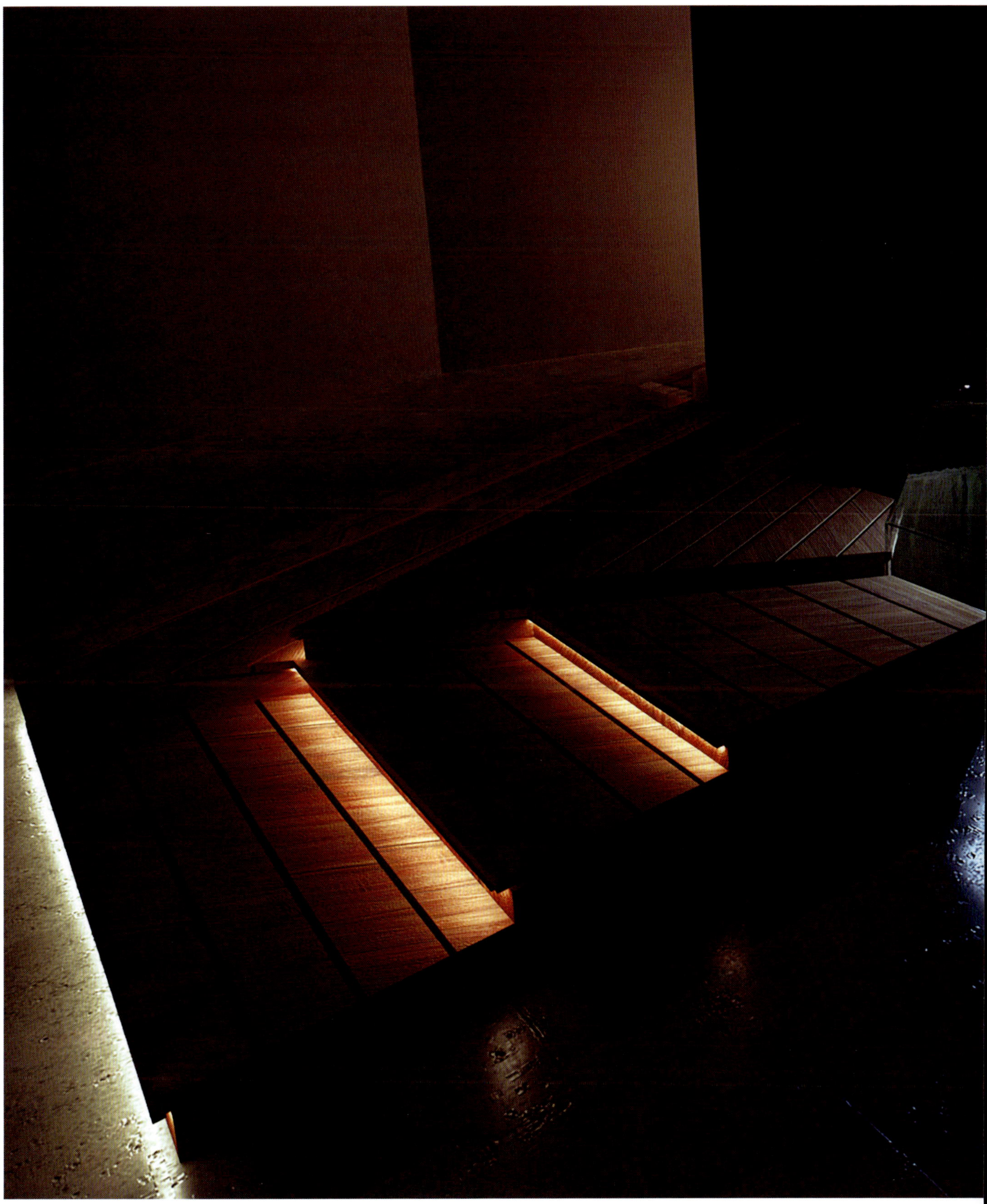

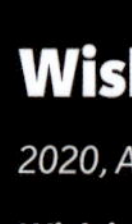

## Wish

*2020, Acrylic, water, dinoflagellates, lights, dimensions variable*

**_Wish_ is an experience activated by the viewer, who is encouraged to make three wishes while throwing a cast sculptural "coin" into a conceptual wishing well—a large sculptural tank filled with bioluminescent dinoflagellates. When the viewer enters a darkened room, there is a low glow that reveals the tank, which exists as a crystal shape. The viewer is given three cast objects in the shape of a coin but with the texture of street rocks, an association with the act of protest. As the tokens fall toward the bottom of the tank, they agitate the dinoflagellates and create a brightly lit trail of their path, a visualization of hope. In this work, the viewers themselves are the agents of visibility; their actions have a direct correlation to the images that appear.**

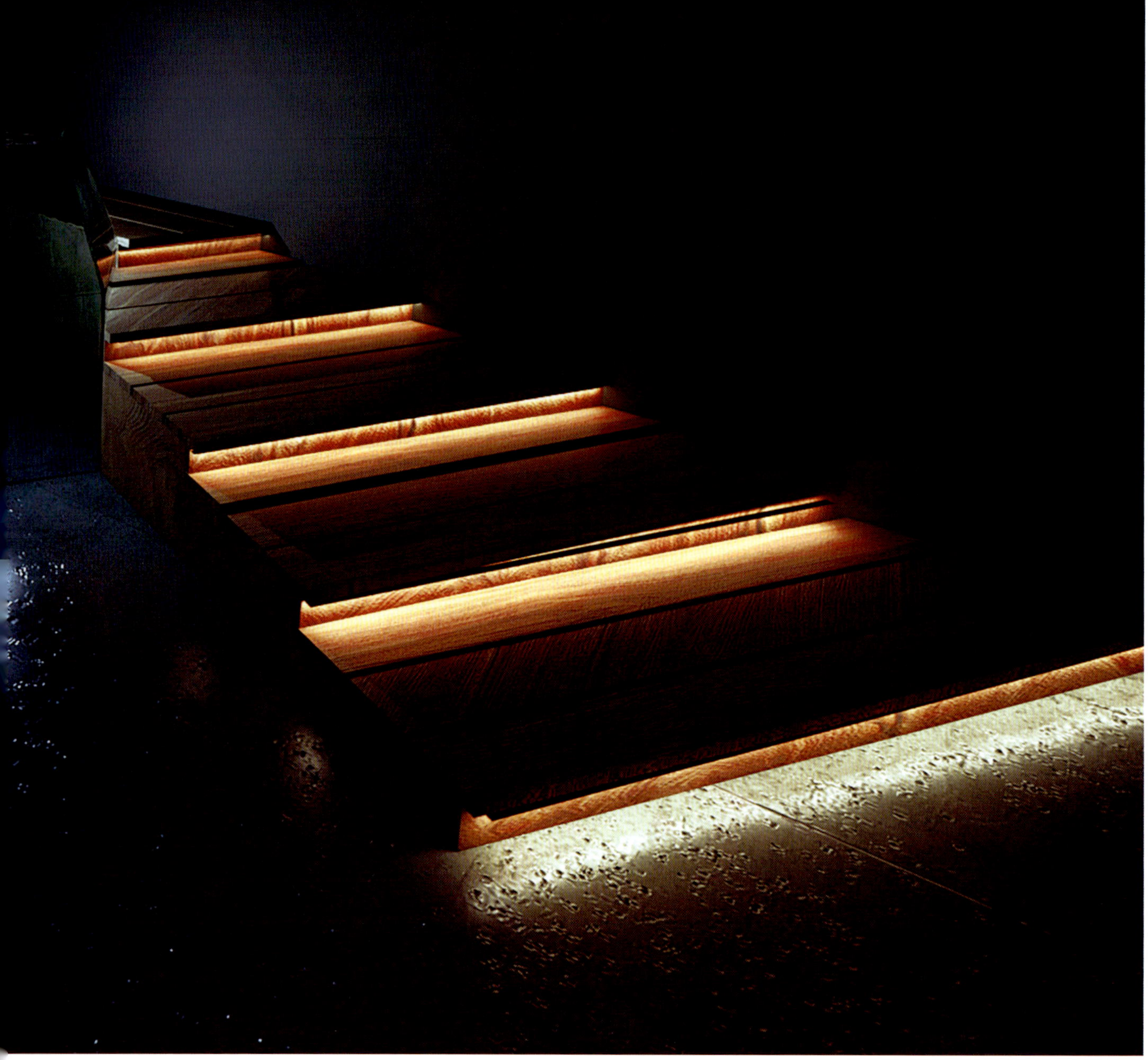

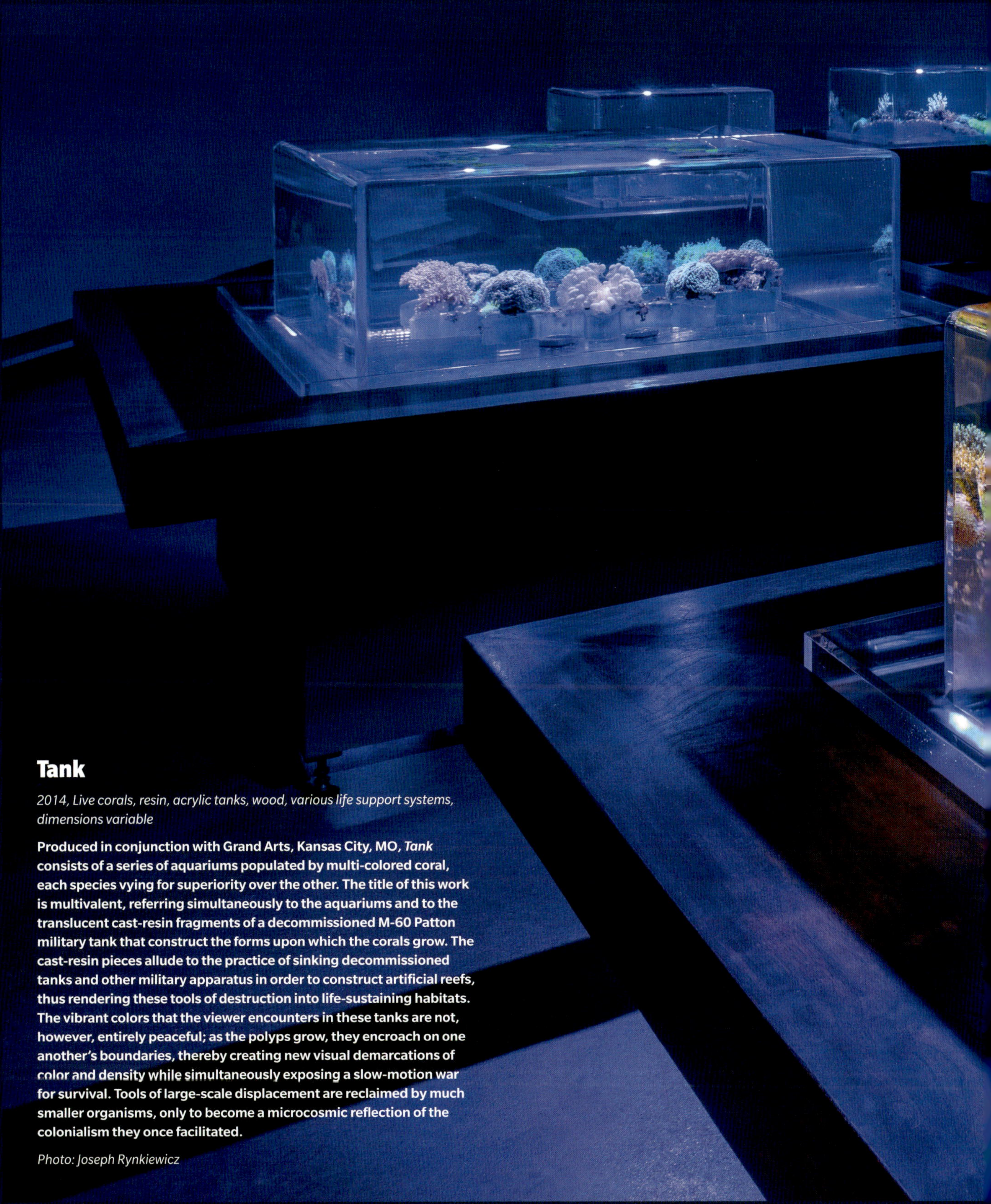

## Tank

*2014, Live corals, resin, acrylic tanks, wood, various life support systems, dimensions variable*

**Produced in conjunction with Grand Arts, Kansas City, MO, *Tank* consists of a series of aquariums populated by multi-colored coral, each species vying for superiority over the other. The title of this work is multivalent, referring simultaneously to the aquariums and to the translucent cast-resin fragments of a decommissioned M-60 Patton military tank that construct the forms upon which the corals grow. The cast-resin pieces allude to the practice of sinking decommissioned tanks and other military apparatus in order to construct artificial reefs, thus rendering these tools of destruction into life-sustaining habitats. The vibrant colors that the viewer encounters in these tanks are not, however, entirely peaceful; as the polyps grow, they encroach on one another's boundaries, thereby creating new visual demarcations of color and density while simultaneously exposing a slow-motion war for survival. Tools of large-scale displacement are reclaimed by much smaller organisms, only to become a microcosmic reflection of the colonialism they once facilitated.**

*Photo: Joseph Rynkiewicz*

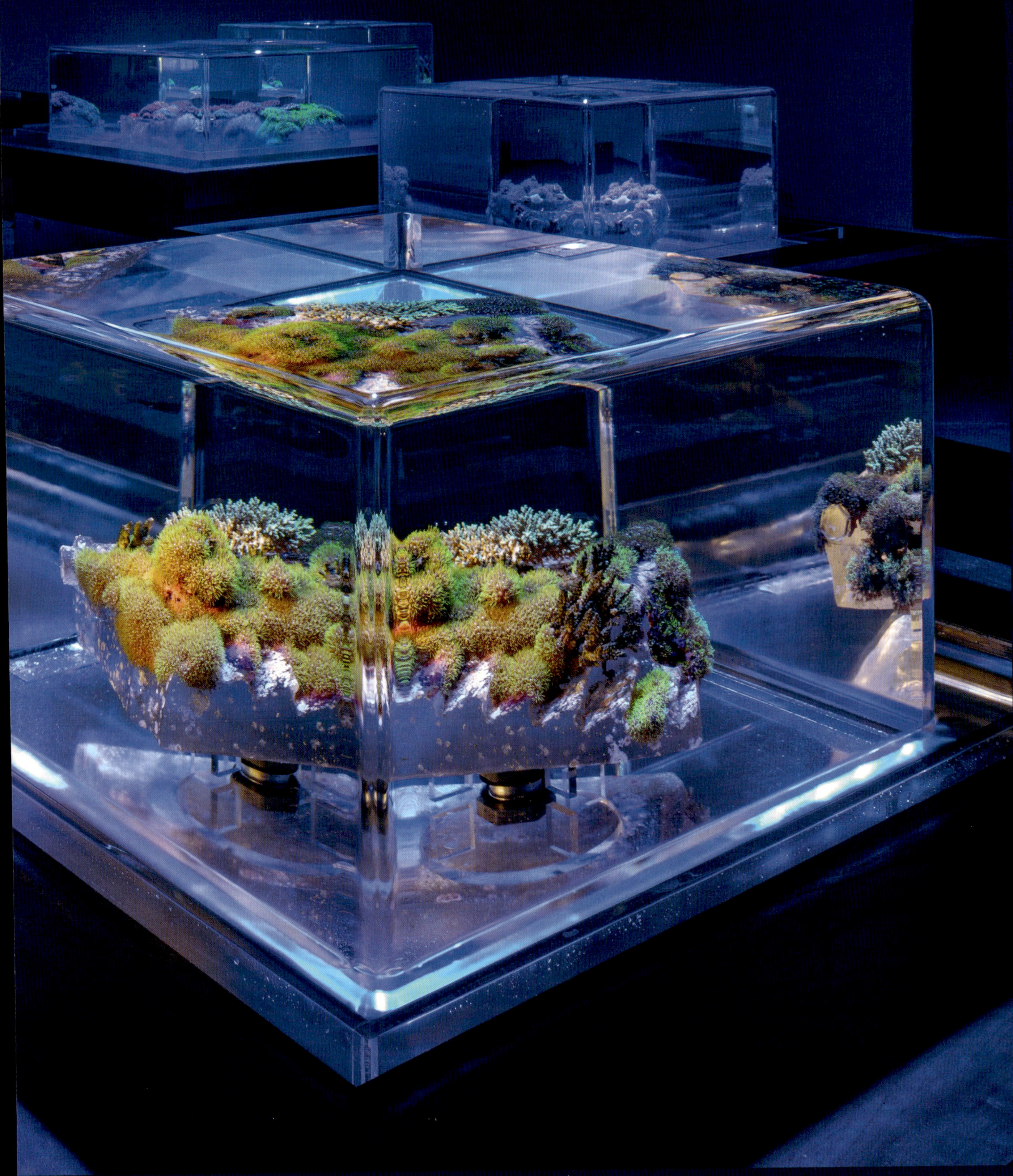

# Changing Course
# **David Gruber**

The vibration of the hum, the larynx shivering. Mm-other, Mm-adre, Mm-oeder. Air extending outward through the lungs. Four hundred million years ago, the lungfish or Sarcopterygians took their first breaths outside of the ocean. These aquatic relatives endowed us our paired limbs, arms and legs, as we took our first hesitant steps out of the sea.

It was once thought that the oceans were a silent world, "*Le Monde du Silence*,"[1] but ancient songs have reverberated beneath the waves from long before we ever considered evolving to stand upright. Our human ears now have the capacity to hear resonating sea urchin skeletons orchestrating coastal ensembles,[2] to listen to millions of lanternfish moving their jaws to "evening choruses" deep among submarine canyons.[3] We now know that eager audiences even consist of fish larvae, which have finely tuned hearing to listen for the "homeward sound" of their acoustical homes.[4] Our collective thoughts and knowledge have shifted to recognize the beat that has been.

Nicolaus Copernicus had few of his mortal breaths remaining in 1473, when he exhaled his idea that the earth is not the center of the universe and that we revolve around a dwarf star that we call our sun. His text titled *De revolutionibus orbium coelestium*, or "On the Revolutions of the Celestial Spheres," was not widely discussed at the time. This idea took centuries to ignite into a hypothesis with ever-mounting clarity and evidence, a heretical revolution of celestial capacity.

I sometimes look up at our dwarf star with squinted eyes. She does not appear dwarf to me, she is our everything-orb, floating high in the sky eighty million miles away. Burning like an inferno; millions of hydrogen bombs igniting and gently providing the nourishment to the green leaf beside me. Plants have the machinery to catch and consume her gentle nourishing photonic magic. It took time for me to accept the duality of the sun's emitted particles, being both particles and waves at the same time. I've studied this time and time again, like analyzing the magic tricks of Harry Houdini (aka Erik Weisz), how he might unshackle after diving into the depths. I've come to understand how the plant embraces and harnesses Lilliputian waves, waves that measure less than a millionth of a meter, not dissimilar to the meter-high ocean waves I joyously played in as a child. James Maxwell deciphered the wave particle dualism wizardry in 1865. In equations, he explained how electric and magnetic fields travel through space as waves and move at the speed of light. Like E=MC2, a natural law that has yet to be disavowed.

Breathe in. Breathe out. Out of our mouths come water and carbon dioxide. In simple terms, plants use carbon dioxide and water to produce sugar and oxygen. Our thoughts and bodies are energized by this sugar and oxygen and we exhale carbon dioxide and water. Once returned to the air, this is eventually taken up by a plant once again. Our star, our plants, our bodies. The cycle, the revolution continues. The sun burns bright until, someday, it doesn't.

Stephen Hawking predicted in 2014 that the full development of artificial intelligence, combined with robotics and other technologies, "could spell the end of the human race."[5] Why would we continue down a path that leads to the demise of our own species? Why not invent the most gentle and connective technology in the world—for example, robots that can embrace a jellyfish without harm?[6] Why end our human cycle prematurely? Going backward is not an option on our mortal timescales. We cannot return to the sea in our lifetimes, in the way that marine mammals have slowly done. Our noses gradually becoming blowholes; our ears becoming more acute than our eyes; our heartbeats

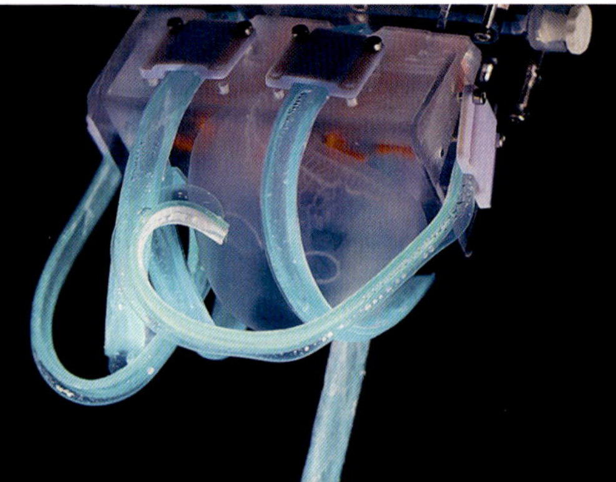

**Ultra-gentle soft robot with "linguini fingers" that can interact with fragile life, such as jellyfish, using less force that our eyelids exert while resting on the eyeballs. Engineered by Dr. Nina Sinatra of the Harvard Microrobotics Laboratory.** *Photo: David Gruber*

slowed down; and with the ability to conserve oxygen for prolonged breath-hold dives. We cannot leave the past behind, unexamined. We need a new way forward; one that reckons with how we got here.

Nikki Giovanni's 2010 poem, "Quilting the Black-Eyed Pea (We're Going to Mars)," comes to mind:

> *When the rocket red glares the*
> *astronauts will be able to see*
> *themselves pull away from Earth...*
> *as the ship goes deeper*
> *they will see a sparkle of blue...*
> *and then one day not only will*
> *they not see Earth...*
> *they won't know which way to look...*
> *and that is why NASA needs to*
> *call Black America*
> *They need to ask: How did you calm*
> *your fears...*
> *How were you able to decide you*
> *were human even when everything*
> *said you were not...*[7]

While we can go to Mars, are we ready to go to Mars? Are we ready to relinquish our training wheels of intraspecies and interspecies dialogue here on earth? As Glenn Kaino states in *In the Light of a Shadow*, it is more evident than ever that we must fight "to dismantle the repressive frameworks of power that have shaped our relationship to our planet, and each other."[8]

Have we considered the vitreous fluids in our eyes and *how* they will respond to life in space? How the change in gravity will affect the ebb and flow of the cerebrospinal fluid in our brains and spinal cords?[9] I find hopeful essences embedded in life's symbioses. The meandering relationship to a plus/plus (+, +) stands as an example of beauty and magnificence. Examples of this include the coral and *Symbiodinium* dinoflagellate union that leads to reef structures that can be seen from space, arising from nutrient-poor oligotrophic watery deserts; the cellulose-consuming microscopic gut community that allows wood to power termites' and insects' engines, a process so powerful it changed biogeochemical cycles and climate; and the plastid inside plants who trace their ancestry back to a union between a cyanobacteria and a protozoa. Or perhaps we don't even have to look far—just inside each of us—to honor the mitochondria inside our cells, these energy factories with their separate mitochondrial DNA having their roots as purple non-sulphur bacteria.

No other species in the history of life on earth has revolved around the conscious situation in which we now find ourselves. How do we move forward collectively toward a bright future? How do we dismantle the repressive frameworks of power that have shaped our relationship to our planet, and each other? We need more than magic to lift the chains on the box that imprisons Schrödinger's cat. As the sun sets, I find hope in the rays of light, composed of particles and waves; in the duality of natural processes; in the prospect of equity and the inevitability of evolution.

Tomorrow is a new day; another possibility to find the light of the shadow.

[1] *Jacques-Yves Cousteau and Louis Malle,* Le Monde Du Silence, *1956, 86 mins.*

[2] *Craig A. Radford, et al, "Resonating sea urchin skeletons create coastal choruses," in* Marine Ecology Progress Series *(June 2008), 362, pp. 37–43.*

[3] *Robert D. McCauley and Douglas H Cato, "Evening choruses in the Perth Canyon and their potential link with Myctophidae fishes," in* Journal of the Acoustical Society of America *(2016), 140(4), pp. 2384-2398.*

[4] *Stephen D Simpson, et al, "Homeward Sound," in* Science *(2105), 308, p. 221.*

[5] *Rory Cellan-Jones, "Stephen Hawking warns artificial intelligence could end mankind," December 2, 2014, www.bbc.com/news/technology-30290540.*

[6] *Michael Tessler, et al, "Ultra-gentle soft robotic fingers induce minimal transcriptomic response in a fragile marine animal,"* Current Biology *(2020), 30(4), pp. 157-158.*

[7] *From Nikki Giovanni,* Quilting the Black Eyed Pea: Poems and Not Quite Poems *(William Morrow, 2010).*

[8] *From Kaino's proposal text for this MASS MoCA exhibition, 2020.*

[9] *Vincent Koppelmans, et al, "Brain structural plasticity with spaceflight,"* npj Microgravity 2 *(2016).*

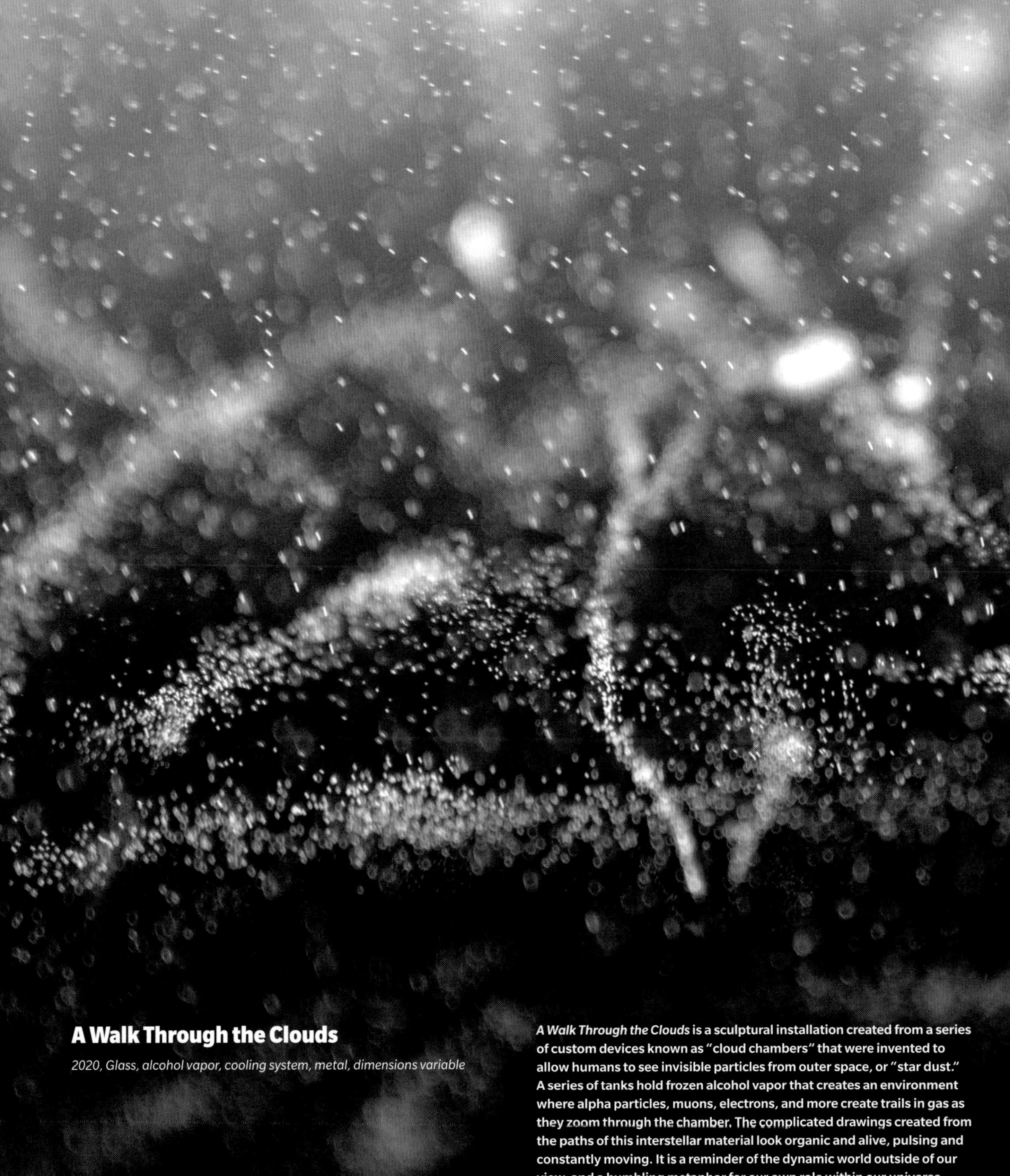

## A Walk Through the Clouds

*2020, Glass, alcohol vapor, cooling system, metal, dimensions variable*

*A Walk Through the Clouds* is a sculptural installation created from a series of custom devices known as "cloud chambers" that were invented to allow humans to see invisible particles from outer space, or "star dust." A series of tanks hold frozen alcohol vapor that creates an environment where alpha particles, muons, electrons, and more create trails in gas as they zoom through the chamber. The complicated drawings created from the paths of this interstellar material look organic and alive, pulsing and constantly moving. It is a reminder of the dynamic world outside of our view, and a humbling metaphor for our own role within our universe.

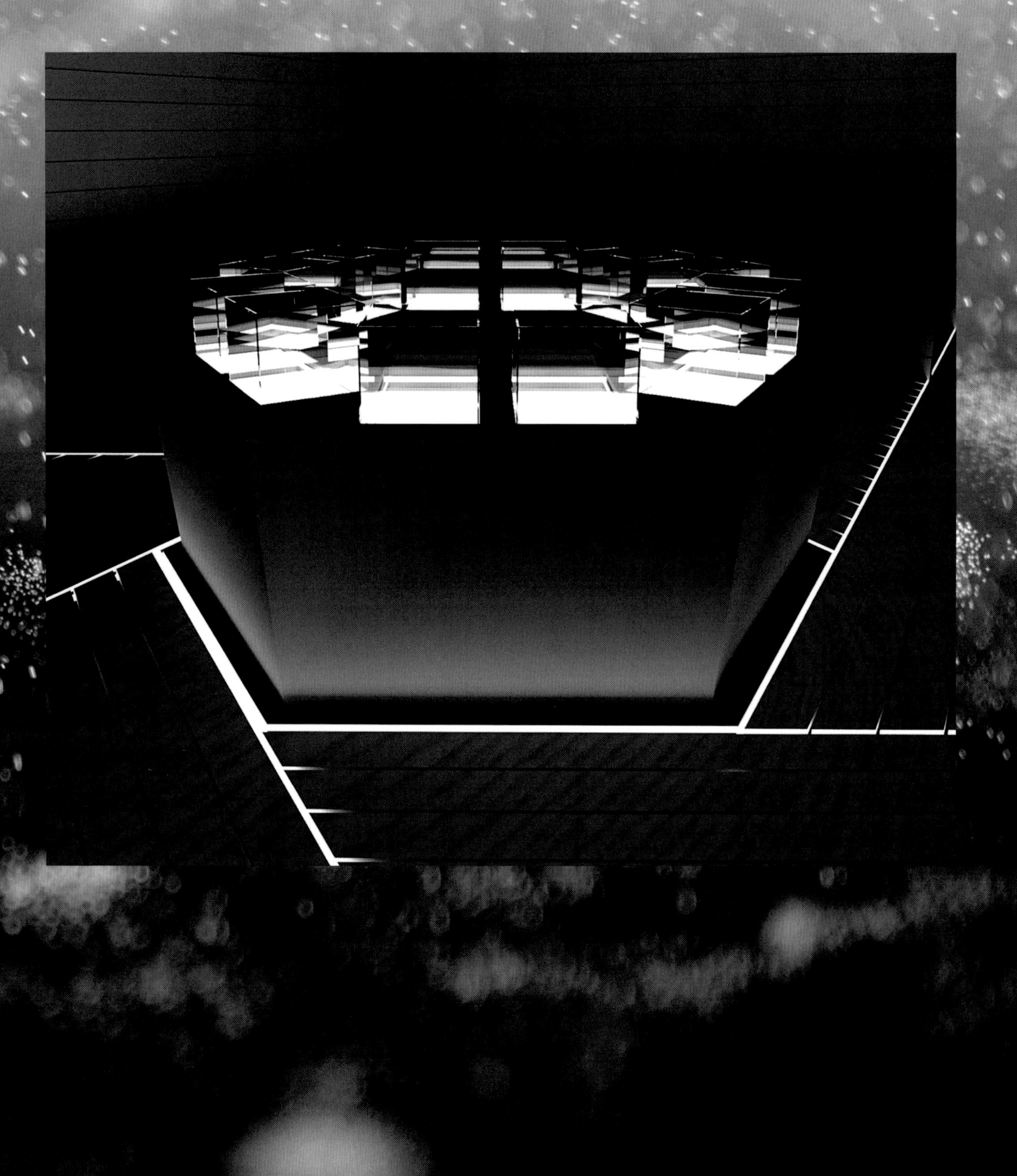

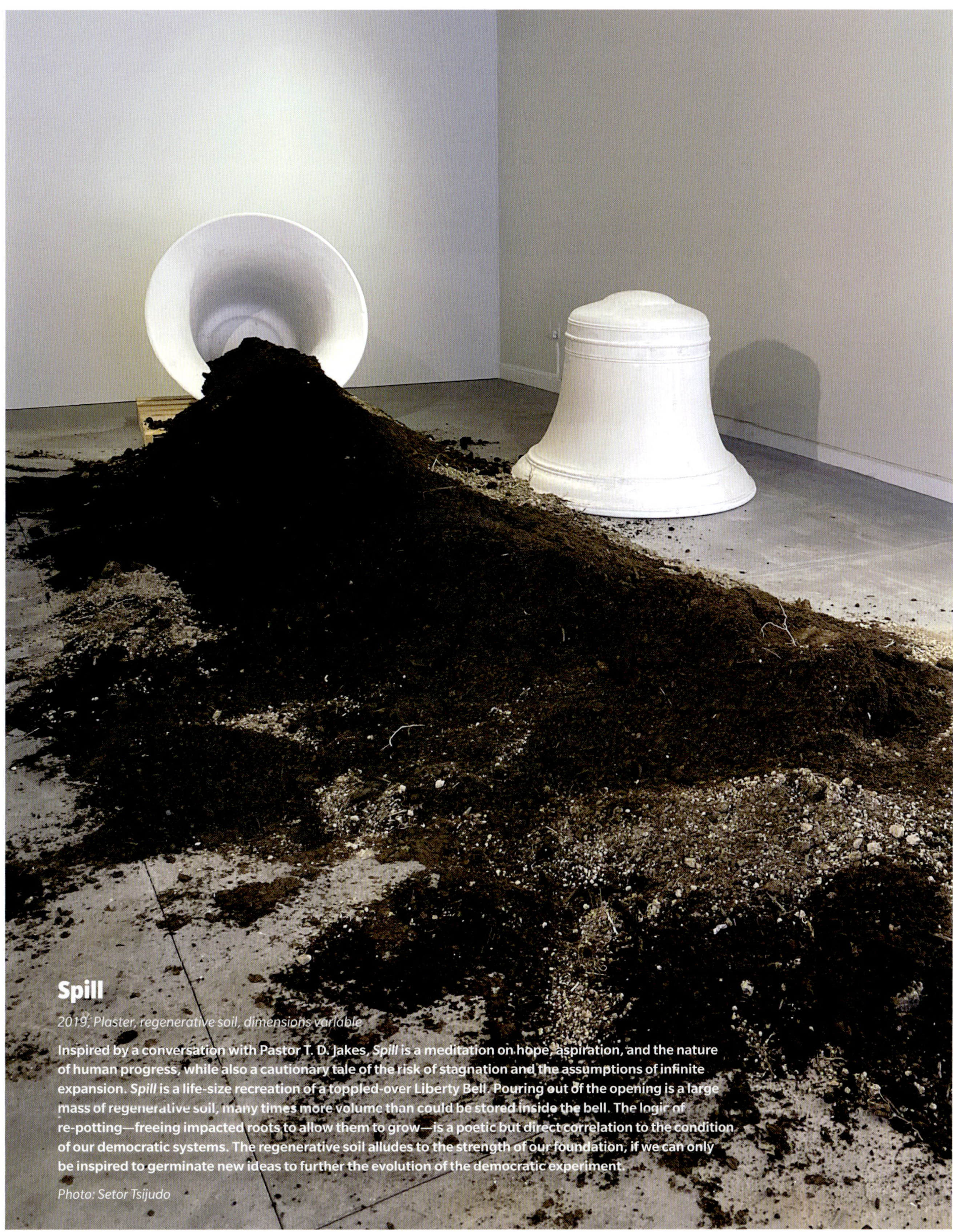

## Spill

*2019, Plaster, regenerative soil, dimensions variable*

Inspired by a conversation with Pastor T. D. Jakes, *Spill* is a meditation on hope, aspiration, and the nature of human progress, while also a cautionary tale of the risk of stagnation and the assumptions of infinite expansion. *Spill* is a life-size recreation of a toppled-over Liberty Bell. Pouring out of the opening is a large mass of regenerative soil, many times more volume than could be stored inside the bell. The logic of re-potting—freeing impacted roots to allow them to grow—is a poetic but direct correlation to the condition of our democratic systems. The regenerative soil alludes to the strength of our foundation, if we can only be inspired to germinate new ideas to further the evolution of the democratic experiment.

*Photo: Setor Tsijudo*

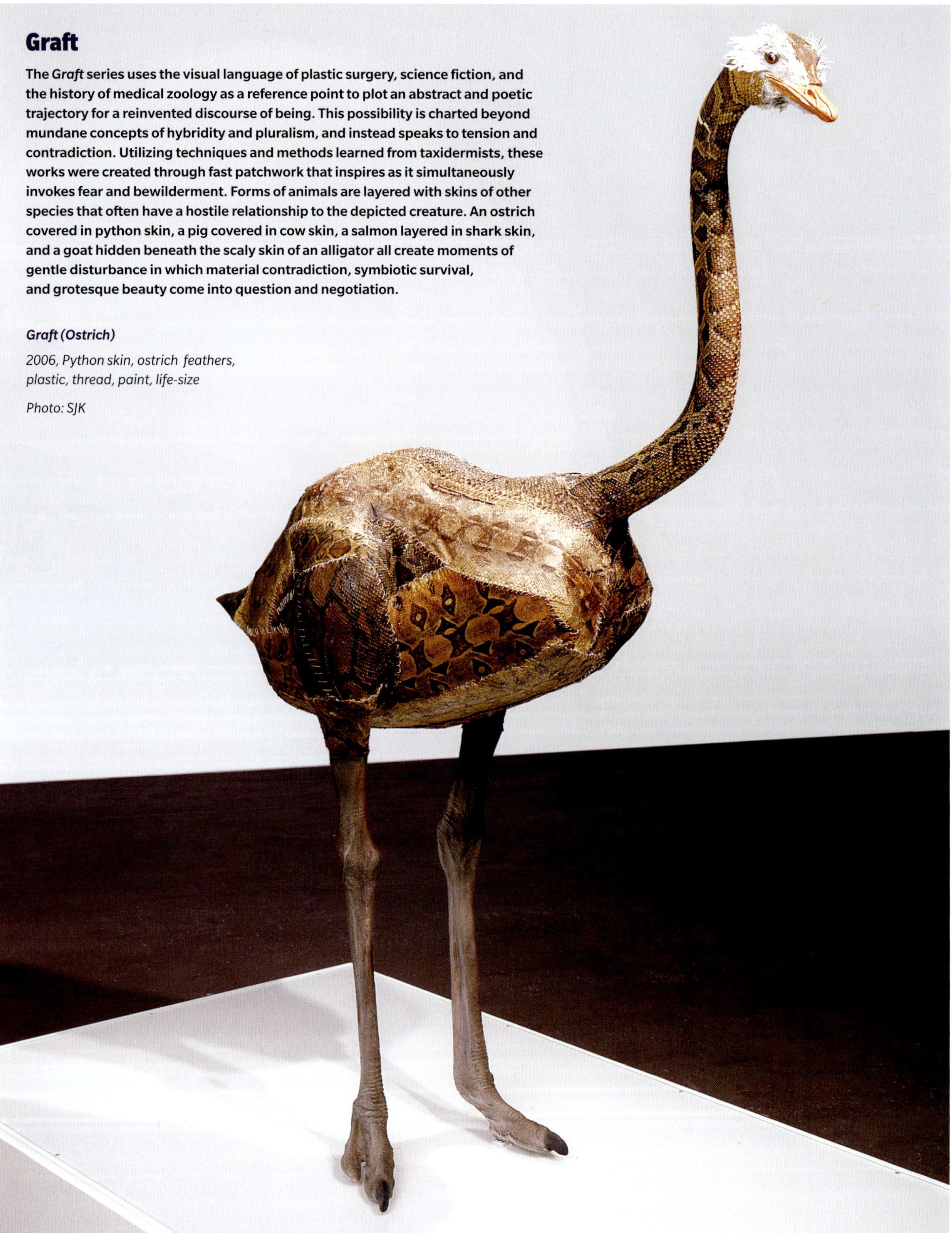

# Graft

The *Graft* series uses the visual language of plastic surgery, science fiction, and the history of medical zoology as a reference point to plot an abstract and poetic trajectory for a reinvented discourse of being. This possibility is charted beyond mundane concepts of hybridity and pluralism, and instead speaks to tension and contradiction. Utilizing techniques and methods learned from taxidermists, these works were created through fast patchwork that inspires as it simultaneously invokes fear and bewilderment. Forms of animals are layered with skins of other species that often have a hostile relationship to the depicted creature. An ostrich covered in python skin, a pig covered in cow skin, a salmon layered in shark skin, and a goat hidden beneath the scaly skin of an alligator all create moments of gentle disturbance in which material contradiction, symbiotic survival, and grotesque beauty come into question and negotiation.

***Graft (Ostrich)***

*2006, Python skin, ostrich feathers, plastic, thread, paint, life-size*

*Photo: SJK*

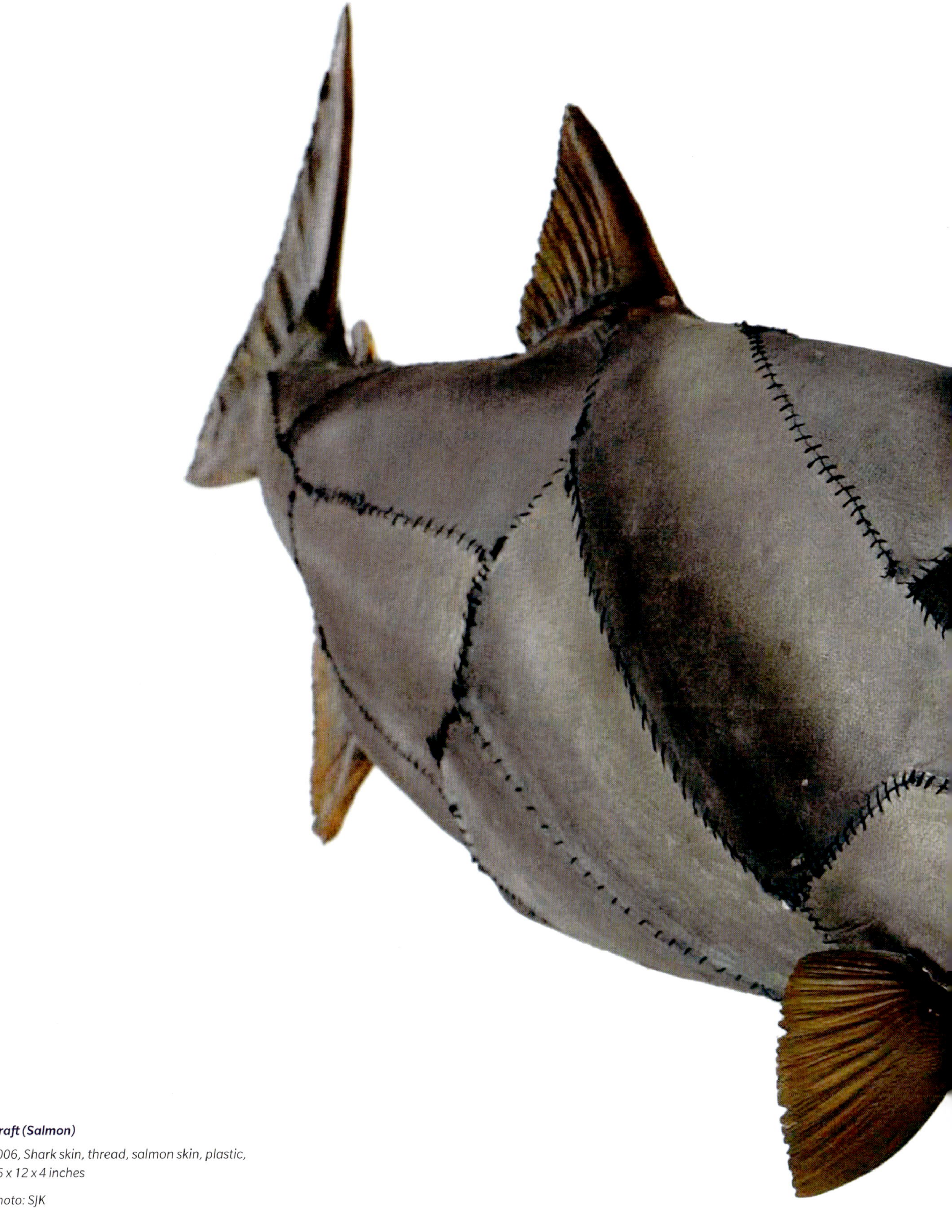

***Graft (Salmon)***

*2006, Shark skin, thread, salmon skin, plastic, 36 x 12 x 4 inches*

*Photo: SJK*

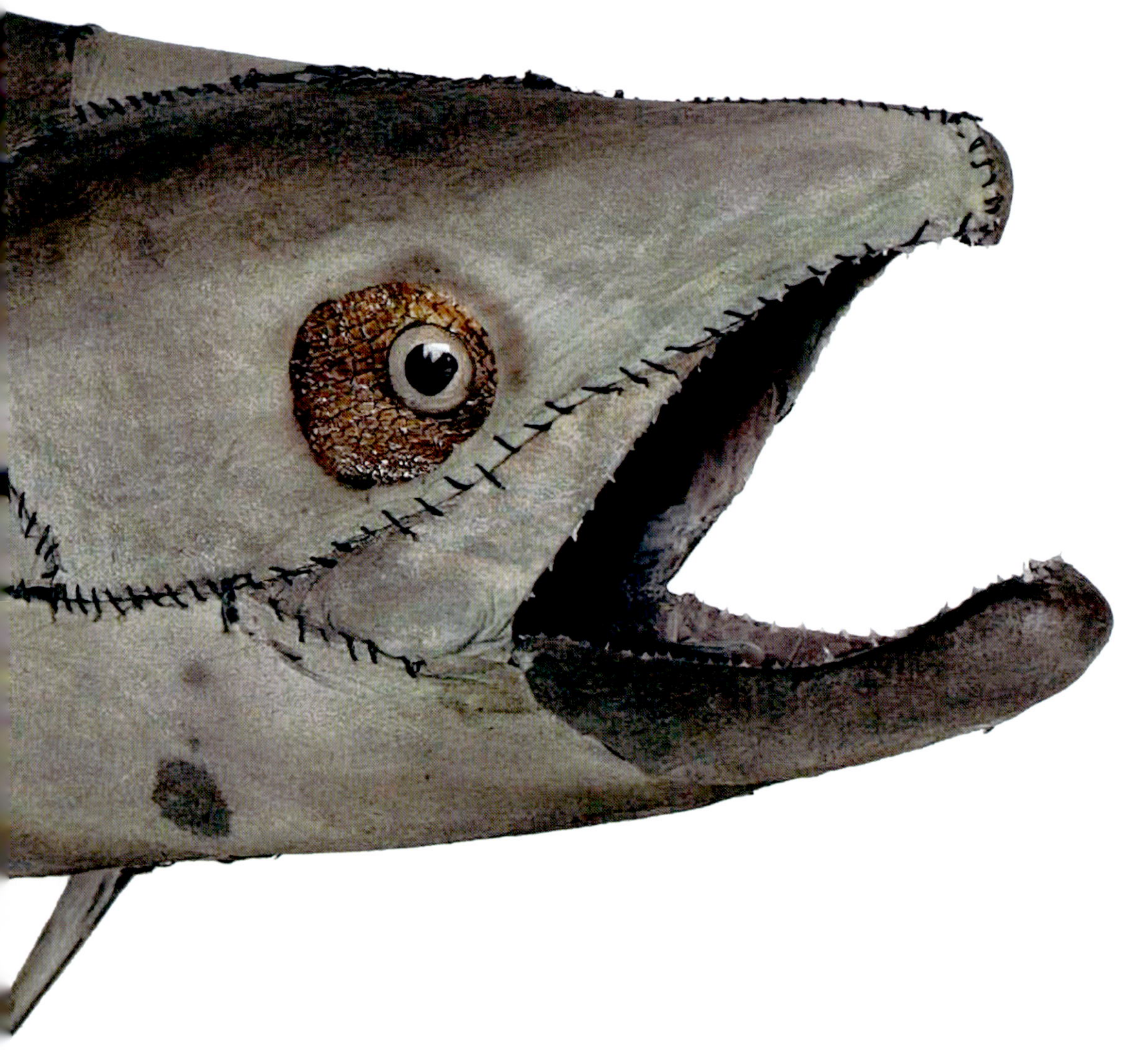

# Chapter 6

# Deep Rivers: Glenn Kaino's Rhizomatic Collaborations

Laura Fried

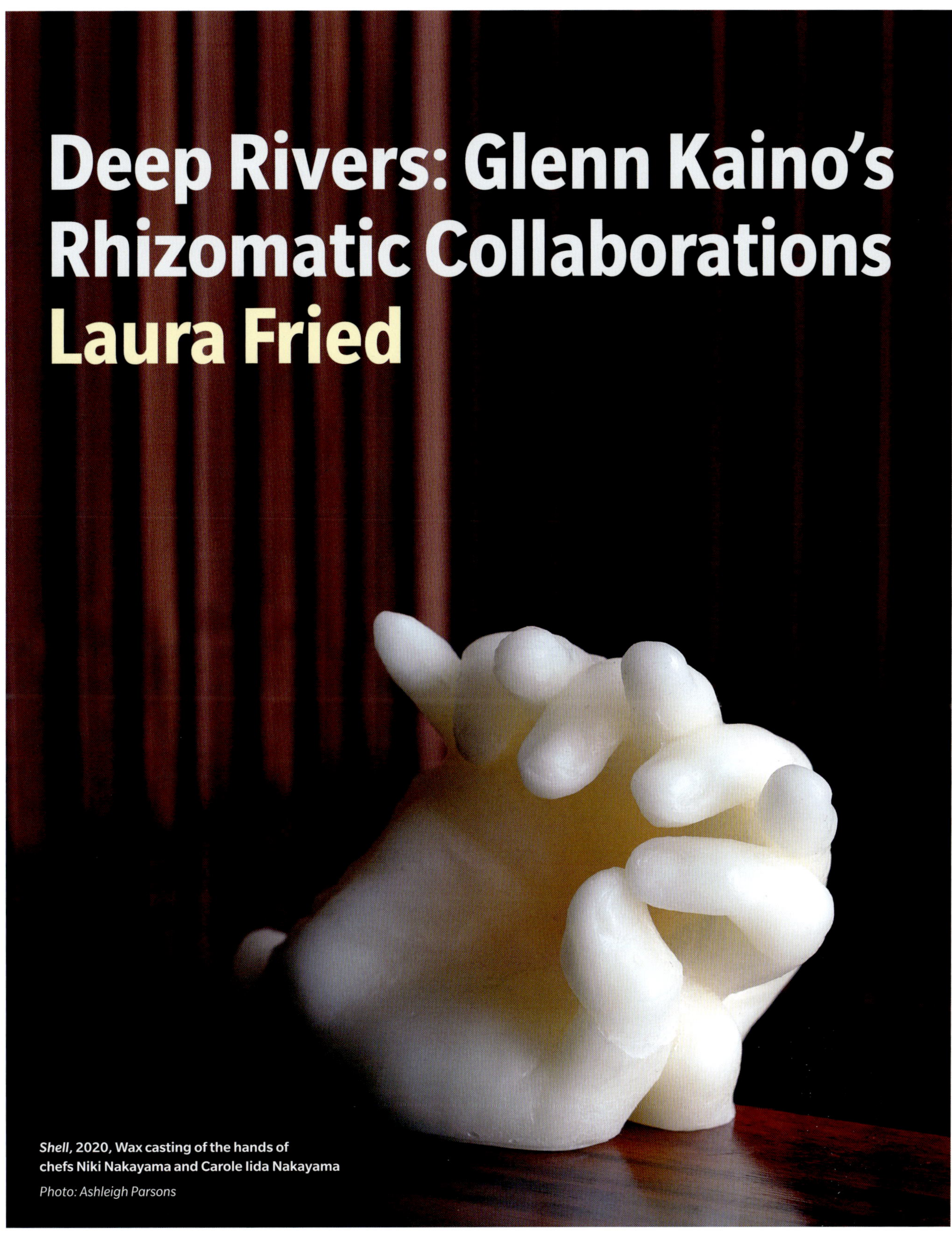

***Shell*, 2020, Wax casting of the hands of chefs Niki Nakayama and Carole Iida Nakayama**

*Photo: Ashleigh Parsons*

On a warm October night in 2018, in San Miguel Chapultepec, Mexico City, a group of sixteen friends and strangers sat, elbows brushing, along a long table in a dark and narrow room—the original space of a restaurant called Masala y Maiz, founded by the activist chefs Saqib Keval and Norma Listman. Now, over the crowded glasses of natural wines and tequila, the guests turned to Glenn Kaino, who was ready to share a toast. The toast came in two parts. First Kaino thanked the chefs and welcomed our esteemed group to a new performance art project: a supper collaboration called *The MSG Club*, conceived with Niki Nakayama, one of the world's greatest living chefs, and her wife, Carole Iida Nakayama. Among the guests were the designer Carla Fernandez; poet Luigi Amara; political activist Deon Jones (who left an internship in Vice President Joe Biden's office to work in Kaino's studio); cinematographer Afshin Shahidi; chef Jesús Salas Tornés; Niki and Carole; and the Olympic sprinter and activist Tommie Smith and his wife, Delois. We were gathered, Kaino told us, to participate in a taste-memory club, where together we would break bread and face our food fears—a delectable opportunity to upend explicit cultural and culinary biases, and to inspire a meaningful dialogue about inclusion and equality in the world. The second toast was directed to Smith. That evening marked the fiftieth anniversary of his black-gloved salute to human rights on the podium of the 1968 Mexico City Olympic Games. We raised our glasses to Smith and looked down at our first course, which had just been delivered by two servers clad in light denim-blue coats (designed by Fernandez), on the back of which—by sheer coincidence, or perhaps providence—was embroidered the large silhouette of a raised fist.

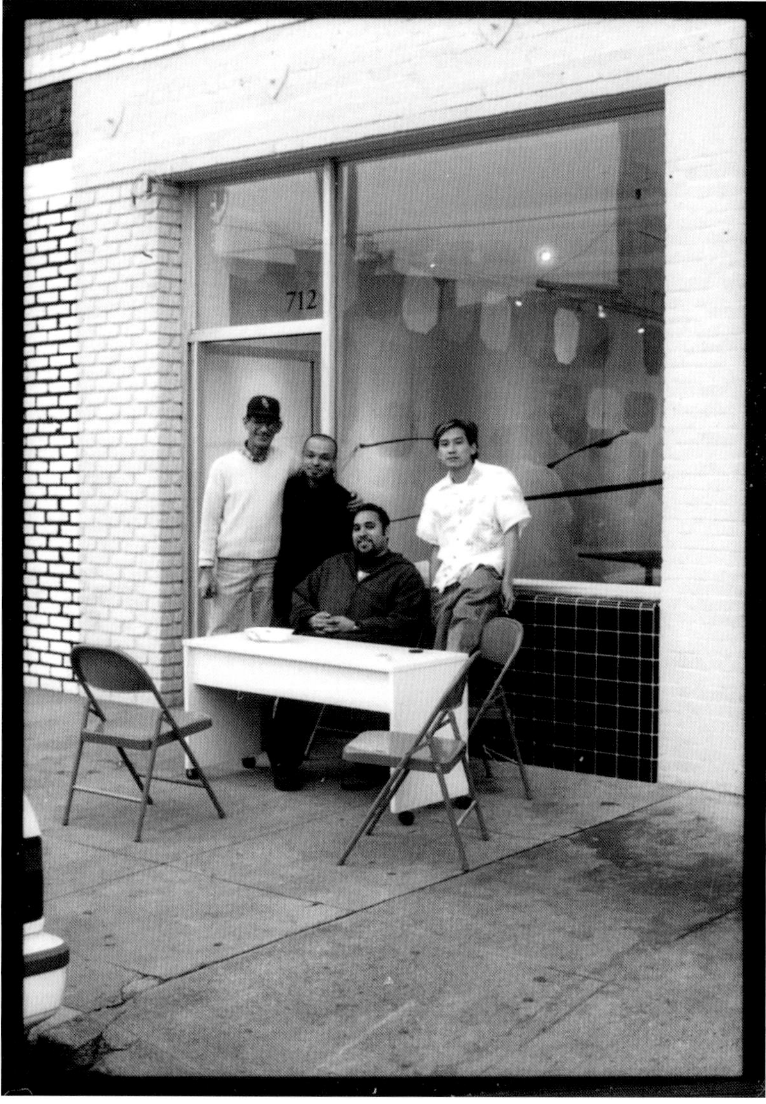


## Deep River

**Deep River (1997–2001) was a five-year project initiated by artists Rolo Castillo, Kaino, Daniel Joseph Martinez, and Tracey Shiffman. Neither commercial nor nonprofit, Deep River was 325 square feet of exhibition space, located at 712 Traction Avenue in Los Angeles, which presented an experimental laboratory conceived as a "social sculpture." The Deep River space focused on local concerns, cultural diversity and differences, putting forth an alternative model wherein temporality eschewed the logic of institutionalization. Deep River's embodiment of a collective and infinite model, which subverted the operations of both the museum and the market, represents a significant contribution to the legacy of alternative spaces in LA and beyond.**

**Left to right: Joel Bloom, Daniel Joseph Martinez, Rolo Castillo, and Kaino in front of Deep River, 1997**

*Photo: Daniel Joseph Martinez*

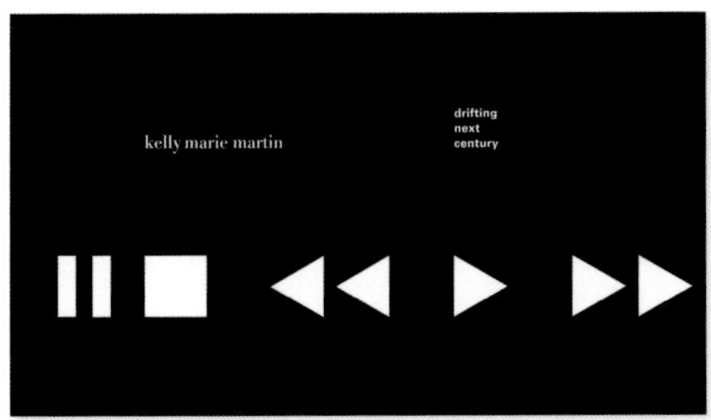

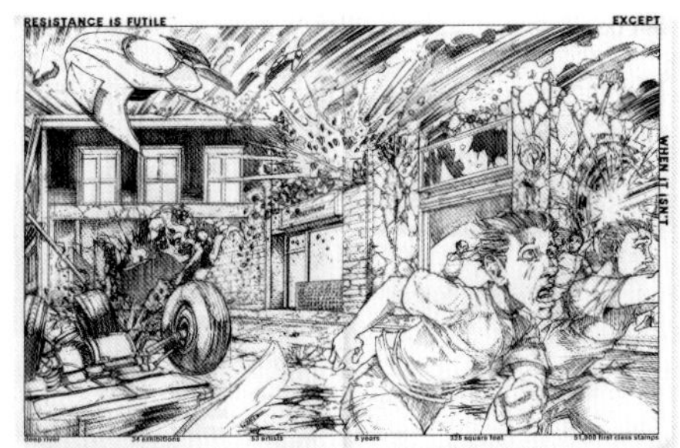

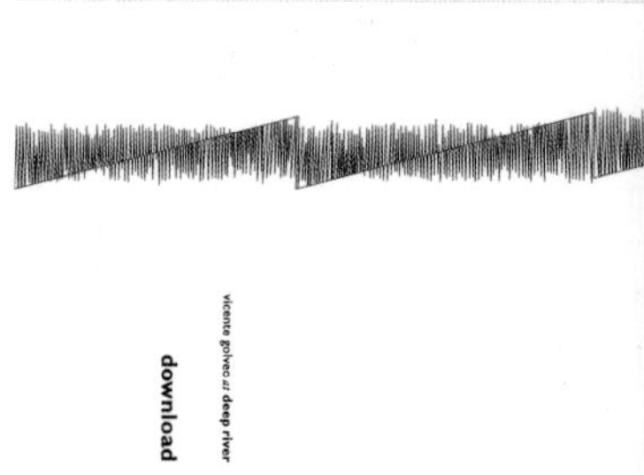

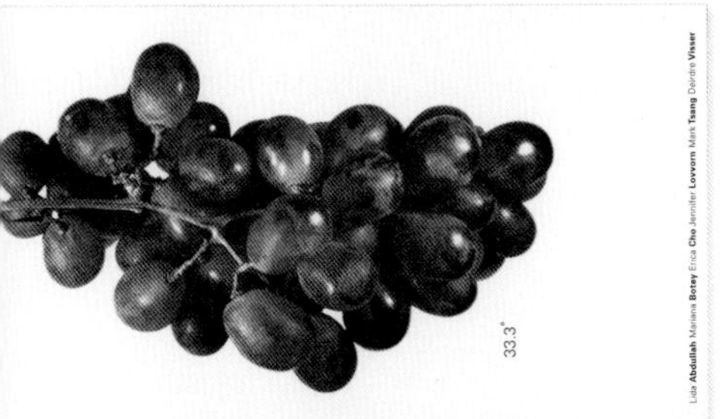

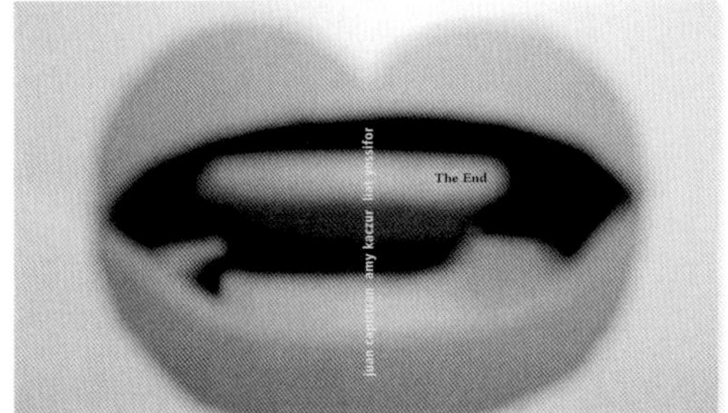

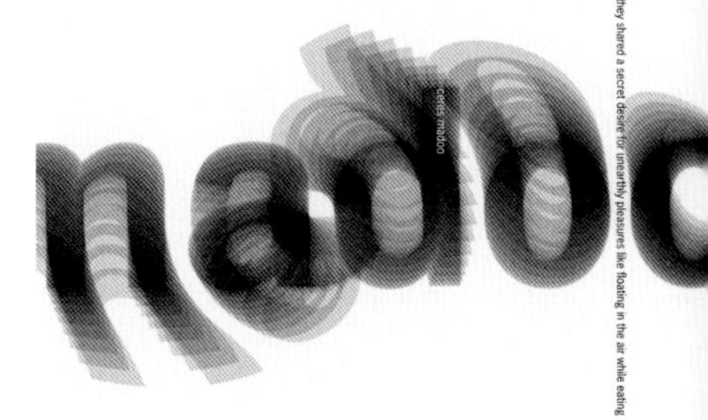

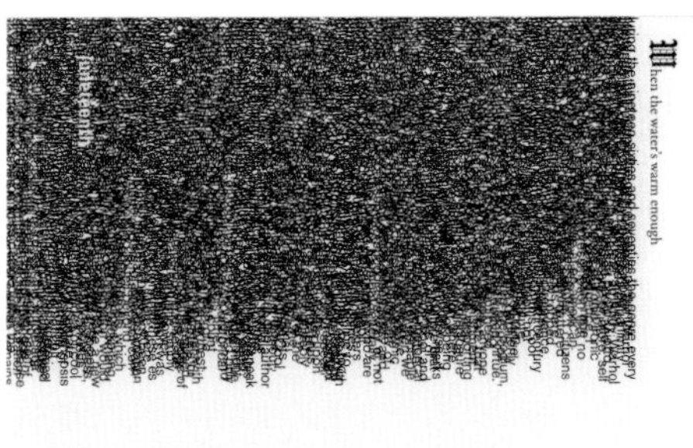

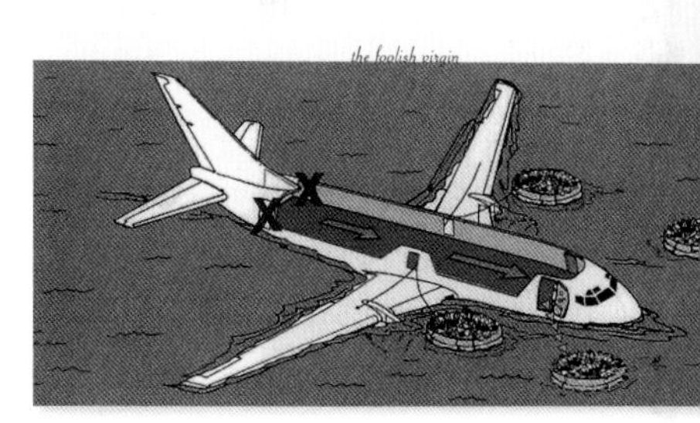

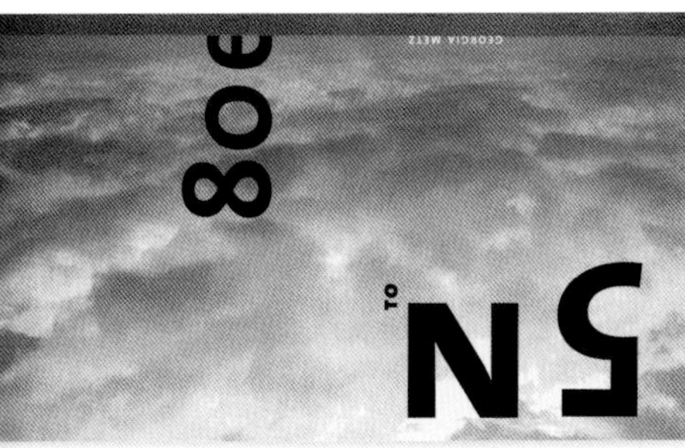
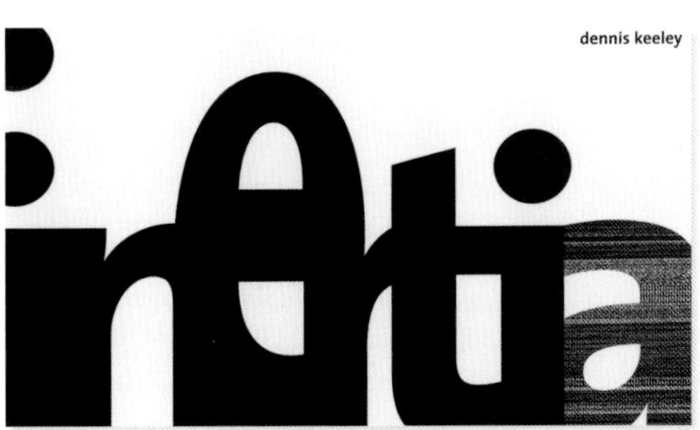

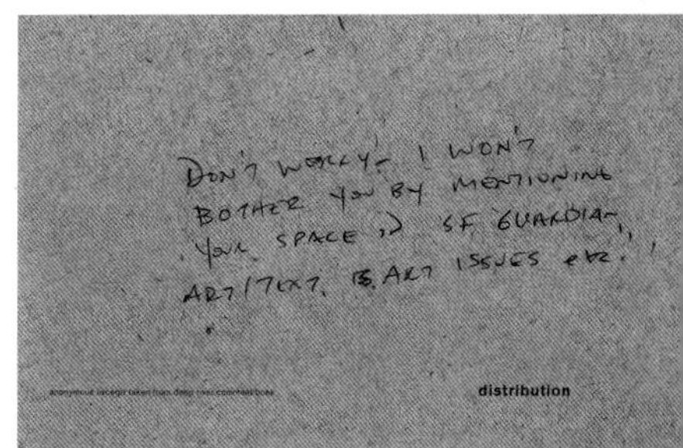

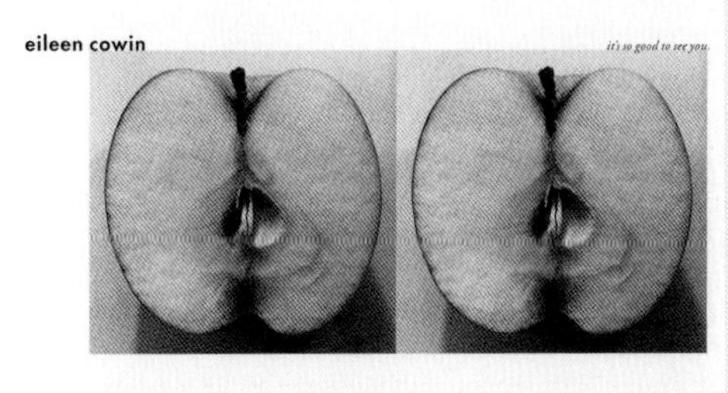

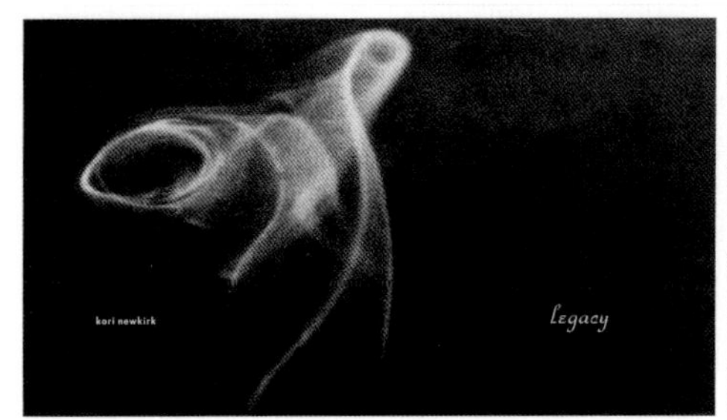

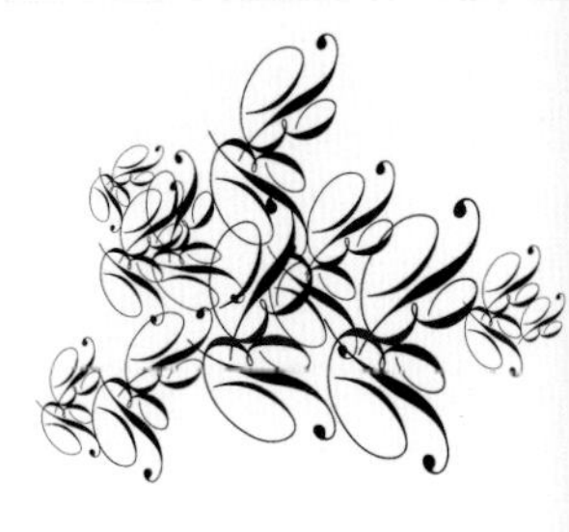

**Deep River invitations designed by Tracey Shiffman, 1997–2002**

Over powdered-liver-dusted potato chips and *chicatanas y ahuautle*, Kaino, Shahidi, and Jones recounted their trials and triumphs of the day, filming with Tommie in his first return to the stadium since that October night in 1968. It was both a return and a rebirth, and Kaino and Smith had ruminated on what it meant to reclaim that space. At the time, Kaino and Shahidi were still deep in production on the film *With Drawn Arms* (2020), a meditation on Smith's life and an exploration of how his salute—and indeed, his right hand—has been appropriated, reproduced, and invoked over five decades, and continues to be a vital touchstone for athletes using their platform for protest today. Meanwhile, Chef Tornés recounted tales of bribing corrupt officials with his family's heritage moonshine in order to protect and import the indigenous ingredients and traditions from his hometown, Ayutla de los Libres, that comprise the staples of his cooking and wholesale business in Mexico City. Fernandez and Amara swapped stories of their deepest food fears, and we talked about how a taste memory might be transformed by new synesthetic gestures.

It is characteristic of nearly any encounter with Kaino to find oneself in a room punctuated with virtuosic folks spanning a spectrum of heterogenous fields. I remember feeling dizzy after my first studio visits, years ago, trying to weave together in my head the network of experts Kaino was engaging at any one time. ("If the social condition is about ideas, and communication, and inspiration, I want the experts in inspiration," he has told me.[1]) His ambitious, multi-year projects typically overlap and are often deeply interconnected. And within these projects, Kaino not only attracts collaborators considered leaders in their fields (say, the greatest magician of a generation, or the politician organizing the most effective grassroots campaign to fight systemic voter suppression in history). To that end, many of his works are underpinned by a mission to make new space not only for art, but to offer possibilities for structural change in the fields and systems within which his collaborators practice. As it did on that evening, *The MSG Club* reflected an artistic practice that is perpetually focused on connecting systems of knowledge, forms of production, and activist-minded experts who rarely have opportunities to connect. As both performance and conceptual artwork, *The MSG Club* proposed a condition for discourse and experience unbound by the strictures of an often more limited definition of social practice. This is possible, I would argue, not because it existed outside the closed system of the art world and its embedded class politics, but because the project itself was not an autonomous social experiment. Indeed, on the one hand, this particular dinner could be an apposite symbol for the horizontal nature of the artist's collaborations that in their essence root Kaino's practice: *The MSG Club* guests were neither actors nor subjects in a discrete performance, but themselves agents of forms of cultural production that often sublimate the artist's authorship in favor of holding s pace *collectively*. On the other, *The MSG Club*, and projects such as *With Drawn Arms*, are themselves imbricated threads in the artist's career-long undertaking to make and sustain space.

Over the years, I have come to visualize Kaino's practice as a kind of hybrid rhizome. At the central stem is an ethos of transformation. The heterogenous nature of his work is a natural result of his collaborative practice, undergirded by common refrains towards ethics, justice, visibility, and magic. Among the many works of his ambitious oeuvre—spanning sculpture, public art, installation, performance, painting, film, theatrical production, social gatherings, digital platforms, and mobile apps (and this list is far from exhaustive)—are the material manifestations of a core conceit that is persistently hopeful about the potential for change. Largely unseen, however, is the root system of the studio, inexhaustibly bearing lateral shoots and new plants, which are often cultivated to be self-sustaining beyond their germination in the studio. And indeed, one of the most fundamental and emblematic branches of Kaino's rhizomatic work is also the least visible and most underexamined: spacemaking, and with it, structural transformation. For one, the film *With Drawn Arms* is just one piece of a complex network of connected projects with the Olympian, all emanating from Kaino's studio, to recuperate Smith's legacy within the public imagination and liberate it from the systemic racism and oppression of corporate institutions that for decades disavowed Smith and suppressed his ability to profit from the appropriation and licensing of his image and his gesture. As we celebrated Smith that night in Mexico City, *The MSG Club* was among the first public projects of Active Cultures, a new nonprofit space that Kaino and I had recently founded in Los Angeles.

Since the beginning of his career, Kaino has explored the real possibilities for building and revolutionizing infrastructure—particularly to foster visibility and inclusivity—as a conceptual and artistic gesture. Notably, over the last two decades Kaino has assumed powerful roles that have helped shape the trajectory of inclusion in tech, a biographical detail not often revealed. He once worked to create the first streaming music service (as chief creative officer of Napster); and he would go on to run all digital production for a major media platform (as senior vice president, digital, at the Oprah Winfrey Network). While these activities have long undergirded and been extensions of the practice itself, they have yet to be recorded or explored in examinations of his work. And to appreciate the expansive nature of his work in spacemaking is to understand that it has rooted his practice and politics since the early nineties. Kaino's investment in the interplay between group and individual identity-- along with an interest in how one can disrupt mechanical, digital, and social phenomena—has informed his thinking since art school. Following his MFA at the University of California, San Diego, he moved to downtown Los Angeles and, in lieu of fashioning a traditional studio space, borrowed $5,000 from his parents to buy a computer, a server, and a T1 line with the intention of making internet sites. Indeed, as Kaino has said, this is where his core conceptual concerns, particularly around a decolonial approach to art-making and cultural production, began to grow.[2]

In 1993, Kaino co-founded FAVELA!, one of the first-ever art websites, and the first-ever digital space designed to increase visibility for creators of color. The website was named in homage to the radical and experimental American architect Lebbeus Woods (1940–2012), whose famous visit to the favelas of São Paulo informed a visionary practice that modeled principles of heterogeneity and multiplicity while splicing architecture, philosophy, and mathematics into his designs. Reconfiguring architectural space in environments of crisis, Woods asserted that in a relentlessly changing world, we must face disaster to imagine new ways of living, and the spaces we create for ourselves must allow for that work.[3] With the same sense of urgency, Kaino and his six collaborators, including artist Daniel Joseph Martinez (who had been his teacher during Kaino's undergraduate work at UC Irvine) and the writer Susan Otto, embarked on a project fundamentally tied to heterogeneity and politics. FAVELA! was a platform to offer visibility to artists of color within early search databases, such as Yahoo.com, to publish scholarship and manifestos, and to make censored artworks publicly available. FAVELA! itself was ill-fated—personal dynamics among the group torpedoed the endeavor—but it propelled Kaino and his collaborators forward in work that centered on visibility for marginalized communities of artists, as well as the empowerment of art and artists to influence institutional systems. This extended across early and high-level technology consulting for major corporations establishing web-based presences, as well as the punk-inflected grassroots projects that simultaneously radiated out of the studio: Cyber Ethnics (created with Martinez, Betty Lee, Rolo Castillo, and Ulysses Jenkins); [4] the prankster/agitprop project FUKA with Matthew Fukuda; and Uber.com, which offered free websites and media production software to musicians and artists.[5]

Deep River (1997–2001) came soon after. Castillo, a club promoter and silkscreener who had started a gallery called 50 Bucks, called Kaino to say that he had just been given the keys to an empty space in the American Hotel on Traction Avenue, in a tumbledown stretch of downtown LA. He took Kaino and Martinez to see the tiny, raw, vermin-infested storefront, and as soon as they saw it imagined, as Kaino put it, "325 square feet of dopeness." After scoping out and indexing the lighting, trim detail, fixtures, and floors of galleries and museums across the city, Kaino and Martinez invested in making a pristine white pocket cube with the help of philanthropist and collector Eileen Harris Norton. With a five-year plan and a $600 budget for printing, stamps, and wine, Deep River was conceived as a non-commercial, impactful space for artists who were not seeing opportunities elsewhere at the time. Deep River hosted Mark Bradford's first solo show in 1998, followed by exhibitions with Kori Newkirk (1999), Ken Gonzales-Day (2000), and Mario Ybarra Jr. (2001). A tiny label on the front door, "No Critics Allowed," signaled their collective fracturing of the existing systems of validation that persisted in reifying and canonizing the careers of not just white male artists, but also particular cabals of artist communities in the city. (As Kaino tells it, the sign nettled a prominent *Los Angeles Times* art critic so much that he complained he could only peer in through the windows to see the shows.) With Deep River, Kaino and Martinez imagined an inclusionary, equitable platform where artists of color could make their work in an elevated (if tiny) space and context, visible to Los Angeles and to the art world at large.

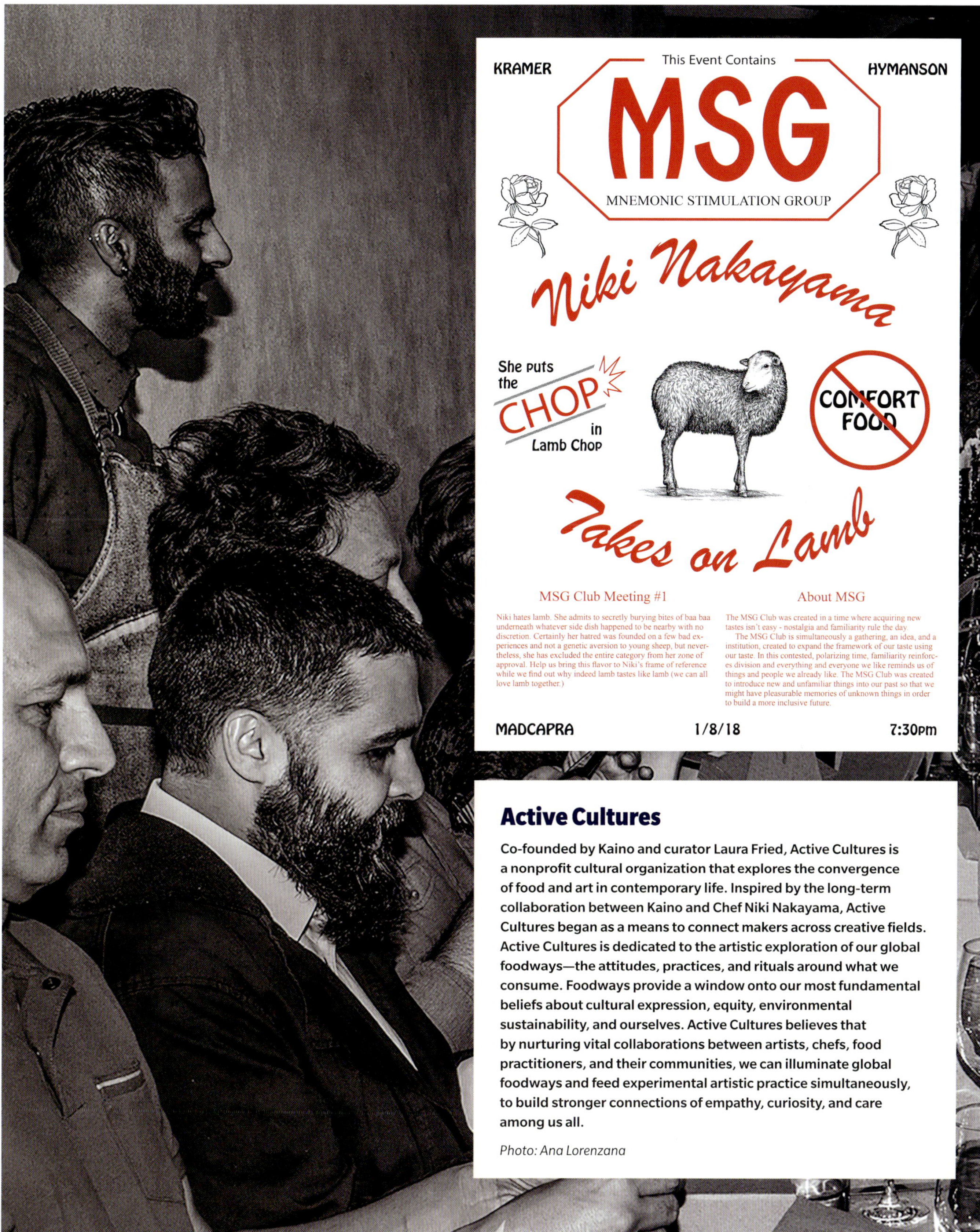


## Active Cultures

Co-founded by Kaino and curator Laura Fried, Active Cultures is a nonprofit cultural organization that explores the convergence of food and art in contemporary life. Inspired by the long-term collaboration between Kaino and Chef Niki Nakayama, Active Cultures began as a means to connect makers across creative fields. Active Cultures is dedicated to the artistic exploration of our global foodways—the attitudes, practices, and rituals around what we consume. Foodways provide a window onto our most fundamental beliefs about cultural expression, equity, environmental sustainability, and ourselves. Active Cultures believes that by nurturing vital collaborations between artists, chefs, food practitioners, and their communities, we can illuminate global foodways and feed experimental artistic practice simultaneously, to build stronger connections of empathy, curiosity, and care among us all.

*Photo: Ana Lorenzana*

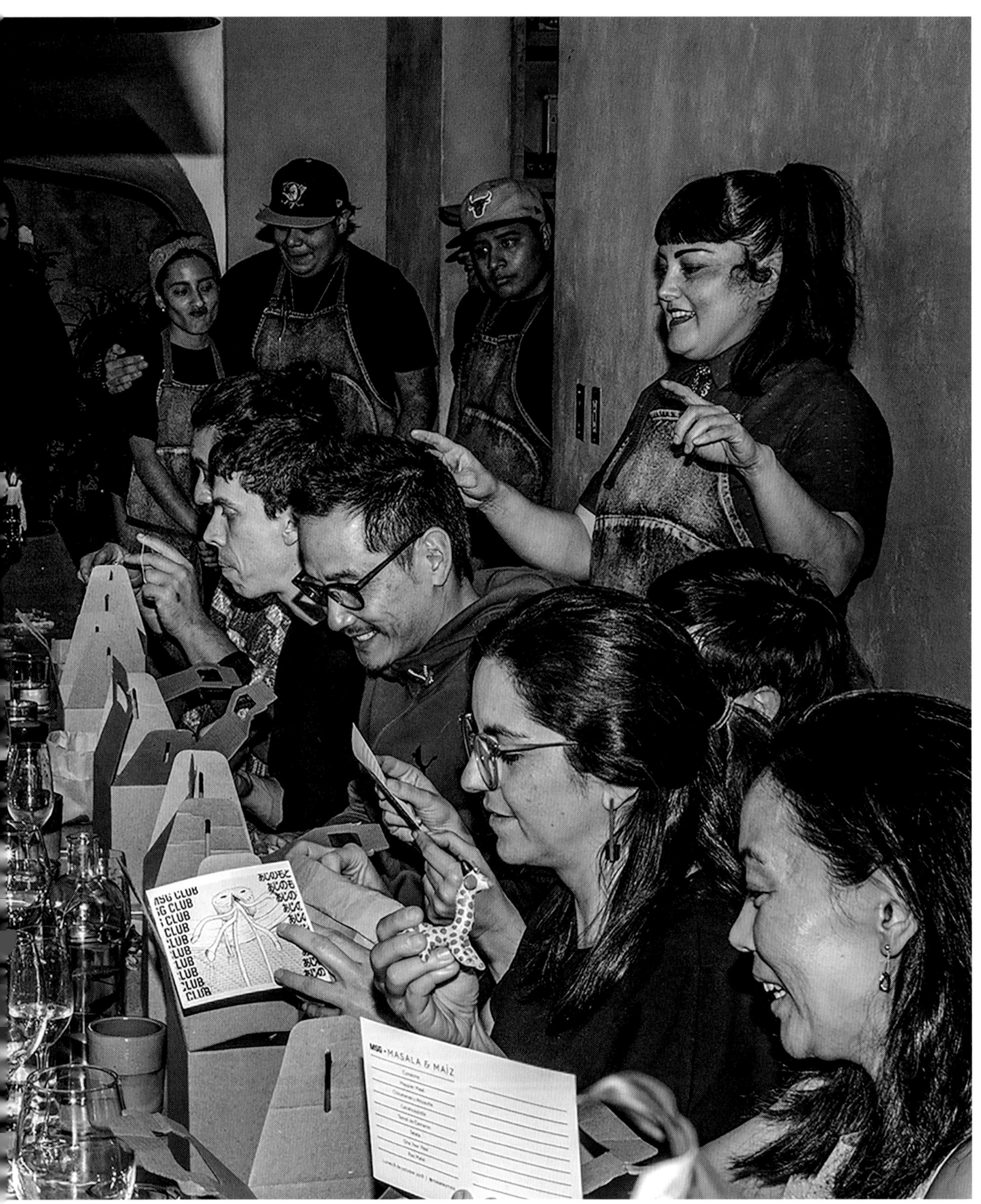
MSG • MASALA & MAÍZ

Deep River was at once a collective action and a social sculpture: a finite model that proposed to challenge the market and whose legacy marked a paradigmatic shift in the landscape of exhibition spaces, and not just in Los Angeles. Deep River was conceived to foreground "local concerns, cultural diversity and difference, putting forth an alternative model wherein temporality eschewed the logic of institutionalization."[6] It also spurred new models in the ecosystem. Christian Haye, founder of The Project—a seminal commercial gallery in Harlem in the late 1990s that in its time was the first gallery to represent Black artists and artists of color in the majority—was known to credit Kaino and Deep River for his inspiration.[7] Kaino was one of the youngest artists represented in The Project, which also played a pivotal role in the careers of artists like Paul Pfeiffer, Julie Mehretu, William Pope.L, Newkirk, and Romuald Hazoumè, to name a few. Then, in 2005, curator Lauri Firstenberg recruited Kaino and Martínez to join the board of a new space she was founding in Los Angeles, which, she said, she intended to model after Deep River. With the philanthropist Dr. Joy Simmons and the support of The Project, they helped raise the funds for a five-year rent cycle: a new model for supporting and sustaining infrastructure for the brand-new, artist-centered exhibition space. Kaino served as a long-time board member and close advisor to Firstenberg in the formative years of LAXART.

In 2012, curator Cesar Garcia, who had organized an exhibition of Kaino's at LAXART, founded a new organization with his support. Garcia wanted to name the space after a recent magic performance project Kaino had created under the collaborative moniker A.Bandit with magician Derek DelGaudio: The Mistake Room. For two years, Garcia and Kaino incubated The Mistake Room from an office in the latter's former longtime Hollywood studio, which sat above a magic shop and half a block down from LACE, one of Los Angeles's longest running alternative art spaces. The founding conceit of The Mistake Room was to make a truly international space in LA: one that was democratic, that foregrounded broader representation among artists, and that created access in Los Angeles to the international network of curators and scholars the space would bring to the city. Through Kaino's advocacy and with the infrastructural support of the studio, The Mistake Room was founded with a majority BIPOC board of directors, the most diverse of any visual arts organization in Los Angeles.

If Deep River was an artist-driven conceptual project created out of Kaino's studio, born of the same core concerns as all of his work as an artist, the other roles he has played since then—to develop, support, and counsel institutional bodies—are similarly inextricable from his studio practice. While he cut his teeth on the board of the Los Angeles Center for Photography—even before founding Deep River—over the last decade he has deepened his role on several boards throughout the city. His appointments to the Board of Advisors at the Hammer Museum and the Board of Directors at the Music Center began to shape his perspective on the scalability and reciprocal tactics of institutional governance and its relationship to cultural production. Indeed, as Kaino persistently strives to shift from theoretical interrogations of power to concrete maneuvers that can transform real power structures, he has long worked to plant those strategies within nonprofit leadership. Now, Kaino typically serves on three boards at any given time, representing a range of institutional modes and scales. For each role, he imagines opportunities to challenge notions of entrepreneurialism and sustainability. In

his work with LAXART and The Mistake Room, as with Active Cultures and his recent role on the board of the Fathomers, another small LA-based nonprofit, he cultivates and places value on new approaches to financial stability. And indeed, the heterogeneity of Kaino's practice has allowed for innovative business models to be applied across fields of knowledge, especially within the arts and culture nonprofit sector. This can be transformative in a landscape where organizations are extremely vulnerable at every stage of their life cycle, and where founding curator-directors often have little to no grounding in business planning or alterative fundraising models.

As Kaino's work in technology, media, music, and branding weaves through the activity and output of the studio, and textures his object-making, so is it the warp and weft of his conceptions of spacemaking and industry transformation. With the spaces he has co-founded, the conceptual exercise, for Kaino, has been to make space for curators, artists, and scholars to produce culture—through the lens of inclusion and equity—while deploying the tools and best practices of technology, connectivity, collaboration, and access to a more diverse group of patrons to bolster and enrich that space simultaneously. From the early days of LAXART's founding up through his role on the Hammer board today, Kaino has actively participated in the remodeling of governing boards, both in their actual representation of racial equity, and also in the education and commitment of their members toward diversity and inclusion in organizational infrastructure and power. It is worth noting that artists do not often recruit other board members. Yet for Kaino, this work in particular reflects the same heterogeneous, activist-driven work that underpins all other facets of his practice. By bringing a diverse group of thought-leaders into the boardroom, collective forms of knowledge can transform the symbolic into the material; decolonialist work can be made manifest; and new spaces can be made to consider how people access, experience, and engage with culture.

Above all, Kaino's work in any media and within any system is often characterized by his obsessive investment in technical virtuosity, functionality, and legitimacy; and by the depth of his commitment to his collaborators, whom he frequently engages over long periods of time. For the past decade and a half, Kaino's studio has typically housed a complex network of highly specialized practices at any given time. At a desk in one corner of the studio, web developers build platforms for Oprah's website and for V|S|B|L|T|Y, his technology and media collaboration with actor and activist Jesse Williams that has created mobile applications like Ebroji, BLeBRiTY, and Ya Tu Sabes. In another, fabricators test the machinery underlying a new magical illusion. A young composer at another monitor mixes new sound for an upcoming film. Kaino is an artist whose practice is never solitary, rarely autonomous, and in its depths relies on the sublimation of authorship for its productivity, impact, and legacy. The notion that the holistic output of the studio—not defined or authored by the artist alone—can manifest ideological and actual space is perhaps why this aspect of his practice has been largely invisible. In Kaino's and DelGaudio's production (and now film) *In & Of Itself*, DelGaudio tells his audience, "I am not just defined by what you see. I am also defined by what you will never see." The slippage between visibility and invisibility, presence and absence, continually ripples throughout Kaino's practice. There is a quiet radicality in the recognition that revolutionary change does not often come in one person's lifetime, in one artist's career. Kaino says: "The fight is way too big for one space. The fight is way too big for one studio. The fight for justice and for equality and for inclusion is way too big." On the other hand, it is the very nature of his collaborative work—and his inconspicuous tactics—that have allowed for, as Lebbeus Woods might have it, radical spacemaking for new ways of being and making. As Kaino reminded me, "This entire body of my practice is an effort to prove that our collaborations are not zero-sum."

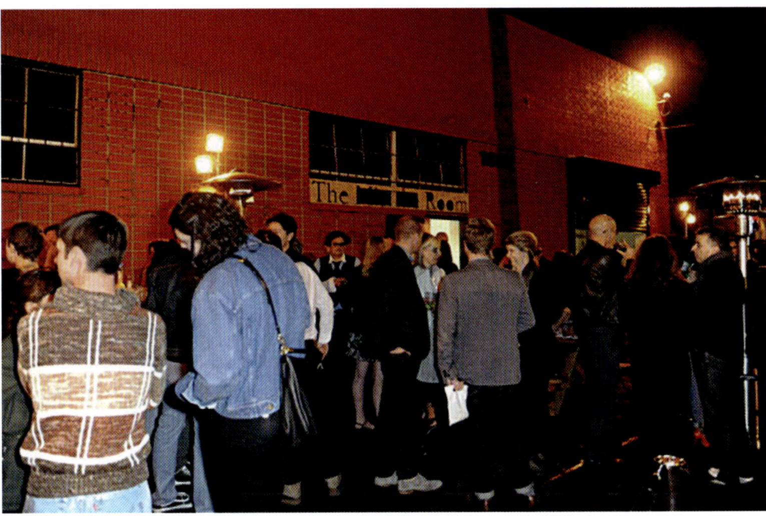


**The Mistake Room. *Oscar Murillo: Distribution Center* VIP Opening Reception, January 17, 2014**

*Photo: Joshua Blanchard/WireImage. Courtesy of Getty Images*

Kaino's work establishing equitable cultural platforms in digital and physical space both prefigures and runs concurrently with a spate of artist-driven nonprofit projects that have emerged over the past decade, propelled largely by artists of color. And as it has been with spaces shepherded by Kaino, these newer organizations go much further in seeking to serve and transform their communities than the institutions born out of the alternative space movement that gained steam in New York in the early 1970s.[8] Theaster Gates founded the Rebuild Foundation to transform buildings and neighborhoods on the South Side of Chicago in 2009; Noah and Karon Davis created the Underground Museum in Arlington Heights in Los Angeles in 2012 as a space to share world-class exhibitions, events, dialogue, and artist collaborations with the neighborhood's predominantly working-class residents; Mark Bradford (along with activist Allan DiCastro and philanthropist Norton) founded Art+Practice in Leimert Park in Los Angeles in 2014 to work with nonprofit social service providers to support the needs of eighteen- to twenty-four-year-old foster youth and provide free access to museum-curated contemporary art celebrating artists of color; Titus Kaphar (along with Jason Price and Jonathan Brand) founded NXTHVN in in 2017 to build an alternative model of art mentorship and career counseling through a specially designed curriculum, and to simultaneously set into motion significant opportunities for emerging local entrepreneurs in the Dixwell neighborhood of New Haven, Connecticut. This list only scratches the surface, and in Los Angeles there is a particular concentration of radical new spaces and organizations, such as Lauren Halsey's Summaeverythang or the Crenshaw Dairy Mart, co-founded by Patrisse Cullors, Alexandre Dorriz, and noé olivas, that are being birthed to bridge cultural work and advocacy in South Los Angeles. Set against this backdrop, it is remarkable that, since the 1990s, Kaino has founded or played a seminal role in the creation of no less than five arts organizations in Los Angeles alone. One could argue that he has shaped the contours of an entire cultural sector of a single city, in a way that is likely without peer. While Deep River is a recognized and emblematic beginning for the wave of spaces artists have founded across the country since,

Kaino's expansive imprint has transformed a landscape through its roots. And ultimately, because this facet of his practice has gone unseen and unrecorded for so long, Kaino's persistent (and rare) commitment to work selflessly for the visibility of others has long come at the expense of his recognition in the space of spacemaking.

Kaino and I founded Active Cultures together in 2017, at our second meeting to discuss what would become *The MSG Club*. Those early studio visits quickly evolved into two years of intensive discussions—often around the table at *The MSG Club* itself—among curators, artists, chefs, activists, and philanthropists about the future of public institutions, the promise of that work, and, above all, how art and foodways together can be mutually nourishing modes of cultural production and experience. We founded Active Cultures as a new public arts organization to explore the confluence of art and consumption in contemporary life. As a new model committed to interdisciplinary artistic and creative practice, our mission is to cultivate empathy and foster social justice by building accessible platforms for shared experience. In that conviction, Active Cultures creates opportunities for sustained engagement with diverse facets of our culture: in the kitchen, at the table, and within spaces for art. Our purpose is to treat food, alongside art, as vital cultural production, while embedding the values of radical hospitality in our work. Through digital platforms, live public programs, shared meals, and persistent, long-term collaborations, Active Cultures creates space for artists and for folks in foodways to experiment and explore—and for new and more accessible ways of thinking about equity, about justice, about visibility, and about cultural consumption. That night in Mexico City, as we celebrated Smith and chefs Listman and Keval for their indefatigable activism, we began to sketch the possibilities for making space to hold and sustain work like theirs. In many ways, we aspire to model the same kind of radical space Kaino has been creating for nearly thirty years.

[1] *Interview with Glenn Kaino, January 23, 2021.*

[2] *Many of the stories and all Kaino's quotations in this essay are from our January interview. Thank you to Anna Cho-Son for her assistance in additional research.*

[3] *Tracy Myers, "'The Possibility of the Exceptional': Lebbeus Woods's Passionate Provocations," in* Lebbeus Woods, Experimental Architecture, *ed. Tracy Myers (Carnegie Museum of Art, Carnegie Institute, 2004), p. 20.*

[4] Cyber Ethnics *(1994–96)—which fed in many ways directly into* Deep River*—was a working group built around, as Kaino has put it, "the intention of sharing artwork, scholarship, and research about the utilization of and relationship to technology in communities of color."*

[5] Uber.com *came before the Uber we know today.*

[6] *From the exhibition description of* Remembering Deep River: Resistance is Futile Except When it Isn't, *LAXART, Los Angeles, January 10-February 28, 2015, http://archive.laxart.org.*

[7] *As related by Kaino in our interview on January 23, 2021.*

[8] *Spaces such as 112 Greene Street (which later became White Columns), founded in 1970 by Jeffrey Lew, Alan Saret, and Gordon Matta-Clark (who would also co-found the seminal restaurant and social project FOOD a year later), were mainly focused on providing non-commercial exhibition opportunities to a wider range of artists and practices than were being represented in commercial galleries.*

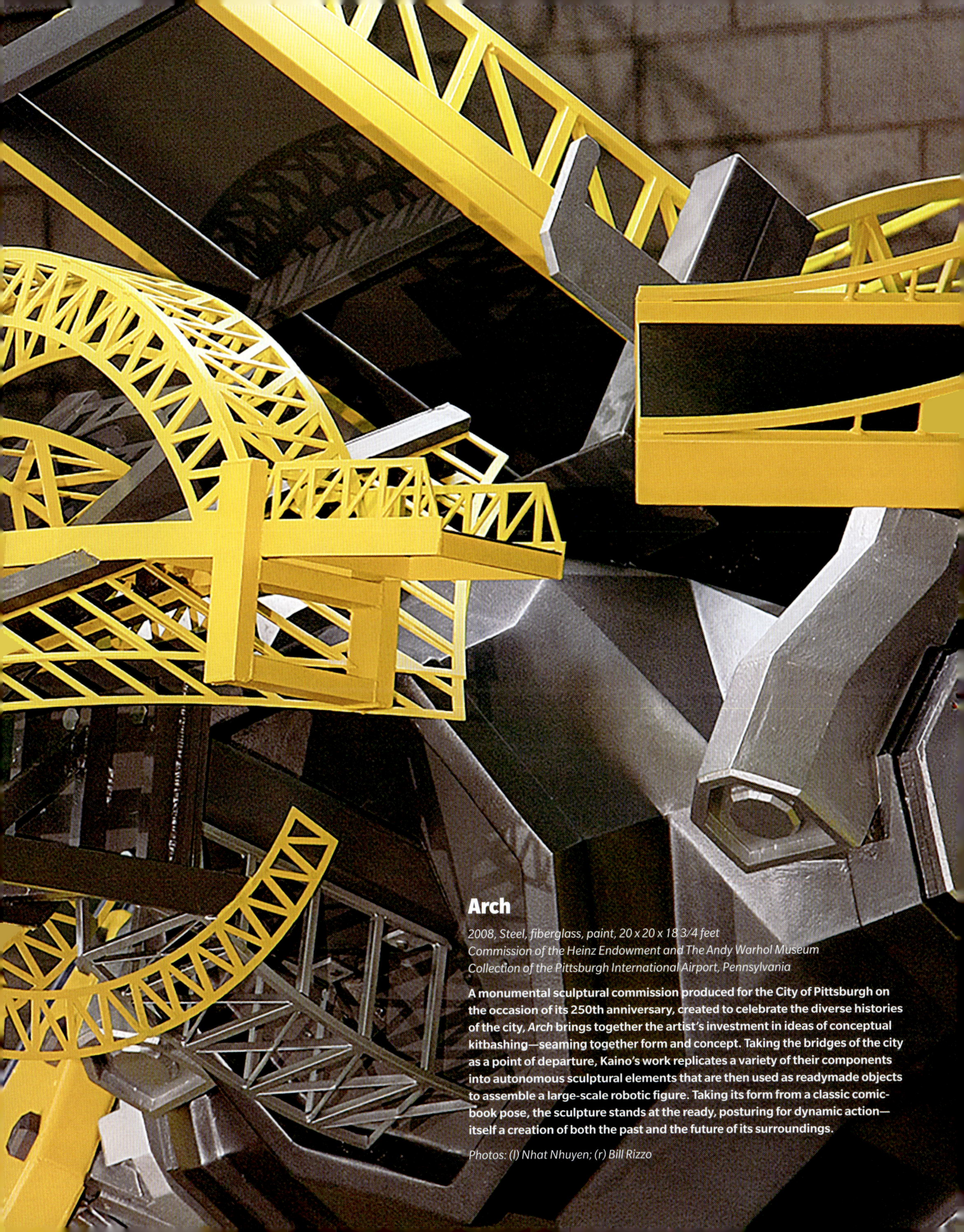

## Arch

*2008, Steel, fiberglass, paint, 20 x 20 x 18 3/4 feet*
*Commission of the Heinz Endowment and The Andy Warhol Museum*
*Collection of the Pittsburgh International Airport, Pennsylvania*

**A monumental sculptural commission produced for the City of Pittsburgh on the occasion of its 250th anniversary, created to celebrate the diverse histories of the city, *Arch* brings together the artist's investment in ideas of conceptual kitbashing—seaming together form and concept. Taking the bridges of the city as a point of departure, Kaino's work replicates a variety of their components into autonomous sculptural elements that are then used as readymade objects to assemble a large-scale robotic figure. Taking its form from a classic comic-book pose, the sculpture stands at the ready, posturing for dynamic action—itself a creation of both the past and the future of its surroundings.**

*Photos: (l) Nhat Nhuyen; (r) Bill Rizzo*

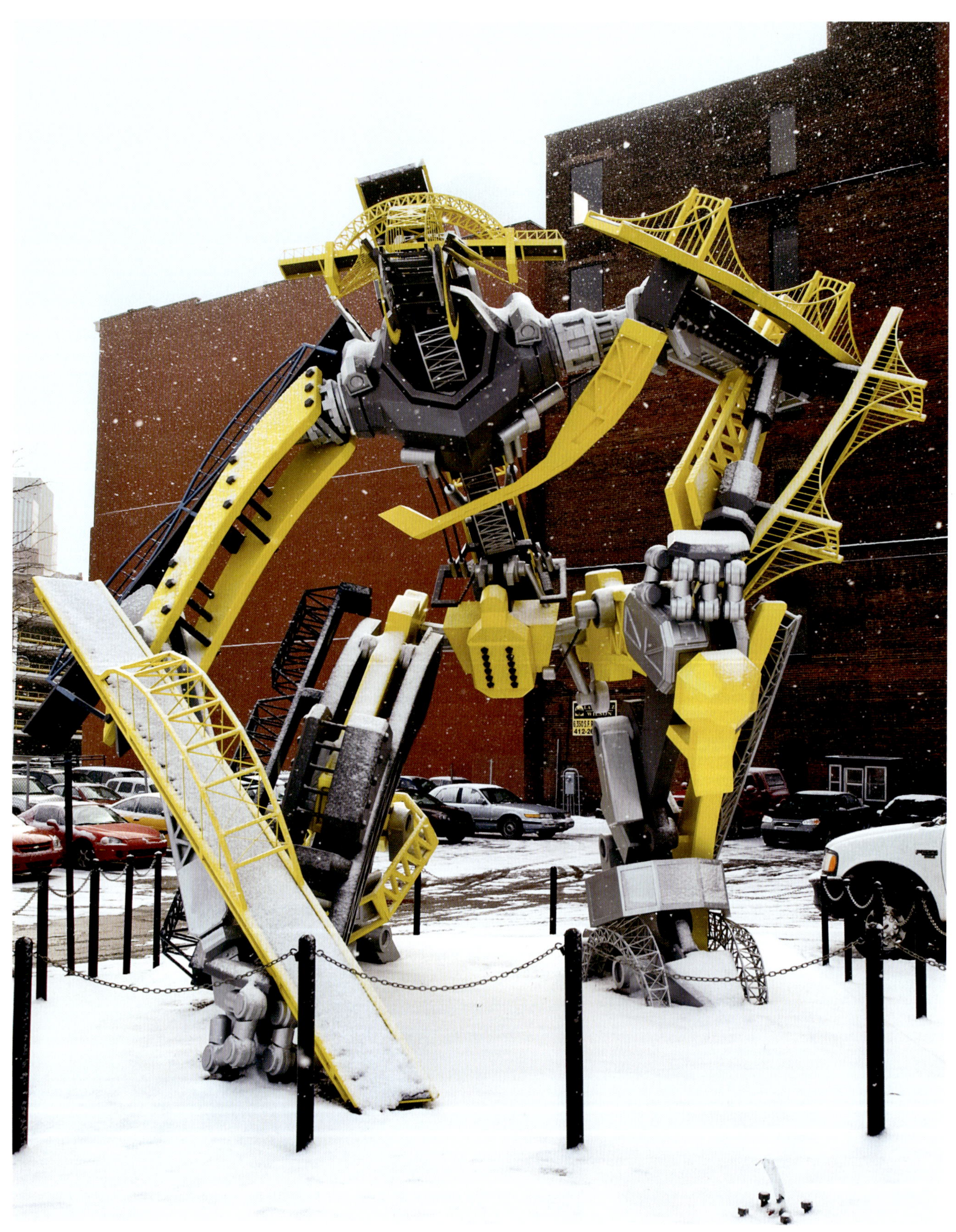

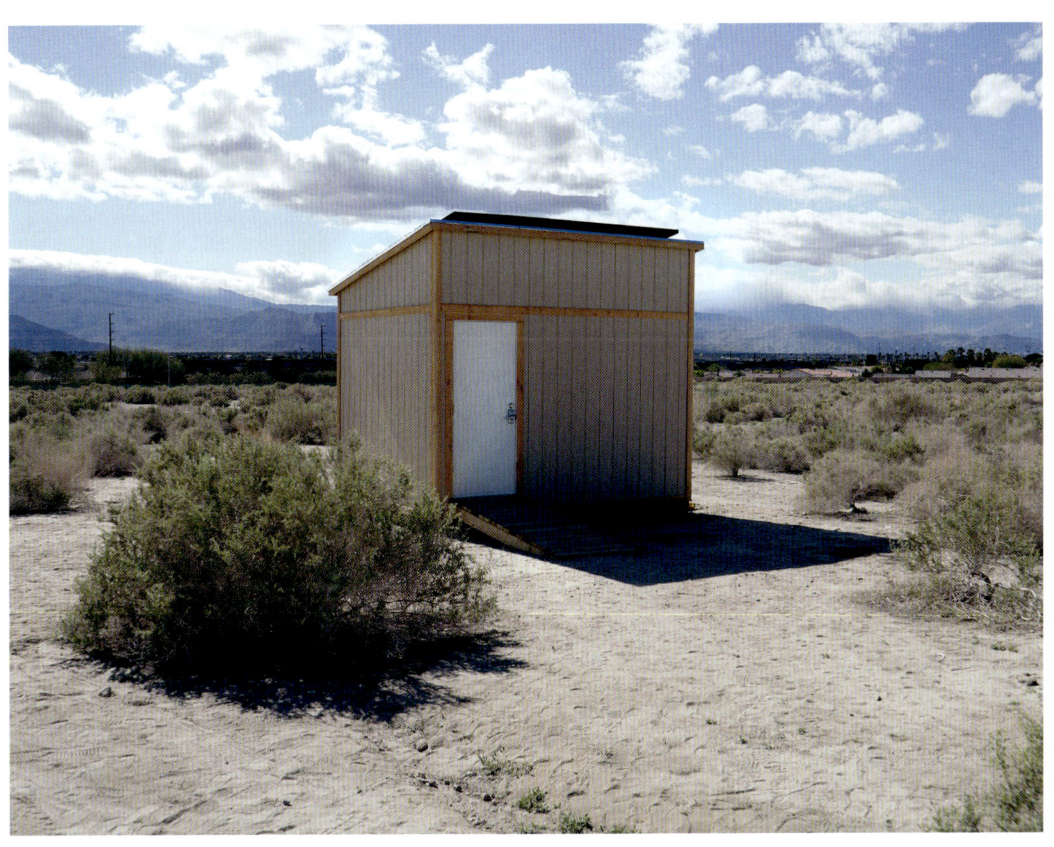

## Hollow Earth

*2017, Wood, glass, lights, dimensions variable*

**_Hollow Earth_ is a sculpture that creates the illusion of a tunnel descending deep into the earth, housed in an abandoned shed in the California desert. Once inside the darkened space, visitors become uneasy as they peer down a brightly lit and very deep-looking hole that drops away into infinite darkness. Kaino's work is a contemplative gesture that explores the complicated and diverse history of tunnel making, from the secret tunnels between Egypt and the Gaza Strip to the common childhood (and Orientalist) fantasy of digging a hole through the planet and ending up in China. The title, referencing the numerous legends of a subterranean land, invokes the idea that the world is inside out. Paradoxically, as the viewers stare down at the piece, wondering about the depth of the tunnel, they are actually staring at themselves as seen through a series of mirrors. In this ironic case, art directly reflects (their) life and the meaning, value, and power that they assign to it.**

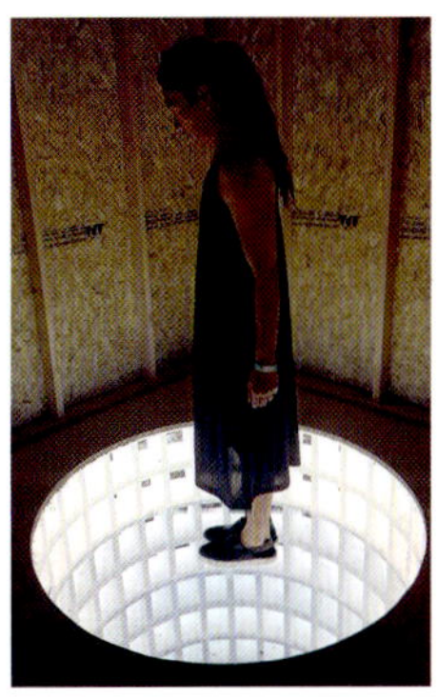

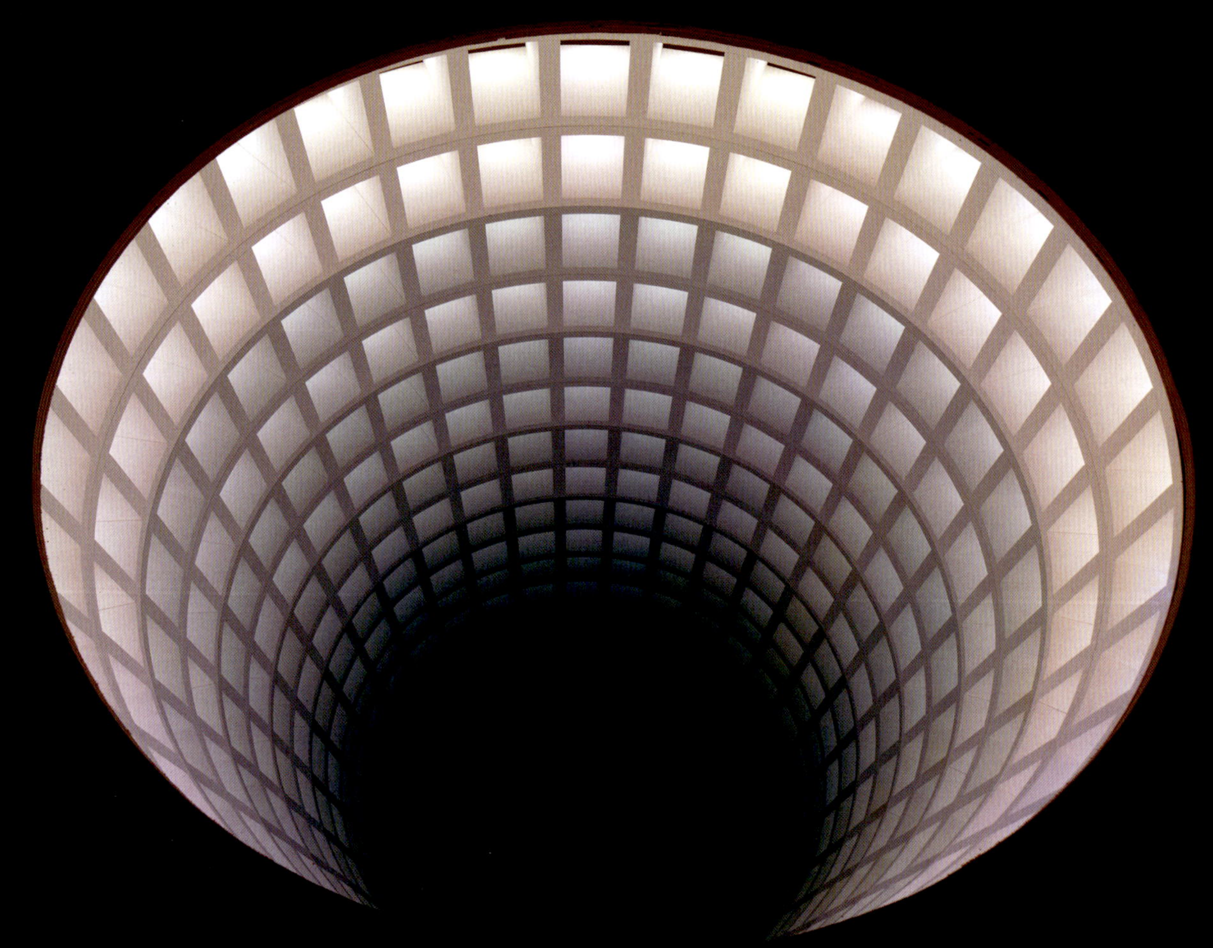

## Desktop Operation: There's No Place Like Home (10th Example of Rapid Dominance: Em City)

*2003, Wood, paint, plastic tarp, sand, water, 96 x 168 x 84 inches*

**Resulting from an ongoing interest in the ephemeral qualities of materials and solids, and the ability to make visible intangible forces, *Desktop Operation: There's No Place Like Home (10th Example of Rapid Dominance: Em City)* takes the form of an eight-foot-high sand sculpture that evokes the Emerald City of Oz. Using techniques and strategies learned from master sand sculptors, the work juxtaposes delicate materials with monumental scale to create a moment that is both powerful and fragile. Interrogating ideas of permanence, the work poetically speaks to the rapid dissolving of utopic possibilities, functioning as a monument to fleeting hopes and dreams deferred.**

*Photo: Erma Eastwick*

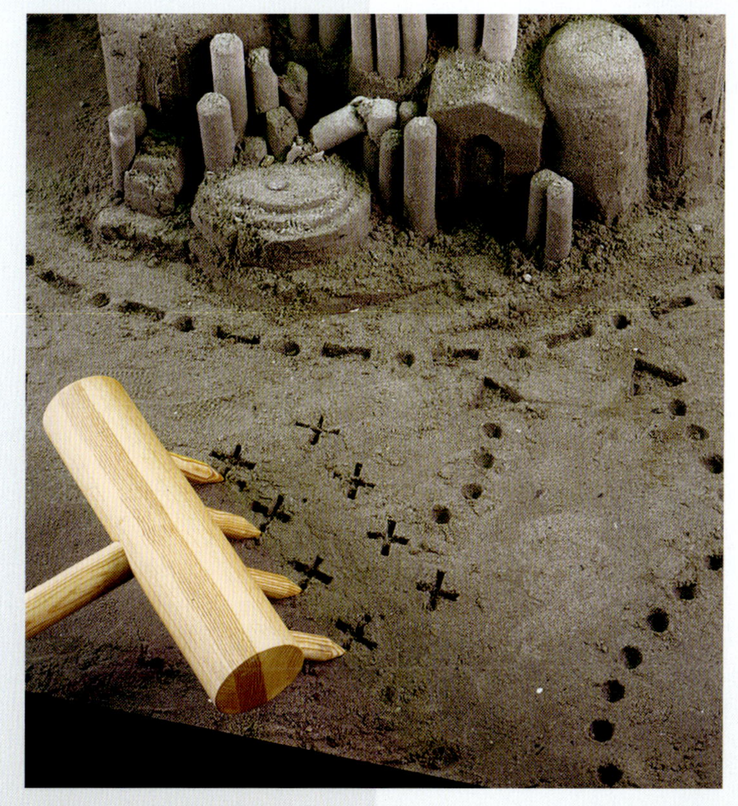

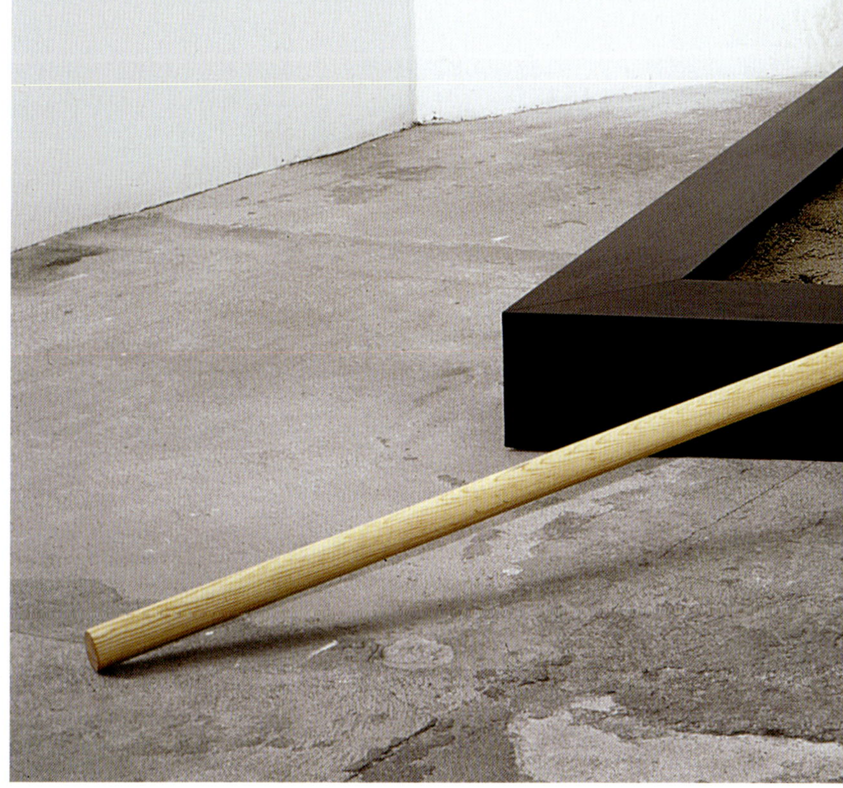

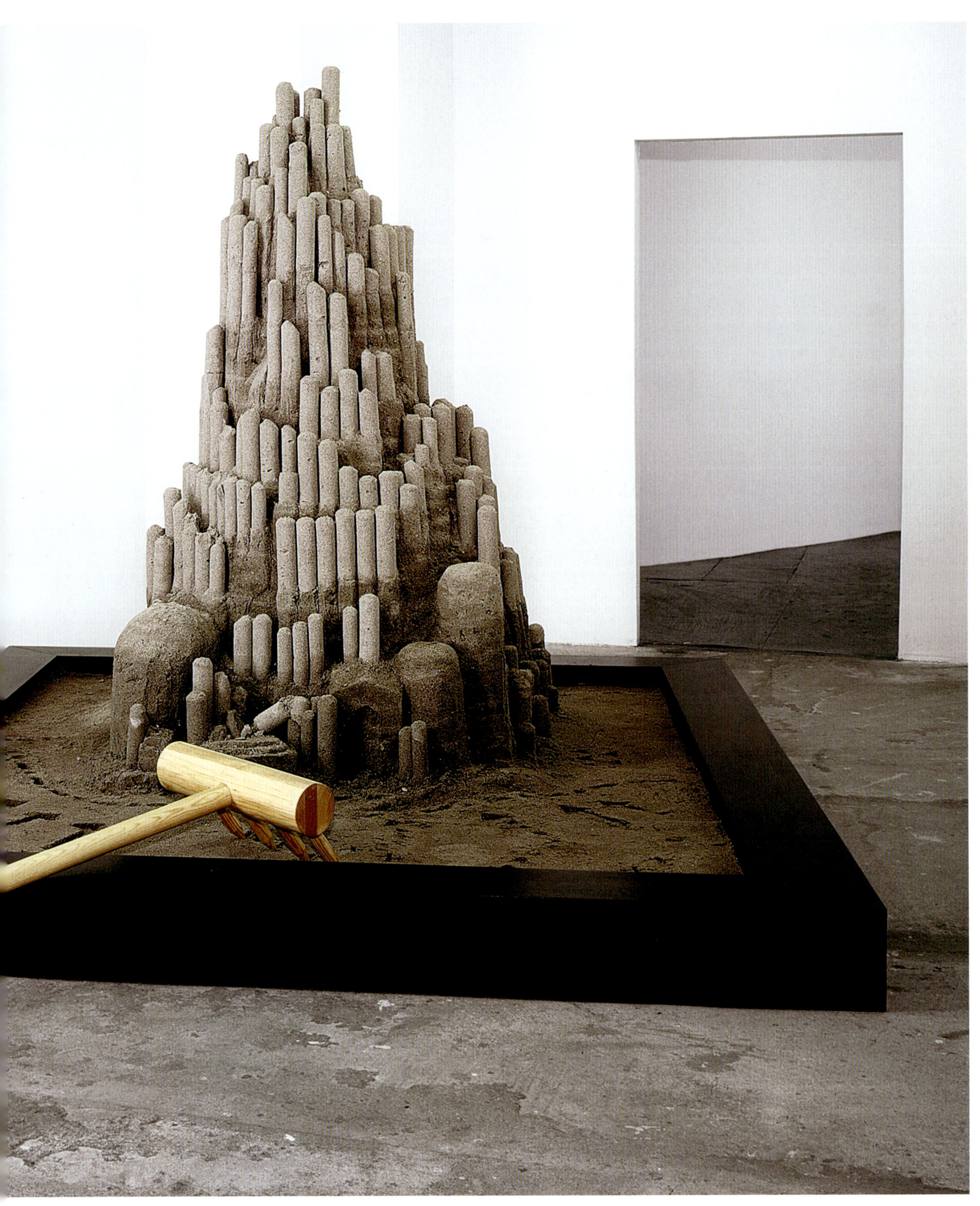

## Knowledge Transfer

*2011, Inkjet transfer on paper, 19 x 25 inches*

***Knowledge Transfer*** **consists of a suite of transfigured drawings that begin with maps sketched by Turkish pirate Piri Reis in the 15th century. These seemingly abstract drawings—the recordings of an outlaw—eventually became standardized maps after Reis joined the Ottoman fleet as an admiral, following a death threat by the emperor. Through inventive constructions that aim to reconcile gaps with imagination, Kaino prints images of these maps on a film that he then releases onto paper using an alcohol-based technique similar to a Polaroid transfer. Physically distressing the images with his hands, fingers, and nails, Kaino layers the original images with new itineraries and locations, creating roadmaps for worlds we have yet to know.**

*Photo: Joshua White*

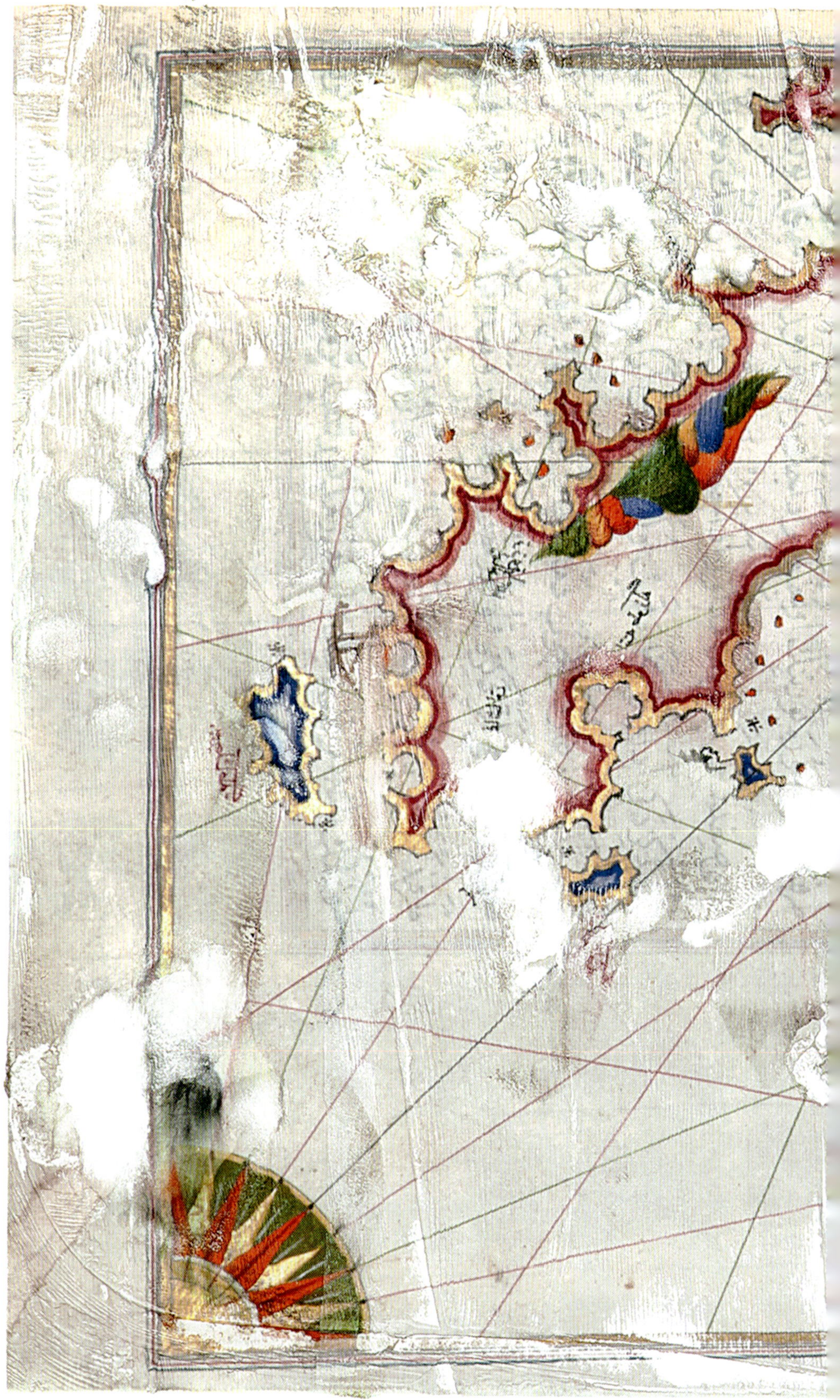

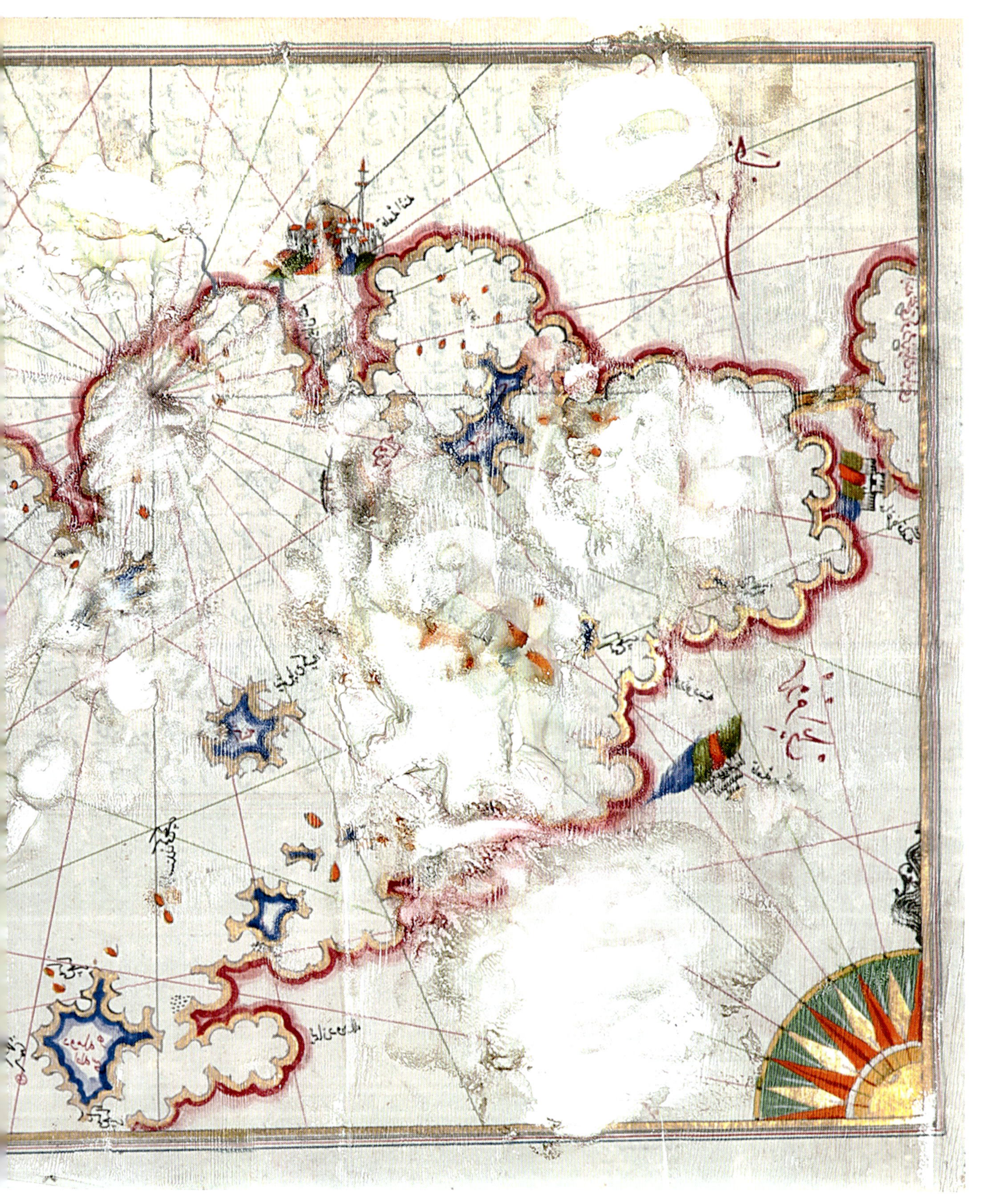

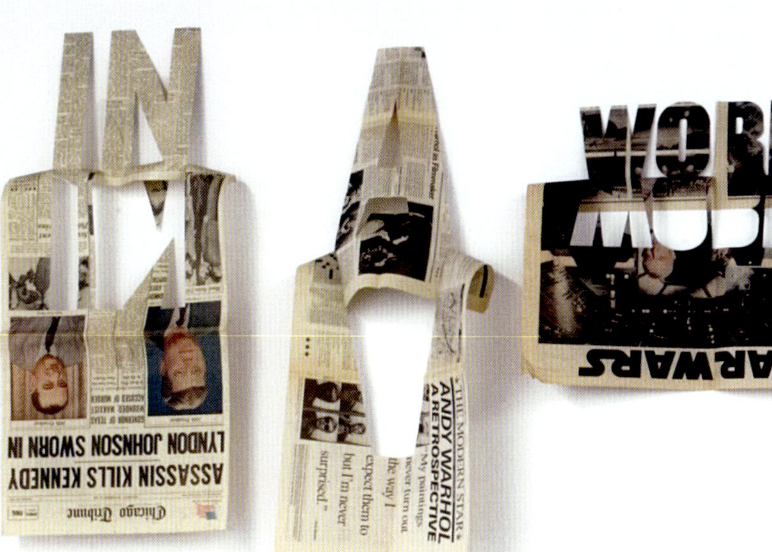


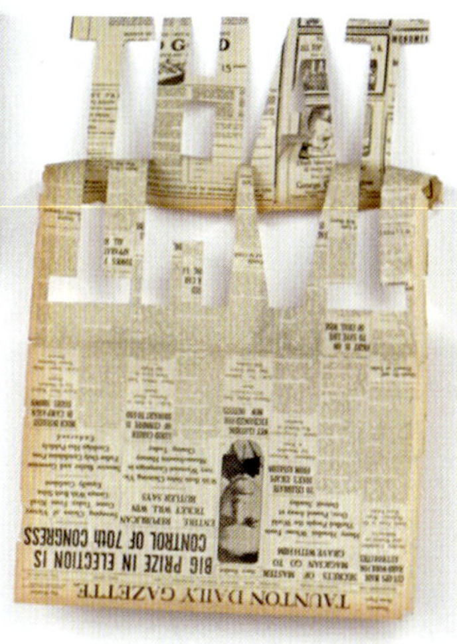


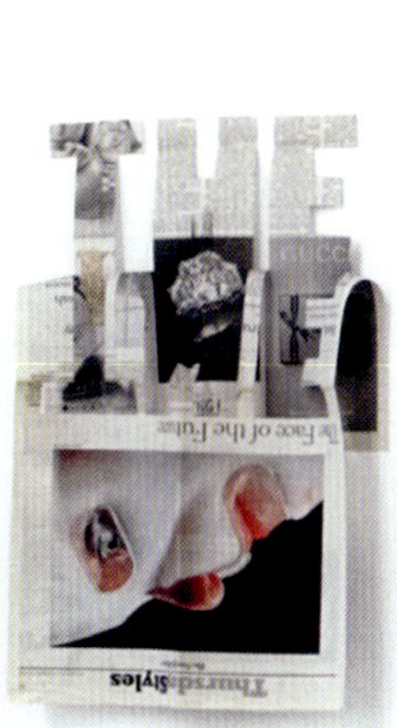


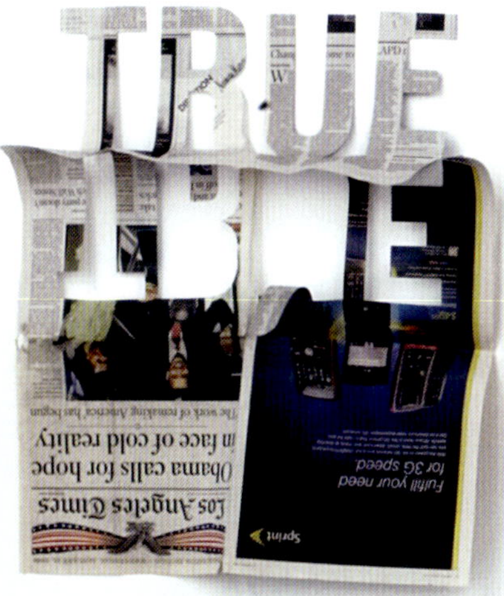


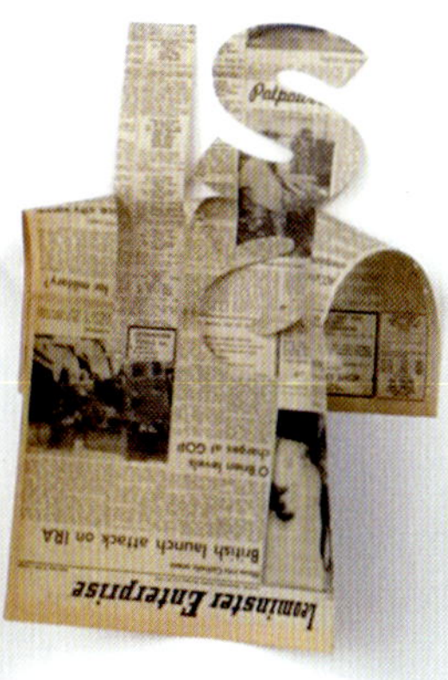


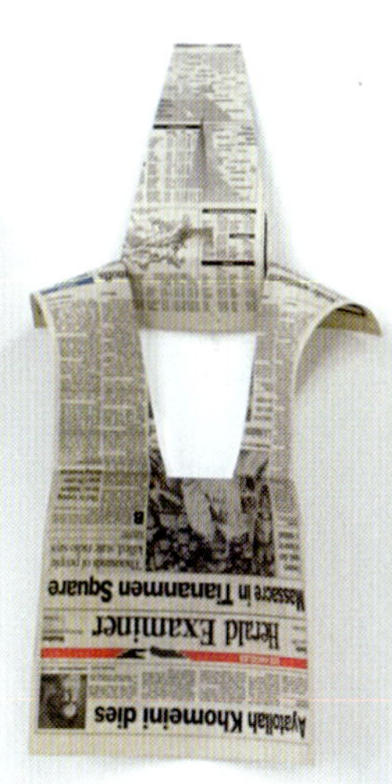


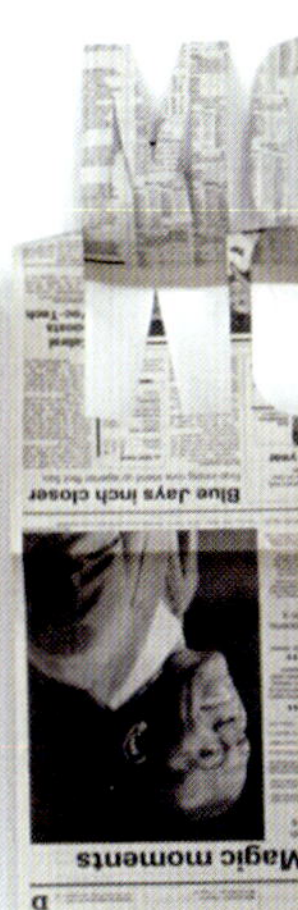


## Torn and Restorn

*2010, Cut and found newspaper, dimensions variable*

**There is one magic trick that has always intrigued Kaino since he initially experienced it. The effect starts with a magician tearing up a newspaper and then magically healing it before our eyes. Kaino initially believed that his attraction to the trick was due to its visual effect—seeing the paper restore itself. Magician and author Max Maven shared additional perspective with Kaino about the conceptual history of magic, in particular, the ways in which certain tricks get trapped into fundamental narratives. The newspaper trick then becomes a story of resurrection. Already a collector of vintage newspapers, Kaino began to cut the alphabet into them, crafting the ways in which the pieces hang from the shapes of the letters. *Torn and Restorn* is Kaino's version of the classic magic trick, half-performed. In the end, the work becomes many things: torn historic markers of a distraught world; ideas and people that are dead and dying, pre-resurrection; and a crisis of suspended animation, implicating the audience as witness at the moment of observation.**

*Photo: Kelly Barrie*

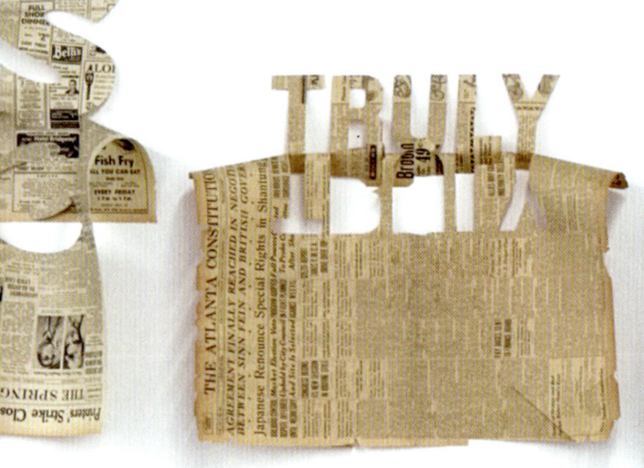
TRULY
THE ATLANTA CONSTITUTION
Japanese Renounce Special Rights in Shantung
Fish Fry

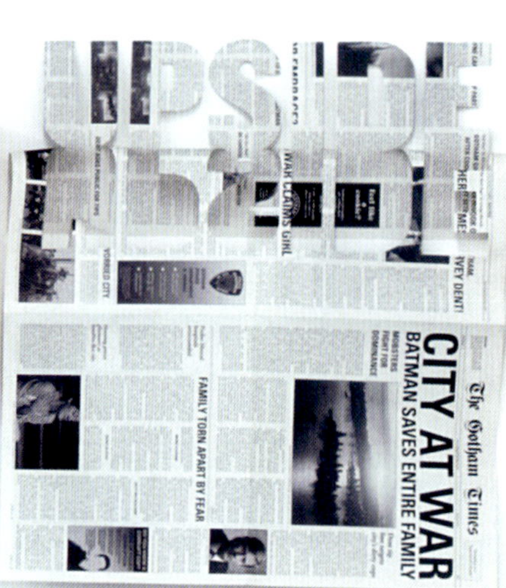
UPSIDE
The Gotham Times
CITY AT WAR
BATMAN SAVES ENTIRE FAMILY
FAMILY TORN APART BY FEAR

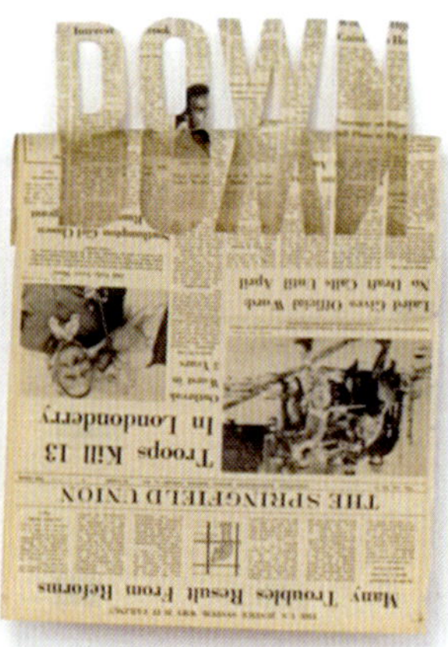
DOWN
THE SPRINGFIELD UNION
Troops Kill 13 In Londonderry
Many Troubles Result from Reforms

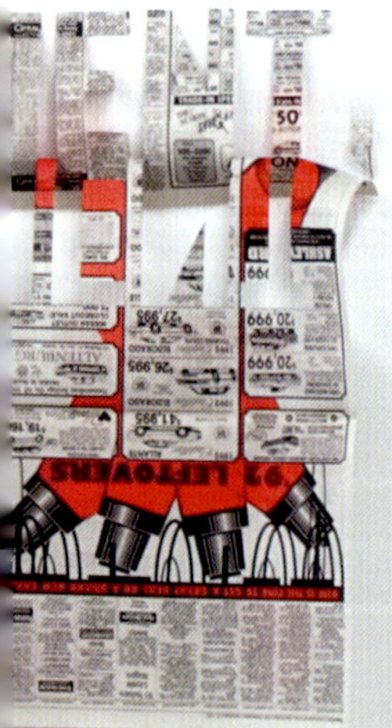
'97 LEFTOVERS

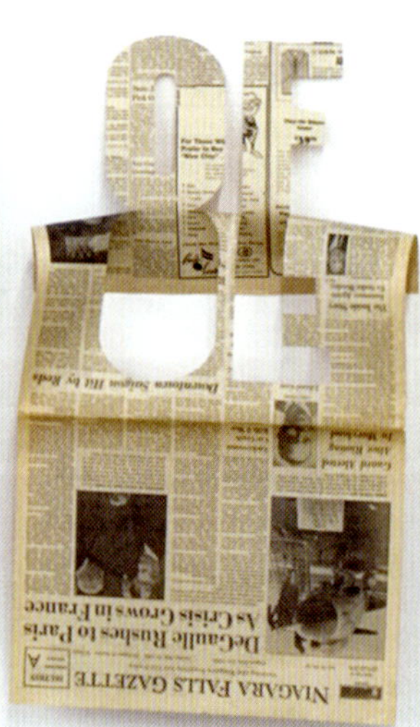
OF
NIAGARA FALLS GAZETTE
DeGaulle Rushes to Paris As Crisis Grows in France

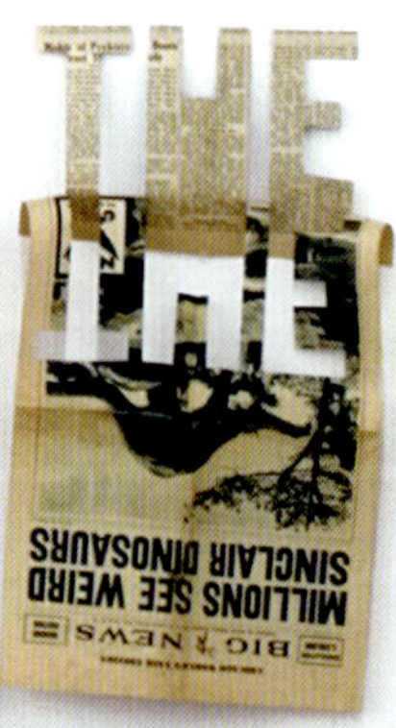
THE
MILLIONS SEE WEIRD SINCLAIR DINOSAURS

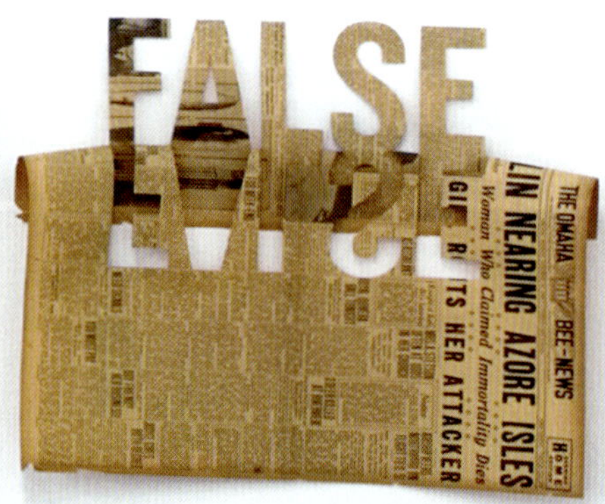
FALSE
THE OMAHA BEE-NEWS
NEARING AZORE ISLES
Woman Who Claimed Immortality Dies
HER ATTACKER

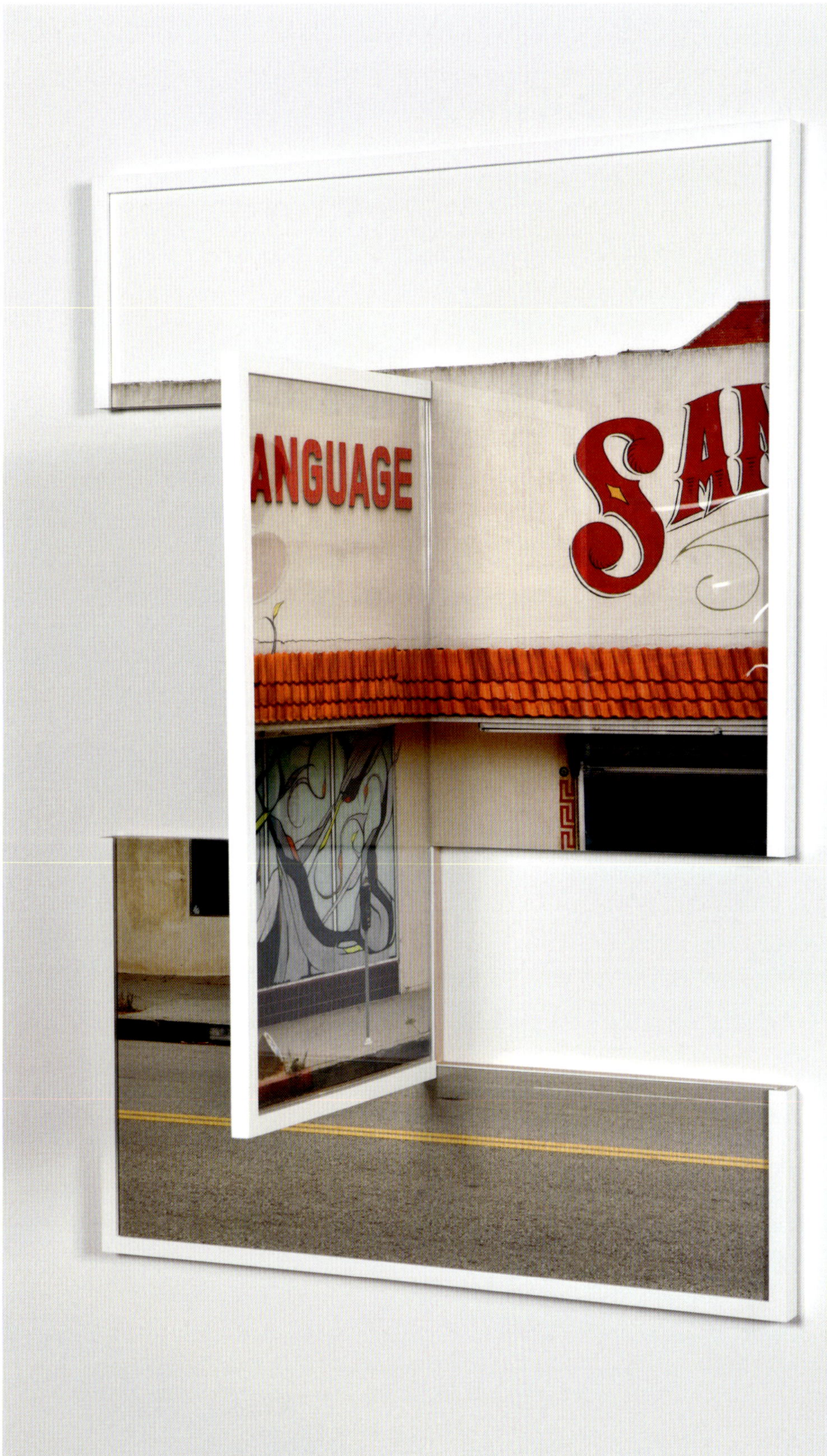


## Temporary Autonomous Zones

*Temporary Autonomous Zones* is a series of photographs of independent art spaces in Los Angeles that have been transformed so that when viewed from the front, the galleries appear to have vanished from the landscape. Yet when seen from the side, the photographic prints seem to have an impossibly expanded middle section, within which the architecture of the exhibition spaces resides. This metaphoric illusion alludes to both the ephemeral nature of artist-run galleries and simultaneously to the cultural defenses they often create for themselves: an underground area of creative production, or a temporary autonomous zone.

*Photo: Joshua White*

***Temporary Autonomous Zones (Slanguage)***

*2011, Digital Print on archival paper, wood, 49 x 33 x 18 inches*